Cognitive Behavior Therapy for OCD in Youth

Cognitive Behavior Therapy for OCD in Youth

A Step-by-Step Guide

Michael A. Tompkins, Daniela J. Owen,
Nicole H. Shiloff, and Litsa R. Tanner

AMERICAN PSYCHOLOGICAL ASSOCIATION
Washington, DC

Published by
American Psychological Association
750 First Street, NE
Washington, DC 20002
https://www.apa.org

Order Department
https://www.apa.org/pubs/books
order@apa.org

In the U.K., Europe, Africa, and the Middle East, copies may be ordered from Eurospan
https://www.eurospanbookstore.com/apa
info@eurospangroup.com

Typeset in Meridien and Ortodoxa by Circle Graphics, Inc., Reisterstown, MD

Printer: Sheridan Books, Chelsea, MI
Cover Designer: Beth Schlenoff, Bethesda, MD

Library of Congress Cataloging-in-Publication Data

Names: Tompkins, Michael A., author.
Title: Cognitive behavior therapy for OCD in youth : a step-by-step guide /
    by Michael A. Tompkins [and three others].
Description: Washington, DC : American Psychological Association, [2020] |
    Includes bibliographical references and index.
Identifiers: LCCN 2019026733 (print) | LCCN 2019026734 (ebook) |
    ISBN 9781433831850 (paperback) | ISBN 9781433831867 (ebook)
Subjects: LCSH: Obsessive-compulsive disorder in children. | Cognitive
    therapy for children.
Classification: LCC RJ506.O25 T66 2020 (print) | LCC RJ506.O25 (ebook) |
    DDC 618.92/891425—dc23
LC record available at https://lccn.loc.gov/2019026733
LC ebook record available at https://lccn.loc.gov/2019026734

http://dx.doi.org/10.1037/0000167-000

Printed in the United States of America

10 9 8 7 6 5 4 3 2 1

CONTENTS

ACKNOWLEDGMENTS

This book would not have been possible without the support and encouragement of many people who have contributed to our thinking and practice over the years.

Michael A. Tompkins: I wish to thank my colleagues at the San Francisco Bay Area Center for Cognitive Therapy (Jonathan Barkin, Emily Berner, Joan Davidson, and Monique Thompson) for their continued support of my professional development. I also wish to thank Jacqueline B. Persons, who has been, and continues to be, a steady source of support and encouragement to lean out of my comfort zone. Thanks to my partner, Luann L. DeVoss, for her love and tolerance of another book project, and thanks to our daughters, Madeleine and Olivia, who have been asking for years that I write a book for kids. They wanted to have something to talk about during show-and-tell at school. Although I doubt this book is what they had in mind (and they have certainly outgrown show-and-tell), it is a book that I hope will help kids. I know they would think that is a good thing.

Daniela J. Owen: I would like to acknowledge the various people who were important in the writing of this book. First, I would like to thank all of the professors, supervisors, and clinicians who have taught me about how to assess, conceptualize, and treat OCD. Thanks to my partners at the San Francisco Bay Area Center for Cognitive Therapy (Michael A. Tompkins, Joan Davidson, Jonathan Barkin, Monique Thompson, and Emily Berner) for their support of my professional activities as well as their ongoing guidance and consultation on cases. Special thanks to Michael A. Tompkins for inviting me to be a coauthor of this book. I'd like to acknowledge my other coauthors, Litsa R. Tanner and Nicole H. Shiloff, for working hard putting this book together.

I want to thank my wonderful family for their constant support and love. Last and most important, I would like to acknowledge and thank my patients, who teach me every day about OCD and how to work together to manage this challenging disorder.

Nicole H. Shiloff: I wish to thank Michael A. Tompkins, without whom this book would not have been possible. Michael has supported my professional development over many years, and I appreciate the opportunity to participate in this book project with him. I also wish to thank my other coauthors, Daniela J. Owen and Litsa R. Tanner. I appreciate their support and encouragement as we worked together on this book. Daniela kept us on track, and Litsa ensured that we laughed a bit along the way. It has been a pleasure working with them. Last, I wish to thank my parents, who in infinite ways helped me get to where I am today. In addition to educating me about the health benefits of brussels sprouts and broccoli, they taught me the importance of perseverance. Coauthoring a book requires perseverance, and my ability to persevere through the ups and downs of writing this book is a tribute to them. Although my father passed away before we completed the book, on days when the sun shines brightly, I imagine he is looking down, beaming with pride.

Litsa R. Tanner: I want to thank the late Paul and Arna Munford for providing me with an amazing foundation in how to use exposure response prevention to treat OCD. Without their excellent guidance I would have never found my way down the path of becoming a specialist in treating this condition. I would also like to thank my cofounder of the Santa Rosa Center for Cognitive Behavioral Therapy, Jennifer Shannon, for encouraging me to not pass up the opportunity to coauthor a book on the treatment of pediatric OCD. I would like to acknowledge all the dedication and hard work of my coauthors who have remained determined and focused in making sure this project became a reality. Last, I want to thank my friends and family for tolerating, at times, my gleeful excitement about new exposure ideas and my standard response to their squeamish responses to germs, bugs, spiders, and other creepy crawlies: "You know, exposure therapy would be great for that."

As we plunged into the writing, Susan Reynolds, senior acquisitions editor at APA Books, supported and encouraged us along the way. Her thoughtful insights regarding the structure and development of the book were invaluable. In addition, Susan was tremendously patient with us. Oh, such patience. We think patience must be a primary trait of editors, particularly senior ones, and it is a trait that Susan has in spades. Thank you, Susan.

We wish to thank Ida Audeh, who is an amazing development editor. Ida has a very gentle hand when it comes to guiding authors through the development process. It is quite remarkable the way she suggested changes to the manuscript. We often congratulated ourselves for coming up with a fantastic idea that, truth be told, was really Ida's idea. Masterful!

Finally, we are deeply grateful to the many kids and families with whom we have worked over the years. To hear the giggles of children as they boss back that nasty-naughty-no-gooder OCD or to watch them try things that only weeks before seemed beyond their reach is a true gift. We thank you all.

Cognitive Behavior Therapy for OCD in Youth

Introduction

Obsessive–compulsive disorder (OCD) affects an estimated one of every 200 children in the United States, and as many as 50% to 60% of the youth diagnosed with OCD experience severe impairment in their personal, social, and academic life. Although researchers and clinicians have recognized for many years that cognitive behavior therapy (CBT) is an effective treatment for adults with OCD, the application of this treatment to youth lagged until 1989, when John March and his colleagues developed a CBT protocol specifically for the unique needs of youth with this debilitating disorder. In 1998, March (with Karen Mulle) published the treatment protocol and his findings from the research study in the book titled *OCD in Children and Adolescents: A Cognitive-Behavioral Treatment Manual*. The book is a landmark in the treatment of pediatric OCD and is responsible for introducing clinicians around the world to the power and benefits of this approach.

However, treatment protocols, such as the one designed by John March and his colleagues, are primarily for researchers, not necessarily for clinicians. To test the efficacy of a psychological treatment, researchers ensure that all subjects in a study receive the psychological interventions at the same intensity, in the same order, and in the same manner. The process of standardizing treatment results in protocols that limit to some degree the clinician's flexibility and creativity. The view of many clinicians that they must "follow the book" to provide evidence-based treatment often prevents them from accepting these treatments into their clinical practice. At the same time, although many clinicians hold this view, we know that this view is not quite accurate.

http://dx.doi.org/10.1037/0000167-001

Cognitive Behavior Therapy for OCD in Youth: A Step-by-Step Guide, by M. A. Tompkins, D. J. Owen, N. H. Shiloff, and L. R. Tanner

Our experience is that clinicians (outside of standardized treatment studies) who provide evidence-based treatments rarely follow the book and instead flexibly and creatively apply the components or interventions within the treatment approach based on a comprehensive case conceptualization. In other words, flexibility and creativity are between the lines of every treatment protocol, but most clinicians are not aware of this. We have written this book to reach these clinicians and to describe explicitly the flexibility and creativity inherent in CBT for pediatric OCD.

What do we mean by *flexibility* and *creativity*? By *flexibility*, we mean the thoughtful selection and application of the core strategies that are part of CBT for pediatric OCD. These evidence-based core strategies include prolonged exposure and response prevention primarily, but also other strategies such as engagement, decreasing family accommodation behaviors, and relapse prevention. At the same time, most treatment protocols do not, in our opinion, provide clinicians with sufficient guidance to understand when and how to apply these core strategies. This is the job of case conceptualization. A comprehensive case conceptualization enables the clinician to pick and choose, in a thoughtful and flexible manner, what to include in the treatment and to what degree. Most protocols or treatment manuals assume clinicians have a firmer and more comprehensive understanding of CBT and cognitive behavior conceptualization than many clinicians do. We have written this book not only to underscore the importance of a case conceptualization-driven modular approach and the value it brings to the treatment of pediatric OCD, but also to explain how to do it, particularly across a range of symptoms, co-occurring conditions, and developmental ages of youth.

By *creativity*, we mean the ability to think on ones' feet, that is, to creatively apply the core evidence-based strategies to the unique strengths and weakness of a particular youth while engaging the youth in the active application of these strategies to the problem at hand. Many clinicians believe that a treatment protocol limits their creativity with youth. They believe a treatment protocol boxes them into thinking about OCD in a certain way and doing CBT for it in a lockstep fashion. However, we know that to be effective, clinicians need to feel free to think outside the protocol box and to do what they love to do—to be creative and do what makes clinical sense while at the same time applying the evidence-based core strategies. We want clinicians to focus less on doing the steps of the treatment "right," and instead focus on engaging the child in a treatment approach we are confident can help. Above all, we want clinicians to feel as if they can still have fun with the child while using an evidence-based approach.

ORGANIZATION OF THE BOOK

We have divided the book into three parts. This is a nuts-and-bolts book, and the parts mirror our clinical approach to the problem of pediatric OCD. We diagnose and assess the condition, develop a case conceptualization that results in a treatment plan, then apply the core strategies based on that plan.

In Chapter 1, we review the nature of pediatric OCD and review the efficacy of CBT and medications for the condition in youth. In Chapter 2, we summarize the treatment plan described in this book, describe key intervention modules and the empirical evidence that supports them, and describe case conceptualization and the structure of sessions. We intentionally separated Chapters 1 and 2 from Parts I through III that focus on assessment and treatment of the condition. Although it is important that clinicians understand the nature of OCD, we also recognize that busy clinicians may have little time to read information about the phenomenon of pediatric OCD (and there is a great deal of it). Fortunately, it is not necessary for clinicians to know all of the research literature on pediatric OCD to treat the condition effectively. Therefore, we limit the information to what we believe is necessary to answer the typical questions that youth and parents ask regarding the condition and its treatment.

In Parts I and II, we walk clinicians through the diagnostic and assessment processes and describe how to implement the core strategies for a wide range of symptoms and with a variety of youth and their families. In Chapters 3 to 9, we introduce the core strategies in a manner that builds on skills and concepts. Although engagement is crucial early in treatment, engagement is an ongoing process that is sensitive to the ups and downs of motivation on the part of both youth and parents as well as to the developmental age of youth.

In Part III, starting with Chapter 10, we present three cases to illustrate the evaluation and treatment process, from assessment, case formulation, and treatment planning, and from the beginning to the end of treatment. We have selected these cases to illustrate the flexible and creative application of the approach across a range of symptoms, and developmental, cultural, and family factors. In Chapter 11, we describe the commonly prescribed medications for pediatric OCD and how clinicians can include medications in CBT for the condition. Again, we present only the information we believe is necessary to answer the typical questions that youth and parents ask regarding medications for the condition and guidelines for clinicians who wish to include medications within CBT for pediatric OCD. Last, in Chapter 12, we describe typical problems that arise when providing CBT for pediatric OCD and offer ways to overcome them.

The descriptions of youth and parents in this book are composites or contrived and do not describe any particular real-life youth, parent, or particular circumstance. Throughout the book, we refer to materials that we have found helpful in our own clinical practice. They are available for download at http://pubs.apa.org/books/supp/tompkins.

CONCLUSION

The American Academy of Child and Adolescent Psychiatry recommends CBT as the first-line treatment for youth with OCD, whether alone or in combination with medications for the condition (Geller, March, & AACAP Committee on Quality Issues, CQI, 2012). At the same time, parents can search many years before they find a clinician with sufficient experience and training to provide CBT for the condition. Why is that? The answer to this question is complicated, as are most questions about mental health and mental health services, but part of the answer may be that more clinicians would learn CBT for pediatric OCD if it were a better fit for the way they work. In this book, we describe a treatment approach for pediatric OCD that is effective yet flexible, fun yet focused, and based on solid clinical science yet speaks to the innate creativity, genuineness, and personal style of clinicians. In describing this approach, we hope to encourage more clinicians to treat pediatric OCD and thereby help more kids.

We now move to the first chapter of the book, in which we present the epidemiology and phenomenology of the disorder in youth, including the range of symptoms, typical co-occurring conditions, and the developmental and cultural factors that influence the expression of OCD in a pediatric population. We believe clinicians who have a basic understanding of the condition can more effectively diagnose and treat it.

1

Overview of Obsessive-Compulsive Disorder in Youth

In this chapter, we describe the features of obsessive–compulsive disorder (OCD) in general and how the condition presents in youth[1] in particular. The extant literature on pediatric OCD is quite extensive; therefore, we limit the information regarding the condition and its treatment to that we view as necessary for clinicians to answer with confidence and clarity the typical questions parents[2] or youth ask about the condition and how cognitive behavior therapy (CBT) might help, such as "How much improvement can we expect in our child's condition?" "How long can we expect our child's improvement to last?" "How does the treatment you provide compare with other treatments like [medication, family therapy] in terms of response?" "What are the risks of your treatment?" "Could my child's condition get worse?" "What happens if we don't treat my child's problem now?" and "Might my child get better without treatment?"

To that end, we present up-to-date epidemiology and phenomenology of the disorder in youth, including the range of symptoms and typical co-occurring conditions. In addition, we describe cultural, familial, and temperamental factors that influence the expression of behaviors, as well as developmental factors

---

[1]Throughout this book, we use the term *youth* to refer to children and adolescents.
[2]Throughout this book, we use the term *parent* to refer to caretakers, which can include biological, adoptive, and foster parents, or other caretakers who act as parents even though they are not the youth's actual parents.

http://dx.doi.org/10.1037/0000167-002
Cognitive Behavior Therapy for OCD in Youth: A Step-by-Step Guide, by M. A. Tompkins, D. J. Owen, N. H. Shiloff, and L. R. Tanner

that clinicians can misattribute to OCD but are features of typical child development. It is essential that clinicians understand the epidemiology and phenomenology of pediatric OCD in order to diagnosis the condition accurately and efficiently. For example, it is rare for a young child to exhibit sexual obsessions, and the clinician who identifies thoughts and images with a sexual content from a youth may wish to rule out other conditions or circumstances that could account for this. Similarly, because children with OCD are more likely than adults to have concomitant attention-deficit/hyperactivity disorder (ADHD), the clinician may wish to screen carefully for these conditions in youth with OCD.

DIAGNOSIS

Although OCD affects 2% to 3% of children (Rapoport et al., 2000), many clinicians fail to accurately detect and diagnosis the condition (Fireman, Koran, Leventhal, & Jacobson, 2001). OCD is highly disruptive to the typical psychosocial development of youth and can result in impairment in academic performance, friendships, and family[3] relationships, and it can place youth at risk of developing other serious problems, such as substance abuse and self-harm behaviors (Adams, Waas, March, & Smith, 1994; Piacentini, Bergman, Keller, & McCracken, 2003).

In the fifth and most recent edition of the *Diagnostic and Statistical Manual of Mental Disorders* (*DSM–5*; American Psychiatric Association, 2013), OCD is under the broader category termed obsessive-compulsive and related disorders, along with body dysmorphic disorder, hoarding disorder, trichotillomania (hair-pulling disorder), and excoriation (skin-picking) disorder. OCD is characterized by recurrent obsessions and/or compulsions that cause marked distress and/or interference in the youth's life. To merit a diagnosis of OCD, the youth can have obsessions or compulsions, although most youth have both (Storch et al., 2004).

Obsessions are recurrent and persistent thoughts, images, doubts, or impulses that intrude into the youth's awareness that they, for the most part, view as senseless. Obsessions tend to trigger negative affect, such as fear, disgust, anxiety, or a feeling of incompleteness and distress. *Compulsions* are observable repetitive behaviors, such as washing or checking, or unobservable mental acts, such as counting or replacing an undesired thought with a positive or neutral one, to neutralize or alleviate the distress youth experience because of the obsession. *Rituals* are compulsions performed in an exact way or according to certain rules, such as the youth who washes her hands by starting with the thumb on her left hand and repeats the process for each finger before moving

---

[3]Throughout this book, we use the term *family* to refer to the many constellations that constitute the families of today, from nuclear families to extended unrelated people who support and care about the youth.

to the right hand. In addition, youth attempt to ignore, suppress, or conceal from others the obsessions and overt neutralizations. To reiterate, we use the term *neutralization* rather than *compulsion* throughout this book to refer to any internal or external action youth consciously use to neutralize an obsession and the accompanying distress it causes. Over the years, we have observed clinicians who are new to the assessment and treatment of pediatric OCD assume that compulsions are only observable behaviors and thereby miss the many internal mental actions youth with OCD use to neutralize distress. In the past, clinicians described this presentation as "pure *O*," or purely obsessional. However, by definition OCD includes both obsessions and compulsions or neutralizations, and for some youth, mental actions dominate the clinical presentation.

Because many youth, particularly young children, engage in compulsive-like behaviors, such as counting their steps or repeating phrases or snippets of songs, clinicians would not give these youth a diagnosis of OCD unless their symptoms are distressing, are time-consuming (e.g., taking up more than 1 hour per day), or are significantly interfering with their ability to participate in school, social activities, or important relationships. Unlike adults, youth do not have to recognize the senselessness of their obsessions and compulsions, although most do, to meet criteria for the diagnosis. Many youth with OCD, particularly developmentally young people, view their OCD symptoms as reasonable more often than do adults (Geller et al., 2001). At the same time, to receive a diagnosis of OCD, the youth must recognize at some point in the illness that the obsessions originate within his mind and are not simply excessive worries about real problems. Similarly, the youth must see that their compulsions are excessive and unreasonable. Youth need to have adequate "insight" regarding the unreasonableness of their obsessive and compulsive symptoms to benefit from CBT for the condition. In addition, clinicians would not give a youth the diagnosis of OCD when the content of the obsessions is a feature of another disorder, such as guilty thoughts because the youth is depressed, or delusional thoughts because the youth has a psychotic disorder.

PREVALENCE, ONSET, AND COURSE

The prevalence of OCD among youth in Western countries, particularly Anglo-Saxon and Anglo-Celtic ones, is quite consistent at 1% to 3% (Shaffer et al., 1996; Zohar, 1999), whereas rates across Asians and other ethnic groups vary considerably. The lack of data from many countries (e.g., Africa, South America, Western Europe) and different assessment methods make it difficult to determine categorically that there is a relationship between the prevalence of OCD and culture and sociodemographic factors (Sica, Novara, Sanavio, Dorz, & Coradeschi, 2002). Among adults with OCD, one third to one half develop the condition during childhood (Rasmussen & Eisen, 1990), and about 20% of all affected persons in the United States suffer from manifestations of the disorder at age 10 or earlier, although children as young as 5 or 6 years old can develop the condition (Kessler, Berglund, et al., 2005; Kessler, Chiu, Demler, & Walters, 2005). In a clinical sample, the modal age of onset of OCD was 7 years and the average age at onset was 10 years (Swedo, Rapoport, Leonard, Lenane, & Cheslow, 1989), with a possible age distribution that includes a first peak at age 11 years and a second peak in early adulthood (Delorme et al., 2005). For boys, onset of OCD is more likely to occur prior to adolescence, whereas for girls onset is more often during adolescence (Tükel et al., 2005). Typically, more boys than girls suffer with OCD (in a ratio of about 3:2; Chabane et al., 2005), but by adolescence, the prevalence in boys and girls is the same. There appear to be no differences in prevalence as a function of ethnicity or geographic region for adults (Flament et al., 1988), although the discrepancy between prevalence rates for OCD in clinical and epidemiological samples may be due to the difficulty recruiting minority families into child mental health treatment centers. European American youth are diagnosed with OCD more often than are African American youth (Rasmussen & Eisen, 1990).

The typical course of OCD without treatment is chronic and deteriorating. Symptoms routinely wax and wane over time and may even disappear completely with or without treatment, although sustained remission is rare (Leonard et al., 1993; Riggs & Foa, 1993). With well-delivered treatment, most youth achieve meaningful symptom relief that can substantially improve functioning and positively influence the developmental trajectory of youth with the condition (Pediatric OCD Treatment Study [POTS] Team, 2004).

TYPICAL SYMPTOMS IN YOUTH

Common obsessions for youth with OCD are fears of contamination, fears of harm to self, fears of harm to a familiar person, and urges for symmetry and exactness (Garcia et al., 2009). Common and corresponding compulsions in youth are washing and cleaning, followed by checking, counting, repeating, touching, and straightening (Swedo et al., 1989). Hoarding compulsions appear to be common in youth too (Geller et al., 2001). One or more negative affects drive these compulsions or other neutralizations and include fear, doubt, disgust, urges, and "just so" feelings, which some have labeled *sensory incompleteness* (Goodman, Rasmussen, Foa, & Price, 1994). Furthermore, to treat OCD effectively, it is essential that clinicians clearly identify the functional relationships and the affect that drives neutralizations. For example, a child may wash her hands because she fears that she will become sick or make others sick. In that case, the compulsion is in response to anxiety or fear. Another child, however, may wash her hands in response to a sensory-affective experience, feeling "sticky," rather than to fear and without an obvious obsession or cognitive trigger. Both children, however, may feel anxious prior to encountering the triggering situation or object. In the first case, the child is anxious about triggering the cognition or obsession. In the second case, the child is anxious about triggering the sticky feeling.

Most youth have more than one OCD symptom at any time, and many youth experience nearly all the classic OCD symptoms by the end of adolescence (Rettew, Swedo, Leonard, Lenane, & Rapoport, 1992). It is rare that youth have only obsessions (Swedo et al., 1989). More likely, children without overt neutralizations (i.e., compulsions) have instead covert internal mental neutralizations, such as praying, counting, and "do-overs" by which the youth attempts to "undo" a feared harm in some way. Other subtle mental neutralizations may include attempting to reason an obsessive doubt away, such as an adolescent who says to himself repeatedly "it's just my OCD" in response to an obsession. In addition, young children may have trouble distinguishing between an obsession and a mental neutralization because both are mental events. For this reason we recommend that the clinician assume youth have mental neutralizations even if they cannot report them.

INSIGHT AND OVERVALUED IDEATION

To meet criteria for a diagnosis of OCD, youth must view their obsessional fears and compulsive behaviors as unreasonable (American Psychiatric Association, 2013); in these cases, the diagnosis includes a specifier "with poor insight." Many children lack insight about their obsessions and compulsions and attribute a "magical" quality to them. For example, a 6-year-old girl insisted that her shoes felt lonely and that was why she arranged them (and rearranged them) so that they touched: "That way they know a friend is close by." The tendency to anthropomorphize objects is common in young children and is even encouraged through children's literature and films. Teacups talk and dance, and trains talk to passengers and to one another. At the same time, the extent to which children view their thoughts and behaviors as unreasonable varies considerably (Snider & Swedo, 2000).

Although the research suggests that children with OCD exhibit diminished insight (Geller et al., 2001), this observation may reflect several factors. For example, very young children may have poor emotion regulation skills that make it difficult for them to tolerate anxiety and regulate their emotional state. In the presence of high underregulated negative affect, youth may have difficulty maintaining adequate insight during acute episodes of OCD symptoms. Also, youth may fear disclosing particular thoughts because they fear that parents, teachers, peers, or the clinician might ridicule or criticize them for having nonsensical thoughts and fears. In addition, youth may feel embarrassed and even ashamed that they have thoughts or actions that they cannot stop or resist. Careful, developmentally appropriate and sensitive assessment of the youth's true level of insight is essential to an effective case conceptualization and treatment plan for pediatric OCD (Storch, Geffken, & Murphy, 2007).

PSYCHOSOCIAL FACTORS THAT INFLUENCE ONSET AND MAINTENANCE OF PEDIATRIC OCD

A number of factors influence the development and expression of OCD in youth; they include both biological and psychosocial factors. Later in the chapter, we also describe common co-occurring conditions that not only affect a youth's risk of developing the disorder but also can affect the course of the condition. Furthermore, a comprehensive treatment plan will include these factors and enable the clinician to respond flexibly and effectively to the many nuances that arise when providing CBT for pediatric OCD.

Developmental Influences

Identifying OCD in youth is particularly challenging because of developmental influences on the expression of the condition. Ritualistic and superstitious behaviors are common in early childhood (Snider & Swedo, 2000; Zohar & Felz, 2001). For example, a child may want a parent to read the same book to her and in the same manner before bed, or she may pray that her parents, siblings, or pets sleep safely through the night. These behaviors are similar to obsessive–compulsive symptoms in youth and seem to peak between the ages of 2 and 5 years, although they may continue in some form throughout childhood and adolescence (Rutter & Sroufe, 2000). For this reason, it is essential that clinicians tread with caution when diagnosing youth with OCD, particularly very young children.

Cognitive processes, such as abstract and causal reasoning, can influence the expression of the condition in youth. For example, very young children (less than 5 years of age) may have low insight into the reasonableness of their obsessions and compulsions. That may be because of the limited ability of young children to think abstractly and to understand what is meant by reasonable or unreasonable. In addition, the limited verbal ability of developmentally very young children can make it difficult for them to describe their symptoms clearly. Therefore, young children may have trouble stepping back from their compulsions and stating that they are inappropriate. However, beliefs about personal responsibility appear to develop early in youth (5 to 7 years), and for this reason children at this age are susceptible to beliefs of inflated responsibility that can play a role in the development of childhood OCD (Sameroff & Haith, 1996). At the same time, the ability to think about one's thoughts (i.e., metacognition) develops over a wide developmental age range (perhaps not fully until early adolescence) and often is a function of broader intellectual development (Alexander, Fabricius, Fleming, Zwahr, & Brown, 2003). Therefore, the cognitive development of very young children may not be adequate to fuel the beliefs that certain thoughts are important and for that reason must be controlled.

Other neurodevelopmental factors may influence both the expression of the condition as well as the treatment itself. Because young children may lack adequate abstract and inferential reasoning, they may not benefit from meta-cognitive interventions for their OCD. Furthermore, the prognosis is poorer for youth with poor insight because these youth may be less willing to resist an urge to perform a neutralization during CBT for the condition (Storch et al., 2008) or to participate in exposure tasks.

Development seems to influence the presentation of symptoms, patterns of co-occurring conditions, and sex differences (Geller, 2006; Kalra & Swedo, 2009). For example, harm and sexual obsessions and hoarding compulsions are less common in youth with OCD than in adults with OCD (Geller et al., 2001). A young boy may first exhibit harm obsessions and later, at the time of puberty, exhibit harm obsessions with a sexual quality, such as fear of impregnating a girl or acting on a sexual urge to fondle or kiss her. This shift in symptom expression may reflect the youth's typical sexual development as he experiences developmentally appropriate sexual urges, fantasies, and images. Similarly, as a child matures and becomes aware of the concept of death, she may exhibit existential obsessive doubts about death, such as what happens to our soul when we die. Obsessions that center around sexuality, morality, or death require higher order reasoning not available to young children (Rachman, 2003). In addition, youth on the autism spectrum often exhibit stereotypical movements and self-stimulating behaviors, and they rigidly follow specific routines. It is important for clinicians to distinguish these core features of a developmental disorder from the rigid compulsions in which youth with OCD engage.

Development seems to play a role in the expression of other conditions that tend to occur in pediatric OCD. For example, ADHD and tics are most often associated with childhood onset of OCD, whereas depression and other anxiety disorders more often develop during or after puberty (Mancebo et al., 2008). Males with childhood-onset OCD have higher rates of comorbid tic disorders (Swedo et al., 1989), a higher frequency of compulsions not preceded by obsessions (Geller et al., 1998), and a greater genetic contribution to the disease than adults with the condition as shown in monozygotic and dizygotic twin studies (Pauls, Alsobrook, Goodman, Rasmussen, & Leckman, 1995).

Temperamental Influences

Temperament refers to aspects of a youth's personality that are innate rather than learned. Youth with OCD may exhibit certain temperamental features (Carter & Pollock, 2000). For example, in a study of temperament of youth with OCD, investigators identified elevated levels of emotional reactivity and behavioral inhibition compared with a nonclinical sample of youth of the same age and sex (Ivarsson & Winge-Westholm, 2004). *Emotional reactivity* refers to the characteristics of an emotional response, including the intensity of the response and the threshold of stimuli required to generate the emotional response (Davidson, 1998). That is, for youth with high emotional reactivity, it takes less to trigger an emotional response, and, once triggered, the emotional response is more intense than for youth with low emotional reactivity. These data suggest that although certain temperamental profiles may be more likely in youth with OCD than in control subjects, youth with OCD exhibit considerable variability with respect to the temperamental variables in the study. These findings suggest that the interaction of temperament and environmental stress may better predict the development of OCD in youth than temperament alone.

Temperamental factors may influence the course of treatment in CBT. For example, youth with high emotional reactivity may benefit from less anxiety-evoking exposure stimuli and greater control over the exposure process than youth with lower emotional reactivity. Similarly, the interaction between the youth's temperament and temperament of his parents may influence how the clinician works with the youth's parents, who coaches the youth's exposure tasks, and the extent with which the clinician works with parents to adjust their parenting styles relative to their child (see Chapter 6, this volume).

Cultural, Social, Family, and Peer Influences

Although the phenomenology of OCD appears to be relatively consistent across cultures (Weissman et al., 1994), cultural, social, and familial factors may play a role in shaping the content of a youth's obsessions and compulsions. *Culture* refers to past learning that results in shared patterns of behavior that overlap more with behavior of members of a particular culture than with members of another culture. That is, culture refers to behavior patterns and value systems shared by a group of people (Seiden, 1999). Culture may influence the content of obsessions and the form compulsions take (Tseng, 1997). For example, 20 to 30 years ago in the United Kingdom, people with OCD commonly reported fears of contamination by asbestos, and in more recent years they were more apt to report fears of HIV/AIDS (de Silva, 2006). Similarly, researchers reported a predominance of aggressive obsessions in Brazil and speculated that the rates of violence there may influence the rise in aggressive obsessions in people in Brazil with OCD (Fontenelle, Mendlowicz, Marques, & Versiani, 2004).

The central religious themes and practices within certain religions within cultures can also shape the nature of obsessions and compulsions for individuals with OCD. For example, in India, purification rituals are common to the Hindu faith and reflect a preoccupation with matters of purity and cleanliness. Thus, people in India more often exhibit obsessions and compulsions that reflect themes of dirt and contamination (Chaturvedi, 1993). Similarly, according to their faith, Muslims must pray five times each day, preceded by a ritualized ablution or cleansing. People with OCD in Egypt were more likely to exhibit symptoms that reflected this preoccupation with purity and cleanliness within their Muslim culture (Okasha, Saad, Khalil, El Dawla, & Yehia, 1994).

Unlike with adult-onset OCD, the family environment, among other factors, may play a role in the development of OCD in childhood (Steketee & Van Noppen, 2003; Waters, Barrett, & March, 2001). Family factors, however, likely play a more significant role in maintaining the condition (Allsopp & Verduyn, 1990; Amir, Freshman, & Foa, 2000). Research consistently supports that the family context affects the nature of the youth's OCD and that the youth's OCD affects the family context (March, 1995). The families of youth with OCD are often characterized by high levels of expressed emotion (e.g., high levels of expressed criticism and overinvolvement; Hibbs et al., 1991) and with low levels of emotional support, warmth, and closeness (Valleni-Basile et al., 1995). In addition, parents of youth with OCD may have less confidence in the youth's abilities, less often reward the youth or encourage his or her independence, and less often orient the youth to problem-solving strategies than parents of youth with a non-OCD anxiety disorder (Barrett, Shortt, & Healy, 2002). Instead many parents, particularly anxious parents, step in too quickly to assist youth to escape their distress, or they accommodate or participate in the youth's compulsions and pleas and demands for relief.

The family may also shape the nature of obsessions and compulsions for youth with OCD. According to social learning theory, people learn vicariously, without direct experience (Bandura, 1977). Caregivers may communicate to the child through their actions or their words that certain situations or objects are dangerous and must be avoided at all costs. For example, a child with a biological predisposition to OCD may develop germ obsessions and washing compulsions if one or both parents are physicians and insist on scrupulous handwashing and hygiene. In this way, the parents model an overanxious response to germs and fail to model for the child that the body, particularly a young body, has a robust protective response to germs.

The role of peers in the development and maintenance of pediatric OCD is not well understood, although the negative effect of OCD on peer relationships is well documented (Langley, Bergman, McCracken, & Piacentini, 2004; Piacentini et al., 2003; Storch et al., 2006). Furthermore, it is not clear whether the observed negative effects on peer relationships is primarily because of OCD or other anxiety disorders, or temperamental attributes of the youth, or other common comorbid conditions, such as ADHD. Therefore, it is unlikely that peer difficulties are a risk factor particular to OCD; more likely it is a common feature of most childhood psychiatric disorders. At the same time, youth with disabilities are highly vulnerable to bully victimization (Blake et al., 2016). Bullying by peers may influence the extent and severity of OCD symptoms as well as the development of other emotional and behavioral problems and conditions that can complicate the treatment (Storch et al., 2006).

Stress and Trauma Influences

Although there is some evidence for the relationship between exposure to stress and increases in intrusive thoughts (Rachman, 1997), trauma and stress are nonspecific risk factors for the development and aggravation of a great number of psychiatric conditions. It is unlikely that these risk factors are specific to the development of OCD, as many youth experience stress and trauma without developing OCD. Similarly, certain psychiatric conditions, such as bipolar disorder or schizophrenia, increase the likelihood that individuals will experience trauma when they are in an acute phase of their illness where their judgment is poor and their impulsivity is high (Assion et al., 2009; Cusack, Grubaugh, Knapp, & Frueh, 2006). Therefore, it appears that trauma and stress play a role in the onset of some cases of pediatric OCD, but not in all cases.

COMMON CO-OCCURRING CONDITIONS

Comorbid conditions are common in youth with OCD (Geller et al., 2001). Differential diagnosis between OCD and other psychological conditions can be difficult because OCD shares some features with other conditions (March, Franklin, Leonard, & Foa, 2004). For example, the attempts of youth with OCD to suppress obsessions or to resist engaging in compulsions can drain attentional resources. This can result in the youth's attention problems misdiagnosed as features of ADHD. Although the youth may have ADHD in addition to OCD, it is important that clinicians not diagnose a youth with ADHD without a careful and comprehensive diagnostic evaluation.

Similarly, clinicians may misdiagnose youth with OCD who avoid a range of social situations with social anxiety disorder. However, following a careful evaluation, the clinician may determine that the youth avoids social situations because people trigger obsessive fears that he might hurt someone.

Attention-Deficit/Hyperactivity Disorder

ADHD is common in youth with OCD. Perhaps 30% of youth with OCD also meet criteria for ADHD (Geller, Biederman, Griffin, Jones, & Lefkowitz, 1996), and the onset of ADHD precedes the onset of OCD for more than 80% of youth with both conditions (Geller et al., 2002). Furthermore, youth with both OCD and ADHD experience greater impairment than youth with only OCD, particularly in the areas of school problems, social functioning, and depression (Sukhodolsky et al., 2005). Youth with OCD and ADHD present additional challenges to clinicians treating pediatric OCD. Youth with significant attentional difficulties may have trouble engaging fully in imaginal exposures, for example, or remembering to engage in other treatment strategies and therefore may benefit from treatment of the comorbid ADHD prior to beginning treatment for the OCD.

Other Anxiety Disorders

The prevalence of other anxiety disorders in youth with OCD may be 50% to 60% (Geller et al., 2001; Zohar, 1999). Generalized anxiety disorder (16%) and separation anxiety disorder (7%; Geller, 2006; Leonard et al., 2001) are the most common anxiety disorders (Geller et al., 1996). Other anxiety disorders often precede the onset of OCD in youth (Rasmussen & Eisen, 1990). Social phobia appears also to be common in youth with OCD and its prevalence may range from 2% to 25%, depending on the age of the youth. Interestingly, the longer youth have struggled with OCD, the more likely they are to develop social phobia, perhaps because of the shame and secrecy that are common experiences of youth with OCD (Diniz et al., 2004).

Mood Disorders

Children with OCD are at considerable risk of experiencing depressive symptoms and the onset of mood disorders (Peterson, Pine, Cohen, & Brook, 2001). Rates of major depressive disorder in youth with OCD in clinical samples range from 10% to 26% (Hanna, 1995; Swedo et al., 1989), and depression in early adolescence is a possible predictor of risk for developing OCD in young adulthood (Douglass, Moffitt, Dar, McGee, & Silva, 1995). This is not surprising, because OCD can significantly derail the social, emotional, and academic development of youth with the condition. Furthermore, researchers suggest that the ruminative nature of OCD may place youth at risk for developing the depressive cognitions associated with a mood disorder (Carter & Pollock, 2000; Douglass et al., 1995). In addition, pediatric clients that develop both OCD and bipolar disorder tend to have earlier onsets of OCD than do pediatric clients without a bipolar mood disorder (Masi et al., 2004).

Tourette and Tic Disorders

The rate of occurrence of tic and Tourette spectrum disorders (TSDs) in youth with OCD is quite high. For example, 20% to 60% of youth with TSD have a comorbid OCD, whereas 7% of youth with OCD have comorbid TSD and 20% have tics (Coffey & Park, 1997). Tics and TSD are the most common comorbid psychiatric illness for pediatric OCD (Leonard, Lenane, Swedo, Rettew, Gershon, & Rapoport, 1992). Researchers have found a strong association between tic disorders and OCD (Peterson et al., 2001) and therefore have argued that tics and TSD and OCD may have a common genetic substrate (genotype) that in interaction with other factors may influence the expression of the genetic substrate (phenotype) as one disorder or the other (Pauls et al., 1995). In other words, OCD and Tourette disorder may be different expressions of the same underlying genetic abnormality (Zohar, 1999). In addition, because of the high rate of co-occurrence of tics and OCD in pediatric populations, researchers have proposed that childhood-onset OCD may be a tic-related subtype of OCD (Eichstedt & Arnold, 2001). Furthermore, the presence of tics in childhood and early adolescence predicts an increase in obsessive–compulsive symptoms in late adolescence and adulthood (Peterson et al., 2001; Leckman & Cohen, 1999).

Oppositional Defiant and Conduct Disorders

Many youth with OCD exhibit disruptive or "pushback" behaviors, and perhaps 25% of these youth exhibit behavioral disorders, such as oppositional defiant disorder (ODD) and conduct disorders (Geller et al., 1996; Hanna, 1995). The prevalence of behavioral disorders in this population may reflect the difficulty parents have in managing pushback from youth who are desperate to avoid situations that evoke their anxiety, or who are unwilling to "go with the flow," in general, but particularly when a situation triggers their OCD. It is not easy to differentiate OCD and ODD, as the rigidity of compulsive behavior can mimic oppositional behavior of youth with ODD. However, a diagnosis of ODD in youth with OCD predicts for poorer response to pharmacotherapy (Geller, Biederman, Stewart, Mullin, Farrell, et al., 2003) and can complicate cognitive behavior treatment as well.

Eating Disorders, Impulse-Control Disorders, and Autism Spectrum Disorders

Eating disorders co-occur in youth with OCD (Becker, Jennen-Steinmetz, Holtmann, El-Faddagh, & Schmidt, 2003). The lifetime prevalence of anxiety disorders (particularly social anxiety disorder) and OCD is 30% to 65% in youth with anorexia nervosa and bulimia nervosa (Herzog, Nussbaum, & Marmor, 1996; Johnson, Cohen, Kotler, Kasen, & Brook, 2002). In addition, pediatric anxiety disorders, in general, predict substance abuse in later adolescence and adulthood (Essau, Conradt, & Petermann, 2002). For this reason, we recommend that clinicians routinely screen for substance use and abuse in youth with OCD.

Impulse-control disorders and OCD share an excessive preoccupation with certain thoughts and accompanying urges to act in order to decrease tension and physiological arousal (Grant & Kim, 2007). Unlike with OCD, youth with impulse-control disorders also experience pleasure or gratification when carrying out impulsive acts. For example, pyromania is an impulse-control disorder that involves intentionally setting a fire for gratification. Prior to setting the fire, youth experience intrusive thoughts or images that result in tension and then relief once they set the fire. The prevalence of pyromania in youth is unknown, but over 60% of cases of fire-setting in the United States occurred before the youth reached 15 years of age (Blanco et al., 2010). Kleptomania, another impulse-control disorder, is characterized by strong urges to steal. Youth with kleptomania do not steal for personal gain, such as revenge or money, nor do they steal because of another disorder, such as bipolar disorder. Kleptomania appears to be rare and is more common in females than in males (Grant & Odlaug, 2008).

Autism spectrum disorders (ASDs) are pervasive developmental disorders that begin in early childhood and are characterized by significant deficits in the ability to communicate and interact effectively with others. Many individuals with ASD exhibit repetitive and stereotypic behaviors that may be linked to fixed interests common to youth with ASD, but they can also exhibit obsessive–compulsive symptoms common to OCD, particularly somatic obsessions (overawareness of body sensations or functions, e.g., blinking, breathing) and repeating compulsions (Russell, Mataix-Cols, Anson, & Murphy, 2005). The prevalence of OCD in youth with ASD is near 37% or higher (Lewin, Wood, Gunderson, Murphy, & Storch, 2011).

OBSESSIVE–COMPULSIVE SPECTRUM DISORDERS

Researchers recognize that OCD is likely a heterogeneous condition. Attempts to classify symptoms into homogeneous and mutually exclusive types or categories related to neurobiological variables, genetic transmission, and treatment response have yielded mixed results. At the same time, investigators suspect that OCD and other obsessive–compulsive spectrum disorders may share a similar underlying neurobiological substrate (Mataix-Cols, Rosario-Campos, & Leckman, 2005). In recognition of the common features of obsessive preoccupation and repetitive behaviors of certain disorders, as well as their distinction from anxiety disorders, researchers have subsumed OCD and several other conditions under the broad class of obsessive–compulsive spectrum disorders (American Psychiatric Association, 2013). Along with OCD, disorders in this class include body dysmorphic disorder (BDD), trichotillomania (TTM; hair-pulling disorder), excoriation disorder (skin-picking disorder), and hoarding disorder.

BDD is characterized by persistent and intrusive preoccupations with a perceived defect in appearance. Youth with BDD can dislike any part of their body, such as their hair, skin, nose, chest, or stomach. Typically, the perceived defect is only a slight imperfection or irregularity in size, shape, or color. Nonetheless, youth with BDD are very distressed by the perceived imperfection and may avoid social encounters, refuse school, or plead parents for plastic surgery or other interventions. BDD most often develops in adolescence. The prevalence is approximately 1% and appears to be about equal in both males and females (Becker et al., 2003; Grant, Kim, & Crow, 2001). Research suggests that BDD is not a clinical variant of OCD and often has relationships with other disorders, such as mood, social anxiety, and eating disorders (Frare, Perugi, Ruffolo, & Toni, 2004). Furthermore, key differences between OCD and BDD directly influence the course and treatment of the condition (Phillips, Menard, Pagano, Fay, & Stout, 2006). For example, the beliefs about defects in appearance for youth with BDD are ego-syntonic (consistent with sense of self), whereas for the vast majority of youth the OCD-related beliefs are ego-dystonic (alien to sense of self). Furthermore, in BDD there is a high rate of delusional conviction in the beliefs about defects in appearance that are not typically present in OCD (Castle & Groves, 2000; Jefferys & Castle, 2003).

Trichotillomania, or hair-pulling disorder, is characterized by recurrent and compulsive hair pulling, leading to noticeable hair loss and significant distress and functional impairment. Youth primarily pull hair from the scalp, eyebrows, and eyelashes, although they can pull hair from any part of the body with hair. Youth may use their fingernails to pull, as well as tweezers, pins or other devices. Typically, but not always, adults report a sense of tension before pulling hair that leads to strong urges to pull and gratification or relief after pulling. Most children, on the other hand, deny feeling this sense of tension (Oranje, Peereboom-Wynia, & De Raeymaecker, 1986). The prevalence of TTM in youth with OCD is significant (Fontenelle, Mendlowicz, & Versiani, 2005; Stewart, Jenike, & Keuthen, 2005), although the rates among younger children are largely unknown (Tolin, Franklin, Diefenbach, Anderson, & Meunier, 2007). The peak age of onset of TTM is 9 to 13 years of age, and the lifetime prevalence of the disorder is 0.6% to 4.0% in the general population (Huynh, Gavino, & Magid, 2013). The condition is generally chronic, although symptom severity tends to wax and wane (Christenson, Mackenzie, Mitchell, & Callies, 1991). Most cases of TTM begin in childhood (Schlosser, Black, Blum, & Goldstein, 1994).

Developmental age may play a role in the progression of the disorder as well as the presentation of particular features of the condition. For example, there appears to be a progression across developmental age in the type of pulling itself. There are two distinct types of hair pulling: automatic and focused (Franklin et al., 2008). Automatic pulling is pulling that occurs outside awareness. Focused pulling, by contrast, is pulling with awareness and typically occurs in response to negative emotional states (e.g., sadness, anxiety, anger), intense thoughts or urges, or as an attempt to establish symmetry. Younger children more often engage in automatic unfocused pulling, with little awareness of the behavior and its antecedents. As youth mature, they experience more focused and frequent urges to pull and greater awareness that they are engaged in hair pulling (Panza, Pittenger, & Bloch, 2013). In addition, younger children are much more likely to pull from one site than are adults, and many younger children do not describe urges before, and relief after, hair-pulling behavior (Panza et al., 2013).

Excoriation disorder (ECD) is characterized by recurrent skin picking that results in skin lesions and clinically significant distress or impairment in functioning (Wilhelm et al., 1999). The primary location of skin picking is usually the face, but any part of the body can be involved. Youth may pick at normal skin variations, such as freckles and moles; at pre-existing scabs, bumps, or blemishes; or at imagined defects in the skin. Youth typically pick the skin with their fingernails, but they can use their teeth, tweezers, or pins. Skin-picking behavior can result in bleeding, infections, or permanent disfigurement of the skin. The lifetime prevalence of ECD in adults is at least 1.4% to 5.4% of the general adult population (Lang et al., 2010; Odlaug & Grant, 2010), and approximately 75% of individuals with ECD are female (Odlaug & Grant, 2010). It is not clear what the prevalence of ECD in youth is, although adolescence may be the most common age of onset of the condition (Andreoli, Finore, Provini, & Paradisi, 2008). As in the case of TTM, skin picking is sometimes preceded by tension and strong urges to pick and can be followed by a sense of relief or pleasure. Skin picking, as in the case of hair pulling, can be focused or unfocused.

Hoarding disorder (HRD) is characterized by persistent difficulty discarding or parting with possessions, regardless of the value others may attribute to these possessions. The large number of possessions and the difficulty organizing and discarding them results in highly cluttered living spaces; at times, those living in the residence face significant health and safety risks. While some people with HRD may not be particularly distressed by their behavior, their behavior can be distressing to other people, such as family members or landlords.

Investigators estimate the prevalence of HRD in the general population to be between 2% and 5% (Iervolino et al., 2009; Timpano et al., 2011). Hoarding symptoms typically appear in childhood (Tolin, Meunier, Frost, & Steketee, 2010), with hoarding symptoms relatively prevalent in adolescents, particularly in girls, which cause distress and/or impairment. Exclusion of the clutter criterion (as adolescents do not have control over their environment) increased the prevalence rate to 3.7%. Approximately one third of youth with clinically significant hoarding symptoms reported excessive acquisition (Ivanov et al., 2013).

PEDIATRIC AUTOIMMUNE NEUROPSYCHIATRIC DISORDERS ASSOCIATED WITH STREPTOCOCCAL INFECTIONS

Pediatric autoimmune neuropsychiatric disorders associated with streptococcal (PANDAS) infections refers to a subset of prepubertal children with rapid onset or exacerbation of OCD or tic disorders following group A beta-hemolytic streptococcal (GABHS) infection (an infection of a beta-hemolytic species of Gram-positive bacteria that is a response for a wide range of infections). Researchers propose that an initial autoimmune reaction to a GABHS infection produces antibodies that interfere with basal ganglia function, causing symptom exacerbations (Snider & Swedo, 2004). This autoimmune response can result in a broad range of neuropsychiatric symptoms. In addition to OCD or tic disorder symptoms, youth may exhibit increased emotional lability (rapid and tense fluctuations in mood), enuresis (involuntary urination), anxiety, and deterioration in handwriting (Boileau, 2011; de Oliveira & Pelajo, 2010; Moretti, Pasquini, Mandarelli, Tarsitani, & Biondi, 2008). Although there is some evidence to support the link between streptococcus infection and onset in some cases of OCD and tics, this causal link is by no means established, making the diagnosis of PANDAS controversial (Maia, Cooney, & Peterson, 2008; Murphy, Kurlan, & Leckman, 2010; Shulman, 2009). Furthermore, debate continues whether PANDAS is a distinct entity that differs from other cases of Tourette syndrome disorder and OCD (Boileau, 2011; Felling & Singer, 2011; Robertson, 2011; Singer, 2011). Adding to the debate, researchers have raised concerns that clinicians may be overdiagnosing PANDAS in pediatric populations without conclusive evidence and clear diagnostic criteria (Shulman, 2009). At this time, PANDAS is not considered a disease entity and therefore is not listed as a diagnosis by the *International Statistical Classification of Diseases and Related Health Problems* (*ICD*) or as a syndrome in the *DSM* (Pichichero, 2009).

Given the controversy regarding the etiology of PANDAS and the absence of clear and agreed-upon diagnostic criteria, researchers proposed pediatric acute-onset neuropsychiatric syndrome (PANS) as an alternative to PANDAS (Swedo, Leckman, & Rose, 2012). PANS includes youth with acute-onset OCD, but also acute-onset neuropsychiatric disorders without an apparent environmental precipitant or immune dysfunction. Researchers hope that the new criteria captured within PANS will assist researchers and clinicians to discriminate better between traditional childhood-onset OCD and the sudden and severe onset of symptoms that characterizes youth with PANS (Swedo et al., 2012).

The research on the topic of PANDAS/PANS is limited, and what is known about its diagnosis and treatment is speculative at best. For example, we do not know if OCD-like symptoms for children with an acute onset are always PANDAS/PANS or are never PANDAS/PANS. We do not know if PANDAS/PANS symptoms remit spontaneously later in adolescence, nor do we know whether these symptoms result in treatment-resistant OCD secondary to permanent damage to the basal ganglia. At this time, we have many more questions about acute-onset pediatric OCD than we have answers. Current treatment recommendations for PANS/PANDAS include simultaneously treating the infection with medication and the OCD symptoms with exposure and response prevention therapy (a form of CBT that involves youth with OCD facing their fears and refraining from engaging in compulsions or rituals; see Chapter 2), with or without psychotropic medication (Thienemann et al., 2017). For additional information on PANS/PANDAS, check the NIMH website (http://www.nimh.nih.gov/health/publications/pandas/index.shtml) and the International OCD Foundation (IOCDF) website (http://www.iocdf.org). Also, when discussing PANS/PANDAS with parents, clinicians can download the PANS/PANDAS handout (see http://pubs.apa.org/books/supp/tompkins, Web Form 1.1).

COGNITIVE BEHAVIOR MODEL OF OCD

Conceptualization of pediatric OCD begins with the nomothetic conceptualization of the disorder in general. A *nomothetic conceptualization* is a theory about the primary variables that maintain OCD for anyone. That is, nomothetic conceptualization is a general theory about the mechanism that drives and maintains the condition. Fortunately for clinicians, to treat the condition it is not necessary to know what caused a child to develop OCD. It is only necessary to know the hypothesized factors that maintain the symptoms. These hypothesized factors are the targets of CBT for pediatric OCD. The goal of CBT is to reverse or undercut these factors and thereby weaken the existing mechanism thought to maintain the condition.

The cognitive behavior nomothetic conceptualization of OCD proposes that dysfunctional beliefs and interpretations of normally occurring intrusive thoughts result in obsessions and compulsions (Rachman, 1997). That is, although thoughts, images, or impulses that intrude into consciousness are normal mental events (Rachman & de Silva, 1978), youth with OCD transform these normal intrusions into highly distressing obsessions through a series of maladaptive evaluations, primarily evaluating these thoughts as highly significant and a threat that only they can prevent. For example, the belief that one has the special power to cause, or the duty to prevent, negative events or outcomes (i.e., inflated responsibility) and the belief that it is necessary and possible to be completely certain that negative events or outcomes will not occur (i.e., intolerance of uncertainty) are two of the most common maladaptive OCD beliefs. These misinterpretations cause individuals to become preoccupied, overly focused, and desperate to control normal thoughts. For a comprehensive list of maladaptive OCD beliefs, see Abramowitz, 2006 (Table 3.2, page 68).

Youth without OCD think very little about their thoughts. They consider most thoughts to be meaningless: "It's just a thought." They understand or believe, although they are likely to be unaware of this, that thoughts are random mental events that do not influence outcomes or one's actions and in themselves are meaningless and harmless (i.e., mental noise). However, youth with OCD attach a high degree of importance to a thought. For example, as James, who does not have OCD, speaks to his math teacher, he has the urge to spit in the teacher's face. James immediately labels the thought as silly and does not assume that thinking the thought means that he may spit in his teacher's face. Nor would James assume that the thought meant anything about the teacher. However, his best friend, George, who has OCD, labels the thought that he might spit in his teacher's face as significant. He then feels very anxious and leaves the classroom abruptly before he acts on the thought, as he believes he might do. As he exits the classroom, he touches the right and left sides of the doorway with his right and left shoulder to get the thought out of his mind.

Repeated appraisal of normal intrusive thoughts in this way triggers anxiety and distress. The youth then attempts to suppress the unwanted thought or, through actions and mental actions, attempts to prevent the feared event from occurring. George both escaped the classroom and engaged in a compulsive behavior to prevent the feared outcome (i.e., spitting in his math teacher's face).

According to the cognitive behavior model of OCD, avoidance and escape behavior, as well as mental and behavioral neutralizations (e.g., compulsions), maintain the condition in several ways (see Figure 1.1). First, because avoidance, escape, and neutralizations do indeed result in an immediate decrease in distress and anxiety, these actions (both mental and behavioral) are reinforced and maintained through operant conditioning (negative reinforcement). For example, if you enter a room that is hot and stuffy and you adjust the thermostat in the room until you feel cool and comfortable, the next time you enter the room when it is hot and stuffy, you will go immediately to the thermostat to adjust it. The immediate relief you experience increases "go to the thermostat" behavior when you are uncomfortable in that way.

FIGURE 1.1. Comprehensive Cognitive Behavioral Model

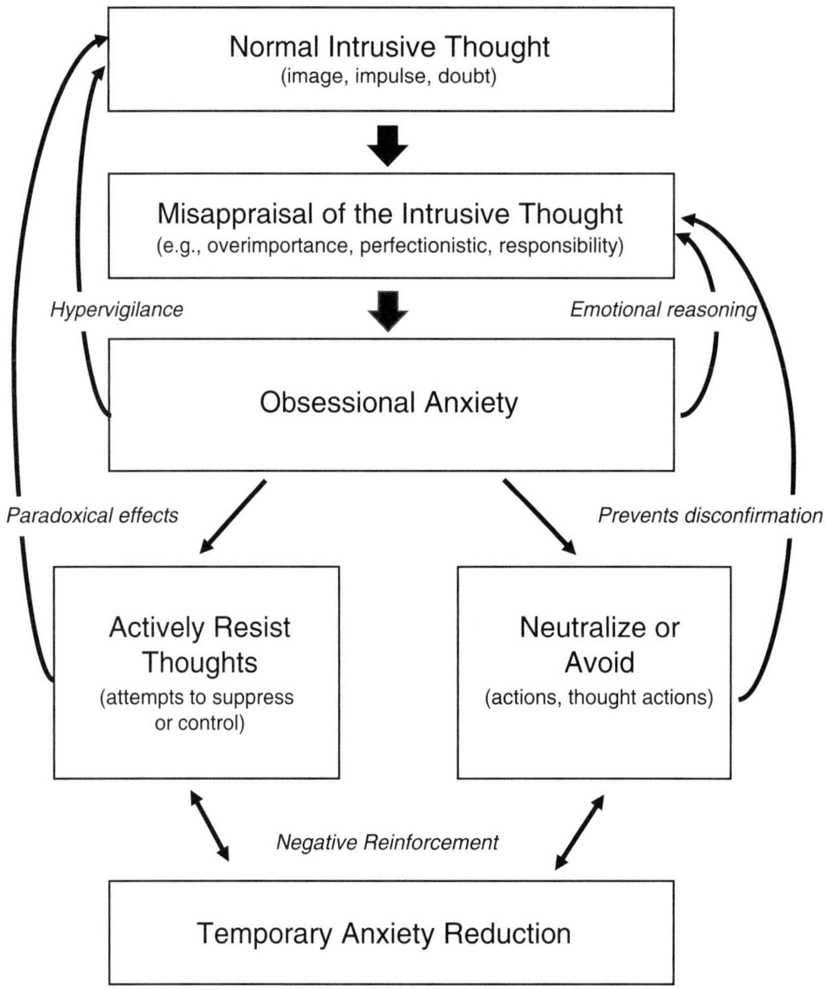

From *Understanding and Treating Obsessive-Compulsive Disorder: A Cognitive Behavioral Approach* (p. 86), by J. S. Abramowitz, 2006, Mahwah, NJ: Lawrence Erlbaum Associates. Copyright 2006 by Lawrence Erlbaum Associates. Adapted with permission.

Second, because avoidance and neutralizations result in an immediate, although temporary, reduction in anxiety, these maladaptive anxiety management strategies interfere with the natural attenuation of the fear response that occurs when individuals remain in the feared situation for longer periods. Also avoidance and active neutralizations preserve dysfunctional beliefs and misinterpretations of obsessional thoughts. That is, when the feared consequence does not occur after completing a neutralization, the individual attributes this outcome to having engaged in a neutralization. For example, if George leaves the classroom quickly or engages in compulsions (e.g., touches the doorway with his right and then his left shoulder), he will not learn that having the thought and urge to spit in his teacher's face does not mean that he will do it, whether he engages in the compulsive behavior or not. To learn that his expectations are incorrect, George must remain in the situation without engaging in any neutralization.

Third, attempts to avoid, suppress, and neutralize intrusive obsessions increase the frequency of obsessions. This is quite counterintuitive to most individuals with OCD who believe that these maladaptive actions decrease the frequency of their obsessions. Instead, avoidance and neutralizations serve as reminders of obsessional intrusions and thereby prompt their occurrence. For example, George repeatedly swallows the saliva in his mouth. He believes by keeping his mouth free of saliva, he will not be able to spit in his teacher's face. However, each time George swallows, the act of swallowing triggers intrusions about spitting in his teacher's face.

To summarize, the cognitive behavior model hypothesizes that the process of maintaining OCD begins with an evaluation of normal intrusions as highly meaningful (e.g., posing a threat to oneself or to others for which the individual with OCD is responsible). This evaluation results in the individual feeling anxious, who then attempts to remove the intrusive thought from consciousness or prevent the feared consequence. This process paradoxically results in an increase in the frequency of the intrusions and the perpetuation of these mental events. Neutralizations (actions and thought actions) maintain the frequency and intensity of the undesired intrusions and prevent the individual from learning that the appraisals, including the predictions of catastrophic events, are incorrect. Clinicians can download an illustration of the model (see http://pubs.apa.org/books/supp/tompkins, Web Form 1.2) to use when discussing the model with older youth and parents.

CONCLUSION

Nearly half of all cases of OCD arise in childhood (Rasmussen & Eisen, 1990). Pediatric OCD appears to be a heterogeneous disorder with a variety of factors that influence the onset, expression, and maintenance of the condition and thereby challenge the clinician's ability to diagnosis, conceptualize, and treat the condition. For this reason, it is important that clinicians understand the particulars of the condition, as well as the developmental and environmental factors that can influence the course of the disorder and the youth's response to CBT for it. When pediatric OCD is untreated, its course is chronic and deteriorating (Stewart et al., 2004), which places many youth at greater risk to develop other psychiatric disorders in adulthood (Bolton, Luckie, & Steinberg, 1995; Hanna, 1995). However, with appropriate treatment, either CBT alone or in combination with medication, conducted by knowledgeable and qualified clinicians, most youth exhibit significant long-term improvement (Stewart et al., 2004).

In the next chapter, we describe the modular treatment that is the focus of this book.

2

Modular CBT for Pediatric OCD

Cognitive behavior therapy (CBT) for pediatric obsessive–compulsive disorder (OCD) is the psychological treatment of choice for youth (ages 7–18) with mild to moderate cases of OCD (March, Frances, Carpenter, & Kahn, 1997; Weisz et al., 2012). In this chapter, we describe a modular treatment approach that is the focus of this book. We begin with a description of protocol-driven versus modular-driven CBT for pediatric OCD, followed by what we view as the advantages of a modular-driven CBT approach for the condition. We then describe the key modules, or intervention packages, that we flexibly apply in the treatment of pediatric OCD, and the empirical evidence in support of these interventions. We also describe the vital role of case conceptualization in modular-driven CBT and conclude with the general phases of modular-driven CBT and the structure of typical sessions.

PROTOCOL-DRIVEN CBT APPROACH

Protocol-driven CBT for psychological disorders includes a standardized step-by-step list of interventions, primarily exposure and response prevention. Generally, these interventions are implemented in a particular order and in a particular manner regardless of the particular youth and parents. Over several decades, psychotherapy researchers have developed many protocol-driven, evidence-based treatments for childhood problems, such as anxiety and depressive disorders, and conduct disorders (Weisz et al., 2012; Weisz & Kazdin, 2010).

http://dx.doi.org/10.1037/0000167-003
Cognitive Behavior Therapy for OCD in Youth: A Step-by-Step Guide, by M. A. Tompkins, D. J. Owen, N. H. Shiloff, and L. R. Tanner

In spite of strong empirical evidence in support of the efficacy of protocol-driven CBT, many clinicians have not accepted these treatments into their routine clinical practices (Borntrager, Chorpita, Higa-McMillan, & Weisz, 2009). Clinicians report that the inflexibility of a standardized protocol-driven CBT approach is not relevant to the population with whom they work nor to the way they work (Palinkas et al., 2013). They are concerned that protocol-driven CBT limits their ability to select the most clinically relevant problems and intervene effectively, and that adhering to a protocol disrupts the therapeutic process and alliance. Understandably, these concerns have likely decreased the dissemination of these evidence-based treatments into routine clinical care.

Several researchers have suggested that the poor dissemination of standardized protocol-driven treatments is a result of poor implementation and accompanying poor fidelity to the treatment protocol (Ougrin, Tranah, Leigh, Taylor, & Asarnow, 2012). Other researchers have suggested that the complexity of youth and parents in routine clinical practice such as community-based clinics may contribute to the poorer results of traditional evidence-based treatment protocols with this population (Weisz et al., 2012). This is the long-standing opinion of many clinicians who argue that the participants in these research studies significantly differ from youth who present in everyday clinical practice. Their clients often present with multiple complex problems (e.g., developmental issues, family difficulties, trauma histories) and one or more co-occurring disorders (e.g., depression, autism spectrum disorder [ASD], attention-deficit/hyperactivity disorder [ADHD], social anxiety disorder), which may require greater flexibility and individualization in the selection and application of interventions than are typically included in standard protocol-driven CBT.

MODULAR-DRIVEN CBT APPROACH

By *modular-driven*, we mean key strategies packaged as modules, such as exposure, response prevention, or cognitive restructuring. The modular approach involves the flexible application of a specified set of intervention modules to the unique clinical characteristics of each client (Chorpita, Daleiden, & Weisz, 2005b). For example, while most parents benefit from some parent training in CBT for pediatric OCD, not all parents require the same "dose." Some parents accommodate to the youth's OCD symptoms seldom and therefore require very little training in responding adaptively to the youth's symptoms. Other parents may directly or indirectly undermine treatment, such as a father with OCD who refuses to attend parent meetings because he is worried that his wife will insist that he seek treatment for his own OCD, or an anxious mother who cannot resist reassuring her daughter with OCD that she is not ill. Not only does a modular-driven CBT approach address many of the concerns clinicians have regarding the implementation of protocol-driven CBT, but there is growing evidence that modular approaches result in greater efficacy, efficiency, and acceptance by clinicians in routine clinical practice (Weisz & Chorpita, 2012; Weisz et al., 2012).

The concept of modular treatment is not new (Lazarus, 1974; Liberman, Mueser, & Glynn, 1988), and the approach has been applied to a variety of psychological conditions (Annon, 1975; Falloon, 1988). The majority of these approaches fall under the heading of "prescriptive" approaches. For example, Beutler and colleagues proposed a therapeutic approach for the treatment of adult depression designed to work across theoretical orientations and to allow clinicians to match particular strategies or styles to client characteristics (Beutler & Harwood, 2000; Norcross, 2011). The authors described a set of overarching principles that clinicians apply within different therapeutic approaches. Similarly, Persons and colleagues outlined a method for systematically developing an intervention based on a cognitive behavioral case conceptualization (Persons, 1989; Persons & Tompkins, 1997). Building on strategies from the behavioral assessment literature, this approach requires clinicians to develop a working model of the internal and external factors that maintain a specific client's problems.

Recently, however, researchers have formalized modular-driven CBT to include a set of core principles (Chorpita, Daleiden, & Weisz, 2005a), including the notion of structured flexibility. Structured flexibility is a critical and overarching principle of modular-driven CBT. Clinicians can deliver modules as needed but they are based on a case conceptualization that recognizes the particular characteristics of the child, parents, and context. Although flexible, however, the module content includes specific procedures that adhere closely to the procedures in protocol-driven CBT for which there is strong evidence in support of treatment effects (Weisz, Donenberg, Han, & Weiss, 1995). We believe that there are a number of advantages to modular-driven CBT.

Increasing Efficacy of Evidence-Based Treatment

A number of studies suggest that individualized treatments tailored to the unique strengths and weakness of pediatric clients may result in greater efficacy than protocol-driven treatments. For example, 50% to 75% of children who did not respond to protocol-driven CBT exhibited treatment gains after CBT was more individualized (Ollendick, 2000). In addition, research has demonstrated that modular-driven CBT is effective for pediatric anxiety disorders (Chorpita, Taylor, Francis, Moffitt, & Austin, 2004) and depressive disorders (Chorpita et al., 2013). Furthermore, modular-driven CBT appears to transport well into real-world clinical settings (Weisz & Chorpita, 2012). For example, modular-driven CBT for depressed, anxious, and disruptive youth in community-health settings outperformed usual care and standard evidence-based treatments across multiple outcome measures (Weisz et al., 2012).

Increasing Efficiency of Evidence-Based Treatment

A number of studies suggest that treatments tailored to client characteristics can result in improved responses in a shorter period of time (Eisen & Silverman, 1998). Efficient therapies are more cost-effective because clinicians achieve good outcomes in less time. This is particularly important for clinicians providing services within community clinics with limited funding and high demand.

Increasing Child and Parent Engagement in Evidence-Based Treatment

Efficient treatments are less taxing for child and parents. Fitting therapy appointments into already busy schedules is not easy for many families, and fewer appointments means that it is more likely that families will attend all sessions required for a good treatment outcome. Furthermore, fewer effective therapy appointments may decrease therapy dropout, increase the engagement of youth in evidence-based treatments, and reach more youth who are suffering.

Increasing Clinician Engagement in the Evidence-Based Treatment

A reality of clinical practice is that most clinicians do not use protocol-driven CBT (Addis & Krasnow, 2000). Perhaps they favor creativity and flexibility over empiricism and evidence. To reach more youth with evidence-based treatments, we believe that it is essential that one recognize this reality and strive to meet clinicians where they are. Modular-driven CBT recognizes that clinical judgment guides the selection of interventions and the staging of them. Modular-driven CBT gives clinicians a greater say in which interventions make sense for a particular youth and parent, how long to spend on the intervention, and when in the course of therapy to introduce it. However, flexibility does not mean less structure. Modular-driven CBT limits the range of interventions and stages interventions in a specific order that builds understanding and skills in a stepwise progressive manner. For example, in this book, we introduce psychoeducation and the rationale for treatment prior to building the exposure and response prevention (ERP) hierarchy because these components increase the youth's willingness to participate in the design of an ERP hierarchy and to engage fully in the exposure process.

ROLE OF CASE CONCEPTUALIZATION

Modular-driven CBT is not a collection of techniques that clinicians throw at youth randomly and hope that one sticks. The approach is more thoughtful than that. We believe that a comprehensive case conceptualization is essential to treat pediatric OCD effectively, modular-driven or otherwise. In modular-driven CBT, not every youth will receive the same core strategies, or at the same dose, and not in the same order for the same period of time. Therefore, modular-driven CBT depends on clinicians making a myriad of clinical decisions over the course of treatment.

Of course, the first clinical decision is whether the youth has OCD and is therefore a candidate for CBT. However, once diagnosed, there are other factors that influence the general treatment plan, for example, whether to include medications or not, or whether treatment is even possible. Can youth and parents engage in treatment, and can they meet regularly? What other factors might affect the youth's treatment response (insight, degree of parent accommodation and the willingness of parents to change it)? Are there other conditions that influence the youth's response to treatment, such as co-occurring ADHD, ASD, or Tourette disorder (TSD)? What is the degree and severity of oppositional behaviors, if any, and how might they influence the youth's willingness to participate fully in treatment?

A comprehensive, thoughtful, and relevant conceptualization guides clinicians through the decision-making process. Clinicians develop a case conceptualization utilizing information gathered during the diagnostic and assessment processes (see Chapter 3, this volume), which includes multiple data sources (clinical interviews, measures, behavioral observations, collateral contacts, and recording completed by youth and parents). In a sense, the case conceptualization is a story that explains the primary factors hypothesized to maintain the internal and external symptoms, in this case, the intensity and frequency of obsessions and compulsions, and the degree youth avoid situations that trigger these internal and external experiences. Clinicians then focus the core strategies on these hypothesized perpetuating factors.

Once clinicians develop the case conceptualization, they then develop a treatment plan with youth and parents. However, the case conceptualization evolves or changes in response to the youth's progress in treatment. Therefore, it is essential that clinicians monitor the frequency and severity of the youth's OCD symptoms and modify the case conceptualization in response to the youth's response to treatment (Stoddard & Williams, 2012). We describe later in this book the process of monitoring treatment outcome and its link to case conceptualization (see Chapter 4).

CORE STRATEGIES

A *principle* in science is a fundamental, primary, or general rule or fact of nature that explains how something works or why something happens. For example, "behavior is maintained through contingent reinforcement" is a principle. "Cognition moderates emotional responses" is a principle. A *strategy* is an application of a principle. For example, imagery is a strategy. At the same time, one clinician might utilize the strategy of imagery to evoke feelings of safety and comfort and another clinician might utilize imagery to evoke feelings of awareness or even negative affect, as in the case of exposure. Then there are *techniques*. A technique is a specific procedure, such as imaginal exposure (in which the client imagines feared situations, thoughts, and memories) or selective ignoring (in which parents actively ignore undesirable behaviors to decrease the frequency of those behaviors). Many clinicians view CBT as a handful of techniques without recognizing that they rest on guiding principles and are also a part of broader psychotherapeutic strategies and a case conceptualization (Persons, 2008; Persons & Tompkins, 2007). In fact, clinicians can apply a technique in a variety of ways and in line with various strategic objectives. For example, in the treatment of OCD, the clinician may use the strategy of exposure via a number of exposure-based techniques: situational, imaginal, or interoceptive. Thus, principles, strategies, and techniques differ in terms of their specificity, along a continuum, from least to most specific (Beutler & Harwood, 2000). Although it is important that clinicians know the CBT techniques required to treat pediatric OCD, we believe it is as important that they understand the principles on which the strategies rest.

We describe the modules in this treatment as evidence based for two reasons. First, certain strategies are linked to a principle with strong, direct empirical support, such as the principle of extinction (VanElzakker, Dahlgren, Davis, Dubois, & Shin, 2014). Second, other core strategies have indirect empirical support because they are repeatedly included in evidence-based protocols, such as psychoeducation in CBT for anxiety disorders (Bandelow, Michaelis, & Wedekind, 2017) or CBT for depression (Schotte, Van Den Bossche, De Doncker, Claes, & Cosyns, 2006). Because not all strategies have strong empirical support of the underlying (hypothesized) principle, we favor the term *modular-driven* rather than *principle-driven*.

The modular-driven approach we describe in this book depends on the effective implementation of core strategies shown to be effective in the treatment of pediatric OCD (March, Mulle, & Herbel, 1994) as well as pediatric anxiety disorders (Ollendick & Francis, 1988; Ollendick & King, 1994). At the same time, clinicians may find that there is considerable overlap between core strategies. For example, educating youth and parents about OCD and socializing them into the treatment approach are engagement strategies, as is the collaborative process of developing the case conceptualization and treatment plan with youth and parents, or even the use of a hierarchy to direct the exposure plan. Our decision then to include an intervention in one class of core strategies rather than in another is arbitrary. The application of these core strategies, however, is not.

In the next chapters, we describe the proper implementation of the fundamental core strategies that form the evidence-based treatment for pediatric OCD. Later in the book, we describe typical problems that can arise as clinicians implement the core strategies and tell how to overcome these problems. However, when a problem arises in this treatment, we encourage clinicians to first establish that they have implemented the core strategies correctly and effectively before assuming that poor treatment response is due to another factor.

Engagement

Engagement is the willingness of youth and parents to participate in the tasks and goals of therapy. Sufficient engagement on the part of youth and parents is required to benefit from CBT for pediatric OCD. Therefore, engagement is a critical core strategy that directly influences treatment outcome. Youth and parents cannot benefit from treatment unless they are attending therapy sessions and participating fully in therapeutic tasks, such as exposure strategies.

Typically, youth and parents with poor engagement have trouble adhering with the tasks of therapy and the general treatment plan. For example, poor adherence to the tasks of therapy involves failure to complete, or complete correctly, out-of-session ERP tasks, to record symptoms, or to limit parental accommodation behaviors. Poor adherence to the general treatment plan involves failure to meet at the frequency recommended by the clinician or to adhere with other aspects of the treatment plan (e.g., follow-through with a medication evaluation or plan). Frequent cancellations of appointments or missing appointments without notice are the most common signs that youth and parents are about to drop out from treatment. Furthermore, there is a relationship between poor task adherence and attrition or dropout. Youth and parents who do not complete the tasks of therapy, such as exposure with response prevention, are not likely to improve and therefore are more likely to withdraw from treatment.

Several factors increase the risk of poor engagement (Armbruster & Fallon, 1994; Kazdin, Holland, & Crowley, 1997; Kendall & Sugarman, 1997): socio-economic factors, co-occurring conditions, treatment credibility, and level of insight. Interestingly, relationship with the clinician is not strongly related to treatment dropout. Clinicians can focus on some of these engagement factors, such as treatment credibility, the therapeutic relationship, and at times the general treatment plan to account for co-occurring conditions. Clinicians have less influence over other factors, such as socioeconomic factors, that include, for example, difficulty finding childcare services for other children in the family so that parents and youth can consistently attend therapy sessions.

Treatment credibility and expectancies play an important role in treatment adherence. *Treatment credibility* refers to youth and parent evaluations of how believable, logical, or reasonable treatment is for a particular problem (Nock, Ferriter, & Holmberg, 2007). *Treatment expectancies* refer to the improvements youth and parents expect to achieve through participation in a particular treatment approach (Kazdin, 1979). These distinct but related constructs are important in therapeutic engagement because they predict clinical changes in treatment approaches of all kinds (Nock, Ferriter, & Holmberg, 2007). In the treatment of pediatric psychological conditions, parent beliefs about treatment are particularly important in determining the degree and quality of the youth's engagement in treatment (Arch, Twohig, Deacon, Landy, & Bluett, 2015). For example, parents typically initiate treatment, pay for treatment, and see to it that the youth attends treatment. Furthermore, parents play a role in the maintenance of the youth's psychological problems, such as accommodating to the youth's wish to avoid situations that trigger obsessions or to engage in compulsions, and therefore must participate in treatment in order for the youth to benefit from it (Kazdin, Bass, Ayers, & Rodgers, 1990).

To improve treatment credibility and expectancies, clinicians can do two simple things. First, they can increase treatment credibility by explaining the nature of pediatric OCD, particularly the factors hypothesized to maintain the condition. Clinicians generally provide this information during the psycho-education phase of treatment. However, we recommend that clinicians revisit psychoeducation throughout the treatment process and to evaluate what youth and parents expect during each phase of treatment or during specific tasks of therapy: "Why do you think reassuring your child less might help decrease your child's OCD symptoms?" Second, youth and parents are more likely to complete therapeutic tasks if they understand how completing the task will help youth reach their treatment goals (Addis & Jacobson, 2000). For this reason, we recommend that clinicians explain the rationale for each inter-vention before asking youth and parents to complete the task. Furthermore, we recommend that clinicians provide the rationales repeatedly throughout treatment. For example, for each ERP task, the clinician might explain,

> Remember that facing your fear shows the OCD bully that he can't push you around. Each time you act brave, you get stronger and the OCD bully gets weaker. You're doing great. I can see that you're getting stronger and stronger. So, are you ready to show the OCD bully just how strong you are?

Engagement is an ongoing process that includes any number of strategies. For example, the ERP ladder clarifies the path forward for youth and parents. Knowing that exposure will proceed in a stepwise fashion decreases the youth's anxiety about future ERP tasks and increases the youth's willingness to participate in each exposure step. Clinicians can also increase engagement through collaboration, soliciting feedback from youth and parents, and other standard features of CBT. Last, contingency management plans play a key role in increasing the willingness of youth to participate in the tasks and goals of therapy. Simply said, the goal of contingency management is to increase the youth's approach behavior while decreasing avoidance and safety behav-iors. Part of this plan includes training parents to accommodate less to their child's OCD symptoms while learning to manage reassurance seeking and various pushback behaviors, such as tantrums, complaining, and refusal to follow parental instructions.

Psychoeducation

The objectives of psychoeducation are to provide accurate information regard-ing the OCD diagnosis and treatment of the condition; the nature of thoughts; the role of avoidance and physical and mental neutralizations[1] in maintaining obsessive fears and the condition itself; and, most important, the vital role of ERP in the process of therapeutic change, and instilling in youth the idea that

---

[1]Throughout this book, we use the term *neutralization* to refer to any physical or mental act that youth use in an attempt to lessen obsessive fear or discomfort. Neutral-izations include physical and mental compulsions and rituals, safety behaviors, and attempts to suppress and conceal covert thoughts and mental actions from others or oneself or to redirect attention from these mental events.

they play a pivotal role in decreasing their OCD symptoms. So important is psychoeducation to the treatment process that clinicians introduce psycho-education at the first session and continue psychoeducation throughout the treatment process, often revisiting key points along the way.

Before moving to ERP, it is essential that youth and parents understand the mechanism that maintains the youth's OCD symptoms and how ERP can decrease the symptoms and thereby the condition. Psychoeducation, as so many other elements of the treatment, serves to increase the willingness of youth and parents to engage fully in the treatment process. Exposure is difficult, and few youth and parents will engage in the treatment unless they understand how treatment works and their respective roles in the treatment process. Further-more, parents benefit from understanding the role of accommodation in the maintenance of their child's OCD and how to go about eliminating those behav-iors (Lebowitz, Panza, Su, & Bloch, 2012).

Several studies illustrate the value of psychoeducation in the treatment of a number of psychological conditions (Cuijpers, 1998; Donker, Griffiths, Cuijpers, & Christensen, 2009; Houghton & Saxon, 2007; Parikh et al., 2012), although studies that examine psychoeducation as a distinct and stand-alone intervention for pediatric OCD have not. However, psychoeducation is included in every study of the efficacy of ERP for pediatric OCD and in the earliest manuals on CBT for the condition (March & Mulle, 1998).

Self-Monitoring

In self-monitoring or self-recording, the youth or parents notice and record occurrences of problem behaviors as they occur, usually in the natural envi-ronment (Korotitsch & Nelson-Gray, 1999). In the case of OCD, the youth notices and records occurrences of the situations that trigger obsessions and compulsions and the specific features of these symptoms. Clinicians might ask youth to record the frequency of a particular compulsion, such as handwashing, and the duration of each handwash. Clinicians might ask parents to notice and record how they respond to their child's OCD episodes (what they said and did). Clinicians might ask parents to notice and record the frequency with which their child seeks reassurance from the parent and how the parent responds, or record the frequency of their child's tantrums in response to OCD and what they did and how well it worked.

In addition to collecting data for the assessment process, self-monitoring can function as an intervention too. Most youth are not entirely aware of the extent to which they engage in problem behaviors such as compulsions. Sim-ilarly, parents are not entirely aware of the extent to which they reassure their child or exhibit other problem parent behaviors. Behaviors such as these become automatic, and youth and parents often respond out of habit. How-ever, when youth and parents begin systematically to observe carefully their own behaviors, these behaviors often change. The reasons self-monitoring changes behavior are not well understood. One theory is the reactive effect of self-monitoring: if the individual is asked to monitor the occurrence of behaviors that depart from a culturally, socially, or self-imposed standard, then the individual may change the behavior to meet the standard (Kanfer, 1977). For example, after the clinician explains that seeking reassurance and giving reassurance depart from the goal of decreasing OCD symptoms, the youth may decrease the frequency of reassurance-seeking and parents may decrease the frequency of giving reassurance actively or passively to their child. Similarly, the careful observation of a desired behavior may result in an increase in the behavior through reinforcement of the behavior. For example, after the clinician asks parents to record when they praise their child, the frequency of praise can increase. Researchers have applied self-monitoring to a variety of problem behaviors, such as cigarette smoking, overeating, nail-biting, tics, and anxiety disorders (Cone, 1999).

There are several advantages to self-monitoring strategies. First, self-monitoring is a practical, inexpensive, and practice-friendly strategy to gather important information to assist treatment planning. Second, it is often the only way to gather information regarding covert or internal mental activities, such as mental neutralizations, obsessions, or sensory experiences. Third, self-monitoring can decrease the frequency of problem behaviors, such as reassurance seeking or compulsions, through the reactive effects of monitoring (Nelson, 1977). For example, it is common for the frequency of parents reassuring their child to decrease when they are asked to record each incidence of reassurance. Furthermore, instructing parents to monitor their responses to their child's OCD symptoms can identify targets for parent effectiveness training, such as assisting parents to resist arguing or reasoning with youth who are in the midst of a tantrum. Last, self-monitoring can build self-awareness. In the case of youth, self-monitoring builds awareness of situations that trigger obsessions and with this information the youth is better prepared to resist compulsions as they arise. In particular, it assists youth to identify mental neutralizations. Most youth with OCD who experience mental neutralizations do not quite understand that they function in the same way as behavioral compulsions (i.e., they serve to decrease the anxiety and distress youth experience when a situation triggers their obsessive fears). In part, youth do not understand the relationship because they are unaware of these mental actions or neutralizations. Instead, they are more apt to describe both obsessions and mental neutralizations as "obsessing." If youth are to resist mental neutralizations it is necessary that they are both aware of them and understand the function of them. Self-monitoring helps with this.

Graded Exposure and Modeling

The effective treatment of OCD rests on two core strategies: (a) exposure to reduce anxiety or distress associated with obsessions and (b) response prevention to block mental or behavioral neutralizations of the anxiety or distress to facilitate extinction (Meyer & Levy, 1973; Meyer, Levy, & Schnurer, 1974). The other core strategies, from building a graded-exposure hierarchy to training parents to effectively reinforce approach behavior and manage escape and avoidance behaviors, are in the service of enhancing the youth's willingness to engage in exposure. Therefore, it is essential that clinicians master exposure and response strategies, and for that reason we have devoted a considerable portion of this book to the effective implementation of ERP.

ERP is an effective treatment for pediatric OCD and involves evoking the obsession in a systematic, planned, prolonged, and repeated manner (exposure) until anxiety decreases (habituation). At the same time, it is essential that the youth not engage in any behaviors (actions) or mental acts (thought actions) to decrease the anxiety before the anxiety decreases naturally. Although some habituation on the anxious response occurs with response prevention only (Turner, Hersen, Bellack, Andrasik, & Capparell, 1980), exposure has little effect on behavioral compulsions (Mills, Agras, Barlow, & Mills, 1973), and effective exposure depends on the combination of exposure and response prevention (Foa, Steketee, Grayson, Turner, & Latimer, 1984; Foa, Steketee, & Milby, 1980). Evidence-based reviews support that exposure and response prevention is the psychosocial treatment of choice for pediatric OCD (Barrett, Farrell, Pina, Peris, & Piacentini, 2008; Freeman, Garcia, et al., 2014).

Exposure is the act of approaching the feared stimulus either in real life or via imagined scenarios (Watson, Gaind, & Marks, 1971). The goal of exposure, along with active modeling on the part of the clinician, is to alter the youth's interpretations of certain thoughts and images that drive the youth's anxiety and fearfulness. Altering these interpretations lessens anxiety and thereby decreases urges to engage in neutralizations (physical actions and mental actions). Over time, the youth has fewer obsessions and when he does have obsessions, he views them as less important (Rachman, 1997). The now less important thoughts must compete with equally unimportant thoughts or with thoughts that are truly more important (e.g., "I have a math test tomorrow") for the youth's attention. The result is fewer and less intrusive obsessions and to a small degree fewer and less disruptive compulsions.

Exposure strategies take several forms, and all involve modifications of the intensity, duration, or order of stimuli. In vivo exposure involves the direct confrontation of a fear-evoking stimulus, and requires youth to rehearse or actively interact with the actual feared object or situation, such as petting a dog (May, Rudy, Davis, & Matson, 2013), giving a speech in front of others (England et al., 2012), or touching a bathroom floor (O'Kearney, 2007). At times, clinicians may prefer to have the youth imagine the feared object or stimulus, a procedure commonly referred to as *imaginal exposure*. This usually involves a clinician describing a scene involving the stimulus, while the youth listens and imagines the details of the scene as fully as possible. Such strategies can be particularly helpful for exposure to stimuli or events that are not easily performed in vivo. For example, a child who has a fear of an upcoming surgery might be exposed in vivo to the hospital setting or other related stimuli, but confrontation with the event itself (i.e., surgery) is more easily performed through imaginal exposure. Exposure has been shown to be effective in the treatment of pediatric OCD (Abramowitz, 1996; Foa, Steketee, Turner, & Fischer, 1980).

Typically, exposure is graded or graduated, although it is not clear whether graded exposure results in larger effects than ungraded in which the individual confronts the most anxiety-evoking stimulus immediately (Steketee, 1993). However, graded exposure offers several practical advantages. First, exposure requires considerable willingness from youth, and graded exposure may enhance the willingness of youth to approach feared situations when the process involves stepwise approximations. Second, a graded exposure hierarchy provides a path forward for youth. In our experience, a stepwise process lessens the anxiety of youth and parents about the exposure process itself. They are less likely to feel overwhelmed by the exposure process and thereby more willing to move ahead with treatment. Last, anxious youth demand a great deal from parents. Parents who understand that the exposure process proceeds in small steps are reassured that they and their child can tolerate the treatment.

Heretofore, emotional processing theory (EPT) has been the dominant theory put forth to explain "corrective" learning and the improvement observed in exposure-based psychotherapy, such as ERP for OCD (Foa, Huppert, & Cahill, 2006; Foa & Kozak, 1986; Foa & McNally, 1995). The theory proposes that in order for corrective learning to occur through exposure, the exposure process must first activate a "fear structure" that resides in memory and then provide information that is incompatible with that fear structure. This incompatible information is then integrated through corrective learning such that non–fear-based associations replace or compete with fear-based associations. The reduction in fear or habituation (Groves & Thompson, 1970; Watts, 1979) is thought to reflect that corrective extinction learning is taking place. However, whereas habituation refers to a reduction in fearful responding through repeated presentations of a stimulus (e.g., nonassociative learning) during exposure therapy, extinction refers to the associated learning that occurs on repeated confrontation with fear-evoking stimuli. Therefore, although the process of habituation and extinction are related, they are not equivalent (Abramowitz, Deacon, & Whiteside, 2011).

Inhibitory learning theory (ILT) is a model to explain the process of extinction (Lang, Craske, & Bjork, 1999; Myers & Davis, 2007). Although ILT is not a new model, its application to understanding the process of change in exposure therapy has intrigued many clinicians familiar with exposure-based therapy and has direct and important clinical implications. According to ILT, the association between stimulus and fear that is learned during fear acquisition is not erased or replaced by new nonthreat associations during exposure therapy, as EPT suggests. Rather, the feared stimulus becomes an ambiguous stimulus with two meanings, and both remain in memory and compete for retrieval. The original fear-based meaning acquired during the acquisition of the fear remains in memory as does a new nonaversive meaning acquired during extinction learning. The theory posits that the new nonaversive meaning can inhibit but not eliminate the original fear-based meaning (Lang, Craske, &

Bjork, 1999). This hypothesis is supported by the observation that fear can return following successful exposure therapy (Craske & Mystkowski, 2006).

A complete description of the clinical implications of ILT is beyond the scope of this book. We refer readers to several fine articles (Craske et al., 2008, 2014) on the topic and, in particular, a review of the theory and possible clinical implications in the treatment of OCD (Jacoby & Abramowitz, 2016). However, a common theme in the application of ILT to the implementation of exposure therapy is captured in two ideas: first, to introduce "desirable difficulties" into the exposure plan to foster an attitude of tolerating fear rather than controlling it; second, to use acquisition of new and adaptive learning as the index of change during exposure therapy rather than fear reduction.

Desirable Difficulties

The application of ILT in exposure therapy is in the service of enhancing psychological flexibility (i.e., the willingness to experience obsessive fear and discomfort). Although the goal of ILT remains the facilitation of new learning, the focus of the learning is on beliefs about the ability to tolerate negative emotional experiences (Bluett, Homan, Morrison, Levin, & Twohig, 2014). Clinicians accomplish the goal of enhancing fear tolerance through the introduction of desirable difficulties (Bjork, 1994). Desirable difficulties take the form of introducing real-world challenges, such as encountering multiple fear cues (e.g., a dirty sink, a dirty hand towel, and no soap in the dispenser) that clients likely will encounter in life. These desirable difficulties are thought to strengthen fear tolerance (Craske et al., 2008) and maximize the retrieval of newly learned information (Bjork, 1994). Combining exposure strategies (e.g., imaginal and situation) and conducting exposure tasks in multiple contexts are two ways to enhance fear tolerance. For example, a youth with obsessive fear of acting on sexual thoughts and urges might make a trip to a playground while listening to an imaginal exposure that describes him acting on a sexual urge with a child. Multiple contexts might include any situation in which the youth might encounter children: playgrounds, school yards, toy stores.

Expectancy Violation or Disconfirmation

New information is learned when there is a discrepancy between the outcome that is predicted or expected and the outcome that actually occurs, and this element of surprise is critical to the learning process (Rescorla & Wagner, 1972; Rescorla, 1988). To optimize inhibitory learning (and treatment durability), clinicians will think in these terms and ask youth to clarify their anxious prediction. For example, "What do you expect will happen if you touch the floor and then don't wash your hands immediately?" Furthermore, clinicians will keep expectancy violation in mind when they engineer exposures. The most effective exposures will be those that maximally and irrefutably violate the youth's expectation. This is particularly true when working with youth who expect negative outcomes far into the future, such as going to hell. This is an untestable prediction. On the other hand, clinicians may be able to set up an exposure that violates the youth's expectation regarding not knowing whether he is going to hell or not. How anxious will the youth feel if he cannot be certain whether he will go to hell or not, and how long will his anxiety last?

Modeling is the process of learning through observing the actions of others (Bandura, 1977). In the case of fear, youth can learn to fear certain situations or objects if they observe others interact in a fearful way to these same situations or objects. The opposite is true too. Youth can learn to fear situations or objects less if they observe others interact in a nonfearful way (Mineka, Davidson, Cook, & Keir, 1984). Modeling-alone treatment effects are superior to no-treatment control and wait-list conditions (Blanchard, 1970; Murphy & Bootzin, 1973).

For example, a clinician might hold an insect to demonstrate to a child that the insect is not dangerous and therefore that there is no reason to fear it. Typical modeling strategies include live, symbolic, and covert. We typically include all three modeling strategies in the treatment of pediatric OCD. In live modeling, the model performs the behavior directly while the youth observes (Murphy & Bootzin, 1973). For example, the clinician treating a youth with OCD who fears germs might eat a candy off the floor while the youth observes. In symbolic modeling, the clinician might show a video or a photograph to the youth that shows another youth with similar physical characteristics eating candy off the floor (Lewis, 1974). In covert modeling, the clinician asks the youth to imagine rather than observe the model interacting with the feared stimulus (Cautela & Kearney, 1990). For example, the clinician might ask the youth to imagine eating candy off the floor.

Clinicians use modeling in conjunction with exposure strategies in what is termed participant modeling. In this strategy, the youth first observes the model interacting with the stimulus, and the model (clinician) then asks the youth to do what the youth observed the model (clinician) do (Ritter, 1968). For example, the clinician first eats a candy off the floor while the youth observes (modeling). The clinician then asks the youth to repeat the behavior while the clinician observes (in vivo exposure).

Response Prevention

Response prevention alone can reduce compulsive behaviors (Mills et al., 1973); the addition of exposure after preventing or blocking compulsive behavior does not further reduce compulsive behaviors (Turner et al., 1980). Furthermore, exposure alone appears to have little effect on the frequency of compulsive behaviors (Mills et al., 1973). At the same time, response prevention alone results in some reduction in obsessive anxiety, and adding exposure further reduces obsessive anxiety (Foa, Steketee, & Milby, 1980). The results of these studies and others support the importance of the addition of response prevention to exposure strategies and vice versa and the concept that separate mechanisms influence exposure and response prevention processes (Foa et al., 1984).

Strict, rather than gradual, response prevention appears to result in greater responses when combined with exposure strategies (Foa, Kozak, Steketee, &

McCarthy, 1992). In *strict* response prevention, the youth immediately discontinues *all* mental and behavioral neutralizations. For example, clinicians instruct youth with extensive washing and cleaning compulsions to stop all handwashing (except in unusual circumstances, as in the case of touching feces), to take a 10-minute shower once or twice per week, and to resist any other cleaning. In our experience, many youth and parents have trouble following strict response prevention guidelines and favor or trend toward graded response prevention strategies. In addition to the lower effectiveness of graded response prevention, it is not easy to implement. For example, trying to gradually decrease the frequency of compulsive behaviors requires youth and parents to track carefully these behaviors when experiencing greater levels of discomfort or changing circumstances (e.g., trips away from home). Therefore, we typically recommend strict response prevention and work with youth and parents to adhere to the strict approach. If youth and parents refuse strict response prevention, we develop a graded response prevention plan and work toward strict response prevention as soon as is reasonable in treatment.

Response prevention takes two general forms: supervised versus self-controlled. In supervised response prevention, family members (Emmelkamp, de Haan, & Hoogduin, 1990) or clinicians supervise the youth's adherence to the response prevention plan (Abramowitz, 1996). Although supervised response prevention results in greater treatment effects, self-controlled response prevention may result in better long-term improvement than supervised methods (Emmelkamp & Kraanen, 1977) in part because youth learn a skill that helps them maintain their treatment gains. Therefore, the most effective response prevention strategies are those that maximize the youth's involvement in resisting physical and mental neutralizations while at the same time insuring that all neutralizations are consistently and adequately blocked (Steketee, 1993).

Two key outcomes result through successful response prevention for youth: tolerance of uncertainty and expectancy disconfirmation. As youth engage in ERP practices, their tolerance of uncertainty increases because they do not do the response that ensures a reduction in distress. They instead learn that they can tolerate the uncertainty of what will happen as a result of the exposure. Their tolerance of the distress associated with uncertainty increases as they choose to sit with uncertainty with each ERP practice (Arch & Abramowitz, 2015). When youth engage in ERP, their beliefs about what will occur in the presence of the trigger without the neutralization (or response) are often disconfirmed. In learning that their expected feared outcome does not necessarily result and that their distress is tolerable rather than so intolerable that they cannot handle it, youth begin to question the necessity of the response (Arch & Abramowitz, 2015). Inhibitory learning allows youth to incorporate this new information and discover that they do not need the response to tolerate the obsession. Together, tolerance of uncertainty and expectancy disconfirmation allow youth to practice more and more difficult exposures without engaging in neutralizations, thereby managing OCD.

Relapse Prevention

Many controlled studies of CBT for pediatric anxiety disorders conclude with a module that reviews treatment gains with youth and parents and describes strategies that help to maintain these gains (Cohen, Deblinger, Mannarino, & Steer, 2004; Kendall et al., 1997). The inclusion of relapse prevention in the treatment of OCD appears to maintain treatment gains as well (de Haan, Hoogduin, Buitelaar, & Keijsers, 1998; Pediatric OCD Treatment Study [POTS] Team, 2004).

OCD is a chronic condition that waxes and wanes even following a successful treatment. The goal of relapse prevention is to involve youth and parents in preventing the recurrence of the disorder. Relapse prevention generally includes two features. First, youth and parents review the treatment process and the most important skills they learned that resulted in the youth's recovery from OCD. The skills include those skills learned and practiced by the youth, those skills learned and practiced by youth and parents, and those skills learned and practiced by the youth's parents. Second, youth and parents, with assistance from the clinician, develop a plan to practice these skills as the clinician tapers or decreases the frequency of meetings with youth and parents. Practicing these skills independent of the clinician's guidance and support enhances the self-efficacy of youth and parents (Bandura, 1988) and builds their confidence that they can manage OCD into the future on their own.

Working With Families

Parents and other family members play a critical role in their child's recovery from OCD (Renshaw, Steketee, & Chambless, 2005). Furthermore, the effectiveness of family-based CBT demonstrates the importance of including, to some degree, parents in the treatment for pediatric OCD (Comer et al., 2014; Freeman, Sapyta, et al., 2014; Piacentini et al., 2011). The primary goals when working with parents are to decrease accommodation; increase and maintain approach behaviors; manage pushback behaviors, such as tantrums and refusal to comply with parent instructions' and train parents to be effective coclinicians.

Decrease Accommodation Behaviors. Most parents of youth with OCD report that they engage in accommodating behaviors, at least to some degree and often every day (Lebowitz, Scharfstein, & Jones, 2014). Accommodation behaviors include two types: participation in behaviors related to OCD symptoms and modification of family routines.

Participation behaviors include providing reassurance, participating in compulsions, and providing items youth require to engage in compulsions (e.g., extra soap). For example, parents of a child with fears about harming animals might comply with the child's insistent direction to no longer consume meat and remove all leather items from the home. Similarly, parents of a child with contamination or germ fears might comply with the child's directions that they wash their hands in a ritualized way before they touch the child's food.

Modification of family routines include modifying family schedules and roles and routines to minimize their child's distress (Lebowitz et al., 2012; Lebowitz, Vitulano, & Omer, 2011), for example, asking siblings to do chores that the child with OCD refuses to do, or excusing the child from doing school-work. Similarly, a parent might shorten her workday to pick up the child from school early.

Accommodation behaviors such as these can create great distress for everyone in the home and significantly disrupt the family's day-to-day function. Furthermore, the level of accommodation behaviors is associated with poorer treatment response (Ferrão et al., 2006), more severe OCD symptoms (Caporino et al., 2012), and greater impairment of the child (Storch et al., 2010). Targeting parent accommodation behaviors in CBT for pediatric OCD results in greater improvement in the child's symptoms (Merlo, Lehmkuhl, Geffken, & Storch, 2009; Piacentini et al., 2011).

Increase and Maintain Approach Behaviors. The success of CBT for pediatric OCD centers on youth altering their attitudes toward the things they fear. Rather than avoiding situations, objects, and activities that trigger their obsessions, youth learn the value of actively approaching and remaining in these situations when anxious or uncomfortable. Contingency management strategies facilitate this learning process. Contingency or behavioral contracting is a core strategy that clinicians use to decrease the frequency of avoidance behaviors and increase the frequency of approach behaviors (Barmish & Kendall, 2005; Ginsburg & Schlossberg, 2002). Contingency contracts specify details of a specific ERP task, when youth will do the task, the specific reward the parent gives youth (contingent on execution of the ERP task as determined ahead of time), and when the parents deliver the reward. Explicit contingency contracts are particularly helpful when working with youth with extensive pushback behaviors or with parents who engage in reassurance and accommodation behaviors. Contingency contracts reduce conflict and negotiation regarding ERP tasks and signal to parents that they are primary change agents in decreasing their child's OCD.

Manage Pushback Behaviors. Oppositional and disruptive behaviors, such as tantrums or direct refusal to comply with parent commands, are common in youth with OCD (Lebowitz et al., 2011). Effective treatment of pediatric OCD then depends on managing these behaviors in order to assist youth to engage in the core strategies of CBT, particularly exposure with response prevention. As mentioned, clinicians use contingency management strategies to decrease the occurrence of pushback behaviors, including contingency contracts (Kazdin, 2001). Clinicians will use other contingency management strategies, such as time-out from positive reinforcement, shaping (Storch, Geffken, Merlo, et al., 2007), and at times, response cost, such as "the sit-in," which delays parental response to the youth's aggressive behavior (Lebowitz & Omer, 2013).

Train Parents to Be Effective Coclinicians. CBT for pediatric OCD takes a transfer-of-control approach to treatment (Silverman, Pina, & Viswesvaran, 2008). The transfer-of-control approach has been applied to pediatric anxiety and phobic disorders (Silverman & Kurtines, 1996) as well as with other pediatric problems (Israel, Guile, Baker, & Silverman, 1994; Israel, Stolmaker, Sharp, Silverman, & Simon, 1984). The approach assumes that long-term psychotherapeutic change involves the gradual transfer of control of key core therapeutic strategies from clinician to parents to child over the course of treatment. Furthermore, because parents often contribute to the maintenance of OCD symptoms, training parents as coclinicians can shift parent responses that favor therapeutic change, as well as facilitate the generalization of treatment gains (Barmish & Kendall, 2005).

Within the transfer-of-control approach, the clinician is the "expert consultant" who has the skills and knowledge necessary to produce therapeutic change. These skills include knowledge about pediatric OCD and the variables that maintain the condition and how to effectively implement ERP, the key change-producing strategy. Therefore, clinicians will train parents to implement ERP between therapy sessions, as well as respond effectively to the child's distress when the OCD is triggered outside of therapy sessions. Furthermore, as coclinicians, parents will assist youth to follow through with other key core strategies, such as prompting youth to record OCD symptoms, to accept response prevention guidelines, and to tolerate changes in parent responses to OCD symptoms (e.g., decreased accommodation behaviors).

Transfer of control implies that clinicians first train parents in contingency management, followed by clinicians gradually lessening their participation in the implementation of core change strategies as parents take the lead. Finally, clinicians encourage parents to lessen their participation in the implementation of ERP so that youth take ownership of the treatment and their recovery. Contingency contracting assists with this process whereby parents reward youth for effective implementation of ERP tasks. In addition, near the end of formal treatment, contingency contracts focus on self-controlled exposures (Emmelkamp & Kraanen, 1977) to maintain treatment gains. In self-controlled exposure, youth select ERP tasks themselves from within a range of contracted exposures. Similarly, youth are rewarded for impromptu "act brave" behaviors when they complete and record instances of facing a fear observed but not prompted by parents. These strategies all focus on enhancing the self-efficacy (Bandura, 1988) of youth as they near the end of treatment.

Monitoring Progress

Progress monitoring is an essential part of any evidence-based treatment and serves several important purposes (Persons, 2008). The clinician can monitor both the process and the outcome of treatment. In the beginning of treatment, clinicians monitor the youth's symptoms to collect information to develop a case conceptualization and treatment plan. During treatment, the clinicians monitor the youth's response to treatment and refine the treatment plan, if appropriate. Progress monitoring not only provides clinicians with an index of the youth's progress in treatment but, when treatment is going well, can enhance motivation on the part of both the youth and parents. In addition, monitoring progress enables clinicians to identify poor progress early in treatment and then alter the case formulation and treatment plan to get the treatment back on course. Given the crucial role that progress monitoring plays in these various domains, it is perhaps not surprising that there is a growing body of research showing that monitoring treatment progress may actually improve treatment outcomes (Lambert, Harmon, Slade, Whipple, & Hawkins, 2005).

STRUCTURE OF THE TREATMENT

CBT, in general, is a structured, problem-focused therapeutic approach, whether clinicians are treating pediatric mood disorders, anxiety disorders, or OCD. In fact, many experienced practitioners of modular-driven CBT suggest that the highly structured nature of this approach is the primary reason for its efficiency and brevity (J. S. Beck, 1995).

Structure of Therapy Sessions

Each modular-CBT session is structured yet flexible. A structured session assists clinicians to manage time in order to carry out interventions effectively. Also, a structured session models for youth and parents an active, solution-focused attitude toward problems. The youth and parents are oriented to working on the problem of OCD with the skills the clinician teaches them.

The session begins with a check-in. Typically, the check-in includes youth and parents, although clinicians will decide with whom to meet based on their clinical judgment. In the check-in, the clinician asks about the week in general and specifically asks about success. By successes, we are interested in the successful application of core strategies that were not part of the out-of-session action plans (therapeutic homework).[2] For example, the parents report that the youth sought very little reassurance over the past week, or the youth reports several instances in which he "bossed-back" the OCD bully. Next, the clinician bridges content of the prior session to the therapeutic goals: "Last session we focused on the ways your mom and dad feed the OCD bully by reassuring you when the OCD bully scares you. Feeding the bully like that makes OCD stronger, when we want to make him weaker." Last, the clinician and family review out-of-session action plans, typically ERP tasks and whether youth and parents encountered any problems carrying out the action plan.

---

[2]We use the term *action plan* to describe therapeutic out-of-session homework. Use of the term *action plan* avoids the negative association some youth have to the word *homework* as well as signals the essential role of action or behavioral change in the process of therapeutic change.

For example: "We agreed on a plan to starve the OCD bully. How did that go?" Also, the clinician reviews any action plan the parents were to complete. Typically, this includes practicing communication skills and managing accommodation behaviors, reassurance seeking, and pushback behaviors. At times, the clinician may wish to reserve the review of parent skills for a separate meeting with parents or a very brief check-in with parents prior to inviting youth into the check-in segment of the session.

Next, we excuse the parents and set the agenda for the session with the youth. Before meeting with the youth alone, the clinician often gives the parents a handout to read, a measure to complete, or other tasks to occupy them while they wait in the waiting room. If the clinician is meeting with the parents alone, the clinician and parents set the agenda for the meeting. During parent meetings, the clinician may include a topic that the youth asked the clinician to place on the agenda of the parent meeting.

Generally, the agenda focuses on reviewing ERP tasks, troubleshooting any problems that arose, and identifying an ERP task to complete in session. Early in treatment, the agenda may include psychoeducation, building the ERP hierarchy, or a contingency management plan. Near the end of treatment, the agenda typically includes developing a relapse prevention plan. The session with youth concludes with clinician assisting youth to develop an out-of-session action plan, usually continuing the ERP tasks completed in the session or an alternative ERP task.

At the end of the session, the clinician invites parents to rejoin the youth. The clinician then summarizes the main points of the session, what youth and clinician worked on together, and describes the agreed-upon out-of-session ERP task. The clinician explains the role of parents in ensuring that the youth completes the out-of-session ERP task and then troubleshoots with youth and parents any problems that might interfere with youth competing the out-of-session ERP task. The session ends with the clinician soliciting feedback from the youth and parents about the session, for example: "What did you like about our meeting today? What didn't you like? Is there anything you'd like us to do a little differently next time we meet?" Also, we recommend that clinicians ask youth and parents what they learned, for example: "If someone asked you what you learned today that was helpful, what would you tell him?" Last, we recommend that clinicians ask the youth and parents for feedback regarding the clinician's performance in session: "What grade would you give me today?" and "How could I be a better clinician when we meet again next week?"

Beginning of Treatment

In the early phase of therapy, the clinician works to engage youth and parents in the treatment process and begins the assessment process. The clinician also socializes the youth and parents into the structure of therapy sessions, sets treatment goals, and begins the psychoeducation process. In the early phase, the clinician also trains youth and parents to self-monitor and begins the process of building the ERP hierarchy.

Middle of Treatment

The middle phase of treatment generally focuses on ERP and skill development. Parent meetings focus on skills to manage pushback behavior, to reinforce the youth's approach behavior, improve communication with youth, and fade accommodation behaviors. With youth, skill development primarily focuses on increasing approach behavior (exposure) but also includes strategies to resist mental and behavioral neutralizations.

End of Treatment

The end phase of treatment includes self-initiation practice, whereby the youth is encouraged and reinforced for initiating ERP without the prompting or assistance of clinician or parent. The clinician introduces a taper plan, the role of booster sessions, and then develops with youth and parents a relapse prevention plan. The treatment concludes with a graduation ceremony.

CONCLUSION

The treatment approach presented in this book includes well-tested core strategies, grounded on solid empirical evidence, with an eye to the creative and flexible application of these strategies to the problem of pediatric OCD. Furthermore, the effective implementation of these core strategies depends on a thoughtful and comprehensive case conceptualization that considers the unique strengths and weakness of the particular youth and family with whom the clinician is working.

In the next chapter, we describe the process of diagnosing pediatric OCD and assessing the many factors, described previously, that can influence the design and implementation of a treatment plan for the condition. The chapter includes gold-standard assessment strategies, such as the Children's Yale–Brown Obsessive Compulsive Scale (CY-BOCS), as well as other simple assessment strategies that busy clinicians can integrate into their practices.

I

ASSESSMENT, CASE CONCEPTUALIZATION, AND TREATMENT PLANNING

INTRODUCTION

In Part I, we present two essential steps in cognitive behavior therapy (CBT) for pediatric obsessive–compulsive disorder (OCD). The first step is to diagnose the condition and then gather relevant information about the condition and the particular factors that influence its course and its treatment (Chapter 3). The next step is to take this information and develop a case conceptualization (Chapter 4). A comprehensive individualized case conceptualization is essential for the effective treatment of pediatric OCD. By comprehensive, we mean that the conceptualization identifies the salient exposure and response prevention targets, as well as other factors that influence the staging and implementation of the core strategies for the condition, such as developmental age, co-occurrence of other psychiatric conditions, degree of parental accommodation, and the effectiveness of parents.

3

Gathering Information

Pediatric obsessive–compulsive disorder (OCD) is a relatively common childhood disorder that affects approximately 1% to 3% of children and adolescents (Douglass, Moffitt, Dar, McGee, & Silva, 1995; Rapoport et al., 2000). However, many more youth with OCD are likely undiagnosed or misdiagnosed by mental health professionals (Merlo, Storch, Adkins, Murphy, & Geffken, 2007). The failure of mental health providers to identify pediatric OCD, particularly in young children, is a major obstacle in allaying the suffering of likely hundreds of thousands of youth in the United States (Hollander et al., 1996). This reality underscores the importance of thoughtful diagnosis and assessment of the condition.

The chapter begins with a description of the importance of assessment in cognitive behavior therapy (CBT) for OCD. The goals of assessment are to diagnose the condition and then to assess the many factors that maintain the condition that are the targets of treatment. We view diagnosis and assessment as different but overlapping processes. Assessment reaches far beyond the criteria required for the diagnosis of OCD and identifies all factors, or at least the most important ones, that are necessary to develop and implement an effective treatment plan for pediatric OCD. The chapter presents a number of assessment strategies, such as clinical interviews, inventories, questionnaires, and clinician rating scales that we believe most clinicians can easily integrate into their practices.

http://dx.doi.org/10.1037/0000167-004
Cognitive Behavior Therapy for OCD in Youth: A Step-by-Step Guide, by M. A. Tompkins, D. J. Owen, N. H. Shiloff, and L. R. Tanner

In this chapter, we also describe features of the diagnostic and assessment processes, as well as the role and rationale for a consultation process. The goals of consultation are different from the goals of the initial assessment or intake. We spend some time describing these goals and the distinctions and how we speak with youth and parents regarding the process of diagnosing and assessing the condition.

INITIAL CONSULTATION MEETING

In our practices, we begin the diagnostic and assessment processes with a consultation meeting with parents. A *consultation* is a meeting (and at times several meetings) with an expert or professional to seek advice about a problem. An *assessment*, on the other hand, is a meeting or series of meetings to evaluate the problem and develop a plan to resolve it. Often, particularly in community clinics, intake and assessment are the same. However, we are careful to avoid using the term *intake* to describe the first meeting. Intake implies just that, that the clinician has agreed to treat the youth. We believe agreeing to treat a youth prior to diagnosing the youth is premature.

The goals of the consultation are to gather sufficient information to form a diagnostic impression rather than a firm diagnosis, identify possible factors that may complicate treatment or rule out treatment of the youth, describe evidence-based treatment options, and recommend one treatment option over another. In addition, clinicians may wish to explain CBT to the parents and youth, including the important role of exposure. There are several good reasons to separate the consultation from the assessment process.

First, there are three evidence-based treatment options for pediatric OCD: medication alone, CBT alone, or a combination of the two. Prior to a comprehensive assessment that may take several meetings, clinicians likely do not know which option, if any, they will recommend for a particular youth and parents. Second, clinicians may not agree with the treatment option the youth and parents wish to pursue. For example, the family may wish to pursue CBT alone when the youth is very depressed, while the clinician believes that a combination of CBT and medication is the best treatment option. Third, there may be other reasons, such as a child who is the best friend of a former child client that the clinician treated, that cause clinicians to pause and consider other options, or at least other clinicians. Last, explaining to parents the difference between consultation and assessment prior to the consultation meeting will save clinicians considerable heartache if they must tell parents that they are not prepared for any number of reasons to move ahead with treatment of their child. Furthermore, we do not believe it is good clinical practice to move ahead with a treatment when the clinician does not believe it is the correct treatment, at the correct time, and with the correct clinician.

Prior to the consultation meeting, we send a consultation packet for youth and parents to complete and bring to the consultation meeting. The consultation packet includes a consultation agreement that describes practice policies and the goals of the scheduled consultation, a parent questionnaire, a general self-report, and parent-report symptom measures. To that we add a packet of OCD-specific self-report measures. Youth and parents complete these questionnaires and measures and bring to them to the consultation appointment. There are many advantages to utilizing youth self-report and parent-report inventories and questionnaires. Youth and parents generally can complete these measures quickly and independently. These measures are often sensitive to symptom change, and clinicians can use these to track progress across time.

Typically, we schedule two consultation meetings. The first meeting is 1.5 hours and with the parents alone. We are not rigid about this, however, and may meet with parents alone or parents and youth together, depending on the age of the youth, the openness of the youth to treatment, and other factors. There are several reasons for this approach, but perhaps the most important is that at times the parents do not agree with our impressions and recommendations and then they do not want us to meet with their child. Also, the handling of the first clinical contact with the youth is critical and begins the process of engaging the youth in the treatment if the youth is open to help. In the meeting with parents only, we review measures completed by parents and youth, conduct a clinical interview, and give a tentative diagnosis. We then explain the OCD diagnosis to the parents and the treatment options. At this time, we also recommend a treatment plan that may or may not include CBT or may or may not include us. We then set aside time to answer their questions, and if they wish, we schedule a consultation meeting with youth alone. Generally, we introduce the rationale for consultation to the parents in this way:

> This is a consultation meeting. At this meeting, as I explained to you on the phone, I will review the paperwork you and your child completed and ask a series of questions. At the end of the consultation, I will share my diagnostic impressions and treatment recommendations that may or may not include CBT or may or may not include me. My goal is to give you my thoughts regarding what I think will help your child the most. If I think CBT might help, I will briefly describe the approach and, of course, answer any questions you have about my impressions and recommendations. Also, if I recommend options that do not include CBT or me, I am happy to help you find appropriate resources for you and your child.

At the meeting with the youth alone, we interview the youth and confirm the diagnosis. We then explain the condition and the treatment for it, particularly the role of exposure. At the end of the meeting with the youth, we meet with youth and parents to review our recommendations. Once again, we describe the treatment process, including exposure, and explain next steps, including the formal assessment process. Other clinicians likely have their way of conducting the diagnostic and assessment processes, and they likely have good reasons for conducting the process in the way they do, including the limitations and expectations imposed by their practice settings, but this is how we do it.

Consultation Packet

Next, we provide a brief review of the measures we use in our practices. For a comprehensive review of these measures, including more information regarding psychometric properties and the strengths and weaknesses of each measure, we refer you to Storch, Geffken, and Murphy (2007). The basic consultation packet for youth and parents includes the following:

- Parent Questionnaire. One or both parents complete this questionnaire. The questionnaire solicits information on the social, prenatal, birth, and health history of the youth, as well as developmental milestones. In addition, the parent questionnaire solicits information regarding the respective physical and mental health histories of parents and family members.

- Child Behavior Checklist (CBCL) for Ages 6 to 18 (Achenbach, 1991a). Each parent completes a copy of this checklist. The CBCL is a 112-item parent report questionnaire comprising common symptoms for youth with psychiatric conditions. The CBCL yields age-corrected scores for Internalizing Problems, Externalizing Problems, and Total Problems. The CBCL is widely used and has strong psychometric properties. There is a 113-item teacher report version of the CBCL (Achenbach, 1991a).

- Youth Self-Report (YSR) for Ages 11 to 18 (Achenbach, 1991b). Youth complete the YSR. This is a 112-item self-report questionnaire to screen the youth's social competencies and presence of behavior problems. The Social Competence assessment is composed of the Activities and Social subscales, and a Total Competence scale. The Problem Checklist is made up of eight core syndrome scales, including Withdrawn, Somatic Complaints, Anxious/Depressed, Social Problems, Thought Problems, Attention Problems, Delinquent Behavior, and Aggressive Behavior. The core scales may be grouped into Internalizing and Externalizing scales and a Total Problem scale. The YSR is widely used and has demonstrated strong psychometric properties.

- Children's Depression Inventory (CDI; Kovacs, 1992). Depression co-occurs frequently in youth with OCD. The CDI is a 27-item self-report screening measure for depressive symptoms. The CDI is appropriate for youth aged 7 to 17 years and has excellent psychometric properties.

- Multidimensional Anxiety Scale for Children 2nd Edition (MASC-2; March, 2012). Anxiety disorders are common in youth with OCD and may at times complicate treatment. For that reason, it is prudent to screen for anxiety disorders in youth with OCD. The MASC-2 is a 50-item self-report screening measure for anxiety symptoms. The MASC-2 is composed of four subscales: Physical Symptoms, Harm Avoidance, Social Anxiety, and Separation Panic. The MASC is appropriate for youth aged 8 to 19 and the scores are age and gender corrected. The MASC has excellent psychometric properties.

OCD Assessment Packet

To this basic consultation packet, we add an OCD packet that includes the following:

- Family Accommodation Scale–Parent Report (FAS-PR; Calvocoressi et al., 1995). Family accommodation is a common and critical treatment target for pediatric OCD. For this reason, we recommend that clinicians include this measure as part of the assessment of the condition. The FAS-PR is a 12-item parent report measure to assess the degree to which family members accommodate the youth's participation in obsessions and compulsions during the previous month. Accommodation behaviors include giving reassurance, providing objects necessary to complete compulsions (e.g., soap), decreasing expectations for the youth regarding responsibilities and routines in school and in home, and assisting the youth in avoiding objects or activities that trigger the youth's distress. We recommend that each parent complete the measure. Factor analysis identified two separate yet related subscales (Avoidance of Triggers and Involvement in Compulsions). The FAS-PR exhibits good internal consistency and convergent and discriminant validity (Flessner et al., 2011).

- OCD Disturbance Scale (OCD-DS; Geffken et al., 2005). Some youth are not distressed by their OCD symptoms, at least not as distressed as their caregivers. The OCD-DS assesses the degree to which OCD symptoms are ego-syntonic or ego-dystonic to youth with OCD. The OCD-DS is a 25-item parent report measure. We recommend that each parent complete the measure. The OCD-DS exhibits good—but not strong—psychometric properties as well as adequate internal consistency and evidence of convergent and divergent validity (Geffken et al., 2005). Even in the absence of strong psychometric properties, we include the OCD-DS in the OCD assessment packet because of its clinical usefulness. We find that knowing the degree the youth is a willing participant in treatment prior to the consultation appointment with the parents assists us in exploring explanations for the reluctance as well as what we might recommend as a treatment plan.

- Child Obsessive-Compulsive Impact Scale–Revised (COIS-RC; Piacentini & Jaffer, 1999). The COIS-RC assesses the level of impairment in specific areas of the youth's psychosocial functioning due to symptoms of OCD. The COIS-RC is a 56-item self-report or parent-report measure. The COIS-RC assesses common difficulties in school activities, social activities, and home–family activities. The four final questions assess global impairment across school, social, home–family activities, and going places. The COIS-RC has good internal consistency and construct validity (Piacentini, Bergman, Jacobs, McCracken, & Kretchman, 2002), as well as strong convergent validity with other measures of OCD symptom severity and functional impairment (Piacentini et al., 2003). We particularly like including the COIS-RC in the assessment packet, as it appears to be useful as a pretreatment indicator of response (Piacentini et al., 2002). Furthermore, the COIS-RC is sensitive to treatment effects (Liebowitz et al., 2002; Piacentini et al., 2003), and we periodically request youth and parents to complete the measure to monitor treatment progress. Youth and parents can complete the measure in approximately 10 minutes.

- Children's Florida Obsessive-Compulsive Inventory (C-FOCI; Storch et al., 2009). The C-FOCI is a quick, focused self-report screening instrument for pediatric OCD. The measure includes a 17-item symptom checklist and a five-item impairment scale. Youth can complete the C-FOCI in 5 to 10 minutes. The C-FOCI includes the Obsessions subscale, Compulsions subscale, and a Total Score subscale. The C-FOCI has good psychometric properties with significant correlations between other measures of OCD impairment (Storch et al., 2009).

DIAGNOSTIC PROCESS

We differentiate the diagnostic process from the assessment process. The goal of the diagnostic process is to identify the presence of OCD based on its diagnostic criteria. Although the diagnosis is certainly not sufficient to develop a treatment plan for pediatric OCD it is a critical link to the clinical science regarding its treatment. Information is power, and an accurate diagnosis assists clinicians, parents, and youth in accessing information regarding the condition and treatment options and resources. Furthermore, diagnosis puts the clinician in the conceptualization ballpark from which they can begin the process of developing an individualized conceptualization for the youth.

A detailed semistructured diagnostic interview, such as the Anxiety Disorders Interview Schedule (ADIS) for *DSM–5*—Child and Parent Versions (Silverman & Albano, 2004) is the gold standard for evaluating the presence of OCD symptoms. However, diagnostic interviews are time-consuming and labor intensive. Few clinicians have the time to conduct rigorous diagnostic interviews, and community mental health clinics do not have the personnel to utilize diagnostic interviews on a regular basis. Therefore, we do not often use this time-intensive diagnostic interview except when faced with a particularly complex youth with multiple disorders or when we have difficulty making differential diagnoses. Instead, we depend on a thoughtful clinical interview paired with a variety of questionnaires, scales, and measures.

Developmental Considerations

It is important to view all childhood behaviors through a developmental lens (Singh & Singh, 2001). A developmental perspective helps clinicians to understand the nature and course of OCD and contributes to the case conceptualization for the condition, as well as the implementation of the core treatment strategies. Furthermore, a developmental perspective is essential when the clinician ponders whether a behavior is normal or abnormal (Bell-Dolan & Suarez, 2001).

In the same way that all youth experience fears and worries as part of their normal development, most youth also exhibit what can look like obsessive–compulsive behaviors but are really features of the cognitive inflexibility that is typical of young children. For example, young children often ask parents to read the same story in the same way over and over again or insist on the same bedtime routine or route to school. Other youth acquire and keep useless items in a "treasure drawer." These behaviors typically fade by the time the youth reaches middle-school age and seldom are disruptive or distressing.

Clinicians can discriminate between these normal compulsive or ritualistic behaviors and OCD based on the content, timing, and severity of the behaviors (Leonard et al., 1990). For example, many, if not most, children exhibit compulsive or ritualistic behaviors early in childhood; these behaviors are associated with the mastery of developmental tasks, such as insisting on following the rules of a game or playing it as it was played last time. In contrast, compulsive behaviors related to OCD generally arise later in development, have a "bizarre" quality, and produce significant disruption and distress (March, Leonard, & Swedo, 1995). In addition, the frequency and intensity of OCD-related fears and compulsions in young children tend to increase over time, although the primary symptoms may change (Swedo et al., 1989) and then decrease in late adolescent or early adulthood (Rettew, Swedo, Leonard, Lenane, & Rapoport, 1992). In contrast, the frequency and intensity of normal fears and compulsive behaviors abate as the child develops and matures.

Differential Diagnoses

The co-occurrence of other conditions (e.g., anxiety disorders, attention-deficit/hyperactivity disorder [ADHD], mood disorders) is common in OCD (Brakoulias et al., 2011; see also Chapter 1, this volume). Differentiating OCD from other psychiatric disorders can at times be difficult because OCD shares some features with other disorders (March et al., 2004). For example, clinicians must take care to rule out ADHD, even when youth report difficulty with attention, because youth with OCD may try to suppress obsessions or engage in mental neutralizations and these mental actions can drain attentional resources. In addition, we recommend that clinicians give special attention to ruling out other conditions within the obsessive–compulsive spectrum disorders, such as body dysmorphic disorder, trichotillomania (hair pulling), excoriation disorder (skin picking), and hoarding disorder. These spectrum disorders include symptoms that are similar to obsessions and compulsions, but they are not exactly the same. For example, youth with trichotillomania engage in compulsive hair pulling, and they may have distressing thoughts regarding a feature of a hair. However, in OCD, youth experience only relief from the compulsive behavior. In trichotillomania, for example, youth experience both relief (negative reinforcement) and pleasure (positive reinforcement) from some aspect of the pulling behaviors.

A particularly challenging differential diagnosis is between OCD and tic disorders, such as Tourette disorder. Tic disorders, ADHD, and OCD co-occur at high rates in youth (Kadesjö & Gillberg, 2000), and perhaps 20% to 80% of youth with OCD have a co-occurring tic disorder (Leonard et al., 1992). These comorbidities, particularly ADHD, tend to decrease the efficacy of CBT for pediatric OCD. Furthermore, the presence of co-occurring ADHD, tic disorders, or oppositional defiant disorder (ODD) tend to degrade the response rates to pharmacotherapy for OCD (Geller, Biederman, Stewart, Mullin, Martin, et al., 2003).

Differentiating generalized anxiety disorder (GAD) from OCD is another challenge. In general, we recommend that clinicians, when making differential diagnoses among anxiety disorders, clarify the focus of the youth's anxious apprehension or worry (see Table 3.1). In the case of GAD, the focus of the worry is on a number of worry domains (e.g., health, finances, relationships) about which all people from time to time worry. Also, worry is egosyntonic, whereas obsessions are not. That is, youth do not tend to suppress or push from awareness worry in the way they tend to attempt to push from awareness an obsession. Furthermore, youth with GAD do not experience their worry thoughts as intrusive. In GAD, worry tends to ease into awareness, whereas an obsession abruptly intrudes.

TABLE 3.1. Differential Diagnosis of Obsessive–Compulsive Disorder

Diagnosis	Symptoms that differ from diagnosis of obsessive–compulsive disorder
Generalized anxiety disorder	Recurrent thoughts (worries) tend to be about real-life concerns, finances, and family, whereas content of obsessions in OCD is typically odd or irrational. Youth do not experience worry as intrusive. Youth with OCD worry but typically about encountering an object or situation that triggers an obsession.
Specific phobia	Fear reaction to specific objects and situations; feared object in specific phobia is more circumscribed and rituals/compulsions are not present.
Social anxiety disorder	Feared situations limited to social interactions.
Major depressive disorder	Recurrent thoughts (ruminations) in major depression are usually mood congruent, not experienced as intrusive/distressing, and not linked to compulsive behaviors.
Body dysmorphic disorder	Obsessions and compulsions are limited to concerns of physical appearance.
Trichotillomania	Repetitive behavior limited to hair pulling and not in response to obsessions.
Hoarding disorder	Inability to part with possessions is not in response to obsessions (although youth with OCD can have collecting and saving obsessions).
Anorexia nervosa	Recurrent thoughts and repetitive behaviors limited to body image/weight.
Tic disorder	Typically, tics are less complex than compulsions and not aimed at neutralizing obsessions and premonitory urges do not decrease when motor behaviors resisted.
Psychotic disorders	Both OCD and psychotic disorders can include irrational thoughts, delusional beliefs, and peculiarities of thought: youth with OCD do not present with other psychotic symptoms and tend to recognize that the intrusive thoughts are a product of their mind.
Obsessive–compulsive personality disorder	Enduring pattern of perfectionism/control; lack specific obsessions and compulsions.

ASSESSMENT PROCESS

Once the clinician has diagnosed the youth with OCD and identified co-occurring conditions, the next step is to assess the condition. As emphasized throughout the book, in order for clinicians to flexibly apply the core treatment strategies they must gather the information required to develop a clinically useful formulation of the youth's obsessive–compulsive symptoms within the broader context of all factors that might influence the expression of those symptoms.

The goals of the assessment process are to identify other factors that the clinician did not identify fully during the consultation and diagnostic meeting, details of the co-occurring conditions, and other factors, such as parental accommodation, that the clinician will include in the comprehensive case conceptualization for the youth. Although a comprehensive assessment is essential to the effective treatment of pediatric OCD (March & Albano, 1996), the assessment process needs to be efficient and easy to implement in routine clinical practice. To that end, we present only those measures and assessment procedures that clinicians can learn easily and use in busy clinical practices and in a variety of practice settings.

First Meeting With Youth

A goal of the first meeting is to build rapport and to engage youth in the assessment and later treatment processes. As part of engagement, we use the first meeting to educate youth about OCD, place the condition in a neurobehavioral framework, and explain the treatment process.

Create a Language for Change

By "language for change," we mean that we build a language that we and the parents use to speak about the problem. The language externalizes or places the problem outside the youth. Externalizing the condition decreases shame and embarrassment youth have regarding the condition and begins the process of engaging youth and parents in the treatment process (White, 1986; White & Epston, 1990). Furthermore, placing OCD outside the youth enables the clinician to develop a therapeutic narrative whereby youth, parents, and clinician are on the same team with a shared foe and have a shared goal to push OCD out of the youth's life. Externalizing language then becomes the language to discuss OCD at any point in the treatment. Clinicians can download a blank Map of My Land form (see http://pubs.apa.org/books/supp/tompkins, Web Form 3.1) to use when discussing the youth's symptoms, current level of impairment, and progress during treatment.

Create a Nickname

The first step is to ask the youth to name the OCD. Although adolescents are typically comfortable referring to OCD as OCD, a nickname is a very effective strategy to externalize the condition for younger children. We recommend that clinicians assist youth to come up with their own unique nickname. Over the years, youth have suggested nicknames that were characters in books, movies, and television shows that were popular at the time, as well as their own take on the condition. The best nicknames are those that view OCD as mean, bossy, or tricky. Most important, the best nicknames are those that are neither too formidable nor too scary. Here are a few nicknames we have heard over the years: Count Olaf, Germy, Bossy Man, Trickster, Mr. Worry, Worry Monster, Worry Bug, Danger Man, Nasty Nora, Annoying Nagster, Scary Guy, and Brain Sticker.

Over the years, youth have selected names from current books (e.g., Voldemort from the Harry Potter series), movies (Loki from the *Thor* movies), or television shows (e.g., Ninja Turtles). It is wise to avoid names that the youth experiences as dangerous or powerful. (Of course, the name Voldemort may frighten one child and not another.) However, giving OCD a name provides the youth with some psychological distance from the condition while increasing the youth's confidence that the foe is beatable. The clinician might encourage the youth to give OCD a name in this way:

CLINICIAN: So, Timmy, who is your favorite bad guy?

TIMMY: What do you mean?

CLINICIAN: Well, we want to come up with a name for the bad guy who makes you wash your hands and scares you into believing that you're going to get sick, even when you know you're not. I think he's a big bully, and we're going to get him to leave you alone. Now, some kids call the bully Oscar, from *Sesame Street*— you know, Oscar the Grouch. Some kids call the bully Meany or Bossy. It doesn't matter. It's up to you.

TIMMY: Okay. How about Germinator? My dad and I watched *The Terminator* last night, and it was kind of scary but not that bad. The terminators were these android assassins who want to take over the world. The Germinator wants to take over my world.

CLINICIAN: I love it! From now on, it's you, me, and your mom and dad against the Germinator, and—you know what?—the Germinator doesn't stand a chance against us. Not a chance.

Clinicians will use this language when inquiring about symptoms. For example: "What are the ways that Voldemort scares you?" and "What kinds of things does Voldemort make you do that you don't want to do?" Clinicians will use this language when reviewing treatment progress ("Tell me about some of the times you bossed Mr. Bossy off your land this week"), or when asking youth about new symptoms ("Has the Germinator played any new tricks on you this week?"), or when asking youth to report strategies they used to resist compulsions or face fears ("Who helped you to boss OCD back this week?" "Can you give me an example of how you beat up on OCD this week?").

With older youth, clinicians can use the term OCD to describe the foe and ask about it in similar ways: "When did the OCD start to bug you?" "How does the OCD make your life hard?"

Refer to OCD in the Third Person

Once youth have identified a nickname for OCD, the clinician then assists youth and parents to talk about OCD as if it were another person in the room. For example, when checking with youth and parents regarding progress, the clinician might say, "I'd love to hear how you ignored Mr. Bossy this week," or to encourage youth to resist compulsive urges, the clinician might say, "Go ahead and tell Mr. Germy that you're not going to wash your hands when he tells you to." Externalizing language also is useful when working with adolescents. The clinician can still refer to OCD as a foe, one outside the youth; for example: "Tell me about a couple of times last week that you resisted OCD and didn't wash your hands."

Ask Youth About Symptoms

Most youth with OCD arrive at the diagnostic interview feeling anxious and embarrassed about the thoughts they are having and the compulsions that they are powerless and afraid to stop. For this reason, we recommend that the clinician conduct the initial diagnostic interview with the youth alone. We introduce the topic of symptoms in this way:

> Obsessions are thoughts, images, urges or sensations that you have that make you feel anxious or upset or even "icky." You probably don't want to have these obsessions and might try to make them go away by doing certain things to feel better or to prevent a bad thing from happening. Sometimes when you feel anxious or upset or icky you might want to do something over and over until you feel just right or complete. We call these compulsions. Or, you might try to avoid certain objects or places that you know make you have these thoughts. We call this avoidance.

With young children, clinicians can inquire about OCD symptoms using the externalizing language they introduced earlier:

CLINICIAN: So, tell me, Sean, what things scare you?

SEAN: What do you mean?

CLINICIAN: I mean what does the worry bully tell you that scares you?

Clinicians can also ask about symptom triggers, such as a red spot on the wall for a youth who fears diseases and thinks the spot is blood. With younger children, we usually ask,

> What kinds of things bring the worry bully around? Are there certain places at home, or school, or anytime you're outside that tends to bring the worry bully around? Sometimes you'll know the worry bully is around because he makes you not do something, like touch another kid, or sometimes the worry bully makes you do something you don't want to do, like wash your hands. We call these triggers, and we want to list all the ways that the worry bully comes and bugs you.

With older youth, clinicians can describe obsessions, compulsions, and triggers and then ask them to list these out. Also, clinicians will obtain this information as they complete the Children's Yale–Brown Obsessive Compulsive Scale (CY-BOCS; Scahill et al., 1997) with youth and parents. We describe this process later in the chapter.

In this first meeting, a matter-of-fact attitude and gentle manner are essential if clinicians are to obtain the information necessary to establish the diagnosis of OCD. Typically, a clinician who communicates "I've heard this before and even scarier and sillier things" does much to decrease the shame and anxiety many youth experience when asked to share these hidden experiences:

CLINICIAN: Hey, Justin, in a minute I'm going to ask you some questions about thoughts that might be bugging you or that you just don't like. Sometimes the thoughts are pretty scary, and sometimes kids are a little embarrassed that they're having scary thoughts. I tell you what: if you can tell me a thought you're having that another kid hasn't told me before, I'll give you this $10 gift card. I want you to be honest, of course, but I'm always interested in learning new things. How does that sound?

JUSTIN: You'll really give me a $10 gift card if I tell you a scary thought I'm having that no other kids have told you?

CLINICIAN: Yep. I know it's hard to talk about your thoughts sometimes, but kids' brains come up with some pretty scary thoughts, and so do grown-ups', but thoughts don't make a kid. They're just thoughts. They're like brain hiccups. Every once in a while, your brain hiccups. Obsession is a fancy name for brain hiccups. Obsessions are thoughts or even pictures that you have in your mind that you don't want. They don't have anything to do with who you are and what you want to do. Some of the scariest brain hiccups kids have are about hurting someone they like or love.

JUSTIN: I hate these thoughts! There must be something wrong with me. I don't think other kids think the things I think.

CLINICIAN: Well, perhaps you could tell me just one thought you're having, and I'll tell you whether other kids have had a thought like that.

JUSTIN: Okay. Well, have other kids told you that they're thinking about stabbing their mom and dad while they're sleeping? Or, thinking that they're going to push their mom down the stairs or in front of a car? Have you?

CLINICIAN: Yes, Justin, I've heard those kind of thoughts from other kids before; lots of times. I guess that means no $10 gift card, but perhaps you could still win it. How about other scary thoughts you're having? You want to try again?

In this case, the clinician's fun and matter-of-fact manner normalizes Justin's experience and comforts Justin enough that he is willing to share more with the clinician. Also, Justin wins either way in this discussion. If he tells the clinician a thought the clinician has not heard before (unlikely), he earns a reward. If he tells the clinician a thought that the clinician has heard before (likely), Justin learns that he is not weird or wicked because he has scary or unacceptable thoughts.

Ask Youth About Sexual or Embarrassing Symptoms

At times, youth will have symptoms, such as sexual obsessions, that they are reluctant to share with anyone, particularly a new clinician. Prior to meeting with the youth, we ask parents for permission to ask their child about sexual obsessions:

> In order to develop a treatment plan, it's essential that I understand what thoughts or images your child is having that make him anxious. From the initial obsessive–compulsive scale, I believe that your child may be having sexual obsessions. I must know the specific content of these obsessions in order to treat them. It's important that we identify these symptoms now, because it would likely be just a matter of time before some other situation outside therapy would trigger them. Do you have questions? If you are not comfortable with me asking questions of your child, then I may not be able to treat the OCD. What would you like me to do?

Once parents have consented, the clinician meets with the youth alone to ask about any sexual or embarrassing symptoms, including thoughts and compulsions. For example, for youth with contamination or germ obsessions, clinicians will want to ask about toileting compulsions, such as excessive wiping, or checking behaviors related to feces or urine. Furthermore, OCD can be involved in many aspects of self-care, such as personal hygiene, diet, sleep, and sexual activity. These can be uncomfortable questions for youth, and it is essential that clinicians introduce the topic in a sensitive but matter-of-fact manner; for example:

> Maggie, sometimes teens have thoughts that are really embarrassing for them. They think they're the only teens who have ever had these thoughts, and because they're embarrassed, they're reluctant to talk about them. I hope you'll give me permission to ask you about these. I'm guessing that just asking you if I can ask about these thoughts might cause you to start having some of them. I apologize for that, but it's important I hear about these kinds of thoughts so that I can help you. Is it okay for me to ask?

INFORMATION TO GATHER

During the assessment process, clinicians gather information regarding the central factors hypothesized to maintain the youth's OCD and factors that may complicate its treatment. As part of the process, clinicians will contact a number of professionals for relevant information: current and prior psychiatric and medical records for the youth and family; educational or neuropsychological evaluations; and reports from classroom teachers, school psychologists and counselors. Once gathered, clinicians organize this data into a treatment plan.

Psychosocial and Medical History

Much of the information regarding the youth's psychosocial and medical history is captured in the Parent Questionnaire. We recommend that clinicians inquire about any family history of OCD and anxiety disorders, because OCD is more common among relatives of individuals with anxiety disorders (Black, Gaffney, Schlosser, & Gabel, 2003). Furthermore, we recommend that clinicians inquire regarding the presence of current or history of other conditions that typically occur in pediatric OCD, such as ADHD and tic disorders. These conditions may influence the outcome of CBT and medication plans.

We recommend that clinicians review the youth's medical history and contact the youth's pediatrician regarding current health status and prior medical problems to rule out medical conditions that can result in anxiety and mood, such as thyroid conditions and autoimmune disorders. In particular, for youth who exhibit sudden onset of obsessions and compulsions, as well as soft neurological signs (e.g., deterioration of handwriting; loss of academic abilities, particularly in visual–spatial areas; tantrums), following exposure to streptococcal virus, the clinician will want to rule out pediatric acute-onset neuropsychiatric syndrome (Chang et al., 2015; Murphy et al., 2004).

Co-Occurring Conditions

An effective treatment plan for pediatric OCD depends on identifying other co-occurring conditions, particularly those that can influence the ability of youth to complete in-session and out-of-session exposure and response prevention (ERP) tasks (see Chapter 2). This is true for parents as well. A mother who has significant ADHD symptoms may not remember to prompt the youth to practice ERP homework tasks or may have trouble remembering and initiating other key tasks, such as assisting the youth to self-record.

Exposure and Response Prevention Targets

Exposure targets include external fear cues (situations, activities, objects that trigger obsessions); internal fear cues (thoughts, images, memories, sensory experiences); external compulsions or safety-seeking behaviors; internal compulsions or neutralizations (suppression, reassuring self, analysis, checking); and active avoidance (situations, activities, or objects).

In addition to completing the CY-BOCS, clinicians may wish to ask youth and parents to describe a typical day. Encourage youth to give a play-by-play description of several recent episodes. We recommend that clinicians inquire about small details, particularly regarding avoidance and compulsions; for example:

CLINICIAN: Justin, if it's okay with you, I want to get more information about how the OCD bugs you during a typical day. I'll probably stop you here and there and ask you some questions to make sure I understand what you were thinking, feeling, and doing at that moment. So try to answer the questions in as much detail as you can. Let's begin with yesterday. What time did you get up yesterday?

JUSTIN: Okay. I got up at seven, I think.

CLINICIAN: Great. Now, did you awaken with an alarm or on your own?

JUSTIN: My mom came in and told me to get ready for school. She leaned over and shook me.

CLINICIAN: Did you get immediately out of bed, or did you stay in bed a little while?

JUSTIN: I stayed in bed for a while.

CLINICIAN: Now, while you were in bed, did you do any compulsions? Perhaps some counting or checking. The OCD often makes you do that kind of thing. Were you doing it then?

JUSTIN: Yeah. I was counting. I had one of those bad thoughts, and I was counting.

CLINICIAN: What was the thought that made you start counting?

JUSTIN: A sexual thought about my mom.

CLINICIAN: Yes. Those are upsetting. What was the thought?

JUSTIN: I thought about touching her breasts. I can't believe I'm thinking that. It's really bad to think that.

CLINICIAN: How did that thought make you feel?

JUSTIN: I felt really bad.

CLINICIAN: Bad as in anxious, or bad as in guilty?

JUSTIN: I guess I felt both. I was scared I was going to do it, and I felt guilty that I was thinking it.

CLINICIAN: So, your mom leaned over you and that triggered the thought about touching her breasts. It sounds like your mom leaning over you was the trigger and the obsession was about touching her breasts. And then you started counting. So, please tell me about the counting. Were you counting to stop the thought or to prevent something bad from happening?

JUSTIN:	I was counting to get the thought out of my head. If I can count to 4 without having the thought, then I can stop.
CLINICIAN:	So how many times did you have to do that?
JUSTIN:	I don't even know. I was counting when my mom came back into my bedroom and yelled at me to get up.
CLINICIAN:	Then what did you do?
JUSTIN:	I got up and went into the bathroom.
CLINICIAN:	Then what did you do? The first thing, I mean.
JUSTIN:	I closed my eyes and started counting again.

This strategy can provide a great deal more detail about the nature of the obsessions and compulsions, as well as avoidance strategies. In addition, clinicians and youth begin to understand the functional relationships among obsessions, feelings, and neutralizations (compulsions).

Often, it can take an entire session to complete a typical day. At times, youth who are anxious and indecisive may have trouble providing details of their symptoms. The youth may have excessive need for exactness or fears of making a mistake. In these cases, we encourage clinicians to instruct the youth to estimate.

In addition, clinicians will identify the feared consequence. This is critical to effective ERP. For example, three youth avoid touching a countertop but for different reasons. One youth avoids touching a countertop because he is afraid that germs on the countertop will make him sick and he might die. Another youth might avoid touching a countertop because he is afraid that germs will make him ill, but he does not fear dying. He fears that he will miss school and fall behind with his schoolwork. Still, another youth might avoid touching a countertop because he does not want to feel dirty but is not concerned about getting ill. We recommend that the clinician inquire regarding feared consequences of the youth's behavior, perhaps in the following way:

CLINICIAN:	So, Tommy, if you couldn't wash your hands, what's the worst thing you can imagine happening?
TOMMY:	What do you mean?
CLINICIAN:	If you don't wash your hands, are you afraid of getting sick from germs?
TOMMY:	No, I know I probably won't get sick from germs. I just don't like feeling germy.
CLINICIAN:	So you mean that you're not afraid of getting sick from germs, but you just don't feel comfortable having germs on you. Is that correct?
TOMMY:	Yeah. I guess I don't like feeling dirty.

Onset and Course of OCD

Information regarding the onset and course of OCD is important to develop a comprehensive conceptualization of the youth's OCD and an effective treatment plan for it. We recommend that clinicians ask youth and parents when the first episode occurred and inquire about any factors that might have influenced the onset of the condition, such as changes in the family, a traumatic event such as a home break-in, or ongoing stressors such as a family member with a serious medical illness. We recommend that clinicians ask about family history of anxiety or OCD (e.g., biological parents or relatives). We recommend that clinicians ask youth and parents whether they have relatives that were "clean freaks" or "hypochondriacs," or "perfectionists."

Clinicians may wish to ask youth and parents to speculate regarding the causes of the youth's OCD symptoms: "How do you think you [or your child] developed OCD?" The story about the onset of OCD can provide particular beliefs that may be the target of ERP strategies. For example, a youth with health obsessions remembered his mother's "devastation" following the death of her mother. The youth was then more afraid of the consequences of his death on his mother than on his actual death.

Parent Accommodation and Functioning Targets

The FAS-PR helps identify these targets. We recommend that clinicians ask parents to elaborate on their responses to FAS-PR items:

> Do each of you respond to your child's distress in the same way? Which of you is more concerned about your child's OCD symptoms? Which of you has the most trouble staying calm when something triggers your child's OCD and your child is distressed?

At times, one parent views the youth's response as disproportionate to the particular situation and the other does not. In this situation, ask the parents how the youth's brother or sister responds to a similar situation: "Does Billy's older sister become as distressed as Billy does when she can't wash her hands immediately after petting the dog?"

Last, we recommend that clinicians explore the effects of the youth's OCD on day-to-day roles and responsibilities. Does the youth help around the home, or have the parents exempted the youth from chores and responsibilities that their other children perform? This kind of accommodation can create considerable distress in the youth's relationships with siblings. Do the parents exempt the youth with OCD from attending family functions, going to school, or completing homework? Also, how well do the parents manage the youth's pushback behaviors? What is the quality of the relationships between the youth and each parent? How well do the parents communicate with each other, their children, and the clinician?

Level of Insight and Motivation

Insight and its relationship to the youth's willingness to engage in the tasks and goals of therapy is critical to a good treatment outcome (Foa, Abramowitz, Franklin, & Kozak, 1999). As discussed earlier, the level of insight exhibited by youth is influenced by their developmental age. Very young youth may not understand that the compulsions do not actually prevent the feared consequence. Furthermore, youth with low insight may experience greater OCD-related impairment and family accommodation and may then require more intensive and multimodal treatment approaches (Storch et al., 2008).

The OCD Disturbance Scale provides clinicians with a sense of the youth's level of insight. We recommend that clinicians explore with parents the degree with which the youth views the obsessions and compulsions as unreasonable or distressing. Some youth, particularly young children, report that they enjoy engaging in their compulsive actions or report little distress (Geffken et al., 2005).

Developmental Factors

In addition to the role of developmental age in factors such as insight, we recommend that clinicians consider the role of core cognitive deficits of youth with developmental disorders (e.g., autism spectrum disorders, intellectual development disorders, or even specific communication disorders) in the treatment of pediatric OCD. For example, youth with developmental disorders may not benefit from abstract cognitive strategies, but they may still benefit from direct and prolonged exposure strategies. Furthermore, youth with autism spectrum disorders may exhibit poor inferential thinking. They may have great trouble generalizing what they learned in one ERP task to a similar task or generalizing what they learned in a session to experiences they have outside of treatment.

Peer Relationships

Youth with OCD are often victims of peer rejection, bullying, and teasing (Storch et al., 2006). Peer victimization may result in greater levels of depression and severity of OCD-related symptoms and thereby complicate the treatment of OCD. We recommend that clinicians screen for peer victimization and clarify its relationship, if any, to OCD symptoms or to other difficulties, such as developmental disorders or tic disorders. Furthermore, youth who are experiencing peer victimization will benefit from a broader plan to address peer teasing and bullying, such as a systemic intervention within the school setting (Leadbeater & Hoglund, 2006). In addition, so that clinicians can identify possible social skills deficits that may complicate treatment of the youth's OCD, we recommend that they inquire regarding the youth's current peer group, their ability to make new friends and keep friends, and any recent changes to the youth's friendship network.

Cultural Factors

The influence of culture on the expression and treatment of pediatric OCD is not well studied. Culture may not greatly influence the specific and typical clusters of OCD symptoms. The exception is religion and religiosity. These cultural factors appear to influence the content of religion-related obsessions and the severity of these symptoms (Nicolini, Salin-Pascual, Cabrera, & Lanzagorta, 2017). For example, the religious practices (rules and rites) of ultra-Orthodox Jews (Okasha et al., 1994) and Muslims (Vinker, Jaworowski, & Mergui, 2014) may influence the nature of OCD symptoms as well as the acceptance of certain behaviors or attitudes, such as the importance of cleanliness, religious obligations, or the difference between right and wrong.

Cultural factors may then influence the motivation of youth and parents to engage in the tasks and goals of CBT for the condition. We recommend that clinicians discuss with youth and parents the cultural appropriateness of OCD-related thoughts and behaviors and compare them with the attitudes and behaviors the family reports are "normal" cultural behaviors. At times, clinicians may benefit from inviting a spiritual expert to consult with youth and parents. For example, we have invited rabbis, imams, deacons, and priests to therapy sessions to help the family understand the line between the condition and the spiritual practice.

Academic Factors

Youth with OCD may have co-occurring learning disorders that complicate treatment. For example, when classroom activities trigger OCD symptoms, youth with a co-occurring learning disorder may experience greater disruption in their abilities to attend, learn, and follow through with academic tasks. We recommend that clinicians inquire regarding the youth's academic history, easy and difficult learning domains (math vs. language), the type of classroom accommodations, if any, the youth has received, and the documented benefit of these accommodations to the youth.

Youth who are struggling to access the academic curriculum, whether they suffer with OCD or not, are at risk of school refusal. Academic difficulties may also direct the targets of ERP. For example, youth who will not touch pencils or paper because of contamination obsessions may benefit, at least temporarily, from classroom accommodations, such as permission to use their own school materials.

Administering the Children's Yale–Brown Obsessive Compulsive Scale

The primary screening instrument for assessing OCD in youth is CY-BOCS (Scahill et al., 1997) and is a downward developmental extension of the adult Y-BOCS (Goodman et al., 1989). Researchers have used the Y-BOCS as a measure of change in studies of the efficacy of psychopharmacology (DeVeaugh-Geiss et al., 1992) and CBT (March et al., 1994). The CY-BOCS follows the same format as the Y-BOCS and consists of two subscales: Obsessions Severity and Compulsions Severity, which are combined to yield a Total Score. The CY-BOCS is administered by the clinician and includes a comprehensive checklist of common obsessions and compulsions, the degree of interference, distress, time consumed, and degree of resistance, and the perceived degree of control over the symptoms. In addition to an assessment of symptoms and symptom severity, the CY-BOCS provides information regarding the youth's ability to resist OCD and gain control over OCD symptoms.

Clinicians will decide whether to conduct the CY-BOCS with the youth alone, with parents alone, or with youth and parents together. Typically, we interview youth and parents together, directing questions to the youth but soliciting feedback from parents as well.

A number of factors may influence the interview format. Older youth who have embarrassing symptoms or low motivation for treatment may prefer separate meetings with the clinician. We recommend that clinicians discuss the interview options with youth and parents in advance of conducting the CY-BOCS interview and decide on a format that is most comfortable with the family. At times, clinicians may wish to meet with the youth alone for certain sections of the CY-BOCS, such as questions regarding sexual obsessions.

We recommend that clinicians begin with the most common obsessions (e.g., fear of contamination, harm to self, harm to a familiar person, need for symmetry or exactness) and compulsions (e.g., washing, checking, repeating, touching, tapping) in youth. One of the most difficult areas of inquiry is to establish the degree of internal neutralizations. These include mental rituals, such as neutralizing a bad thought with a good thought, but also more subtle mental neutralizations, such as repeatedly analyzing a thought, checking for an experience, or reassuring self. Youth may be less aware of these symptoms or confuse neutralizations with obsessions because both are mental events. Clinicians might discuss mental neutralizations in the following way:

> One of the ways OCD bugs kids is to make them think things to prevent the bad thing from happening or to make them feel less anxious. These actions are inside actions. They're different from outside actions, which are the things the OCD bully makes kids do, like washing their hands. Inside actions are thought actions, like thinking through something over and over again to try to convince yourself that you didn't do it. An obsession is the question OCD asks you. For example: "Did I touch something that has germs on it?" The mental action is the kid's way of trying to answer that question. In fact, the OCD question is probably only 1% of what you're thinking. The other 99% of your thinking is trying to answer the OCD questions. I want to see if there is anything like that going on so that I can help you stop doing that too.

GIVING FEEDBACK TO YOUTH AND PARENTS

At the end of the assessment process, clinicians provide feedback to youth and parents regarding the evaluation and treatment plan. During the feedback process, clinicians confirm the diagnosis and explain the model of OCD and how it is treated. At times, parents are reluctant to accept the diagnosis of OCD, particularly the idea that their child has a "disorder." It can help to explain to parents that disorder is defined by four *D*s: disproportionate, distressing, disruptive, and duration:

> Based on my review of the information I gathered, including from my meetings with you and your child, I believe your son meets criteria for the diagnosis of obsessive–compulsive disorder. Understandably, you're concerned about your child's well-being; and, many parents have some trouble with the term *obsessive–compulsive disorder*, and particularly the word *disorder*. I'd like to explain to you what mental health professionals mean when they use the term *disorder*. All disorder means is that your child is experiencing four *D*'s. The first *D* stands for *disproportionate*. By disproportionate I mean that your child's actions are disproportionate to the real threat or danger. For example, your son washes his hands 20 to 30 times per day and takes two showers every day. Each shower takes about 1 hour. I think you'll agree that your son's washing compulsions are disproportionate to the objective risks that he may get sick because of something he touched. The second *D* stands for *disruptive*. Your son's washing compulsions have significantly disrupted his usual routines at home. He is falling behind in school because he must leave the classroom to wash his hands. He is often late to school because of the washing compulsions, and he has started to refuse to go to school. The third *D* stands for *distressing*. Your son is very distressed by the thoughts he has about germs and death, and he's also distressed that he has to wash his hands so many times each day and that he can't stop. The last *D* stands for *duration*. This just means that the first three *D*s have been around in some form for longer than 6 months.
>
> I hope you can see that your son has these 4 *D*s. Also, the goal of treatment is to decrease the obsessions and compulsions so that the *D* disappears. This means that your son may always have a few obsessions and compulsions, but they won't create major problems for him the way they do now.

Since this treatment approach includes meetings with youth alone and parents alone, some clinicians might question whether it is ethical to share information about the youth's treatment with parents. Generally, we favor open communication between youth and parents and model this in our approach to these meetings. At the same time, we recognize the importance of obtaining consent from youth, particularly adolescents, before sharing information. At times, adolescents ask us to withhold certain information from their parents. Unless the youth is at risk of harm, we generally respect this request. However, most times, the youth's wish for confidentiality concerns the attitudes or reactions the parents might have (true or not) about certain obsessions, particularly when the content is sexual, aggressive, or religious.

Generally, we encourage youth to share this information with parents. We explain to youth that withholding information is a suppression (concealment) strategy and that concealment tends to make OCD worse. Also we explain to youth that their parents cannot assist the youth in defeating OCD if the youth continue to hide the content of obsessions. Last, we recommend that clinicians help parents understand that it is normal for adolescents to desire privacy as they move into adulthood.

SELF-MONITORING TO GATHER INFORMATION

Self-monitoring is an effective strategy to gather information regarding the youth's symptoms (or parents' problem behaviors) over time within the environment in which the symptoms and problem behaviors occur.

Clinicians can use several simple strategies to assist youth and parents to comply with the act of self-monitoring, as well as to record accurate and relevant data (Barlow & Hersen, 1984; Nelson, 1977). First, it is essential that clinicians adequately train the client to self-record in the desired manner. If the youth or parent is to use a form, diary, or journal to record responses, we recommend that clinicians take several recent examples of the phenomenon to monitor and complete the form or diary together. When possible, clinicians might trigger the event to record so that the youth or parents can record it. For example, the clinician might ask a youth who counts his steps to accompany him outside the office and to record the occurrence of the compulsion as they take a short walk to the corner. Second, we recommend that clinicians encourage parents or "coaches" to record the same data the youth records periodically. It is important to alert the youth that the parents will do this. At times, clinical judgment will rule against this strategy, but parents' involvement in self-monitoring is particularly important for younger youth. Third, reward youth for accurate self-monitoring. The clinician can ask parents to reward youth (e.g., with praise and a reinforcement token) when youth and parents record the same event in the same way. Last, shape the self-monitoring process. For OCD symptoms that occur frequently throughout the day, instruct youth or parents to record the occurrence of symptoms or the problem behavior during a specific hour during specific days. As youth and parents adhere to self-monitoring, clinicians can then ask youth and parents to increase the periods they self-record.

CONCLUSION

To develop and implement a treatment plan that maximizes the youth's response to CBT for the OCD, it is essential that clinicians identify all factors that maintain the frequency and severity of the youth's obsessions and compulsions, as well as the factors that may influence the youth's response to treatment. To gather this information clinicians will rely on questionnaires, self-report and parent-report measures, and clinical interviews of the youth and parents. The quality of these data rests on youth and parents feeling comfortable with the clinician but also with each other. To that end, we recommend that clinicians build a language for change early in the diagnostic and assessment process. Externalizing OCD can do much to depathologize the condition for youth and parents and thereby enhance willingness to participate in treatment for the condition.

In the next chapter, we describe the process of using the information gathered to develop an individualized case conceptualization and treatment plan. Central to the comprehensive treatment plan is the ERP plan. The ERP hierarchy is a critical piece of the treatment plan for pediatric OCD.

4

Developing the Case Conceptualization and Treatment Plan

Ava is a bright and enthusiastic 10-year-old girl who lives primarily with her mother but spends alternate weekends between her mother's and her father's homes. Ava's parents had a contentious divorce, and although things now are better between them, they still often disagree intensely about the best way to parent Ava and her 13-year-old brother. Several months ago, a psychiatrist diagnosed Ava with attention-deficit/hyperactivity disorder (ADHD). A neuropsychological evaluation confirmed the ADHD diagnosis and identified several specific language-based learning disorders. Ava's parents described her as a bit of a "hypochondriac." Over the years, she has worried about getting sick and has always been more scrupulous with her hygiene than her 13-year-old brother. At times, Ava's handwashing noticeably increased. During these periods, Ava repeatedly asked her mother to feel her forehead to reassure her that she did not have a fever. These behaviors always faded after a few weeks, and her parents were never concerned about her. However, several months ago, Ava began to worry intensely about bee stings. This followed the tragic and sudden death of Will, a boy 2 years younger than Ava, who died from anaphylactic shock after he was stung by a bee in the common area at school. Since then, Ava has repeatedly asked her parents whether she is breathing okay and whether there are bees in the area. Ava had always been very active and played outside with her friends and on a soccer team. She now refused to attend soccer practice or to go outside willingly. Recently, she started to refuse to attend school. Ava has also started to walk slowly while she carefully scans the environment for bees. She repeatedly checks her breathing with a mirror if she feels breathless. Ava has images of suffocating, struggling to breathe, and dying. She refuses to talk about the boy who died, or bees, or about insects in general. A few weeks ago, the

http://dx.doi.org/10.1037/0000167-005
Cognitive Behavior Therapy for OCD in Youth: A Step-by-Step Guide, by M. A. Tompkins, D. J. Owen, N. H. Shiloff, and L. R. Tanner

science teacher excused her from watching a video about rain forests because Ava was terrified that the movie might show bees or other insects. Recently, Ava has started to move her head slowly because she once felt dizzy when she turned her head quickly. She reported other mild symptoms of obsessive–compulsive disorder (OCD), including the need for symmetry regarding special objects in her room (e.g., soccer trophies, spelling bee award ribbons), and "bad" thoughts about God.

Ava is eager to please the clinician, but her inattention and impulsivity make it difficult for her to sit still and answer questions. Furthermore, it has not been easy for Ava to identify and label her emotions, nor has it been easy for her to identify the connections between her thoughts, distress, and actions. In addition, Ava's mother is a first-generation Asian American who places a high value on cleanliness and accommodation to the wishes of others. Her father is an Irish American who values independence and believes it is his job to toughen his children to the inherent difficulties of life.

Youth are complicated, and youth with OCD are no exception. The majority of children with OCD will also receive another psychiatric diagnosis, such as an anxiety disorder or ADHD. Adding to this mix, children with OCD are not exempt from the other complications of life, such as parental divorce, troubled parents, bullying, the death of a loved one, and economic hardship, nor from the cultural, social, and family factors that shape us all.

In this chapter, we describe steps to develop an individualized case conceptualization from the cognitive behavior nomothetic formulation for OCD in youth. We then describe the process of building graded-exposure and response prevention plans. We also describe factors that can influence the implementation of core strategies, such as developmental age and co-occurring conditions. The chapter concludes with the role of progress monitoring in guiding the treatment process.

CASE CONCEPTUALIZATION

In cognitive behavior therapy (CBT) for pediatric OCD, case conceptualization is one of the most complex tasks that clinicians learn and the most crucial to a robust and durable outcome. The individualized conceptualization for OCD includes the youth's particular treatment targets (internal fear cues, external fear cues, focal fear, active avoidance strategies), as well as cultural, family, and developmental factors that can influence the course of the condition and the implementation of the core treatment strategies.

The conceptualization process begins with the cognitive behavior nomothetic conceptualization for the condition. The nomothetic conceptualization identifies the general cognitive and behavioral targets of the treatment. However, the nomothetic conceptualization is insufficient to develop a treatment plan for the particular youth and family that seek the clinician's help. To develop an effective treatment plan, clinicians must transform the nomothetic conceptualization for the disorder into an ideographic conceptualization for a particular youth. The ideographic or individualized conceptualization begins with a comprehensive functional assessment that identifies the particular external and internal fear cues, feared consequences, and neutralizations that the youth uses to attenuate obsessive fear.

DEVELOP THE CASE CONCEPTUALIZATION

The goal of the first few meetings with youth and parents is to develop an initial individualized conceptualization that is sufficient to begin treatment. However, the clinician will refine the case conceptualization over time as he monitors the youth's treatment progress. Monitoring outcome, therefore, is critical to the effectiveness of treatment, and we describe the role of outcome monitoring at the end of this chapter.

Clinicians can expect to spend 2 to 4 hours developing an individualized case conceptualization and treatment plan and longer when youth have several co-occurring conditions, complicated family situations, or complex OCD symptoms. At times, the eagerness of parents and youth to resolve OCD as soon as possible can cause the clinician to rush through this critical phase of treatment planning. We recommend that clinicians reassure parents that it is unwise to rush through the treatment planning process and that a careful and thoughtful plan will save time in the end by creating a targeted treatment.

Identify Treatment Targets and Functional Relationships

The first step in developing an individualized case conceptualization is to identify the relevant treatment targets and the functional relationships among these factors. These factors include the external and internal fear cues, the feared consequence, internal and external neutralizations, avoidance strategies, and dysfunctional beliefs and interpretations. Clinicians may not always target the dysfunctional beliefs and interpretations directly, particularly for young children who may have trouble identifying these cognitive factors during the assessment phase. However, young children with OCD benefit from exposure and response prevention (ERP) tasks and the habituation to distress that accompanies confronting and remaining in anxiety-evoking situations.

Youth with OCD differ considerably in the function of their avoidance and neutralization strategies. For example, one youth avoids touching certain kids because she is afraid that she will become ill. She repeatedly washes her hands to remove germs if she comes in contact with a kid. Another youth avoids touching certain kids because he is afraid that he may take on the negative qualities of the kid. This youth repeatedly washes his hands to remove the "feeling" of the person. Still another youth avoids touching certain kids because she fears that she will hit or push the kid. This youth repeatedly washes her hands to remove the thought of hurting a kid from her mind.

In Chapter 3, we described in detail the process of identifying the factors hypothesized to maintain the OCD mechanism utilizing a combination of symptom measures, clinical interviews, the recording of symptoms, and collateral contacts with teachers and mental health and medical professionals. We recommend that clinicians organize these data with a functional assessment and case conceptualization worksheet. For example, in Ava's case conceptualization worksheet (see Figure 4.1), the clinician listed the factors hypothesized to maintain the youth's OCD symptoms (i.e., external and internal fear cues, external and internal neutralizations, avoidance strategies, and dysfunctional beliefs and interpretations). The internal fear

FIGURE 4.1. Ava's Functional Assessment and Case Conceptualization Worksheet

Name: Ava

Age: 10 years

External fear cues (places, people, things)		
Outside, places in school that remind Ava of deceased boy, common area in school		
Friends of deceased boy, science teacher		
Bees, photos of bees, flowers, lawns, gardens, trees, bushes		
Internal fear cues (thoughts, images, doubts, impulses, physical sensations)		
Contamination	SUD (0–10)	Impact (0–10)
Germs, illness not related to anaphylactic shock	10	9
Feeling "unclean" after touching papers from school	3	3
Harm	SUD (0–10)	Impact (0–10)
Anaphylactic shock	10	10
Face of deceased boy	9	4
Images of bees or other insects	8	8
Images of her suffocating or death	10	10
Incompleteness	SUD (0–10)	Impact (0–10)
Need for symmetry with soccer trophies	2	2
Need for "just right" with spelling bee award ribbons	3	3
Unacceptable thoughts	SUD (0–10)	Impact (0–10)
Blasphemous thoughts about God	5	3

FIGURE 4.1. Ava's Functional Assessment and Case Conceptualization Worksheet (*Continued*)

Avoidance strategies and relationship to obsessive fear (e.g., avoiding bathrooms to avoid germs, avoiding cemeteries to avoid thoughts of death)		
	SUD (0–10)	Impact (0–10)
Avoids going outside, particularly in the common area at school	9	10
Exercise, exertion, dizziness, breathlessness	8	8
Avoids science, science teacher, and talking about deceased boy	6	10
External or overt neutralization strategies and relationship to obsessive fear (e.g., checking backpack six times to avoid misplacing schoolwork; touching doorway with right shoulder, then left shoulder, to feel even; retracing steps to eliminate bad thought to prevent bad luck)		
Compulsions	DTR (0–10)	Impact (0–10)
Seeks reassurance from mother	8	5
Uses mirror to check breath and feels forehead to check for fever	8	6
Straightens possessions in room	6	4
Rituals	DTR (0–10)	Impact (0–10)
Moves possessions six times to neutralize "bad" thought	8	5
Internal, mental, or covert neutralization strategies and relationship to obsessive fear (e.g., repeating phrase "in God's hands" to feel safe, checking whether she is sexually aroused to neutralize sexual thought)		
Repeating	DTR (0–10)	Impact (0–10)
Repeats phrase "no bees, no shock" to feel safe	8	5
Repeats phrase "I'm breathing, I'm okay."	7	5
Checking	DTR (0–10)	Impact (0–10)
Checks breathing with mirror	8	6
Checks forehead for fever	7	6

(*continues*)

FIGURE 4.1. Ava's Functional Assessment and Case Conceptualization Worksheet (*Continued*)

Suppression or distraction (e.g., suppressing thought to prevent acting on thought, distracting away from unwanted thought)	DTR (0–10)	Impact (0–10)
Distracts herself with video games when obsessions are triggered	5	8
Suppresses "bad" thoughts about God to prevent "enjoying" them	3	4

Factors That Influence Implementation of Core Strategies		
Developmental factors		Mild tactile sensitivity
Co-occurring diagnoses	ADHD	Poor planning and organizing tasks needed to live independently, poor task initiation, poor working memory, impulsive
	Specific learning disorder	Poor self-awareness of internal, external states; difficulty reading
Family and cultural factors	Conflict in parental relationship; mother more likely to accommodate to OCD symptoms; significant differences in parenting attitudes and strategies; cultural factors may influence attitudes regarding value of control and cleanliness	
Strength factors	Bright and kind Supportive parents and extended family, two friends Persistent when given a work task Open to prompting and organizational strategies	

Potential Obstacles to Treatment	Interventions to Manage Treatment Obstacles
Poor inferential reasoning	More generalization of exposure tasks
Poor self-awareness	More self-recording with feedback
Poor working memory	More memory supports in and out of session

SUD = subjective units of distress (0 = *low;* 10 = *high*); DTR = difficulty to resist
(0 = *not difficult to resist;* 10 = *very difficult to resist*).

cues (obsessive thoughts, images, doubts, impulses) are organized relative to common OCD symptom subtypes (i.e., contamination, harm, incompleteness, unacceptable thoughts) to organize these data. On the worksheet, the clinician asked youth and parents to rate the distress levels (0 to 10, where 10 is extreme) for each internal fear cue and estimate its impact on a similar scale. Similarly, the clinician identified the youth's current neutralizations and asked youth to rate the difficulty to resist (DTR) as well as the impact of each neutralization on the day-to-day functioning of youth and parents. The most distressing obsessions and difficult-to-resist neutralizations do not always result in the greatest disruption. Gathering estimates of the impact of symptoms can help clinicians identify the symptoms to target first. In addition, the clinician noted other factors (e.g., developmental, family, social, cultural, and co-occurring conditions) that may influence the effective implementation of core strategies and suggestions for managing these obstacles. Last, the clinician added other interventions (e.g., family therapy, academic tutoring) or accommodations (e.g., classroom aides, preferential seating) to the Ava's overall treatment plan. Clinicians can download a blank case conceptualization worksheet (see http://pubs.apa.org/books/supp/tompkins, Web Form 4.1) to organize the conceptualization process.

External Fear Cues

External fear cues are the situations, objects, and activities that evoke the youth's obsessive fears. It is important for clinicians to carefully inquire about the details of external fear cues. Different situations can trigger the same obsessive fear. For example, dogs and cats evoke the obsessive fear of rabies for one youth, whereas for another youth, being around a peer whose family found a rabid bat in their garage triggers the obsessive fear of rabies. For other youth, the same situation may be associated with different obsessive fears. For example, photos in fashion magazines might evoke unacceptable sexual thoughts and urges for one youth, whereas for another youth, the same photos might evoke fears of becoming ill through contact with perspiration, saliva, or other bodily fluids.

Internal Fear Cues

Internal fear cues are the intrusive, senseless, and unacceptable thoughts, images, impulses, and doubts that evoke feelings of anxiety, fear, disgust, or shame. In addition, bodily sensations are internal fear cues for some youth, particularly those with somatic or health obsessions. For example, Ava fears the physical sensations of breathlessness or dizziness because she interprets these sensations to mean that she is in anaphylactic shock.

Identifying internal fear cues can be difficult at times. For example, an 8-year-old girl may refuse to share with the clinician that she has impulses to harm her newborn baby brother because she believes that sharing this information with the clinician means that she is more likely to act on the impulse. Youth with unacceptable thoughts may conceal these thoughts because they are embarrassed or ashamed by the content or frequency of the intrusive thoughts. We recommend that clinicians try to put youth at ease and normalize these experiences and perhaps predict that the youth may feel embarrassed or ashamed that they have certain thoughts or impulses. In Chapter 3, we described a number of strategies clinicians can use to normalize and solicit from youth these upsetting internal events.

Neutralizations and Avoidance

Neutralization and avoidance strategies include the physical (overt) and mental (covert) actions that youth use to decrease obsessive fear or prevent the feared outcome from occurring, as well as strategies to avoid triggering obsessive fears. Neutralization strategies include compulsions, physical and mental rituals, suppression, concealment, distraction, and passive avoidance. The frequency and extent of these neutralization strategies creates considerable distress and disruption for youth. Furthermore, neutralization strategies perpetuate the dysfunctional beliefs and misinterpretations that maintain the condition and interfere with extinction learning.

During the initial assessment, clinicians are likely to identify the primary neutralization and avoidance strategies, at least those that are overt and apparent to parents, teachers, and the clinician. However, it is the rare youth who describes all neutralization and avoidance strategies. Often, youth are not aware that an action is a neutralization because they are subtle (e.g., rubbing hands on pants to remove contamination) or habitual and very quick (e.g., glancing at the corners of the room when entering or leaving to balance an uneven feeling).

Passive avoidance is the intentional avoidance of situations or activities. Again, passive avoidance may be obvious to youth and parents, but they may not understand the function of the passive avoidance. For example, Mason, a 9-year-old boy, refused to do certain activities if he had not done them in a long time because he feared that he would grow younger if he did the activities again. Passive avoidance can also include youth who insist that parents or siblings help them to avoid specific situations and activities, such as the 10-year-old girl who insisted that her younger brother shower immediately after he entered the house to avoid spreading contaminants.

Clinicians can identify passive avoidance through understanding internal and external fear cues. For example, a 14-year-old boy who feared death insisted that his mother drive to school a certain way to avoid the cemetery near their home. He refused to complete his geometry homework because rectangles often appeared on the worksheets. Rectangles reminded the youth of coffins, and coffins triggered thoughts and images of death.

Dysfunctional Beliefs and Interpretations

In Chapter 1, we described the cognitive behavior model of OCD. This model posits that obsessive fear results from misappraisals, misinterpretations, and misperceptions of normal mental events. Through the process of extinction learning (i.e., exposure with response prevention), a new association with the conditioned stimulus forms that competes with the original excitatory association for expression. In other words, through exposure with response prevention, youth form new competing beliefs that override or inhibit dysfunctional beliefs, which results in the decrease of obsessive fear. Therefore, an individualized cognitive behavior conceptualization includes the youth's beliefs, assumptions, and predictions hypothesized to maintain obsessive fear. These misappraisals include overestimation of likelihood and severity of danger, beliefs about the power or value of neutralizations to prevent feared consequence, catastrophic misinterpretations of intrusive thoughts, intolerance of uncertainty, perfectionistic beliefs, and beliefs about emotional responses.

Identifying dysfunctional beliefs, however, is not always possible, particularly with developmentally young youth. Fortunately, young youth benefit from graded exposure with response prevention in which these dysfunctional beliefs are not directly targeted. At the same time, we recommend that clinicians identify dysfunctional beliefs for older youth and target these in the graded exposure with response prevention tasks.

FACTORS THAT INFLUENCE IMPLEMENTATION OF CORE TREATMENT STRATEGIES

Many factors can influence the effective application of the core strategies. We describe the factors we believe are most relevant to routine clinical practice: developmental age, level of motivation, co-occurring conditions, and sociocultural factors.

Developmental Age

Implementing therapeutic core strategies are likely to be ineffective or less effective when delivered without consideration of the youth's developmental level (Kinney, 1991). The idea of incorporating developmental age or level into treatment planning is not new (Ollendick, Grills, & King, 2001). Developmental age influences the degree to which a youth comprehends a therapeutic task or rationale for that task and thereby influences the youth's ability to implement a therapeutic technique (Steiner, 2004). Even adolescents may not have the developmental capacities necessary to grasp some of the abstract and hypothetical constructs involved in therapy, such as understanding the rationale of an intervention. Furthermore, the level of cognitive, social, and emotional development of youth constrain what they can learn from therapy.

Most clinicians who treat pediatric OCD recognize the importance of selecting, designing, and implementing cognitive and behavioral strategies relative to the developmental level of the youth. For example, youth are more likely to be impulsive and have shorter attention spans than adults; therefore, it may help to keep explanations brief and utilize parent prompting for out-of-session therapeutic activities. Furthermore, the youth's zone of proximal development (i.e., the difference between what the child can learn with or without support) will impact the youth's ability to implement new skills without help from the clinician or parents (Vygotsky, 1978). This likely influences the ability of youth without adequate prompting or support to complete out-of-session action plans.

Youth are more limited in their ability to self-reflect than adults, and they often are quiet and less willing to disclose what is troubling them. Clinicians may then wish to provide more training in self-monitoring and rely on collateral sources of information (e.g., parents and teachers). Youth are likely to be more concrete than adults and thereby benefit from self-statements that are linguistically and conceptually simple, such as "I am brave. I can do this." Children younger than 12 years may have trouble imagining feared scenarios (Beidel & Turner, 1998). For this reason, clinicians may wish to emphasize situational exposure tasks over imaginal exposure tasks. Furthermore, developmentally young children may have difficulty labeling an emotion and its intensity, which is necessary to build a graded-exposure hierarchy.

Last, developmental factors influence the degree that youth generalize new learning and skill acquisition. For example, a child may demonstrate mastery of a developmental ability in one situation but may not be able to utilize this same skill in a different situation (Sauter, Heyne, & Michiel Westenberg, 2009). Generalization is essential to enhancing the durability of a treatment. Similarly, delayed inferential reasoning may negatively influence generalization, that is, the ability of a child to apply what was learned in one context to another context.

Level of Motivation

In general, low engagement is a common problem in the treatment of youth with anxiety disorders (Armbruster & Fallon, 1994). For example, approximately 20% to 30% of youth in carefully controlled clinical trials for anxiety disorders drop out of treatment (Chorpita et al., 2013). Dropout rates in community clinic settings or public mental health systems are likely higher because they serve more demographically diverse clinical populations (Southam-Gerow, Weisz, & Kendall, 2003; Wergeland et al., 2015).

A number of factors can influence engagement or motivation. First, family accommodation behaviors can decrease the youth's willingness to engage in treatment, particularly ERP tasks. For youth to engage in treatment, it is necessary for them to experience the consequences of not engaging in treatment. When families accommodate OCD, youth remain comfortable in the OCD symptoms, particularly in the neutralizations that maintain it. As such, family accommodation behaviors tend to maintain low treatment engagement, and it is essential that clinicians target these throughout the treatment process (see Chapter 7, this volume).

Developmental age or level can influence engagement. For example, developmentally young children may have greater difficulty reflecting on past and future patterns of thinking and behaving. For this reason, they may not fully recognize the social consequences of their behaviors and therefore do not see the point of changing these behaviors. Developmentally young children may also exhibit more cognitive rigidity, and for that reason changing specific behaviors may be particularly difficult. Last, development influences the degree to which youth can regulate their emotions, which may result in greater anxiety during mild exposure tasks and therefore a slower progression through the exposure hierarchy.

For very young children in which insight is related to developmental level, good insight may not be necessary for a good outcome, in part because of contingency management. However, low insight in older youth is a predictor of poor treatment engagement, although it does not appear to predict poor response to medication (Eisen et al., 2001). Furthermore, youth with hoarding symptoms may have more limited insight and more magical thinking obsessions than youth with OCD without significant hoarding symptoms (Storch, Lack, et al., 2007).

Co-Occurring Conditions

Certain medical conditions and other psychiatric disorders can influence the implementation of core strategies. For example, typically benign medical conditions, such as asthma, mitral valve prolapse, allergies, and hypoglycemia can exacerbate health or somatic obsessions because the physical sensations (e.g., breathlessness, dizziness) associated with these medical conditions can trigger body-related obsessive fears. Medical conditions such as thyroid conditions or problems with adrenal glands (e.g., pheochromocytoma, a tumor on the adrenal gland) can mimic anxiety and can exacerbate somatic obsessions. Furthermore, interoceptive exposure may not be appropriate for youth with medical conditions, such as epilepsy or exercise-induced asthma. Similarly, certain exposures may be inappropriate for youth with severe food allergies. For these reasons, we recommend that clinicians contact the youth's pediatrician for medical clearance prior to beginning any ERP task.

Co-occurring psychiatric conditions may influence treatment outcome. For example, youth who are severely depressed may have trouble engaging in core treatment strategies, in part because they are easily frustrated or hopeless that anything can be done to help them. In addition, it may be difficult to motivate depressed youth through reinforcement systems because they no longer enjoy once-enjoyable activities or rewards. In these cases, we recommend that clinicians consider treating the depression first, perhaps adding an antidepressant medication to the treatment plan, or begin with behavioral interventions, such as behavioral activation, to decrease the youth's depressive symptoms.

Cultural and Spiritual Factors

Cultural and spiritual practices can influence the implementation of core strategies. For example, the Islamic faith includes a number of regulations regarding hygiene and washing. This code of Muslim hygienical jurisprudence is known as the Q*adaa' al-Haajah*. Muslim youth who adhere to Qadaa' al-Haajah must wash their genital areas with water after defecating or urinating. They must enter the toilet with the left foot and leave the toilet with the right foot and say a prayer on leaving. Clearly, clinicians working with Muslim families are wise to discuss these regulations, if the family practices them, when developing response prevention plans. In some cases, to manage OCD, families receive special dispensation from religious leaders to halt or stop religious practices that can trigger or exacerbate OCD. We recommend that clinicians discuss spiritual and cultural practices with every family in order to guide culturally sensitive implementation of graded-exposure and response prevention tasks.

Socioeconomic factors can influence the implementation of core strategies, particularly engagement in the treatment process and plan. Families with limited financial resources may have trouble paying for adequate treatment or taking time off from work to bring youth to treatment. A family that must take public transportation may find it difficult to attend treatment sessions regularly and on time. Even families who can pay for and attend treatment sessions may have trouble following through with out-of-session ERP practice because they cannot make the time to do one more thing.

DEVELOP THE GRADED-EXPOSURE PLAN

Graded exposure is a core strategy in the treatment of all anxiety disorders and central to the treatment of pediatric OCD. Graded exposure decreases situational and experiential avoidance and the frequency and intensity of obsessional fears. In this section, we describe guidelines for developing a graded-exposure plan. We describe how to identify exposure targets that include internal fear cures (e.g., thoughts and images) and external ones (e.g., door handles) and feared consequences (e.g., "I might kill my parents"). We then describe the steps to build a graded-exposure hierarchy that includes the principle types of exposure strategies (e.g., situational, imaginal, and interoceptive).

Select Items for the Graded-Exposure Hierarchy

The planning of exposure tasks depends on the thoughtful and creative process of engineering situations that evoke obsessive fears. At the risk of stating the obvious, an effective exposure evokes the feared consequence or disaster so that youth can learn that what they fear either did not occur or that they could handle it if it did. In other words, if a child is afraid that dogs will bite him (expectancy), we want to expose the child to the possibility that a dog will bite him so that he learns that the dog does not bite him (expectancy violation). Therefore, the goal of exposure tasks is to engineer a situation in which the child learns this (and is not bitten), by exposing him to a dog that is unlikely to bite.

Effective exposure tasks match the specific features of the cognitive elements of the youth's fear structure as well as the specific features of the situations that evoke the cognitive elements. For example, Ava fears that a bee may sting her and she will die, even though her pediatrician has told her that this is highly unlikely. If Ava believes that it is very likely that a bee will sting her if she walks in her backyard wearing shorts and short sleeves, then Ava needs to do that if she is to learn that it is an unlikely outcome. Exposure tasks that direct her to walk in her yard while she wears long pants and long sleeves will not be effective in modifying Ava's fears because if a bee does not sting her, she will attribute this to having worn long pants and sleeves. However, if Ava is so fearful of bees that she avoids her backyard altogether, then an exposure of walking around first in long sleeves and long pants and then in shorts and a T-shirt could help her build confidence and tolerance to the distress of facing her fear. Therefore, it is essential that every exposure closely match the youth's fear structure. This is the value of developing a case formulation for the specific youth in treatment. In other words, the case formulation guides the selection of each item on the exposure hierarchy.

Build a General Exposure Hierarchy

Clinicians select items for the exposure hierarchy on the basis of information (e.g., internal and external fear cues, avoidance, feared consequences) gathered through assessment and self-monitoring. The process begins with the clinician and youth generating a general hierarchy that lists from 10 to 20 situations that evoke obsessive fears that youth will confront through one or more exposure strategies. There is a great deal of "art" to this process, and it is subject to the discretion of the clinician. Although it is essential that exposure tasks closely match the core elements of the youth's obsessive fear, general hierarchies will not include every possible exposure circumstance. Furthermore, it is not necessary. Learning spreads; youth learn from each exposure, and they then apply this new learning to other situations that were not included in formal exposure practices.

In the case of Ava, the general hierarchy might include "walking outside" as a single hierarchy item. Looking at bees might be another item on the general hierarchy. Feelings in her body might be another item on this hierarchy. Later, the clinician will break down each item into smaller steps linked to specific exposure strategies.

Once the youth has generated a list of trigger situations and stimuli, the clinician introduces the fear thermometer. This is a scaling system referred to as Subjective Units of Distress (SUD) scale (0–100, where 100 is *extremely distressing*; or 0–10 for younger children). The clinician utilizes this scale not only to rank the difficulty of exposure and response prevention tasks but also to provide youth and parents with a framework to monitor progress. Although a decrease in the intensity SUD does not necessarily reflect that youth are learning what the clinician hopes they will learn, the scale is a useful shorthand for the level of distress during ERP tasks (Jacoby & Abramowitz, 2016).

The clinician then directs youth to rank the predicted level of distress or fear they anticipate during an ERP task. We often hand youth a paper thermometer to use in this process. For younger youth, we might encourage the child to draw a fear thermometer with colored markers and construction paper and glitter. The clinician then describes the rationale for the fear thermometer and anchors the scale relative to how the youth might feel at several points along the scale. We might introduce the fear thermometer to younger youth in this way:

> Great job, Ava. We now have a list of all the ways you can show the OCD bully that you're not afraid of him. The next step is to build a ladder with each one of these scary things on a step. We'll use this fear thermometer to do it. Now, do you see how this thermometer goes from 0 to 10? The fear thermometer will help us tell how scared you might feel when you do a step on the ladder. If your fear rating is 0, then you're not at all scared. It's like you're asleep. A fear rating of 2 means that you're a little scared. It's like when you ride the kid's roller-coaster. It's not too high or too fast. It's scary but not too scary. A fear rating of 5 means that you're medium scared. It's like riding a big-kid roller-coaster. It's really high and fast, but it's not as scary as the scariest roller-coaster on the planet. Now, a fear rating of 8 means that you're very scared. You're gripping the safety bar really tight, and maybe you're yelling and screaming to get off. And a fear rating of 10 is like the scariest ride on the face of the planet. It's like the one that swings you around and you're like 500 feet high. I think they call that ride Death Wish, or something like that. If you rode Death Wish with me, our hearts probably would be pounding, and we'd be sweating. Maybe we'd feel like we were going to throw up, so 10 is crazy scary.

For developmentally younger youth, we recommend that clinicians use a concrete strategy to build a graded-exposure hierarchy. First, it is important for the clinician to introduce the fear thermometer. Next, the clinician assists the youth to write each exposure situation on an index card or slip of paper. For example: "walk back and forth in the backyard for 10 minutes." Then, the clinician takes ten index cards on which the clinician has written a number from 1 to 10 that represents the intensity of anxiety that youth predict they will feel, where 10 is terrified. The clinician then places the numbered index cards on the floor or tabletop in ascending order. Last, the clinician asks the youth to place each card or slip of paper with an exposure situation next to the number that corresponds to the predicted level of anxiety or fear.

We recommend that clinicians check with youth regarding SUD ratings, particularly if the youth identifies a rating that does not correlate with the youth's anxiety ratings of other situations. In addition, we encourage clinicians to maximize the fear gradient (e.g., "Let's try to put each scary item on its own step of the fear ladder. We can break down the numbers as small as we want"). The clinician then guides the youth through the process of ranking exposure tasks:

CLINICIAN: Now, I want you to look at the fear thermometer and give each item a number. Let's start with looking at pictures of bees. What would your fear rating be if you looked at a picture of a bee?

	I'd want you to look at it directly and not ask me if you're okay. How scared would you feel?
AVA:	Not too scared. I guess a 2. I'd still be a little scared, you know.
CLINICIAN:	Yes, but if you're not a little scared then you're not showing the OCD bully that you're not scared of him. How about walking barefoot in your backyard? How scared would you feel?
AVA:	I could stay away from the flowers in our yard, right? The bees like the flowers.
CLINICIAN:	How about if you give me two fear ratings? One fear rating for walking barefoot in the middle of your yard and the second fear rating for walking barefoot near the flowers in your garden.
AVA:	Walking barefoot near the flowers would really scare me. I guess that's at least a 7. Walking barefoot in the middle of the yard is maybe 5.
CLINICIAN:	Nice work. How about reading an article about anaphylactic shock and bee stings? How scared would you feel if you did that?
AVA:	Well, it's not as scary as going near the flowers, but it's still pretty scary. Maybe 6.

We recommend that clinicians build an initial hierarchy with sufficient detail to give the youth and the clinician a sense of the nature and difficulty of a variety of exposure tasks. However, at the same time, we recommend that clinicians remain flexible. Over the course of treatment, the clinician is likely to modify, add, or delete exposure tasks based on the youth's response to earlier ERP tasks and as the clinician identifies new information about the youth's fear structure. At the end of the treatment planning meeting, Ava and the clinician developed a general exposure hierarchy (see Figure 4.2).

Build a Hierarchy of Exposure Types

Over the course of treatment, clinicians and youth are likely to create a number of exposure hierarchies that include several of the different exposure strategies. In the case of Ava, the clinician created separate exposure hierarchies for each item on the general exposure hierarchy by breaking down the exposure item into a series of subitems linked to specific exposure strategies (see Figure 4.3). The exposure hierarchy for "walking outside" includes a number of situational exposures (e.g., walking in the backyard wearing long pants and long sleeves, walking in the backyard wearing shorts and short sleeves, walking in the schoolyard wearing long pants and long sleeves, walking in the schoolyard wearing shorts and short sleeves, walking in the backyard near the flowers wearing long pants and long sleeves, walking in the backyard near the flowers wearing shorts and short sleeves).

FIGURE 4.2. Ava's General Exposure Hierarchy

		Item	SUD
1.		Feeling "unclean"	20
2.		Blasphemous thoughts about God	30
3.		Symmetry	40
4.		Illnesses other than anaphylactic shock	50
5.		Memories and associations of deceased boy	60
6.		Feelings of suffocation or dizziness	70
7.		Other insects	80
8.		Outside	90
9.		Bees	100
10.			
11.			
12.			
13.			
14.			
15.			
16.			
17.			
18.			
19.			
20.			

SUD = subjective units of distress (0 = *low*; 100 = *high*).

The exposure item "walking outside" might also include primary imaginal exposures. Ava might listen repeatedly to a recording of the clinician saying the word *bee* or *stung* or the term *anaphylactic shock*. Again, the clinician and youth will rank these imaginal exposure items relative to Ava's anticipated fear level. In addition, the clinician might pair an imaginal exposure with a situational exposure. These secondary imaginal exposures direct youth to listen repeatedly to a recording while engaged in a situational exposure. For example, Ava might listen to the phrase "bees are lurking everywhere" while she walks with long sleeves and pants in the school recess yard. We describe the implementation of these exposure strategies in detail in Chapter 8.

FIGURE 4.3. Ava's Exposure Strategy Hierarchy for Walking Outside

	Type of exposure strategy	Exposure item from general hierarchy: Walking outside.	SUD (0–10)
1.	Situ:	Walk on front porch.	30
	Imag:	Imagine walking on front porch and seeing bee in distance.	20
2.	Situ:	Walk on front lawn.	40
	Imag:	Imagine walking on front lawn and seeing bee in distance.	45
3.	Situ:	Walk in backyard.	55
	Imag:	Imagine insects (not bees) crawling on your skin.	60
	Intr:	Jog in place in backyard.	50
4.	Situ:	Sit in center of backyard, eyes open for 10 minutes.	60
	Imag:	Imagine hearing bees but not seeing them.	60
	Intr:	Breathe through straw.	60
5.	Situ:	Sit in center of backyard, eyes closed for 30 minutes.	65
	Imag:	Imagine hearing bees flying around you but you can't see them.	65
	Intr:	Sit in center of yard, breathe through straw, eyes closed for 30 minutes.	60
6.	Situ:	Sit in backyard, 10 inches away from bushes and flowers, eyes open.	70
	Imag:	Imagine bees crawling on your skin.	65
	Intr:	Do jumping jacks in backyard near bushes and flowers.	60
7.	Situ:	Sit in backyard, 30 inches away from bushes and flowers, eyes closed.	80
	Imag:	Imagine feeling bee sting and trouble breathing.	75
	Intr:	Sit in backyard, near bushes, breathe through straw for 5 minutes.	75
8.	Situ:	Stand in middle of common area.	90
	Imag:	Imagine bee stinging you, then feeling dizzy and short of breath.	90
	Intr:	Run up and down stairs thinking of anaphylactic shock.	85

(continues)

FIGURE 4.3. Ava's Exposure Strategy Hierarchy for Walking Outside (*Continued*)

	Type of exposure strategy	Exposure item from general hierarchy: Walking outside.	SUD (0–10)
9.	Situ:	Stand in common area where Will was stung.	95
	Imag:	Imagine having trouble breathing and losing consciousness.	85
	Intr:	Breathe through straw for 10 minutes while standing in area where the bee stung Will.	80
10.	Situ:	Sit at table in common area at school and think of Will's face.	100
	Imag:	Imagine seeing bees flying around common area.	90
	Intr:	Do jumping jacks in common area.	85

SUD = subjective units of distress (0 = *low*; 100 = *high*); Situ = situational exposure; Imag = imaginal exposure; Intr = interoceptive exposure.

Also, Ava's specific exposure hierarchies include interoceptive exposures. Clinicians use interoceptive exposure strategies to evoke body sensations related to obsessive fears. For example, Ava fears specific body sensations, such as feeling light-headed or short of breath. To Ava, these body sensations mean that she is in anaphylactic shock. Although not every youth with OCD is fearful of body sensations, those with health-related or somatic obsessions often are. Clinicians then use interoceptive exposure strategies to target the physical features of certain obsessive fears, and these appear in Ava's specific exposure hierarchy for the item "feelings in my body." Over the course of treatment, clinicians will likely build a number of hierarchies for specific steps in the general exposure hierarchy. The process of identifying steps and ranking tasks relative to SUD ratings is similar to the process used initially to create the general exposure hierarchy.

Typical Exposure Strategies for OCD Subtypes

As previously noted, there are three fundamental exposure strategies used to treat pediatric OCD: situational, imaginal, and interoceptive. Clinicians will use one or more of these exposure strategies in conjunction with response prevention strategies described in detail in Chapter 8. We present examples of these strategies relative to the particular OCD symptom subtypes discussed next.

Contamination
Contamination symptoms are one of the most common OCD symptom subtypes in youth. Typical situational exposures include touching counters and

floors, licking the bottom of a shoe, or tasting and eating feared foods. Imaginal exposures might include reading or listening to anxiety-evoking phrases or words, such *hepatitis C*, *AIDS*, or *anaphylactic shock*. Similarly, listening to stories of the contamination spreading over and into the body or dying from a disease are excellent imaginal exposures. Interoceptive exposures could target body sensations related to any obsessive fear, but more commonly they would target health or somatic obsessions. For example, youth who fear that they will vomit might benefit from overbreathing to generate feelings of nausea, or youth who fear that they will stop breathing might benefit from breathing through a straw to evoke suffocation sensations.

Harm

Harm obsessions are particularly troubling and terrifying for youth. Situational exposures that target harm obsessions might include holding a sharp knife, standing close behind someone on a balcony, eating food that is 1 day beyond the expiration date, or reading articles about airplane crashes. Imaginal exposures might include reading or listening to certain words or phrases (e.g., *knife*, *death*, "I might go crazy and kill my mom and dad while they sleep"). Imaginal exposures regarding making a mistake are excellent imaginal exposures for harm obsessions. For example, youth might listen to a story of a burglar breaking into the house because the youth did not check the door locks. Likewise, youth might listen to stories of accidentally sending texts that hurt someone's feelings or that include bad words or sexual images. Interoceptive exposures might focus on the feeling of going crazy. For example, a youth who fears going crazy and hurting himself might hyperventilate or stare at a spot on the wall to generate sensations of derealization or light-headedness.

Incompleteness

Obsessions related to a sense of incompleteness, inexactness, unevenness, or imperfection can create considerable distress in youth with these symptoms. Situational exposures for the incompleteness subtype can include touching only one shoulder to a door frame on entering and exiting a room, ending sentences without completing them, writing a paragraph without any punctuation marks, or adding columns of numbers incorrectly. Imaginal exposures might include listening to incomplete sentences, imagining the feeling of incompleteness intensifying, or imagining not completing activities. Interoceptive exposures can be particularly helpful with this subtype when youth report physical feelings associated with the sense of incompleteness. For example, a youth who associates tingling sensations with feeling uneven might benefit from hyperventilation as an interoceptive exposure strategy.

Unacceptable Thoughts

Obsessive fear of particular thoughts can take many forms. Thoughts or doubts about sexual identity, images of sacrilegious acts, and impulses to shout a racial slur are examples of unacceptable thoughts. Situational exposures might include thinking of a racial slur while standing next to a stranger of that race, sitting in a church while thinking about having sex with the priest, or spitting on the sidewalk across the street from a church or synagogue. Imaginal exposures might include listening to recordings of the unacceptable thought or phrase, imagining acting on the unacceptable thought (e.g., touching the priest's crotch), or imagining the humiliation and social consequences of shouting the unacceptable thought in a crowd. Interoceptive exposures would be useful when youth report feared physical sensations associated with the unwanted thought (e.g., hyperventilating with a youth who is afraid that if she feels dizzy and "out of it" then she is more likely to act on her impulse to shout "nasty" words).

DEVELOP THE RESPONSE PREVENTION PLAN

Response prevention is essential if youth are to benefit fully from graded-exposure tasks. In this section, we describe guidelines for developing a response prevention plan with youth and parents. We describe how to introduce the plan to the family, how to prepare family members to support the response prevention plan, and how to develop a plan to manage failures to adhere to the plan. We identify response prevention targets and strategies and conclude with guidelines to create a response prevention hierarchy.

Introduce Response Prevention to the Family

The goal of response prevention is to assist youth to resist all physical and mental neutralizations to prolong the exposure process and thereby to facilitate new learning, including learning that they can cope with their level of distress. We recommend that clinicians carefully and repeatedly explain to youth and parents the vital role of response prevention in the treatment process. For older youth, clinicians can explain the role of response prevention in this way:

> In addition to exposure I'll help you break the habits you use to decrease your anxiety or to prevent the bad thing from happening. These are the things that you do and the things that you think to neutralize or suppress upsetting thoughts, such as checking locks or your backpack over and over. You do these things to make yourself feel safer when you have dangerous thoughts even though most times you know these things are silly and don't really make you safer. Breaking these habits is important if you are to recover from OCD because as you break these habits, you'll learn several important things. First, you'll learn that these neutralizations don't really prevent bad things from happening. For example, as you stop checking your backpack, you'll learn to trust yourself. Second, you'll learn that you don't need to do these habits to decrease your fear. You'll learn that the fear goes away gradually on its own if you wait. Last, and most important, you'll learn that you can handle feeling afraid or anxious even if you don't do the habits. Once you learn that, then everything gets easier. However, the only way to learn these things is to stop the habits. As you stop the habits, you'll begin to weaken the OCD patterns and develop new ways of thinking and acting that don't make your life so hard.

With younger youth, clinicians can explain the role of response prevention in this way:

> In order to win back your land from the OCD bully, you'll do two things. First, you'll face your fears. We'll do this in steps, and with each step you take, you'll show OCD that you're brave and that he can't boss you around. Second, you'll break the OCD bully habits. These habits are the things that OCD tricked you into doing over and over. OCD told you that this would prevent you from getting sick. That's why you wash your hands so much or ask your mom and dad to look at your food before you eat it. If you keep doing these habits, then OCD wins. As long as you do these habits, you'll keep believing what OCD tells you, which isn't true. In order for you to believe what you know is true and stop believing what OCD tells you is true, it's necessary that you stop these habits. So to get back your land from OCD there are two super-important things that you'll learn to do: act brave and stop the habits. Once you do those, OCD will give up and go away. Then things will get a lot easier for you.

Define Reasonable Risk

The goal of ERP tasks is for youth and parents to become more comfortable with reasonable and thereby acceptable risks. Youth and parents often and understandably resist broad, global response restrictions, such as no washing or no checking. To increase the willingness of parents to assist their child to follow response prevention guidelines, we recommend that clinicians introduce the concept of reasonable risk and clarify the goal of response prevention: to assist youth to become more comfortable with what other youth are comfortable with.

> Life is inherently risky. In order to live our lives fully, we typically act according to probability rather than possibility. Although it's possible we could crash on the freeway, it's not likely we'll crash on the highway. If we refuse to accept any possible risk that we might crash, then we'd never drive on the freeway. The goal of response prevention is to help your child become more comfortable with what is possible but not probable. We call this reasonable risk. Therefore, sometimes we'll focus on limiting a neutralization rather than eliminating it. For example, we might restrict your child to one daily 10-minute shower as long as he doesn't engage in any cleaning rituals while he's showering. We'll also want him to touch a feared contaminant, such as the bathroom wall, after he showers.

We recommend that clinicians consider not only what is possible but also what is reasonable relative to hygiene, safety, and health. For example, it is not only reasonable but also advisable for youth to visit their pediatrician once per year. In fact, pediatricians typically recommend wellness visits, particularly when youth are young. However, visiting the pediatrician repeatedly at the first ache or pain may not be reasonable or helpful. Similarly, youth who do not bathe or brush their teeth at all may break cultural norms regarding hygiene. The goal of response prevention is to assist youth to act in accordance with these norms, that is, to match their behaviors to the behaviors of other youth their age and according to cultural and social norms.

Identify and Prepare the Support Person

Response prevention with youth, particularly young youth, typically depends on the assistance of parents. For example, clinicians might instruct parents to supervise their child's handwashes and turn off the water after 30 seconds, if that is the agreed-upon length of time. Similarly, clinicians might direct parents to support their child to check a door once or not at all and then engage the child in an alternative task.

We recommend that clinicians carefully consider which parent is likely to be the most effective response prevention support person. For example, the parent who is overly anxious may have trouble tolerating the child's distress during ERP tasks. Similarly, the parent who is easily frustrated may not make an effective response prevention support person. We suggest clinicians check with the youth regarding the appropriate support person, particularly with older youth who may bristle at any help from an adult, or who may already have a distressed relationship with a particular parent. Typically, an effective support parent will be considerate, sensitive, calm and willing to encourage and at times nudge the youth to resist neutralizations.

We recommend that the support parent or parents participate in response prevention planning and understand the role of response prevention in the youth's recovery from OCD. If possible, we encourage clinicians to include the support parent in early ERP tasks. For example, while the support parent observes, the clinician directs the child to touch a countertop and then instructs the child to resist washing his hands or engaging in stealth washing neutralizations, such as rubbing his hands on his pants.

After the support parent observes the clinician assist the youth in the ERP task, the clinician then instructs the parent to conduct the ERP task. In addition, the clinician can role-play with parents supportive responses to encourage the youth to tolerate distress: "I know it's hard for you, but you're doing a great job." "Wow. I know you really want to wash your hands. What can I do to help you get through the next few minutes?" "Remember that OCD will get bored and go away if you don't do what he wants you to do right now. You can do it."

Clinicians can coach parents to facilitate corrective learning too. For example, "Remember that the urge to wash your hands will go down as you wait. This feeling will pass, just as it's passed before." "Do you really think you can't handle the dirty feeling? I bet you can. Let's give it a few more minutes and see."

Last, clinicians can assist support parents to respond adaptively to their child's wish to avoid fear-evoking situations. For example: "I can see that OCD is telling you not to do this. You can do what OCD says, but that will only make OCD stronger. Or you can show him that you're in charge. I'm here to help you and not to help your OCD. Why don't you try to resist and see how you feel?" At times, youth will simply refuse to resist neutralizations or demand that they avoid situations. We recommend that clinicians coach support parents to remain calm and to resist criticizing, blaming, or arguing with the child. For example: "It's your choice. You can do this or not. I think you can do it. I hope you will try."

Develop a Plan to Handle Response Prevention Infractions

We encourage youth of all ages to take responsibility for resisting neutralizations. However, this is particularly important for adolescents who insist that they do not want parents involved in the response prevention plan and may not always follow the response prevention guidelines. We recommend that clinicians speak with youth and parents regarding an appropriate response to infractions with the plan. For example, the clinician can instruct parents to call and leave the clinician a message when the youth fails to adhere to the response prevention task and then do nothing more. The clinician will speak to the youth at the next appointment about the infraction. Last, because following response prevention guidelines is difficult, many youth will fail to adhere to them, particularly early in treatment. To decrease the likelihood of demoralizing youth, we recommend that clinicians present response prevention as a no-lose proposition:

> At first, resisting handwashing will be a bit harder, but it will get easier with time. That means at first, sometimes you'll resist washing your hands, and sometimes you won't. Even when you give in and wash your hands, you'll learn something that will help you become stronger the next time.

Develop a Written Response Prevention Agreement

We recommend that clinicians formalize the response prevention plan in a written agreement. Written agreements or contracts decrease the likelihood of misunderstandings and arguments and provide clear guidance to parents as they support the response prevention plan. These written agreements often evolve over the course of treatment as clinicians implement ERP tasks and observe how youth and parents respond. However, we recommend that clinicians insist that youth and parents not make any change to the agreement, no matter how small, until they discuss and negotiate proposed changes in appointments with the clinician.

Typically, response prevention agreements include the rationale for response prevention, how parents can support youth to adhere with response prevention, how infractions to the response prevention plan are handled, and the specific response prevention instructions (see Figure 4.4).

Identify Response Prevention Targets

During the assessment phase, the clinician identifies key neutralizations (physical actions and mental actions) the youth typically uses to escape or minimize fear or discomfort. The clinician will use the response prevention targets in two ways. During exposure tasks, the clinician will instruct the youth to resist particular neutralizations identified in the assessment process. Also at times the clinician will focus only on response prevention in a particular exposure situation and shape the youth's response. For example, the clinician might ask a youth to decrease in steps the duration of handwashing after toileting or when entering the house from outside.

FIGURE 4.4. Ava's Response Prevention Agreement

My Response Prevention Agreement

To overcome OCD, I must resist compulsions: Response prevention means resisting compulsions. Although compulsions can make me feel less anxious for a short while, they prevent me from getting better in the long run because they prevent me from learning that I am safe and that I can handle my discomfort without them.

What I will do or not do: I will not seek reassurance, and when I slip, I will accept without complaint or argument your reminders and encouragement to resist seeking reassurance. I come to you and ask you to help me resist a compulsion. Please stay with me until the urge passes, and then praise me for doing this. Encouragement always helps.

What you will do or not do: When you stop cooperating with my OCD, it might try harder to get you to cooperate at first. I will try my best to resist the compulsions, but if I slip, please remain calm and do not give in to the OCD. After a while, the OCD will grow weaker if we both do our jobs.

When you see that I'm doing a compulsion, calmly remind me that the compulsions feed my OCD, and then encourage me to stop. Don't grab me, or threaten me, or yell or nag. Responding in that way just makes me feel more anxious and upset. Remind me that you're on my side and that you want to support me and not the OCD.

At times, I'll slip and ask you to cooperate with the compulsions or even ask you to do them for me. This doesn't help me. Please don't cooperate with the compulsions, even if I insist you do it. I promise that I'll try to resist, but if I slip, please say, "We agreed that cooperating with the OCD doesn't help you. I'm here to help you and not the OCD."

What you can say that will help: I am in charge, and it is my choice to give in to the OCD or not, but you hope that I will resist. Remind me when you see OCD, and encourage me to resist and do something (perhaps with you) while I wait for OCD to go away. Remind me that my urge to do the compulsion is because I believe something that's not true. I'm safer than I feel, and I don't need to do the compulsion to decrease the chances that I'm in danger.

How we will handle slips: I will record the slip on my self-monitoring form and discuss it with the therapist. You will call and inform the therapist of the slip, and I will permit you to do this. I will undo any compulsion in the way the therapist showed me.

I understand that overcoming OCD is my responsibility, but I want your help. This agreement describes our roles and shows our commitment to pushing OCD out of my life.

Signatures   Date

The first step in creating an effective response prevention plan is to identify as many of the neutralizations that youth use to escape and avoid distress as possible. Youth may be aware of many of the neutralizations they use but not all of them, particularly their mental neutralizations. Similarly, parents may be aware of many of the overt neutralizations but not the subtle "below the radar" neutralizations, such as a child's rubbing his hands on his shirt to clean his hands when he is unable to wash his hands immediately.

We recommend that clinicians begin the process of identifying response prevention targets by reviewing the Children's Yale–Brown Obsessive Compulsive Scale (CY-BOCS; Scahill et al., 1997) with youth and parents and adding to the list of neutralizations. The clinician might ask the following: "I have written down all the things you've told me you do to try and make yourself feel better when OCD is making you worry. What other things does OCD tell you to do when you're scared?"

To solicit and encourage youth to share the particulars of their neutralizations, we recommend that clinicians ask, "How often do you do that?" "Do you have to repeat it a certain number of times or just until it 'feels right'?" "How do you know that you've done it right or have finished the compulsion?" These specifics help clinicians create a targeted response prevention plan. It is important to note that youth often have several different neutralizations for a single obsession or the same neutralization for several obsessions. There's no magic recipe for a perfect hierarchy, but order can make a difference. Buy-in is essential; therefore, we recommend that clinicians begin with neutralizations that youth sometimes resist and work to eliminate these first.

Search for Functional Relationships

Typically, there is a logical connection between a neutralization and the obsessive fear. For example, a young girl who has thoughts of stabbing her sister may give her sister a hug every time she has the thought. A boy who fears that someone will break into his house because he left the door unlocked may check the locks repeatedly, or he may ask his parents to check the locks for him. A teen who worries that he will become sick may refuse to shake the hands of people he greets. Understanding the functional relationships between obsessive fears and common neutralizations can guide clinicians as they inquire about neutralizations, particularly covert neutralizations. Clinicians might inquire about covert neutralizations in this way: "Kids who are afraid of harming people sometimes think back over what they did to reassure themselves that they didn't hurt someone. Do you do anything like that?"

However, not all neutralizations appear to have a logical connection to the obsessive fear. For example, a child with obsessions of harming her mother may repeat mundane actions like walking through a door three times to prevent acting on these thoughts and images. A boy with religious obsessions may tap his finger on a table a certain number of times when he thinks of the devil. A girl who has unwanted sexual thoughts about her teacher may wash her hands repeatedly after having these thoughts. However, with additional inquiry clinicians can identify a functional relationship that can guide further questioning. The clinician might say,

> Those thoughts you just shared with me sound like they really bother you. When kids have thoughts that bother them, sometimes they try to do or think things to make the thoughts go away or change. What kinds of things do you do?

Identify Avoidance Strategies

Neutralizations can also involve *not* doing things; for example, youth may open doors with the sleeve of their shirt or with their foot to avoid touching doorknobs. When watching a movie, youth might look away during scenes that involve kissing to avoid triggering a sexual obsession. Therefore, we recommend that clinicians ask youth about possible avoidance strategies:

> Great job telling me about all the things OCD orders you to do to prevent bad things from happening. Is there anything OCD tells you not to do? How about places you try not to go or activities that you try not to do? What kinds of situations tend to beckon the OCD bully and bring him around?

Identify Family Accommodation Behaviors

Youth with OCD often rely on others, such as parents, to complete neutralizations for them. For example, before going to bed, youth may ask their parents to wash their hands before they tuck them in, or they may direct a sibling to check the door. If the family refuses, youth may have a tantrum or become belligerent. Youth may repeatedly seek reassurance from parents, family members, and even teachers that they are safe, that they are not ill, or that the bad thing did not and will not happen. We recommend that clinicians include family members in the process of identifying these accommodation behaviors. In Chapter 7 we describe how to work with family members to drop these behaviors over time.

Create a Response Prevention Hierarchy

It is unlikely that most youth will stop all neutralizations immediately. Typically, the response prevention plan eliminates or alters neutralizations gradually. Once the youth and clinician have listed all neutralizations, the clinician guides the youth in creating a response prevention hierarchy:

CLINICIAN: Now that we've listed all your neutralizations, I want you to think about how hard it would be to resist doing them. Rate each one, where 0 means that it would be super-easy to resist doing and 100 means it is the hardest thing you can imagine to resist doing.

AVA: They are all really hard to resist.

CLINICIAN: Okay, which of your compulsions do you think you might be able to put off doing if you tried really hard?

AVA: I guess I could probably put off asking my mom if the front door was locked on the way to school.

CLINICIAN: Okay, good. So it sounds like that one would not be a 100 but also not really a zero. What would you rate putting off asking your mom if the front door was locked?

AVA: Well, I guess it would probably be a 50, maybe.

CLINICIAN: Great, go ahead and put a 50 next to that one on the list.

The clinician developed a response prevention hierarchy for Ava's reassurance-seeking behaviors (see Figure 4.5). For developmentally younger youth, we might use the index card method described earlier to build the response prevention hierarchy. In this case, however, we use a thermometer to rate difficulty to resist a neutralization rather than the intensity of an obsessive fear.

FIGURE 4.5. Ava's Response Prevention Hierarchy

	Description of Neutralization	DTR
1.		5
2.		10
3.		15
4.		20
5.		25
6.	Resist seeking reassurance from Father for 10 minutes.	30
7.	Resist seeking reassurance from Father for 20 minutes.	35
8.	Resist seeking reassurance from Father for 30 minutes.	40
9.	Resist asking Mother to check if I have a fever for 5 minutes.	45
10.	Resist asking Mother to check if I have a fever for 10 minutes.	50
11.	Resist asking Mother to check if I have a fever for 30 minutes.	55
12.	Resist checking breath with mirror for 5 minutes.	60
13.	Resist checking breath with mirror for 10 minutes.	65
14.	Resist checking breath with mirror for 30 minutes.	70
15.	Resist looking for insects when outside.	75
16.	Resist seeking reassurance from Mother about breathing for 5 minutes.	80
17.	Resist seeking reassurance from Mother about breathing for 10 minutes.	85
18.	Resist seeking reassurance from Mother about breathing for 30 minutes.	90
19.	Resist asking Mother or Father whether there are insects in the area.	95
20.	Resist asking Mother or Father whether there are bees in the area.	100

DTR = difficulty to resist (0 = *not difficult to resist*, 100 = *very difficult to resist*).

The clinician might build several hierarchies for different types of neutralizations when youth engage in multiple neutralizations. For example, clinicians might build a response prevention hierarchy for reassurance seeking, another for checking neutralizations, and still another for washing neutralizations.

Typical Response Prevention Strategies for OCD Subtypes

In general, there are a number of standard response prevention strategies we use relative to particular OCD symptom subtypes. However, we encourage clinicians to be creative, particularly with youth who at times present idiosyncratic OCD symptoms, such as the boy who waved his hands above his head to wash his hands with "clean and good" air.

Contamination

Typical neutralizations for obsessive fear of contamination are washing and cleaning neutralizations. Response prevention strategies for washing and cleaning typically involve limiting the youth's contact with water, such as one daily 10-minute shower that parents or the youth time. The clinician directs the youth to resist washing or cleaning neutralizations during the shower, such as washing the body in a specific order, repeatedly washing a specific part of the body, or repeatedly rinsing. The clinician directs youth to resist washing hands after taking out the garbage, after using the bathroom, or before handling food. Youth may brush their teeth, but not in a specific way, such as back to front. Older youth will shave with an electric razor to minimize contact with water. Youth will avoid other strategies to remove or minimize contamination, such as using handwipes or sanitizing gels. Youth will not wear gloves or use tissues, shirtsleeves, or their feet to touch surfaces or to open doors. Parents, siblings, or other family members will not comply with requests from youth to hand them items or other means that permit youth to avoid contact with items. Youth may wash or clean if their hands or clothes are visibly dirty with grease, paint, or feces. Last, youth recontaminate their hands and body immediately after any washing or cleaning with items from the exposure hierarchy, such as touching the bathroom counter after washing hands or drying hands on the kitchen towel used by all family members.

Harm

Obsessive fears that youth may act on an unwanted impulse to stab a parent or accidentally leave a window open and a murderer enters the home and kills the family while they sleep result in a variety of checking and repeating neutralizations. Response prevention strategies for checking include covering objects that the youth checks, such as taping paper bags over doorknobs so the youth cannot check the locks. Youth who are afraid of making mistakes or writing something hurtful may check emails, notes, or other written items only once, quickly. Response prevention strategies for repeating neutralizations, such as counting to a safe number, praying, or repeating good words aloud or covertly, include counting to the wrong number, praying incompletely, and repeating bad words. Similarly, clinicians instruct youth who covertly review their actions to change the order with which they review an action (begin by remembering the last thing you did) or remember the action incorrectly. Parents, siblings, or other family members will not comply with requests to check for youth when they seek reassurance that doors are locked, that the baby is safe, or that they did not say something mean or nasty to the neighbor.

Incompleteness

Response prevention strategies for the incompleteness subtype include assisting youth to resist reordering, moving, rearranging, or rebalancing objects or even their bodies. For example, clinicians instruct youth who feel the need to touch the doorway with their left and then right shoulder as they enter or exit a room to resist the urge to balance the feeling in their bodies. At times, youth will count to achieve a sense of completeness. Response prevention is then either to resist counting altogether or to count incorrectly or incompletely. Some youth will stare or glance at objects to achieve a sense of symmetry, such as the child who glanced at the eight corners in every room she entered (top right corner, bottom right corner, top left corner, bottom left corner, etc.) in a particular order. Response prevention for this child included first glancing at the corners in the wrong order and later staring at the floor to resist the urge to check.

Unacceptable Thoughts

Neutralization strategies for unacceptable thoughts include a variety of physical and mental actions to undo or "put right" unwanted thoughts. For young youth, the neutralization strategies are often physical actions, such as repeating the phrase "God is good" six times in response to an unwanted or "impure" thought. Response prevention strategies often include directing youth to perform the act incorrectly, such as repeating the phrase three times and incorrectly: "Is God good." Youth can engage in washing and cleaning neutralizations to neutralize unacceptable thoughts. Response prevention strategies in these instances are much the same as those used for contamination symptoms.

Many youth engage in covert or mental neutralizations in response to unacceptable thoughts. These include replacing an unacceptable thought, such as the girl who replaced images of penises with images of rainbows. Older youth with sexual images or thoughts might monitor their bodies for signs of sexual arousal or repeatedly reassure themselves that they are gay or straight. Resisting these covert mental neutralizations is quite difficult for most people with OCD and particularly for youth who may be less clear regarding thoughts and their functions. If youth are to resist mental neutralizations, they must first understand what to resist. That is, it is essential that youth distinguish between the thought or image that caused their fear from the thought or image they used to neutralize their fear. Psychoeducation as well as self-monitoring assist youth with the process of identifying mental neutralizations. Often, the most effective response prevention strategy for mental neutralizations is to flood the youth with the obsessions themselves. Clinicians can instruct youth to listen to recordings of their obsessive thoughts at all times when possible. For example, youth can listen to the recordings with earbuds while eating, walking to the bus, playing video games, and in particular, during activities or in situations that trigger their obsessive fears. Clinicians can also use response prevention strategies that include performing the mental action incorrectly or incompletely the way they would with other OCD symptom subtypes.

Last, some youth engage in religious rituals, such as praying, in response to unacceptable thoughts. This can be complicated terrain for clinicians to traverse with youth and their parents. We recommend that clinicians permit youth and parents to sort out what is appropriate and inappropriate religious behaviors. We recommend, when possible, to include the family's spiritual leader (pastor, priest, rabbi, imam) in these discussions. Typically, we meet with the spiritual leader and parents without the youth first and organize the discussion to distinguish prayer that is driven by fear from prayer that is driven by faith. In our experience, spiritual leaders are well informed and very helpful in assisting youth to adhere to response prevention strategies.

MONITOR PROGRESS

The ERP plan guides the treatment process, and, although it is important to begin with a good plan, the ERP plan is dynamic and will change as the clinician gathers information in response to the youth's progress. Therefore, the active and ongoing process of monitoring progress is central to the effective treatment of pediatric OCD. There are several benefits to monitoring treatment progress. First, regular progress monitoring that includes feedback to the client of objective measures of treatment progress appears to improve treatment outcome (Lambert et al., 2005). Second, ongoing progress monitoring may decrease the rate at which clients prematurely discontinue treatment (Lambert & Shimokawa, 2011). Clients who know that they are improving are more likely to engage in the tasks of therapy and thereby improve more in treatment. Third, clinicians who receive feedback from their clients appear to become better clinicians (Tracey, Wampold, Lichtenberg, & Goodyear, 2014). Last, monitoring outcome helps clinicians modify both the conceptualization and the treatment plan to improve the client's response to treatment (Persons & Tompkins, 2007). We monitor treatment progress using measures that assess severity of symptoms, changes in functioning in school and home, and response to ERP exercises, including changes in SUD and changes in the strength of beliefs that ERP exercises target.

As mentioned earlier in this chapter, we routinely administer the CY-BOCS and the Child Obsessive-Compulsive Impact Scale—Revised (COIS-RC; Piacentini & Jaffer, 1999) as part of the assessment process. However, these measures are sufficiently sensitive to symptom change (Benazon, Ager, & Rosenberg, 2002; Geller, Biederman, Stewart, Mullin, Martin, et al., 2003) that we use both to monitor treatment progress as well. Because the COIS-RC is a self-report measure that takes just a few minutes for youth and parents to complete, we measure treatment progress with the COIS-RC at every appointment. Parents and youth complete the measure while waiting to begin the appointment. We keep this measure in our waiting rooms. Because the CY-BOCS takes considerable time for clinicians to administer, we use the CY-BOCS at the start and end of treatment, and perhaps once midway through treatment.

The NIMH Global Obsessive-Compulsive Scale (Goodman & Price, 1992) and the Clinical Global Impairment Scale and the Clinical Global Improvement Scale (Guy, 1976) are global measures of improvement and impairment. Clinicians complete these measures in 1 to 2 minutes. The NIMH Global Obsessive-Compulsive Scale measures the severity of the youth's OCD rated from 1 (*normal*) to 12 (*extremely impaired*). The Clinical Global Impairment Scale measures the severity of the youth's impairment relative to OCD rated from 1 (*normal, not at all impaired*) to 7 (*extremely impaired*). The Clinical Global Improvement Scale measures the global improvement rated from 1 (*very much improved*) to 7 (*very much worse*). These measures are easy to administer at the beginning of every session during the check-in period. We graph these measures to share with youth and parents. When youth and parents observe that symptoms are decreasing, this can enhance hopefulness and renew willingness to participate in the tasks of therapy. When treatment is not progressing, reviewing the graphs with youth and parents can provide a useful framework for these difficult discussions, including recommendations for changes to the treatment plan.

Another strategy to monitor treatment progress is to periodically rerate the youth's fear or SUD for each step of the ERP hierarchy. Just as the youth's OCD generalizes from a single trigger to a multitude of triggers, the treatment gains generalize as well. This means that through the treatment process youth will report lower fear ratings for ERP tasks near the top of their hierarchy than when they first rated these tasks, even if they have not yet worked on them. This strategy can also motivate youth and parents to continue to work diligently on ERP tasks.

Clinicians can download a blank Map of My Land form (see http://pubs.apa.org/books/supp/tompkins, Web Form 3.1) and assist the youth to complete a new Map of My Land form during each session. For young youth, this is a fun strategy that helps them visualize the progress they are making. Furthermore, we recommend that clinicians save and periodically review with youth all the completed Map of My Land forms. Just a few minutes spent reviewing the youth's Map of My Land forms can quickly reengage and motivate the youth to continue the critical ERP tasks.

Last, periodic conversations regarding the change in the strengths of particular OCD-related beliefs is a useful way to monitor treatment progress. For example,

CLINICIAN: So, Justin, you've worked very hard over the last week. You completed the exposure we started in our session last week over 33 times. When we did the first exposure together you strongly believed that you would get sick if you ate an apple slice off the floor. You rated the strength of your belief at 95% on that

0 to 100 scale. We did that exposure 12 times, and at the end of the twelfth exposure you rated the strength of your belief at about 75%. You then agreed to practice this exposure during the week. Now, how strongly do you believe, on that 0 to 100 scale, that eating an apple slice off the floor will make you sick?

JUSTIN: I guess maybe 30% now. Maybe even a little lower. Maybe 20%.

CLINICIAN: So before the first exposure you believed very strongly that eating an apple slice off the floor would make you sick. Now you believe it much less. From 95% to 20%. Why do you think you believe this less strongly?

JUSTIN: I guess I'm learning what I kind of already knew about my OCD worries: They don't make any sense. Now I'm realizing that I don't have to listen to them, just as you said.

CLINICIAN: Yes, Justin, you're doing a great job. I wonder how strongly you believe now that you would get sick if you ate an apple slice that touched the sidewalk rather than the floor of my office. That step was near the top of your ladder. When we first put your ladder together you rated that at 100%. How strongly do you believe that now?

JUSTIN: Not 100%. Maybe 50%. Yeah. I'm much less scared about that now.

CONCLUSION

In this chapter, we described the process of developing an individualized case conceptualization for pediatric OCD. The case conceptualization begins with the cognitive behavior nomothetic formulation of OCD individualized relative to the particular youth and family with whom the clinician is treating. The individualized case conceptualization, along with careful monitoring of the youth's response to treatment, guide the implementation and refinement of the ERP treatment plan. The chapter then described guidelines for developing a graded-exposure and response prevention plans that when combined provide ERP: the active ingredient in the psychological treatment of pediatric OCD. We concluded this chapter with a description of the many factors that can influence the effective implementation of core strategies, apart from the clinician's skillfulness with these strategies.

In the next chapter, we describe strategies to engage youth and parents in the treatment process. Not every youth or parent requires engagement in the therapeutic process, but most do, at least most do at some point in treatment. Therefore, it is essential that clinicians understand that fluctuations in the motivation of youth and parents are inevitable, and it is essential that clinicians are skilled in implementing a variety of engagement strategies throughout the treatment process.

II

IMPLEMENTING THE CORE STRATEGIES OF THE TREATMENT APPROACH

INTRODUCTION

In Part II, we present the core strategies of cognitive behavior therapy for pediatric obsessive–compulsive disorder (OCD). We begin with strategies to engage youth and parents in the treatment approach itself (Chapter 5). Although we emphasize engagement at the beginning of treatment, engagement continues throughout treatment and particularly when youth or parents disengage from exposure with response prevention (ERP). Next, we describe psychoeducation (Chapter 6). This core strategy serves several functions: engagement, normalization of the condition, and the rationale for the other core strategies. In the next chapter (Chapter 7), we present strategies to decrease family accommodation and push-back behaviors. Assisting parents to decrease family accommodation is critical for the effective implementation of the other core strategies, particularly ERP. The effectiveness with which clinicians implement ERP is critical to a successful treatment of OCD strategy in the treatment of pediatric OCD (Chapter 8). Therefore, we describe these two core strategies in detail. Part II concludes with relapse prevention (Chapter 9). Because OCD is a chronic condition, it is essential that clinicians assist youth and parents to develop an ongoing plan to manage breakthrough symptoms in order to prevent a recurrence of the condition.

5

Engaging Youth and Parents in the Treatment Approach

Maya sat in the clinician's office with her head down, holding her dry and chapped hands a bit out and away from her body for fear of touching her clothes and the furniture in the clinician's office. Maya's mother brought her to the appointment, and it was clear that this polite 12-year-old would not warm to the clinician easily. The clinician wanted to build rapport with Maya as well as to engage her sufficiently to begin the process of gathering information regarding her obsessive–compulsive disorder (OCD) symptoms. Christmas was in 3 weeks, and the clinician knew that Maya's family was Catholic. The clinician suggested that they construct an Advent calendar with colored construction paper, glue, and glitter. The clinician explained that each door was an area of Maya's life that OCD ruled: friendships, relationships with her siblings, schoolwork, and athletics. They labeled four of the doors with these areas. The clinician then explained that inside the doors was what Maya's life looked like with OCD and that outside the doors was what she wanted her life to look like after she pushed OCD out of her life. With colored pencils Maya then drew her "two" lives. As Maya drew, the clinician asked her questions about the ways that OCD bullied her: what he said to scare her and what he made her do. She enjoyed the activity and called it her "OCD house of doors." She and the clinician often discussed the house, particularly when Maya hesitated to try an exposure and response prevention (ERP) task. At the final session, Maya brought her OCD house of doors to the appointment, and she and the clinician sealed each door with glue such that the calendar now displayed only the pictures she had drawn of her life after she pushed OCD off her land.

http://dx.doi.org/10.1037/0000167-006
Cognitive Behavior Therapy for OCD in Youth: A Step-by-Step Guide, by M. A. Tompkins, D. J. Owen, N. H. Shiloff, and L. R. Tanner

In this chapter, we introduce several engagement strategies. Many of the strategies we describe are ones we use as a matter of course when we treat youth with any type of problem. There are a number of considerations to the process of therapeutic engagement. First, engagement is an ongoing process and includes many strategies, including, and most important, a safe, supportive, and encouraging therapeutic alliance with youth and parents. Second, engagement strategies are tailored to the developmental age of youth. Last, engagement is not limited to engaging the youth in the treatment process. Often, clinicians must engage parents too, and we describe strategies to do that.

COGNITIVE BEHAVIOR THERAPY AND ENGAGEMENT

Cognitive behavior therapy (CBT) includes many strategies that enhance engagement and motivation. Although we will not discuss these at length here, we believe that engagement is built into CBT through the principles on which it rests and the techniques that distinguish CBT from other forms of psychotherapy. For example, collaboration is an important feature of CBT. We collaborate with clients (youth and parents) when setting treatment goals, when developing a case conceptualization, when building the agenda for a therapy session, and when creating the ERP plan itself. Furthermore, the principle of collaborative empiricism engages clients in the collaborative examination of the usefulness of their thoughts and behaviors (Dattilio & Hanna, 2012). This process rests on Socratic questioning: thoughtful questioning (rather than telling or lecturing) to guide clients to new ways of thinking about themselves and their problems (Kazantzis, Fairburn, Padesky, Reinecke, & Teesson, 2014).

Last, as we have noted earlier, CBT engages youth by linking the type of engagement strategy to the developmental age of youth. For example, play is appropriate for developmentally young youth. However, play is less appropriate for adolescents who typically possess the higher order neurocognitive processes that enable them to benefit from motivational interviewing or even cognitive change strategies.

THERAPEUTIC RELATIONSHIP

For youth to benefit from CBT for their OCD, it is essential that they engage in the tasks of therapy during and between therapy sessions. There is some evidence that better alliance precedes better outcomes in CBT in certain cases (Klein et al., 2003) and that both the quality of the therapeutic alliance and the quality of CBT skills predict outcome (Podell et al., 2013; Trepka, Rees, Shapiro, Hardy, & Barkham, 2004). CBT includes fundamental counseling skills, such as reflective listening, attending, differentiating, and regulating. These microskills are important regardless of the therapeutic modality (Gillespie, Smith, Meaden, Jones, & Wane, 2004; Ivey & Ivey, 2003) and are implemented within an overarching attitude of empathy, respect, and compassion toward youth and their families.

PSYCHOEDUCATION

Psychoeducation is the process of providing education and information to youth and their families regarding the nature of OCD and the process of treating it. Psychoeducation is critical to engagement. In the case of pediatric OCD, psychoeducation provides accurate information to correct the misappraisals about thoughts and behaviors that maintain OCD symptoms. In a sense, psychoeducation provides the rationale for the core strategies, in particularly the important role of ERP in the treatment of OCD. Youth and parents who understand the role of obsessions and neutralizations (behaviors and mental actions) in maintaining OCD are more likely to engage in a treatment that targets these factors. In Chapter 6 we take up this important topic in detail.

Bibliotherapy is another form of psychoeducation. Youth and parents who learn about OCD and how it is treated are more likely to engage in the goals and tasks of CBT for the condition. Many excellent books written for children and adolescents provide accurate information about OCD, instill hope, and destigmatize the condition, such as *What to Do When Your Brain Gets Stuck: A Kid's Guide to Overcoming OCD* (Huebner, 2007) and *Free From OCD: A Workbook for Teens With Obsessive–Compulsive Disorder* (Sisemore, 2010). In addition, there are books written for parents of youth with OCD, such as *Talking Back to OCD* (March & Benton, 2006) and *Freeing Your Child From Obsessive–Compulsive Disorder* (Chansky, 2000). Typically, these books provide accurate information about the condition and its treatment, as well as strategies parents can learn to support their child to complete ERP tasks and to reduce parent accommodation behaviors. For a list of books and other resources, visit the International OCD Foundation (http://www.iocdf.org).

GRADED EXPOSURE AND MODELING

Graded exposure and modeling are engagement strategies as well as core change strategies. Although research suggests that the order in which clients confront anxiety-evoking situations does not influence treatment outcome (Hodgson, Rachman, & Marks, 1972), most youth favor a graded stepwise approach to exposure tasks. Thus, we view graded exposure, whereby youth and clinician build a hierarchy of ERP tasks ranked from easiest to most difficult, as a way to give youth and parents a sense of control over the exposure process and thereby encourage them to begin.

Modeling also encourages engagement. Youth who watch the clinician and parents engage in an ERP task first are more likely to try it themselves. In fact, we never ask youth to do something that we would not do; thus, modeling not only provides an opportunity to learn through observing others but also can strengthen the therapeutic alliance. Youth learn to trust clinicians when they observe the clinician repeatedly "do it first." In Chapter 8, we describe in detail modeling, an important core strategy.

REINFORCEMENT PLANS AND BEHAVIORAL CONTRACTS

Contingency management strategies, such as reinforcement plans and behavioral contracts, are well-established and powerful methods to increase desired behaviors, such as approaching feared objects and situations. Although youth typically arrive for CBT with differing levels of motivation, in our experience few youth decline rewards when offered. In fact, we are often suspicious of youth who tell us that they are not interested in rewards for the difficult work of ERP. Often, this reflects an underlying perfectionistic attitude that is not helpful in life nor in recovering from OCD (see Chapter 12). In Chapter 7, we describe in detail contingency management strategies to enhance engagement of youth and parents in the treatment process.

MINIMIZING ACCOMMODATIONS

Change is difficult; change that evokes fear and distress is particularly difficult for youth with OCD and their parents. In addition to increasing approach behavior through reinforcement plans, it is also important to minimize the conditions that support avoidance and nonengagement. Family members often unknowingly maintain the youth's OCD symptoms through their participation in neutralizations, such as reassuring youth who are anxious, or permitting them to avoid situations and activities that invoke anxiety or distress. Furthermore, accommodation behaviors create significant disruption in the lives of all family members. In Chapter 7 we describe in detail strategies to minimize family accommodation behaviors and thereby engage youth in the treatment process.

PLAY

The involvement of youth in treatment is an important predictor of treatment outcome (McLeod et al., 2014). Most clinicians who treat children believe that some level of play therapy, or play within a therapy, is necessary to engage youth in what is traditionally a more verbal endeavor, and that is the case with CBT as well. Play facilitates the involvement of youth, particularly young children, in the key interventions of CBT for pediatric OCD, such as ERP tasks.

There are key differences, however, between the way play is conducted in CBT and the way it is conducted in traditional play therapy. In traditional play therapy, the clinician is a neutral observer of the child's psychological process and resists directing or influencing the child. In traditional play therapy, clinicians view direction as controlling the child's psychological process and believe that children will work through, without direction or influence, their problems via the play itself. Therefore, the play clinician does not praise, teach, or educate the child directly. In CBT, on the other hand, the clinician utilizes play to actively guide the child through the tasks and stages of the treatment process. Praise, rewards, psychoeducation, and actively teaching the child skills are central tasks of CBT, and play facilitates the implementation of these tasks. That is, in traditional play therapy, play *is* the therapy, whereas in CBT, play engages the child in the tasks and goals of the therapy.

Play is important in all phases of CBT, including assessment, psychoeducation, ERP tasks, and relapse prevention. For example, during the assessment phase, the clinician might ask youth to use puppets to disclose their troubling or embarrassing obsessions rather than asking youth to disclose this information directly to the clinician. During the relapse prevention phase, youth and the clinician might write a poem or story or draw a picture that clarifies the important lessons learned from the therapy.

Build Rapport

The quality of the client–clinician alliance is a reliable predictor of positive clinical outcome independent of the particular psychotherapeutic approach (McLeod, 2011; McLeod et al., 2014). Furthermore, research suggests that the value of a strong therapeutic alliance may be more important in behavioral therapies than in nonbehavioral ones (Shirk, Karver, & Brown, 2011). Interpersonal factors, such as the clinician's warmth, caring, and genuineness result in a positive client–clinician alliance (Constantino, Castonguay, & Schutt, 2002). Humor can also facilitate the formation of a strong positive therapeutic alliance, in part because an adult who is willing to crow like Peter Pan at the child's successes demonstrates directly to the child that therapy and clinicians can be fun.

Play is a great icebreaker. The Answer Game, in which clinician and child take turns answering questions on cards (e.g., "What is your favorite food?" or "How many brothers and sisters do you have?") is an easy game in which both youth and the clinician share information about themselves. Similarly, games such as I Spy With My Little Eye or charades provide simple, non-challenging ways to break the ice. At the same time, we recommend that clinicians explain the role of play in treatment during these first rapport-building sessions, particularly with children who enter CBT from traditional play therapy and therefore might expect CBT to be similar to the nondirective, free-form play that they experienced in the past.

Engage Youth in Tedious Therapeutic Tasks

Youth seldom refer themselves for treatment. They are usually referred to treatment by parents, family members, teachers, pediatricians, and mental health professionals. In a sense, youth are mandated into treatment, and experienced clinicians expect that youth, particularly adolescents, may not be as engaged as adults who seek treatment themselves. Therefore, it is essential that clinicians find ways to engage youth in the tasks and goals of therapy. Clinicians who are willing to play games and be silly are likely to have fun too, and fun is contagious. In fact, we believe that a creative and playful clinician may do more to encourage and engage a child in treatment than would a tangible reward, such as a sticker or pencil.

Play is particularly important when one strives to engage youth in tedious tasks, such as psychoeducation or developing an exposure hierarchy. For example, during the engagement phase, the clinician might encourage the child to read a Victory Book in which children who completed treatment with the clinician wrote a note (signed anonymously or with only a first name and agreed to by parents) to future children who enter treatment with the clinician. The Victory Book is a fun way to normalize the condition for the child, as well as to motivate the child who feels hopeless that anything can be done to help. Victory Books are a bit like the guest books in small hotels in which guests write a few sentences about their wonderful stay at the hotel. Most youth who recover from their OCD want to "pass it on," and the Victory Book is a great way to do this. Clinicians can then encourage new clients to read the Victory Book early in treatment to build motivation and hope.

Play can engage youth in the process of gathering information for treatment planning too, particularly when one is gathering information that only youth can provide, such as their thoughts, images, or other private events. For example, many youth, particularly young children, may find it difficult to answer questions or share their experiences with strangers. Making information gathering into a game is an effective way to engage youth in this often anxiety-evoking process. For example, the clinician and youth might play Go Fish where they take turns requesting cards. When the clinician or youth correctly requests a card, the clinician or youth instructs the other to do something funny (e.g., "Make your funniest-looking face," "Make the sound of your favorite animal"). Over time, the clinician can ask questions regarding OCD symptoms (e.g., "What is your most upsetting worry?" "What is the most upsetting thing that OCD makes you do?").

Completing self-report measures is another tedious task that clinicians ask youth to complete. In these instances, clinicians can organize a mini-scavenger hunt. The clinician creates clue cards for the hunt. On the back of each clue card, the clinician writes item numbers on the self-report measure (e.g., Items 1–5). The clinician then hides clues in the therapy office, and the youth searches for each clue. For example, the first clue card might read: "Where do we go when we decide to play a game?" The youth would then go to the toy chest where the clinician placed the second clue. Over the course of the game, the clinician includes cards with self-report questions or instructions (e.g., "Complete Items 1 to 5 and then go to the place where you and I greet each other"). The youth then looks for the next clue in the waiting room. For youth who enjoy painted fingers and toes, the clinician allows the youth to paint one nail after completing five questions. In this way, the clinician engages youth in the essential process of gathering information while building rapport and signaling to youth that therapy may not be as boring or as terrifying as they fear.

Last, clinicians can utilize play, particularly arts-and-craft projects, to provide psychoeducation, another core strategy. For example, clinicians can ask youth to draw a map and to color the parts they rule and the parts that OCD rules or to draw a picture of the OCD bully.

Teach Skills

Play engages young children in the process of learning new skills. To teach children to resist compulsive urges, the child and clinician can first develop a list of boss-back talk (e.g., "You're an old meanie, and I don't have to do what you say," "No one likes you, so go away and leave me alone"). Then, the clinician and child play a version of Red Light, Green Light. The child covers his eyes with his hands and counts slowly to 3. The clinician plays the mean OCD and slowly walks toward the child. When the child reaches 3, he opens his eyes and bosses back the clinician with his boss-back talk. The clinician grimaces, snarls, and backs away. As you might imagine, young children love this. Similarly, the clinician and child write boss-back talk on index cards and place the cards on the floor. Then the child and clinician take turns tossing a beanbag toward the cards. When a beanbag lands on a card, the child or clinician shouts the boss-back talk that is on the card.

The clinician and child can use puppets to model adaptive responses (e.g., boss-back talk) or to model effective problem solving or any number of skills. Arts and crafts are always a terrific way to engage young children with learning skills. At the first session, the child and clinician might convert a shoebox into a Strong and Brave box for the child to store the things the child makes during CBT sessions. The child and clinician can make a fear thermometer of colored construction paper with colored glitter to denote degrees of fear while the clinician teaches the child how to use this to report subjective units of distress (SUDs).

Engage Youth in ERP Tasks

An engaged child is more likely to learn from exposures than a disengaged child, and play is central to engagement. Furthermore, exposure with response prevention is a difficult process for most youth, yet these tasks are critical to the effective treatment of OCD. Play that is fun and engaging can help the child not only benefit from the treatment but also remember therapy as a positive experience and thereby increase the child's willingness to return to CBT if OCD symptoms return.

For example, a child with contamination obsessions can play board games (e.g., checkers, Chutes and Ladders) with "contaminated" game pieces as an ERP task with the clinician. Similarly, the clinician and child can play with "contaminated" molding clay or learn to juggle "contaminated" balls. Similarly, the clinician and youth might write a rap song that includes anxiety-evoking words or phrases, or they might play I Spy With My Little Eye to encourage youth to search the office for any red color that evokes thoughts of blood and disease.

Drawing exercises are great ways to engage youth in ERP tasks. For example, Justin, who had many health obsessions, feared that he would have a heart attack like the one that killed his grandfather. The clinician encouraged Justin to complete a series of drawings, beginning with a picture of the clinician dying of a heart attack, then Justin's teacher, then his best friend, and then himself.

Packaging ERP tasks as play is limited only by the creativity of the clinician. For example, an 8-year-old boy with intense need-to-know obsessions could not resist asking his teacher, parents, or friends to repeat instructions, questions, or general remarks. He could not watch a movie without insisting his family jump ahead to a next scene if he needed to know what happened next. The child and clinician agreed to work on his need to know. They devised an ERP task in which the child closed his eyes and selected a colored candy from a bowl, popped the candy into his mouth, and sucked on the candy. Then the clinician asked the child to sit and think about the color of his tongue while he held a hand mirror and resisted the urge to check the color of his tongue. Was it coated in red, in blue, in green? The child and clinician waited and monitored the intensity of the urge to check. After the urge subsided, the clinician asked the child to drink water (to wash away the color) and then to repeat the process. Eventually, the child learned that the urges subsided and willingly agreed to practice this ERP task at home.

Shift Parent–Youth Relationship

For youth to fully benefit from the treatment process, it is essential that they engage in between-session ERP tasks. Typically, this involves parents prompting and assisting youth to begin and complete the ERP tasks that the youth, parents, and clinician devised. However, by the time parents bring youth to treatment, their relationship with their child has often become quite strained, which can undermine the child's willingness to engage in between-session therapeutic tasks with the parent. Play can help moderate this strain and rebuild trust and a sense of fun again in the child–parent relationship. For example, the clinician can teach the parents the boss-back game and ask them to practice the game with the child, or the clinician can demonstrate the colored candy ERP task that the parents then agree to practice with the child. The fun and whimsy inherent in play can reconnect youth and parents in a shared goal to overcome OCD and make the condition and treatment a bit less overwhelming and burdensome.

METAPHORS AND STORIES

Metaphors and stories are powerful engagement strategies. Children, particularly young children, relate to their internal and external worlds through stories and storytelling. Stories and metaphors transform complex principles into meaningful facts about life as youth know it and live it. For example, clinicians can compare the process of habituation through exposure to the experience of jumping into a pool of cold water. At first, it is very uncomfortable, but with some time the youth grows comfortable to what was very uncomfortable at first. Weg (2011) provided 50 examples of stories and metaphors that he uses with OCD clients. Many of the stories are anecdotes from his life that are both disarming and meaningful. Some of the stories are appropriate for any age, but clinicians can adjust the stories to the particular age and interest of the youth. Most clinicians can develop their own stories, as we have, to engage and educate youth in the core strategies of CBT. Here is a story that can help youth understand the role of neutralizations in maintaining OCD symptoms:

> When I was a kid, we inherited a dog named Moe. Moe used to belong to my best friend, Eric. Eric gave me Moe when he moved away. He was moving to a big city, and he didn't think the dog would like that. Moe wasn't a city dog. You could tell that just by looking at him. Anyway, Eric brought Moe to our house around dinnertime and said goodbye to his old friend. Moe sat next to my chair all through dinner. He looked at me with those big, sad eyes and started to whine and whimper. You see, Eric used to feed Moe food from the dinner table, and over the years Moe got bigger and bigger and more and more annoying. Now, if it were left to me, I might have fed Moe from the table too, but my mom and dad wouldn't let me. They said they didn't want Moe hanging around the dinner table anymore. So, I tried to reason with Moe. I told him that people food wasn't good for a dog. I told him that people food didn't taste good, but nothing I said changed Moe's mind. He wanted people food, and he kept coming to the table, whining, whimpering, and generally making a pest of himself. I knew that I couldn't feed him from the table anymore. I felt bad for him, but I didn't feed him. After a couple of weeks, Moe didn't whine so much at dinnertime. He would lie by my chair, which was nice, but I could tell he knew that I wasn't going to feed him. After a few more weeks, I noticed that Moe was losing some weight. He looked better. And he wasn't annoying us so much at dinnertime. After a couple of months, Moe stopped coming to the dinner table at all. It seemed like Moe had kind of lost interest in people food. Now, OCD is a lot like Moe. When you or your mom or dad feed him, he keeps coming to the table, bossing, whining, and complaining, and the more you feed OCD the bigger he gets, just like Moe. But once you stop feeding him, OCD loses interest pretty quickly, just as Moe did, and then doesn't come around so much anymore. And, even when he does come around, his heart isn't really in it. He knows that you're not going to feed him, and after a while he stays away altogether.

CORE VALUES

Values give meaning to our lives. They inspire us, motivate us, and nurture us. Values are not the same as goals (Hayes, Strosahl, & Wilson, 1999). Values are a direction or course (e.g., sailing south along the California coast), and goals are specific destinations or points (e.g., San Francisco, Santa Barbara, Los Angeles, San Diego) along the way as we move in the direction of a given value. Integrity is a value, and speaking truthfully and sensitively to friends is a goal. Health is a value, and eating wisely and exercising regularly are goals. Some values, such as charity or generosity, are in the service of others. Other values, such as creativity or spirituality, are most often in the service of our own welfare and growth.

Youth have values too, and those values direct their lives in deep and personal ways. Identifying core values is a process of reflection and discovery. Few youth (or adults, for that matter) take the time to identify what is truly important to them. This is not to say that their values are not guiding and motivating them. If a youth is passionate about something, whether it's basketball or hanging out with friends, a core value is likely to be leading the way. CBT for OCD is difficult, and it is essential that youth connect to their core values to move ahead in their recovery. There are many fine books for youth that describe the importance of connecting with values when undertaking difficult tasks (Greco & Hayes, 2008; Turrell & Bell, 2016). We describe several strategies we use with the youth we treat.

Past, Present, and Future Game

We developed this strategy to help adolescents enhance their awareness of the discrepancies that exist between life with OCD now, life before OCD started, and the life they want to have in the future. The strategy includes a simple spinner board divided into six sections. Each section represents one of the following domains: family, friends, acquaintances, academics, hobbies and interests, and social activities. The adolescent spins the arrow on the board. Once the arrow points to one of the six domains, the adolescent selects a card from a pile of cards labeled My Past, My Present, My Ideal Future, and My Nonideal Future.

CLINICIAN: So, Paul, I see that the arrow is pointing to the "hobbies and interests" domain and you've drawn a My Ideal Future card. Would you like to talk about your ideal future as it relates to a specific hobby or interest of yours?

PAUL: I want to try out for the soccer team next year, but the OCD is so bad now, I don't think I can play soccer this year. I'm so afraid of getting sick. I couldn't handle being in a gym or on a bus.

CLINICIAN: Why don't you tell me what your ideal life would look like if you tried out for and made the soccer team?

PAUL: Well, I'd be playing with my friends, and we'd take fun road trips to other schools and stuff.

CLINICIAN: Yes. You'd probably be traveling for your away games. You mentioned that these road trips would be fun. Please close your eyes now and picture yourself and your friends on one of those trips. What do you see? What are you thinking and feeling?

PAUL:	I'm laughing. Maybe throwing around the ball. You know.
CLINICIAN:	Now, please open your eyes and tell me what this life feels like.
PAUL:	Well, at first it was really cool, but then I started to feel kind of sad. I can't even imagine getting to a point where I could pass around a soccer ball or sit on the seat of a bus without freaking out because I couldn't wash my hands.

We encourage clinicians to adapt the domains to fit the particular interests of the adolescent with whom they are working. For example, if an adolescent is active in local politics, include "community" as one of the domains. In addition, clinicians could add a "just for fun" section to the spinner board and create a second set of Just for Fun cards, that include items such as "Tell a favorite joke," "Ask your clinician to tell a favorite joke," "Say something in a funny voice," or "Have your clinician say something in a funny voice."

Older adolescents may benefit more than children would from these discussions. However, children can sometimes identify the "motto" they wish to live by, which is often linked to a core value. For example, an athletic 8-year-old girl and *Star Trek* aficionado decided, with the clinician's help, that her motto was "To bravely go where no girl has gone before." The clinician and youth then discussed how the OCD caused her to avoid living her motto. She avoided attending sleepovers or joining a traveling soccer team because of her many time-consuming rituals at bedtime. At the end of the discussion, the girl realized that if she stopped the bedtime rituals, she could do the things she wished to do. The clinician and youth then agreed to begin each therapy session by standing, saluting each other, while the girl stated, "Today, I shall go where no girl has gone before," which ended with plenty of giggles.

Last, clinicians can help youth convert values statements into motivational coaching statements to encourage them to face fear and resist neutralizations. For example, 12-year-old Grace wished to be a nurse, like her mother and grandmother. However, Grace felt quite hopeless that she would be able to achieve this goal because of her germ and contamination fears. The clinician asked her why this goal was so deeply important to her. Without hesitation, Grace stated that nursing was helping. Grace's mother and grandmother spoke to the importance of service to others, and together they crafted her coaching statement: "I willingly take the chance that I may get sick today in order to care for others one day who are really sick."

Develop Values-Driven Smart Attitude Self-Talk

We recommend that clinicians include values-driven smart attitude self-talk to assist youth to approach and remain in feared situations. The function of values-driven smart attitude self-talk is not to reassure or to suppress an obsession but to encourage youth to step toward discomfort and resist neutralizations in order to live a fuller and more meaningful life.

Values-driven smart attitude self-talk includes any phrase that reminds youth of the greater value of changing their attitude toward fear. In the early phase of treatment, the clinician has identified the core values that connect youth to who they really are. These core values are central to a values-driven smart attitude toward OCD. A values-driven smart attitude statement reminds youth of the true and deep reasons that they willingly face and endure anxiety, fear, and discomfort in order to overcome OCD. For example, an adolescent whose OCD symptoms have prevented her from attending sleepaway camps and who identifies herself as someone who loves adventure might encourage herself to face her fears with the phrase "I willingly step toward my fear and accept the chance that I might get sick and vomit, because I want to live an adventurous life." Young children might use a simple personal motto as a values-driven smart attitude statement, such as "I'm a fearless friend."

MOTIVATIONAL INTERVIEWING

Motivational interviewing (MI) is a client-centered directive method for enhancing intrinsic motivation to change by exploring and resolving ambivalence (Miller & Rollnick, 2002). Researchers initially applied MI to address ambivalence about behavioral change in problem drinkers (Miller, Benefield, & Tonigan, 1993) and then applied the approach to a variety of problems, including the treatment of anxiety and obsessive–compulsive disorders (Arkowitz, Westra, Miller, & Rollnick, 2008). A comprehensive description of the principles and strategies of MI are beyond the scope of this book. We refer clinicians to several fine books on motivational interviewing (Miller & Rollnick, 2002; Moyers, Miller, & Rollnick, 1998), particularly its application to adolescent populations (Naar-King & Suarez, 2010). Furthermore, we recommend that clinicians seek training in this engagement strategy through the Motivational Interviewing Network of Trainers (http://www.motivationalinterviewing.org).

Motivational Interviewing With the Adolescent

MI lends itself particularly well to the treatment of adolescents who are often brought to therapy by their parents and may therefore lack the motivation to fully engage in treatment. Although MI with adolescents is much like MI with adults, we have adapted several strategies to enhance engagement when working with adolescents as well as older children.

"Yeah, But" Exercise

This exercise is a version of the Coming Alongside method to respond to resistance (Miller & Rollnick, 2002) and move toward change talk, the first step in changing behavior. The exercise encourages adolescents to argue both sides of their ambivalence: the pluses and the minuses of engaging in treatment.

CLINICIAN: Stephen, you and I have talked a lot about whether you want to work on the OCD or not. On the one hand, you're bummed out by all things that OCD prevents you from doing. On the other hand, you're not sure you have the time or determination to do the exposure tasks that will push OCD out of your life. I'd like to understand both sides of this. How about we have a kind of debate. I'll be the side of you that's against doing the exposures and all the reasons you think you can't do it. You'll argue the other side. I want you to work hard to convince me that I'm wrong and that you can do the exposures. I'll start.

CLINICIAN [against change]: The exposures take up way too much time. I barely have time to finish all my school homework. I can't do my school homework and my therapy exercises too.

STEPHEN [for change]: But you'd have a lot more time for school homework if OCD didn't make you wash your hands so much. You always say that you can't do things, but you always find a way to do them.

CLINICIAN [against change]: Yeah, but I don't really understand the response prevention thing. If I thought I could stop washing my hands, then I would. I just can't.

STEPHEN [for change]: That's not true. It's really hard to stop, but you've cut down your handwashing a little. Doing it in steps makes most things easier. You can start by cutting back the time you wash your hands, one step at a time.

CLINICIAN [against change]: Yeah, but I get so anxious when I try to stop. I just don't think I can handle that much anxiety. I'm not strong enough.

STEPHEN [for change]: Well, the OCD makes you anxious already, and it's stressful to make up excuses and lie to your friends when you're too anxious to hang out with them. Also, how do you know you can't handle this? You've done some really hard things before.

CLINICIAN: Okay, let's stop the debate. What did you learn from this?

STEPHEN: I guess I learned that there are some good reasons to try this. I only think of the reasons for not doing it. I never think of the reasons to do it.

Rulers

The perception of the importance of change, as well as their confidence that they can change, both influence the intrinsic motivation of youth to engage in the goals and tasks of therapy. Through rulers, the clinician can assess both importance and confidence and thereby elicit change talk (Miller & Rollnick, 2002). Ruler questions begin with an initial scaling question, to which the youth responds with a number to reflect the strength of importance or confidence. To encourage change talk, the clinician explores the reasons the youth selected the number. If the youth reports a high number, the clinician simply asks why. If the number is moderately low (3 or 4 on the scale), the clinician asks why the youth did not select a lower number. Alternatively, the clinician can ask the youth what needs to happen for the client to move, for example, from a 5 to a 6, 7, or 8 on the scale. The clinician then summarizes what the youth said and asks about the next steps: "Where docs that leave you now?" "What's the next step for you?" For example:

NALA:	I don't want therapy. I can do this by myself.
CLINICIAN:	On a scale of 0 to 10, how important is it that you work on the OCD all by yourself, where 0 represents that it is not at all important to you that you do it yourself and 10 means that it is extremely important that you do it yourself?
NALA:	I think, maybe a 6.
CLINICIAN:	What led you to choose a 6, rather than a 9?
NALA:	Well, my OCD is really bad right now. I'm trying not to check things but it's really hard to resist all the time.
CLINICIAN:	So the number would be higher if the urges to check were weaker? How confident are you on a scale of 0 to 10, where 0 represents no confidence and 10 is complete confidence, that the urges will get weaker working on your own without any help?
NALA:	Maybe a 3.
CLINICIAN:	So the checking urges are very strong, and you're not very confident that the urges will get weaker without help. Where does that leave you, Nala?
NALA:	Well, I guess if I had a little help, that would be okay, but I want to decide how fast we do the exposures and what kind of exposures I do.
CLINICIAN:	So you want to decide how fast we go and what the ERP ladder looks like. I'm certain that we can work out a plan that gives you more say in how fast we move through the ERP steps. I know that in the past your parents pushed you to stop checking, and that wasn't helpful. Because of that, I understand why it's important that you decide how fast you go and the exposures you do. Your participation is important to me too. Without it, we're both stuck.

CONCLUSION

An engaged child, engaged parents, and an engaged clinician are critical for the effective treatment of pediatric OCD, particularly active engagement in the critical core strategies, such as exposure with response prevention. CBT itself includes a host of strategies that enhance engagement, such as collaborative empiricism, goal and agenda setting, and of course a strong therapeutic alliance. In this chapter, we have covered other engagement strategies, such as play, storytelling, core-value clarification, and motivational interviewing. Other chapters present core strategies that contain within them engagement elements, such as contingency management and parent training. Not every youth or parent requires engagement in the therapeutic process, but most do, at least at some point during treatment. Therefore, it is essential that clinicians know how to enhance treatment engagement and, just as important, know when youth and parents have disengaged and how to quickly correct this.

In the next chapter, we describe the important role of psychoeducation. Psychoeducation is a core strategy of CBT because the cognitive behavior model assumes that OCD is maintained in part through cognitive misappraisals. Psychoeducation strives to correct these misunderstandings, educate youth and parents regarding the condition and its treatment, and thereby engage youth and parents in the treatment approach.

6

Psychoeducation With Youth and Parents

Nine-year-old Sarah was in tears as she told the clinician that she had disturbing images and thoughts about harming her family. She constantly sought reassurance from family members that she had not inadvertently harmed them. She stayed in her room for extended periods when the family was at home to avoid interacting with them. As part of the psychoeducation process, the clinician explained to Sarah that people have many different kinds of thoughts and that sometimes they are important thoughts and sometimes they are unimportant. Sarah's scary thoughts about harming her family, the clinician explained, are called intrusive thoughts and are actually unimportant. Sarah nodded cautiously. The clinician explained to Sarah that "one of our brain's jobs is to sort thoughts into important and unimportant piles. Sometimes the 'thought sorter' hiccups and labels a thought as important when it's really unimportant." The clinician added, "I think that your thought sorter might be confused. It thinks those thoughts about hurting your family are important when they're really unimportant." Sarah nodded vigorously and exclaimed, "Oh! I think my thought sorter is broken! I keep having these unimportant thoughts that my brain says are important. They're really bothering me!" The clinician and Sarah then listed the thoughts that Sarah's brain may have accidentally sorted into the important thoughts pile. The clinician explained, "Sarah, we can fix the thought sorter so that it stops placing unimportant thoughts into the important pile. Then maybe these thoughts won't bother you so much! Would you like to fix the thought sorter?" Sarah left the office smiling and told her mother, "I'm going to fix my brain's thought sorter!"

http://dx.doi.org/10.1037/0000167-007

Cognitive Behavior Therapy for OCD in Youth: A Step-by-Step Guide, by M. A. Tompkins, D. J. Owen, N. H. Shiloff, and L. R. Tanner

Psychoeducation is the process of providing information and education to individuals receiving mental health services and is an essential core strategy of cognitive behavior therapy (CBT). Many youth with obsessive–compulsive disorder (OCD) enter treatment feeling terrified and ashamed of their thoughts. Parents are bewildered and frustrated that rational discussions with their child about the unreasonableness of the youth's thoughts do not help. The goal of psychoeducation is to provide information to correct the misappraisals and misinformation youth and parents have regarding the condition and its treatment, thereby lessening anxiety and shame and enhancing engagement in the treatment approach. Psychoeducation begins in the first session and continues throughout treatment.

In this chapter, we describe key topics covered in the psychoeducation phase of treatment for pediatric OCD. We describe strategies to normalize the condition for youth to destigmatize the condition, to lessen concealment and suppression, and to instill hope that they can recover from this difficult condition. We then describe strategies to explain the nature of OCD to youth and parents and the role of exposure and response prevention (ERP) in the treatment of the condition. The trick, of course, is to present this information in a manner that meets youth where they are developmentally and thereby engages them in the psychoeducation process.

NORMALIZE THE CONDITION

Normalizing the condition is an essential first step to engage youth in CBT for OCD. Youth often believe that they are crazy or weird because they have particular thoughts and engage in meaningless neutralizations, such as compulsions, that they are unable to resist. They often feel deeply ashamed by the thoughts and urges they have, even when they are aware that their fears are unreasonable. Normalizing the condition takes the sting out of OCD, and most youth feel significant relief following just a few minutes of discussion. Clinicians can download the Obsessive–Compulsive Disorder Fact Sheet Handout (see http://pubs.apa.org/books/supp/tompkins, Web Form 6.1) and give the fact sheet to parents, other family members, or professionals (e.g., classroom teachers, pediatricians) involved in the youth's care.

You Are Not Alone

The first step in normalizing the condition for youth is to explain that they are not alone. Most youth think that only they have these upsetting thoughts, urges, images, and behaviors. The onset of OCD typically occurs in childhood. Describing the prevalence rates of pediatric OCD can do much to normalize the condition for youth and parents; for example:

CLINICIAN: We think that one or two out of every 100 kids has OCD. How many kids go to your school?

SOFIA:	Two hundred kids, maybe.
PARENT:	Oh no, sweetie. There are many more than that. Probably 500 kids total.
CLINICIAN:	Okay, so there are about 500 kids in your school, right? So that means there are about five to 10 kids in your school with OCD. Now, how many schools does your town have? How many schools does our state have? How many schools does our country have? There are like 70 million kids in the United States. That means that there are 700,000 to over 1 million kids with OCD. That's a lot of kids. Now, you're one of the kids at your school with OCD, but there have to be at least five other kids with OCD there. Do you know any kids at your school with OCD?
SOFIA:	No.
CLINICIAN:	Right. That's because most kids try to hide OCD, just as you did. They hide the OCD because they think that they're the only kid in the whole wide world that has strange thoughts. But there are a lot of kids with OCD, just like you.
SOFIA:	Wow! I can't believe that there are other kids in my school with OCD. I like knowing that.

Decrease Shame and Increase Hope

Youth with OCD often blame themselves for having obsessive thoughts or images because they think they should not have thoughts that they do not like. Educating youth about the nature of thoughts, particularly that we cannot control thoughts, is an important step to decrease shame and to increase hope that change is possible. A clinician might say the following:

> I'd like to tell you a couple of things about brains: your brain, and my brain, and all the brains we know. Basically, brains are built to make thoughts. Brains are thought-making machines. Our brains make thoughts when we're studying, when we're playing soccer or cards, or when we're walking or running. Heck, our brains even make thoughts when we sleep. We call those thoughts dreams, and sometimes nightmares, depending on the thoughts. But here's the thing. Our brains don't care what the thoughts are. As far as our brains are concerned, they're just thoughts. So then if I have a bad thought, who decides that it's a bad thought? Our brains don't care. If my brain doesn't care, then it must mean that I'm the one who decides whether a thought is good or bad. The thing is, when I start sorting thoughts that way—good thought, bad thought—I'm going to run into trouble. I'm not going to want bad thoughts. But I can't control my thoughts. No one can. For example, close your eyes and try really hard not to think about blue donuts. That's right: the more you try to not have blue-donut thoughts the more blue-donut thoughts you have. Right? So the trick is to let your brain do its job and make thoughts. Then we'll work on not sorting them into good thoughts or bad thoughts. You'll learn to see all your thoughts as just thoughts.

And it will be easier to figure out which ones you need to pay attention to—like understanding your math homework—and which ones you don't—like worrying that something bad will happen because you had the bad thought. Once you see all thoughts as just thoughts, not good thoughts or bad thoughts, you're going to feel much better.

It's also important that clinicians work with parents to shift their attitudes toward their child's OCD symptoms. For example, parents can sometimes blame youth for something that youth cannot control and certainly is not their fault. Parents sometimes believe that youth have more control over their thoughts and compulsions than youth actually do and that they could stop if they tried harder. Psychoeducation with parents can help them let go of the misguided notion that their child can stop the obsessions or stop engaging in compulsive behaviors through sheer willpower.

EXPLAIN THE NATURE OF THE CONDITION

Psychoeducation for pediatric OCD also includes developmentally sensitive explanations of the nature of the condition and covers several important topics such as that intrusive thoughts are normal experiences and how avoidance and neutralizations maintain intrusive thoughts and obsessive fear. Once youth and parents understand the nature of the condition, particularly the factors hypothesized to maintain the condition, psychoeducation then explains the rationale for ERP and its role in undermining the maintaining factors. Throughout psychoeducation, we use developmentally appropriate analogies to engage youth in the psychoeducation process.

Intrusive Thoughts Are Normal Experiences

Perhaps the biggest surprise for youth with OCD is that intrusive thoughts, particularly their intrusive thoughts, are normal mental events (Freeston, Ladouceur, Thibodeau, & Gagnon, 1991; Niler & Beck, 1989; Purdon & Clark, 1993). With older youth, we recommend that clinicians begin with a general discussion of the prevalence of unwanted intrusive thoughts and images in nonclinical populations, such as thoughts of pushing a family member in front of a train or transmitting a fatal disease. For a list of normal intrusions in nonclinical subjects, see Purdon and Clark (1993, Table 1). We often review with youth common normal intrusions and discuss the unwanted intrusive thoughts the youth have or have had in the past. This is an interesting exercise for youth who are often surprised to learn that other people have unwanted strange thoughts that are as strange if not stranger than their own. For example:

JOSÉ: Wow. You mean sometimes mothers think about drowning their babies?

CLINICIAN: That's one of the thoughts on the list you're looking at. You seem surprised?

JOSÉ:	Yeah. I am kind of surprised. Those kind of worries don't bother me. The worries that bother me are the ones about getting sick.
CLINICIAN:	Yes. It's interesting that some thoughts bother you and other thoughts don't. Do you know why?
JOSÉ:	Maybe it's like you told me. The thought isn't the problem. The problem is what I think about the thought.
CLINICIAN:	Yes. The thoughts you have about germs scare you because you think those thoughts are dangerous. If you had thoughts about hurting a baby, you wouldn't think that thought was dangerous, would you?
JOSÉ:	No. I'd probably think that it was silly, but I wouldn't feel scared. Wow. Our brains are weird.
CLINICIAN:	Yes. Our brains are weird and amazing!

Importance of Thoughts and OCD

Following the discussion of the normal nature of intrusive thoughts, we recommend that clinicians then explain how labeling a thought as bad or dangerous makes that thought seem more important than other intrusive thoughts. Once a thought seems important, we search for the thought, and searching for a thought results in more of those thoughts:

CLINICIAN:	Charlotte, how many red cars did you see on your way to our meeting today?
CHARLOTTE:	I didn't see any red cars. At least I don't remember seeing any.
CLINICIAN:	Okay. Maybe we could do an experiment. I'll give you a point as a reward for every red car you see on the way home today. How many red cars do you think you'll see then?
CHARLOTTE:	I guess I'll see more red cars if they're there.
CLINICIAN:	Yes. I think you would too. When I offered you a point for every red car you see, I made red cars important in the way that they weren't important before. Once red cars are important, you'll look for them and likely see them, which will make it seem like there are more of them. The truth is that the number of red cars that drove past you on the way here and the number that will drive past you on your way home might be the same, but if you're looking for them, it will feel like there are more red cars on the highway. That's the way OCD works too. You're making certain thoughts important that aren't really important. When you label some thoughts as dangerous, you make them important. You're making them into red-car thoughts. Once you do that, you look for them in

your brain, and then it feels as if you're having those red-car thoughts all the time.

For younger children, clinicians describe obsessions as brain hiccups, computer glitches, or junk email to decrease the importance those youth attach to certain intrusive thoughts (March & Mulle, 1998):

> You probably know this, but our brains are kind of like computers. Computers usually work great, but sometimes computers will have a little glitch. The screen freezes, or the keyboard locks up, or you move the mouse once and it keeps moving back and forth. Brains are like that too. Most of the time our brains work great, but sometimes they have a little glitch. That's what obsessions are like. It's kind of like your brain hiccuped. We don't want to pay too much attention to a glitch or a brain hiccup, do we?

Similarly, clinicians can use the analogy of junk email to decrease the importance of certain thoughts. Junk email is not important; that's why we place it in a junk folder:

CLINICIAN: Typically, our brains work great, but sometimes our brains make a thought that's a junk email. Do you read your junk email?

ALYSHA: No. Never.

CLINICIAN: Right. There's no point in reading junk email. It's not important and not worth paying any attention to. OCD sends our brain junk thoughts, just like junk email, and tries to convince us that the junk thoughts are important, but they're not. Not at all. Does OCD send you junk thoughts?

ALYSHA: Yes! My OCD sends me junk thoughts about hurting my little brother. I get really scared and don't want to be around him.

CLINICIAN: Yes, but when you're scared and stay away from him, you've read the junk thought. If you don't read junk email, why would you read junk thoughts?

ALYSHA: You're right. I'm not going to read junk thoughts any more.

Catastrophic Thinking Leads to Obsessional Anxiety and Neutralizations

Next, we recommend that clinicians link intrusive thoughts and images to catastrophic thinking and the accompanying obsessive fear. For example, youth with germ or contamination obsessions believe that any contact with germs results in serious illness or disease. With young children, we use the idea of true alarms and false alarms to explain the role of jumping to catastrophic conclusions:

CLINICIAN: Mindy, our brains have alarms, just like the fire alarm at your school. When does a fire alarm go off?

MINDY: When there's a fire.

CLINICIAN: Yes. Now, when a fire alarm goes off, how do you feel? Does your body get really tense? Does your heart beat really fast?

MINDY: Yes, and I cover my ears. The alarms are really loud.

CLINICIAN: Yes. That's your body's danger alarm going off. But sometimes alarms go off when there isn't any fire. There's not even any smoke. What do we call an alarm when there's no smoke or fire?

MINDY: Like a fire drill? That's just practice. If it goes off by mistake, that's a false alarm.

CLINICIAN: Right. But, when we hear an alarm, our bodies don't know whether it's a true alarm or a false alarm. Our bodies signal danger, and that's why we feel scared. That's why you get tense and your heart beats very fast. False alarms feel the same as real alarms. That's one of the ways the OCD bully tricks your brain. It convinces your brain that it's a true alarm, but it's really a false alarm. Now, if it was a true alarm, your teacher would find a fire extinguisher and put out the fire. But what do you do when it's a false alarm?

MINDY: The teacher says, "Don't pay attention to it"?

CLINICIAN: That's right, Mindy. You would ignore it and wait for all the running around to stop. You'd go back to the classroom with your friends, and pretty soon you wouldn't be thinking about the false alarm at all. Now, the things that the OCD bully makes you do, like checking the doors before you go to bed, those are compulsions, and compulsions are a lot like a fire extinguisher. You use them to put out the fire, but if it's a false alarm, you're checking the doors over and over when it isn't really dangerous. It seems like a waste of time. You can continue to put out fires when there isn't any fire, or I can help you wait for a real fire before you do anything. What do you think?

Dropping Safety-Seeking Behaviors and Avoidance Decreases Obsessional Fear Over Time

Youth and parents who understand the role of avoidance and neutralization strategies in the maintenance of OCD will quickly grasp the importance of graded exposure with response prevention. Here's how we explain it to them:

CLINICIAN: Ayden, you repeat certain activities when you have the thought that something terrible is going to happen to you. For example, you told me that yesterday you had a bad thought while you walked down the hallway at school, and you had to walk the hallway back and forth until the thought went away. Because of this you were late to class, and your teacher was upset with you. By the way, did something terrible happen to you that day at school?

AYDEN: Well, my teacher was angry with me. I guess that's pretty terrible, but it was because I was late to class again.

CLINICIAN: I see. So you don't know if something terrible would have happened if you hadn't repeatedly walked back and forth down the hallway. How do you think we could test this theory?

AYDEN: I guess I could stop doing the compulsion, but that's really scary.

CLINICIAN: Yes. I know it scares you to stop the compulsions, but until you do, how will you know if your prediction is true or not? That's how OCD stays in control. As long as you don't test the prediction, you don't know whether OCD is telling you the truth or not. That's how avoidance and compulsions maintain your fear. If you don't test your predictions, then you stay afraid.

Explain the Rationale for ERP

Once parents and youth understand the nature of the condition and the clinician has clarified any misconceptions they have about OCD, it is time to explain how ERP works. Educating and socializing youth and parents into the treatment approach is an essential first step in the treatment process. Some clinicians are reluctant to tell youth that they have OCD because they are concerned that this information will frighten the youth. However, teaching youth about OCD and the treatment process in a thoughtful, developmentally appropriate way helps them understand the nature of the disorder and the treatment process. This is true for parents too. It is essential that youth and parents understand the condition and their roles in the treatment process to benefit from ERP.

Psychoeducation includes explaining to youth and parents the cognitive behavior model of OCD. We present the model to older youth and their parents together and to parents of younger youth alone. Typically, as we explain the model, we draw the model on a large whiteboard. We personalize the model to the youth's particular symptoms. Clinicians can download an illustration of the model (http://pubs.apa.org/books/supp/tompkins, Web Form 1.2) and use the following script when discussing the model with youth and parents:

> Triggers are the events, objects, or activities that trigger a disturbing thought or image. Triggers can be other thoughts too, such as a memory of something that happened. For example, Jason, as you walked home from school, you remembered that your grandmother called yesterday. This triggered thoughts about illness because your grandmother is not in the best health right now. Those thoughts about illness and disease are obsessions. Almost anything can trigger

obsessions. Seeing or remembering a person, an object, or a place can trigger obsessions. For example, the other day you heard on the radio a news story about the Ebola virus. That triggered a disease obsession. Now, once something triggers an obsessive thought or image you feel anxious, afraid, and sometimes disgusted, guilty, or ashamed. Once that happens, you'll try to neutralize the feeling or prevent the bad thing from happening. These are compulsions, and they can be physical actions, like washing your hands, or mental actions, like reviewing in your mind what you touched or didn't touch. After you do this several times, you might feel a little better. Then, next time you feel uncomfortable again, you're likely to do the thing you did before to get rid of the discomfort. For example, if you walked into my office and it was hot and stuffy, you might walk over to the thermostat and turn down the temperature. Soon you'd feel more comfortable, and if it was hot and stuffy in my office the next time you visited, you'd probably go right to the thermostat and turn down the temperature as you did before. Turning down the temperature on the thermostat increased "go to the thermostat when uncomfortable" behavior. That's the way neutralizations work. And they do work, temporarily, but the more you neutralize, the stronger you make the OCD.

Explain Graded Exposure

Next, we recommend that clinicians explain to youth and parents graded exposure and response prevention: two core strategies in CBT for pediatric OCD.

> When we're afraid of something, we don't want to be around the danger. We avoid it or do something to increase our safety. For example, if I was afraid of dogs, I'd probably run away every time I saw a dog. If I keep avoiding dogs, then I'll never learn that most dogs are friendly and don't bite people. If I want to prove to myself that most dogs are safe, I can't keep avoiding all dogs. I'm going to have to hang out with a dog for a while. Then, I'll learn that the dog didn't attack me, and that dogs are usually safe and fun. And the more time I hang out with friendly dogs, the more my brain gets the message that "most dogs aren't dangerous." And the more time I hang around dogs feeling scared, the more times my brain gets the message that "I can handle being around dogs. I can even handle my fear of dogs."

Explain Response Prevention

Next, the clinician explains the critical role of response prevention in overcoming obsessive fear. The combination of graded exposure with response prevention is necessary for youth to fully recover from OCD. Many times, youth have greater difficulty understanding the rationale for dropping out neutralizations than the rationale for graded exposure:

CLINICIAN: I know it's hard. OCD is a big bully and makes you do things you don't want to do. What happens if a bully at school tells you to do something but you don't do it?

CONNOR: I guess he might push me or yell at me.

CLINICIAN: Right. A bully may try harder to get you to do something by yelling or shouting or annoying you in other ways. OCD is kind of like that. When you ignore OCD, it can get louder and more annoying.

CONNOR: Yes, it keeps telling me to do the thing until I finally do it. Then I feel better. Like when I was in the waiting room. My left shoe felt uncomfortable. I tried to ignore OCD, but it just kept telling me to take off my shoe. Finally, I couldn't take it anymore, and I took it off.

CLINICIAN: What if you kept ignoring OCD? Do you think eventually it would stop bugging you?

CONNOR: Yeah. Maybe after a long, long time.

CLINICIAN: Sometimes it helps to tell a bully that you're not going to listen to him. What about if you said, "OCD, I know you want me to take off my shoe, but I am not going to listen to you. You are just bossing me around, but I don't have to do what you say. I am the boss of me. Leave me alone!" After a while, OCD gets bored and starts to go away. Then it gets easier to ignore OCD. Wouldn't that be great?

CONCLUSION

Psychoeducation is the first step to engage youth and parents in treatment as well as to set the stage for all interventions that follow. Psychoeducation serves to normalize the condition, to decrease the youth's shame, to increase hope, and to clarify the path forward. Psychoeducation also explains the nature of the condition and how the active core strategy (ERP) operates to decrease the obsessive fear, avoidance, and neutralizations that create significant disruption in the lives of youth with OCD and their families. Although psychoeducation is introduced early in treatment, it continues throughout the treatment process to maintain engagement in the core strategies that contribute to the youth's recovery from OCD.

In the next chapter, we describe the role of family in maintaining OCD symptoms, and the vital role that parents play in their child's recovery from OCD. We describe strategies to decrease family accommodation behaviors, to manage youth's pushback behaviors, to encourage youth's participation in ERP tasks, and to train parents to be effective exposure coaches for their child.

7

Working With the Family

Tyree came into the clinician's office scowling. When the clinician asked why he looked mad, Tyree responded, "This week was horrible!" When the clinician asked what had happened, Tyree responded, "I was afraid that I would accidentally hit a kid in the head during softball practice at school. My mom wouldn't tell me that I'm a good batter and wouldn't hurt anyone, like she used to. I was freaked out all night, and it was worse Monday morning. She wouldn't even write me a note to sit out of PE. I hate her!" The clinician replied, "It sounds like Mom wouldn't give OCD what it wanted, and that was really hard. But it also sounds like you made it through PE twice this week already. I would call that a big win!" Tyree's scowl began to creep into a grin. The clinician turned to Tyree's mother and added, "Leticia, nice work. You didn't give in to OCD when it was being super-demanding. It's hard to watch Tyree so upset, but you did your part resisting OCD, and that was so important." Leticia replied, "Thank you. It helped to know what to do instead of reassuring him. It was hard, but I'll do anything to help Tyree."

In this chapter, we focus on the roles of family members in the treatment of OCD. When treating youth with OCD, the family often inadvertently maintains the symptoms of the condition. Therefore, working with the family is essential in assisting most youth to recover from OCD. In this chapter, we focus on how to help family members decrease accommodation of OCD, manage pushback behaviors from youth, increase approach while decreasing avoidance behaviors, and become effective exposure coaches.

http://dx.doi.org/10.1037/0000167-008
Cognitive Behavior Therapy for OCD in Youth: A Step-by-Step Guide, by M. A. Tompkins, D. J. Owen, N. H. Shiloff, and L. R. Tanner

DECREASE FAMILY ACCOMMODATION BEHAVIORS

Family accommodation describes the way in which family members of youth with OCD adapt and modify their own behaviors to reduce the youth's OCD-related distress. Accommodation behaviors are most often reported by parents, but siblings and extended-family members often engage in these behaviors. Accommodation behaviors typically include two related changes in parent behavior: participation in behaviors related to the youth's OCD symptoms, including giving reassurance, and modifications to family routines.

Participating behaviors primarily include permitting youth to avoid tasks or activities that trigger OCD symptoms or reassuring youth. For example, youth might insist that parents wash their clothing separately from other members of the family to avoid triggering their contamination obsessions. Or youth with OCD might demand that parents purchase excessive amounts of soap, sanitary wipes, and toilet tissue for the youth to use. Parents might comply with the youth's demands to stay up as long as necessary to complete the nighttime OCD rituals, to check and recheck the youth's homework, or to prepare or cook the youth's food in exact ways. Parents might also drive the youth to school if the youth refuses to take the school bus, or they might write notes to school personnel to excuse the youth from participating in certain school activities or to excuse the youth from school altogether if the youth feels too anxious to attend classes. Parents also will reassure youth when youth fear they made a mistake, did something wrong, are unsafe, or might harm someone.

In addition, parents of a child with OCD often modify, minimize, or eliminate family routines or what they expect of their child because these routines or responsibilities evoke the child's anxiety or distress. For example, parents of an adolescent with obsessions regarding symmetry and the need for exactness might excuse the youth from setting the table for meals because it takes the youth so long to get it exactly right. Parents might also excuse youth from other jobs, such as taking out the garbage or cleaning their rooms because these tasks trigger anxiety and distress. Often, these modifications result in arguments and conflicts among siblings who are upset that they must pick up the slack, doing the jobs that their sibling refuses to do.

In sum, accommodation behaviors not only create significant disruption in the lives of all family members but also serve to maintain the youth's OCD-related compulsions and avoidance behaviors. Family accommodation behaviors thus prevent youth from recovering from the condition. After clinicians have identified all accommodation behaviors as part of the comprehensive assessment, the next steps are to set the stage for working on these behaviors and then to work with parents to decrease these behaviors over time.

Set the Stage to Decrease Accommodation Behaviors

Before we can help parents decrease accommodation behaviors, it is essential that they understand how accommodation maintains their child's OCD and why it is a barrier to the child overcoming the condition. We begin by drawing the Family Accommodation Cycle on a whiteboard (see Figure 7.1). Clinicians can also download a handout illustrating this cycle (http://pubs.apa.org/books/supp/tompkins, Web Form 7.1) and use this when discussing accommodation behaviors with parents. Most families, in our experience, quickly grasp the relevance of this cycle. After all, they have been living this cycle for many months and sometimes years.

We explain to parents family accommodation in this way:

> It's difficult for parents to ignore the requests of a distressed child. You love your child, and you don't want him to suffer. I understand that. At the same time, continuing to give in to your child's demands for reassurance or to help your child avoid the things that trigger his OCD is not helping. It's really hurting. When you reassure your child, you increase the likelihood that your child will come to you for reassurance again. It's not your fault or your child's fault. In fact, your child comes to you again and again for reassurance because it worked. When you reassured him, he felt better. We call this negative reinforcement. Consider for a moment that my office was very cold when you entered today. You might hesitate but then ask me to increase the heat. It's a reasonable request. So I turn up the temperature a little. After all, you're uncomfortable, and the fact that you're uncomfortable makes me uncomfortable. You're my guest, after all, so it makes sense for me to do what I can to help you feel more comfortable.

FIGURE 7.1. Family Accommodation Cycle

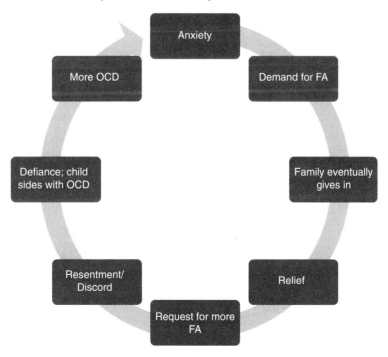

FA = family accommodation; OCD = obsessive–compulsive disorder.

Now, pretty quickly you feel more comfortable. That's good, right? Now, let's say that you return tomorrow and my office is very cold again. Do you think you might ask me to turn up the heat in my office? In fact, this time you might not even hesitate. You just ask me. And if today I said no, you might insist, perhaps even demand, that I increase the heat or you'll leave. You see, the relief you experienced increased the frequency of your "ask for comfort" behavior. That's the way it works for all of us. However, when it comes to OCD, the more you reassure your child or give into his pleas for comfort, the more likely he's to ask again and again and perhaps even demand it or refuse to do things until he gets it. It's really important that we decrease these accommodations to help your child manage his OCD.

Help Parents Identify Reassurance-Seeking Behaviors and Support Youth to Resist

Once the clinician identifies the parent behaviors that maintain the OCD cycle, the clinician then teaches the parents what to do instead of reinforcing OCD, for example, directing the child to resist the OCD. The first step in teaching parents to adjust their responses to reassurance-seeking behaviors is to establish that the neutralizations are indeed neutralizations. This is particularly true when youth suffer with self-harm obsessions and then share with parents that they fear that they might kill themselves. Before asking parents to ignore their child's thoughts of harming self or others, it is essential that clinicians establish that these thoughts are obsessions and have ruled out true suicidal thinking during the initial assessment (and throughout treatment when youth have co-occurring depression with suicidal ideation).

Once the clinician explains to the youth and parents that a particular behavior is an OCD symptom, the clinician develops a plan. There are two steps to this plan. First, the parent calls out or identifies that the child's behavior is OCD, which helps the child step back from the experience and see the behavior as OCD. For example, to a child who asks parents, "Is this okay to touch?" we might instruct parents to respond, "Is that OCD asking if the counter has germs on it?"

Second, the clinician instructs parents to redirect the youth to a valued activity while waiting for OCD's urgency to decrease; for example:

SASHA: Mom, I'm scared. I think I might strangle you and Daddy while you sleep tonight.

MOTHER: Sasha, that's OCD [identify presence of OCD symptom]. I am not going to talk to OCD, and I want you to ignore him too. Let's show him who's in charge. Go ahead and boss back the mean old bossy OCD. You're really good at that [encourage child to resist neutralization]. Why don't you put on your PJs, and we'll watch your favorite show together while we wait for OCD to leave you alone [redirect youth]?

It is important that clinicians explain to the youth and parents that the goal of decreasing accommodation is to encourage the youth to resist neutralizations, such as a ritual, but for the youth to allow and accept obsessions.

This distinction is not always clear to parents. We recommend that clinicians help parents distinguish between redirection, an intentional act, and avoidance, an inevitable act. For example, redirection to a valued activity while accepting that the obsession is present is the goal of this approach, as long as the youth does not do the activity in an attempt to neutralize or eliminate the obsession. This differs from a youth's instinct to avoid an obsession by avoiding triggers or using neutralizations to escape the obsession. Avoidance is part of the youth's pattern of escaping distress.

With youth who seek reassurance by repeatedly asking questions, we recommend that parents answer the question once and then refuse to answer the question again. For example, to the youth's question "Are we going to be late catching the plane flight?" parents might reply, "You already know the answer to that question" or "What was my answer the first time you asked me?" If youth respond that they don't remember, parents can suggest, "If you think about it some more, I'm sure you'll remember my answer." Parents might also encourage the child to resist OCD; for example: "I'm not going to answer OCD's questions, and you don't have to either. Tell OCD to stop bugging you." Similarly, parents might respond, "I am on your side, not OCD's side, so I am not going to reassure OCD."

Whether encouraging resistance to avoidance or neutralizations or refusing requests for reassurance, it is essential that parents respond to their child, who is typically anxious and distressed, in a calm and neutral tone. Refusing to reassure anxious youth is not meant to be punitive. These compulsive behaviors are often automatic, and most youth know that their fears and requests for reassurance are unreasonable. We recommend that clinicians remind parents that their child is not being oppositional when seeking reassurance. Their child just wants to feel less anxious. A calm and concise response is the most effective way to assist their child in the moment. Targeting family accommodation can quickly and dramatically decrease the frequency with which youth engage in accommodation behaviors as well as dampen the intensity of the youth's obsessions, including urges to seek reassurance. Although refusing to accommodate any OCD symptom is the most effective strategy, the clinician and the parents at times may gradually fade the accommodation behaviors, while the clinician works with the youth to resist seeking reassurance in the first place. The clinician might introduce this strategy in the following way:

CLINICIAN: We'll work together to help you stop reinforcing the OCD cycle. Each week we'll agree upon which accommodation behaviors you and Joey will stop. This week Joey has agreed to bring his backpack into the house and leave it in the foyer without asking you to wipe it down. If he asks you to wipe down his backpack, please remind him that you agreed not to wipe down the backpack and that you won't give in to what OCD tells you to do. If Joey becomes upset, redirect him to start his school homework, have a snack, or play a game with you while he waits for his anxiety to decrease. Remember, the only behavior that you're changing this week is wiping down the backpack. That means that for now you will still wash his clothes after school.

PARENT: What if he freaks out?

CLINICIAN: Great question. Our goal is for you to stop all accommodation behaviors. However, even a small decrease in accommodation behavior is a step in the right direction. If Joey is really freaking out, you can limit the accommodation. Perhaps only wipe down part of the backpack. But try to resist anything more than this.

Regardless of the youth's age, clinicians will likely include parents in sessions to help them begin to disengage from the youth's reassurance seeking and other neutralization strategies. The conversation with parents and child might be:

CLINICIAN: Well, Madison, Mom, and Dad, we're here to agree on another piece of our battle plan against OCD. Madison, I know you have a dog. Right?

MADISON: Yeah. His name is Ralph.

CLINICIAN: I love that name. Ralph is a solid name for a dog. Now, what's the rule about feeding Ralph at the table in your house?

MADISON: We don't feed Ralph at the table. Is that what you mean?

CLINICIAN: Yes. So why don't you feed Ralph at the table?

MADISON: Well, if we feed him at the table, then he'll just beg for food while we're having dinner.

MOM: Yes. He'll bug you all night if he thinks he can get something off your plate. He's a sweet dog, but a big and hungry one.

CLINICIAN: Yes, I'll bet. Well, OCD is a lot like Ralph. Once you start to feed OCD, then it keeps bugging you. Then you might feed him more. Over time OCD gets stronger and stronger. That's why it's not good to feed OCD when he bugs you. So we're going to stop feeding OCD, Madison. Every time OCD pushes you to ask your mom whether something is dirty and she tells you that it's clean, OCD gets stronger. So we're going to make a plan to starve OCD. How does that sound?

MADISON: Okay, I guess, but what's the plan?

CLINICIAN: Well, it's our battle plan, and like any battle plan, there's a first line of defense and a second line of defense. The first line of defense is the most important, and you're the first line of defense, Madison. So, when OCD comes around and makes you ask your mom whether something is dirty or not, you're going to boss back OCD and not ask your mom that question. You're going to tell OCD to go away. Tell him that you're not feeding him today—not even a crumb. How does that sound?

MADISON: Okay, but it's hard not to ask.

CLINICIAN: Yes, it is hard not to feed OCD, but remember: the less you feed him, the weaker he gets, and pretty soon he's so weak he stops bugging you. Now, I know that as hard as you're going to try, OCD is tricky, and sometimes he'll sneak past the first line of defense. That's okay because we have a second line of defense. That's where your mom and dad come in. Mom, when OCD makes Madison come to you for reassurance, I'd like you to say, "Hey OCD, I see you. I'm not going to feed you. Not today and not tomorrow. Go away and leave my girl alone." Then, I'd like you to suggest something you and Madison could do for a few minutes while you wait for OCD to go away. I know Madison likes to shoot hoops in the backyard. Perhaps you could do that. What do you say?

MOM: Absolutely. I am the second line of defense, and I will protect my daughter from mean old OCD. I will not feed OCD. Never!

CLINICIAN: It sounds like we have a battle plan. Remember, you're the first line of defense, Madison, and you're the most important member of this team, but if OCD slips through the first line, your mom is there to back you up. That's what teamwork is all about. Right?

INCREASE APPROACH BEHAVIORS AND DECREASE AVOIDANCE BEHAVIORS

Clinicians also strive to encourage youth to approach situations that trigger obsessive fears or distress and to remain in these situations until the fear diminishes. Some youth are highly motivated to overcoming OCD and eagerly take on exposure and response prevention (ERP) tasks. Other youth require extra encouragement to enhance their willingness to engage in ERP tasks as well as the other tasks of the treatment. The use of contingent reinforcement plans is a powerful strategy to achieve these goals.

Contingent Reinforcement

Contingent reinforcement plans include predetermined reinforcers and consequences that follow specific behaviors to increase or decrease the frequency of these behaviors. There are two types of reinforcement: positive and negative. Positive (+) reinforcement adds something positive to reinforce desired behavior. For example, playing a card game with the child following a desired behavior increases the frequency of the desired behavior in the future. Negative (−) reinforcement takes away something unpleasant from youth to reinforce desired behavior. For example, following a desired behavior, parents

excuse the youth from helping to clean the kitchen after dinner. Both negative and positive reinforcers increase the frequency of desired behaviors, such
as engaging in the goals and tasks, particularly ERP, and is the strategy of
choice when working with parents to increase approach behaviors.

To develop reinforcement plans, we recommend that clinicians follow three
steps: (a) select reinforcers for the plan, (b) develop a concrete and explicit
plan for when youth can earn reinforcers, and (c) teach parents to deliver
reinforcers effectively.

Select Reinforcers for Plan

We recommend that clinicians work with youth and parents to develop a list
of reinforcers that includes a range of reward values and choices. Rewards can
be material items and privileges (e.g., staying up late on the weekends, baking
cookies with Dad). More difficult exposures are rewarded with rewards of
higher value as determined by the youth. Creating a list with a variety of
rewards is important. For example, an adolescent girl created a 10-item list
with her parents. For simpler ERP tasks, the girl earned 10 minutes of extra
screen time each day. For medium ERP tasks, she earned money that she could
use to attend movies with friends. For difficult ERP tasks, she earned points
toward a makeup kit that she wanted. For completing her entire exposure
hierarchy, the girl's parents agreed that they would take her to a special cele-
bratory dinner at a restaurant of her choice. Clinicians can download a list of
popular rewards (http://pubs.apa.org/books/supp/tompkins, Web Form 7.2)
and review with youth and parents when developing a list of reinforcers.

Rewards can include any object, activity, or experience that youth desire.
However, a reward is not something the youth already receives for free or for
complying with other responsibilities, such as household jobs or chores. For
example, if parents give their child money each week to attend a movie with
a friend, we do not recommend that they change the rules and now expect
their child to earn that reward for completing ERP tasks. Instead, we recommend that parents provide money to see additional movies each week or to
buy popcorn at the movie. We recommend that clinicians periodically review
with youth and parents the list of rewards to identify those that successfully
reinforce the youth and the rewards, if any, that do not.

We recommend that clinicians not limit reinforcement plans to privileges
and material items. Some youth do not desire more books, dresses, or extra
video game time. Instead, we recommend that clinicians work with youth and
parents to identify special experiences, such as time playing soccer or shooting
hoops with a parent or arranging for a child to hang out with a favorite uncle.
At times, youth report that they are not interested in rewards. This may reflect
that the current reinforcement baseline is too rich (i.e., the supply of reinforcers
is sufficient that the youth is less willing to work for more). In such cases,
clinicians can work with parents to decrease the reinforcement baseline, such
as decreasing the amount of video game time each day, if the youth enjoys
playing video games. Other youth, particularly with perfectionistic beliefs or

suffering from obsessions regarding excessive concern with right or wrong, may reject the idea of receiving rewards for ERP tasks, even though they desire them. They may argue that they do not deserve rewards for doing tasks that they believe they should do. In these instances, clinicians may wish to discuss these beliefs with youth and perhaps target these early in the treatment process.

Choices are also terrific reinforcers for youth; a choice reinforcer can be used either alone or in combination with another reinforcer. For example, the mother of 7-year-old Adam who engaged in excessive handwashing learned to use choice as a simple reward; for example: "Adam, if you don't ask me if you can wash your hands until we get to the restaurant, you can choose the table we sit at."

Last, parents often devalue and thereby underutilize positive attention as a reinforcer. What child does not shout, "Hey, Daddy, look at me!" Smiles, hugs, verbal praise, or fist bumps are all great ways to communicate to youth that parents see and value them.

Develop a Reinforcement Plan

Once the clinician has helped youth and parents identify reinforcers, the next step is to develop the reinforcement plan itself. Clinicians typically develop token economies to organize the reinforcement plan. Token economies are just what they sound like: a system in which youth earn tokens and then exchange tokens for tangible rewards, such as a trip to the mall or a new smartphone. Token economies can include stickers or poker chips, for young children, and good old hard currency for older youth. Although this system can be very effective, many parents, even those who understand the value of token economies, complain about the time it takes to track points or the difficulty they have in keeping track of stickers or poker chips. This is particularly true for parents who are busy and overwhelmed by their child's OCD symptoms. Therefore, we recommend that clinicians devise very simple reinforcement plans. One of the simplest and easiest is Connect-the-Dots.

Connect-the-Dots is a system that tracks and organizes reinforcement. It provides full and partial reinforcement, does not require parents to purchase tokens or keep them on hand, and is a difficult system for youth to game. Also children tell us that thinking about the reward they are striving for helps them remain strong against OCD, and Connect-the-Dots keeps the rewards in full view of youth. To develop a Connect-the-Dots plan, first clinicians assist youth and parents in identifying a big prize or reward. The type of big prize, of course, depends on the resources of the family. The big prize for one family may be a family trip to Disneyland, whereas for another family the big prize might be a sleepover with a few friends. Next, either draw a silhouette of the prize on graph paper or cut a silhouette of the prize and place it on the graph paper and then draw an outline in pencil of the silhouette. Where the silhouette of the big prize touches a line of the graph paper, draw a dot. The outline of the prize will look similar to the dot-to-dot drawings in children's coloring or activity books. Instruct parents to post the drawing in a place that the child can easily see and reach. Explain to parents that each time the youth completes a therapy task that the clinician assigns as an out-of-session action plan, such as an ERP task, the parents direct the child to connect two of the dots with a line. When the youth has connected all the dots, the child receives the big reward depicted in the drawing. The number of dots to include and the number of dot connections a youth can earn in a day depend on the youth's ERP practice plan. For youth who can earn 10 or even 20 connections in a day, the dot-to-dot drawing may require hundreds of dots. For youth who can earn one connection in a day or maybe not even that, the dot-to-dot drawing may require only 10 to 50 dots.

Because it is often difficult for young children to tolerate waiting the many weeks and months it can take to connect all the dots, the Connect-the-Dots strategy provides a way for youth to receive intermittent reinforcement. Clinicians can instruct parents to reward the child with small rewards, such as going to the grab bag that contains inexpensive prizes from the Dollar Store, every time they connect the third or fourth dot. For youth who are instructed to complete many ERP tasks each day, they may receive a small prize every sixth or eighth dot. Special time (one-on-one time with a parent in which the parent devotes 100% of his or her attention to the child), even 5 minutes, is a great reward. Parents can include certificates in the grab bag for special time.

Puzzle Pieces are another easy and visual way to reinforce children, particularly young children, immediately for a desired behavior while they work toward a longer-term reward. Like Connect-the-Dots, with Puzzle Pieces parents and youth identify a big reward and then draw or find a picture that symbolizes the reward. For example, for a child who loves animals, a picture of a cat or a dog might represent the big reward of a trip to the pet store or zoo. For a child who loves to play video games, a picture of Mario, from *Super Mario Brothers* and other super-successful video games, might represent the big reward of video game time or a new game. The picture is then cut into puzzle pieces based on the desired frequency of the behavior. In the case of ERP tasks, if the clinician wishes the child to complete one ERP task each day, the puzzle would have seven puzzle pieces to earn a prize at the end of one week. If the clinician wishes the child to complete three ERP tasks each day, the puzzle would have 21 puzzle pieces to earn a prize at the end of one week, and so on. To keep the puzzle pieces in place, parents can attach Velcro to the back of puzzle pieces or simply use two-sided tape.

We recommend that clinicians shape approximations to approach behavior, particularly early in treatment when the clinician and family have not yet determined the level of anxiety youth will tolerate when attempting a particular ERP. With Connect-the-Dots, the clinician might suggest the child earn one dot connection for a genuine attempt at the ERP task even if the child fails to complete it and three or four dot connections for successful completion of the ERP task as the clinician defined it. We explain to parents that they will not reward their child with a full reward for substandard efforts, for example, engaging in the ERP task more briefly than planned, trading one ritual for another (e.g., saying a phrase rather than counting), engaging in a neutralization after completing the exposure (e.g., washing hands), or substituting mini-strategies for typical neutralization strategies (e.g., rubbing the hands on pants when not washing). As mentioned, we recommend that parents and clinicians always praise youth for initiating and completing the planned and agreed-upon ERP tasks.

Teach Parents to Deliver Reinforcers

The best reinforcement plan in the world will not work if parents do not deliver reinforcers effectively. We recommend that clinicians review with parents the principles of effective reinforcement, answer their questions, and when possible practice the four *C*s of effective reinforcement: contingent, consistent, contiguous, and contains praise.

It is essential that reinforcers are delivered contingent upon the desired behavior. In order to effectively do this, it is essential that youth and parents clearly understand the desired behavior. We recommend that clinicians, particularly early in the treatment process, write a clear description of the ERP task, such as "touch the bottom of your shoe, and do not wash your hands until just before you sit down to eat dinner." Even when shaping ERP tasks, it is essential that parents reinforce for the specific approximation. For example, when working to delay a youth's washing compulsions, clinicians might recommend that parents reward the child with one puzzle piece after a 10-minute delay and two puzzle pieces after every 10-minute delay thereafter, up to 60 minutes. This would involve a many-piece (e.g., 30-piece) puzzle, of course. However, we do not recommend that parents reward youth contingent on changes in fear ratings. Youth do not control the rate at which their fear decreases. Youth do, however, control whether they engage in the ERP task as defined by the clinician. Therefore, we recommend that parents praise and reward their child's approach behavior each and every time.

In order to increase approach behaviors, it is essential that parents consistently reward their child for completing (as defined by the clinician) each and every ERP task, particularly early in treatment when youth are likely to be more anxious regarding ERP tasks. Consistent reinforcement quickly builds motivation to engage fully in ERP tasks. Inconsistent reinforcement can leave youth wondering whether their parents believe that the ERP tasks are necessary and important, and that is not the message we want youth to receive.

Contiguous reinforcement means that parents and clinicians deliver the reinforcer as soon after the desired behavior as possible. In the case of ERP tasks, we recommend that parents praise the child immediately and escort the child to the Connect-the-Dots graph where the child connects the earned dot. Alternatively, when youth and parents do not have the Connect-the-Dots graph easily available (e.g., when shopping together at the mall), parents can use brightly colored tokens or interesting and fun objects (e.g., marbles, pennies) as transitional reinforcers that the child trades for a dot on the Connect-the-Dots graph when parent and child return home. Similarly, when using the Puzzle Pieces strategy, parents can immediately praise and give their child a puzzle piece when the child completes an ERP task.

Last, we recommend that clinicians remind parents to praise their child's desired behaviors. Praise is a powerful reinforcer that costs parents nothing. At the same time, it is important that parents praise effectively. We recommend that parents praise the specific desired behavior (e.g., "I love the way you touched the counter and didn't whine or complain"). At the same time, we direct parents to give praise appropriate to the task. Rather than having the parents say, "You touched the counter and didn't wash your hands. You're amazing! You're the bravest kid in the world," we suggest they use more appropriate praise (e.g., "You touched the counter and didn't wash your hands. Great job. I knew you could do it"). Of course, we recommend that parents give their child all the big smiles and warm hugs that they wish.

Reinforcement plans do not motivate all youth, even when clinicians develop reasonable plans and parents reinforce effectively. When youth repeatedly avoid participating in ERP tasks, consistently do only the minimum the clinician asks, or undermine the therapy in general, that reflects unwillingness on the part of youth, parents, or both. Ineffective treatment results in poor response, and if clinicians ignore these signs of low willingness too long, it can cause parents and youth to believe that ERP does not work. For that reason, we recommend that clinicians step back from the treatment plan and consider other options to enhance engagement, such as medication supports (see Chapter 11, this volume) or an intensive outpatient program for youth with OCD. Furthermore, we recommend that clinicians revisit other engagement strategies (see Chapter 5) or review with youth and parents the treatment model, approach, and rationale for ERP tasks (see Chapter 6).

If youth and parents remain unwilling to engage fully in the treatment, however, the clinician may wish to take up with the family the difficult topic of discontinuing treatment. We often recommend that the family, particularly those suffering from therapy fatigue, take a break from therapy and check back in a few months or a year. We do not ever close the door to treatment. We only suggest that it might not be the right time to continue with a treatment that is not working, especially for families who are struggling with other problems, such as the loss of a job, the death of a loved one, or an upcoming divorce. At these times, we encourage youth and parents to call for check-in appointments (or even to schedule them) to see how the youth is doing and if the youth's readiness and willingness to resume treatment have increased.

TIME-IN

Time-in is when parents and the child spend time together during which the parents pays 100% of their attention to the child. Time-in can last for 1 minute or for many minutes. Attention from a parent is a powerful reinforcer for most youth, particularly young children. To reinforce desired behaviors, parents can use time-in every time youth exhibit a behavior (contingent) or use time-in spontaneously irrespective of the youth's behavior (noncontingent). As a contingent reinforcer, parents reward the child with attention such as playing a game the child chooses for an agreed-upon period of time. Clinicians may wish to encourage parents to include time-in as a reward in their child's reinforcement plan.

An example of noncontingent time-in occurs when a parent plays with a child a game of the child's choosing and follows the child's lead for a set period of time. Although noncontingent time-in is not a reinforcement strategy per se, it is a powerful strategy to strengthen the bond between child and parent. Even the most effective parenting strategies rest on a positive child–parent relationship. Youth with OCD can be difficult at times, and their behaviors often take a toll on the child–parent relationship. We recommend that clinicians work actively to help parents protect and nourish their relationships with their child, and noncontingent time-in is a great way to do that. Furthermore, noncontingent time-in provides parents with an opportunity to model adaptive behaviors for their child, such as positive problem solving. For example, 5-year-old Jennifer was already exhibiting perfectionistic tendencies. She often became very upset with any mistake she made and cried and wanted to stop the game. When playing Pick-Up Sticks with Jennifer, her mother would say following any mistake she made, "Oh, well. I'll get another chance when it's my turn."

Often parents have difficulty playing with their child in a nondirective manner. They tend to take over the task, saying things like "This is the tricky part. Let me do it," or directing the activity, saying, for example: "Let's build a spaceship." We recommend that parents narrate what the child does rather than instruct. For example, they could say, "Let me guess. You're drawing an elephant," rather than, "Why don't you draw an elephant?" Most important, it is essential for parents to set aside all other activities during time-in. If parents are sending text messages or folding laundry, it is not time-in. We recommend 10 minutes a day of noncontingent time-in during which parents give the child their full attention.

MANAGE PUSHBACK BEHAVIORS

Pushback behaviors include tantrums, name-calling, delaying, arguing, cursing, physical aggression, and refusal to comply with parents' instructions. Pushback behaviors do not include the compulsive behaviors youth with OCD exhibit in response to feeling anxious or uncomfortable. Neutralizations are a feature of the condition, and we do not recommend that clinicians instruct parents to manage their child's compulsions in the same way they manage pushback behaviors. Anxious youth often oppose parent instructions when anxious and when asked to do something that will make them anxious. Not every child with OCD engages in pushback behaviors, but it is essential that clinicians teach parents to manage these behaviors when they do occur. We cannot effectively treat pediatric OCD in the presence of pushback behaviors, and, even in the absence of OCD, these skills are essential for parents to master to effectively parent any child.

Teach Parents to Deliver Effective Directions and Commands

Effective parenting begins with the ability to clearly and effectively direct the child to comply with a parental request. Many parents, particularly anxious ones, can have trouble with this straightforward parenting skill. However, parents who master the task of delivering effective directions will soon learn that their child can and will comply with their instructions and discover the paradox: effective commands result in fewer additional and often escalating commands. We recommend that clinicians teach parents to follow several simple guidelines for delivering clear directions to their child.

First, and most important, we recommend that clinicians tell parents to avoid giving to their child directions that they are not prepared to enforce. Parents who threaten rather than enforce teach youth that protesting loudly and long enough will allow them to escape doing what parents instructed them to do. For example, 6-year-old Winston often refused to sit still while his mother read him a story at bedtime. His mother threatened numerous times that "if you don't settle down, no more story time tonight." Winston would plead, "No! No!," and his mother would warn him again, "Then you'd better settle down." A few minutes later, Winston begin to wiggle and fidget again, and the cycle repeated. But Winston's mother never stopped story time early, as she had threatened. When his mother finally stopped reading and left his bedroom so he could go to sleep, Winston threw a tantrum that often lasted for an hour. Follow-through is the key to effective commands.

Second, we recommend that clinicians teach parents to direct rather than request. A request or question (e.g., "Would you like to go to bed now?") presents the child with a legitimate choice, and sometimes the answer to that choice is no. We recommend that parents never ask a child to do something unless they are prepared to accept no as an answer. Instead, teach parents to direct their child. We recommend that parents give clear, specific directions with a time frame for completion of the task. "Take your plate to the sink now" or "put your clothes away before I call you to dinner" can avoid the child responding, "You mean now?"

Furthermore, with young children or older children with significant difficulties paying attention to requests and instructions, we recommend that parents break requests into smaller requests. Rather than say, "Take out the garbage, then sweep the kitchen, and then put away the clean dishes," for example, parents should say, "Take out the garbage, then come to me, and I'll tell you the next thing I want you to do." Also, we teach parents to avoid long explanations or rationales for requests in favor of short, specific requests.

Often children fail to follow through with directions because by the time the parent finishes explaining why it is important to do the task, the child has forgotten the task itself. If the child is particularly inattentive, we teach parents to ask the child to repeat back the directions to ensure the child heard and understood the directions correctly. Of course, we recommend that parents immediately praise the child's compliance with a request and make sure that the praise is specific and appropriate; we also encourage big smiles and hugs.

Third, although we believe in the value of parents teaching to their child politeness, we also recommend that parents distinguish between a "polite please" and a "pleading please" when directing their child to do something. Pleading sends the signal that the child can choose to comply or not comply with the request.

Last, we recommend that parents avoid suggesting that they will help the child complete the task unless they are prepared to do so. In other words, if a parent says, "Let's clean up your room," the parent needs to actually complete the task with the child and not just start cleaning the room with the child and then walk away. Parents who fail to honor implicit agreements with a child not only mislead the child but also model incomplete follow-through.

Teach Parents to Ignore Pushback Behaviors

Paying attention to desirable behaviors and ignoring undesirable behaviors is a highly effective way to shape behavior. However, many parents unknowingly reinforce undesirable behaviors by giving an undesirable behavior, and their child, time and attention. Effective ignoring removes all attention from the child. We recommend that clinicians teach parents to avoid making eye contact with their child, to instruct the child with as few words as possible, and to ignore their child's tears, whining, and arguing. For example, prior to bringing 5-year-old Amy in for treatment, Jan permitted her daughter to avoid tasks that triggered excessive handwashing or cleaning rituals. Over the course of CBT, Amy's fears of germs and handwashing had decreased, but she still refused to do many tasks. Some of these tasks were completely unrelated to past fears of germs, like putting away clean clothes. Amy, like most children, quickly learned that whining and arguing permitted her to avoid triggering her obsessions as well as any task that she did not want to do. The clinician explained to Jan that she and Amy had fallen into an unhelpful pattern. At the suggestion of the clinician, Jan began to ignore Amy's whining and tears. When Jan asked her to do simple tasks, such as putting away the crayons she was using or coming to dinner, Jan continued what she was doing as if nothing was happening. Jan did not look at or speak to Amy, regardless of Amy's reaction. As soon as Amy completed the task, Jan looked at her daughter, smiled, leaned in, and praised her on-task behavior.

When instructing parents to ignore, we recommend that clinicians consider several guidelines. First, we recommend that clinicians not ask parents to ignore dangerous or destructive behaviors, such as hitting a sibling. Second, we recommend that clinicians explain to parents that it is important to ignore the full intensity of an undesired behavior. For example, Jan was able to ignore her daughter's whining and crying until Amy began to sob and scream. Jan then fell into the old pattern again, saying, "Amy, it's not the end of the world. Just put your crayons away." By giving Amy attention, Jan taught Amy that louder and longer whining would get her what she wanted. Third, we recommend that clinicians explain to parents that a bigger fire gets more water. As they begin to ignore an undesired behavior, the behavior is probably going to get worse before it gets better. For example, as Jason ignored his son's tantrums, crying became writhing and screaming on the floor. Jason continued to ignore these intensity bursts and soon his son quieted down and complied with his direction.

Teach Parents to Deliver Effective Time-Outs

Time-out is a strategy most parents use at some point in their child's life, and it is an effective strategy when parents use it correctly. Unfortunately, many parents, even smart, capable ones, do not always implement time-outs properly. The first step in teaching parents how to do time-out is to assist them in identifying the target behaviors to extinguish. We recommend that parents focus on only one or two specific behaviors at a time, such as hitting or refusing. Time-out is often used to manage problem behaviors or noncompliance with parent instructions. We recommend that clinicians instruct parents to give a command (e.g., "Please pick up your shoes now"), and if the child does not begin to comply with the command within 5 full seconds, the parent directs the child to time-out. Parents, if they wish, may give the child a warning after waiting the full 5 seconds: "Please pick up your shoes now, or you will go to time-out." If the child does not begin to comply within another 5 full seconds, the parent directs the child to time-out. For other targeted behaviors, particularly aggressive behaviors, parents alert the child ahead of time that they will always give the child a time-out when they observe a particular behavior; for example: "If you push or hit your brother, you immediately go to time-out."

When parents direct their child to time-out, it is important that they do not give the child any additional attention. We recommend that parents look away from the child with a neutral expression and calm voice. Also we instruct parents to ignore other behaviors that are not the agreed-upon target behaviors, such as crying, pleading, or arguing. For example, in response to time-out, some children apologize and promise that they will not do it again, or they comply with the request after the parent tells them to go to time-out. We recommend that parents accept and praise their child's remorse but then have them complete the time-out (e.g., "Thanks for the apology. Now, please go to the time-out spot"). If the child hesitates or refuses to go to the time-out spot, the parent gently escorts the child to the spot while looking away and ignoring other behaviors. We help parents identify the best time-out environment, usually a spot in the home that is quiet, safe, and some distance from family activity. Because time-out is most often used with young children, time-out periods are brief, typically 1 minute per 1 year of age.

Teach Parents to Deliver Response Cost

There is a place in any contingency management plan for response cost, but we recommend that clinicians and parents use it sparingly and always strategically. Response cost is the removal of a previously earned reward or reinforcer in response to a pushback behavior. For example, a child who earned 15 tokens for completing his morning chores might lose 10 tokens when he pushes his brother. When using Connect-the-Dots, we recommend dot detours. That is, parents add a loop of several dots that begins and ends on the last dot connected. The child must now connect this new string of dots before returning to the dots of the initial pattern. Similarly, when using Puzzle Pieces, parents remove one of the puzzle pieces or cut new pieces in half so it takes longer to complete the puzzle. Parents can use response cost along with time-out. For example, if a youth refuses to go to the time-out spot or if the youth tends to kick, bite, or hit the parent, we recommend that the parent implement response cost whereby the parent warns the child that the child will receive a consequence that is less desirable than time-out; for example: "If you do not go to time-out now, I will not take you to the park this afternoon."

We teach parents several guidelines regarding response cost. First, we recommend parents ignore rather than fine youth for undesired behaviors until the reinforcement plan has been up and running for 2 to 3 weeks. Using response cost too soon can delay the growth of desirable behaviors. Second, we recommend parents avoid "punishment spirals." This occurs when parents fine the child and then the child complains, and parents then fine the child again, and so on, resulting in additional undesired behavior and additional fines. At some point, in the face of large fines, youth stop caring and continue to engage in the undesired behaviors. A more effective alternative is to encourage parents to pivot to an alternative response cost that is even more undesirable than lost tokens, such as grounding. If their child is in a rage and consequences do not penetrate this activated state, we suggest that parents give themselves time-out from their child until their child is calmer and can be reasoned with.

Train Parents to Be Effective ERP Coaches

We recommend that clinicians teach parents to be effective coclinicians, particularly exposure coaches. Effective exposure coaches understand the principles of exposure with response prevention and the strategies to manage pushback behaviors, implement the reinforcement plan, and resist accommodation behaviors. An extensive list of instructions is available from March and Mulle, 1998, Appendix III.

At the same time, knowing when and how to include parents as exposure coaches in the treatment plan is not always clear and straightforward. We recommend that clinicians consider the following when deciding on the role of parents in the treatment process.

Availability for In-Session Parent Coaching

At times, parent participation is essential in ERP, particularly for younger youth who may not be capable of implementing ERP tasks on their own. In these cases, clinicians invite parents to observe while the clinician conducts ERP tasks, delivers reinforcement, and encourages the child to tolerate distress and resist neutralizations. Next, the clinician invites parents to conduct another ERP task in session while the clinician observes. The clinician then provides corrective feedback to parents and asks parents to repeat the ERP task until clinician, parents, and youth are confident that parents understand the ERP process.

Parental Anxiety

Parental anxiety is another factor that determines a parent's effectiveness as an ERP coach and even whether it is appropriate to include parents in sessions when the clinician is conducting ERP tasks with the youth. If the parent is highly anxious, we recommend that the clinician delay including the parent in the ERP sessions. Once the clinician and youth have participated in a number of ERP tasks, the youth who has become more comfortable and confident with the ERP process can educate the parent, with the clinician's assistance, regarding the usefulness of ERP and, more importantly, that the youth can tolerate the experience. With this reassurance, many anxious parents are able to direct out-of-session ERP tasks with their child.

Parents Taking Over the ERP Plan

Once parents observe their child's OCD symptoms decrease through the power of ERP, they may push their child to move through exposures faster than the youth is ready to undertake. We recommend that clinicians validate the parent's wish to help their child feel better as quickly as possible while also underscoring the disadvantages of forced or surprise exposures. Remind parents that their child's willingness to try ERP tasks is, in part, because the child has selected the ERP task and believes that the task is difficult but doable.

CONCLUSION

It is essential that clinicians include and collaborate with parents in the process of treating pediatric OCD. Even the smartest and most well-meaning parent can inadvertently collude with OCD symptoms. Clinicians who teach parents to decrease their accommodation behaviors, to increase their child's willingness to approach rather than avoid what their child fears, to manage their child's pushback behaviors, and to become effective ERP coaches can quickly turn the tables on OCD. Parents who were once overwhelmed and demoralized can quickly become effective coclinicians in the battle against their child's OCD.

In the next chapter, we describe the process of building an individualized graded exposure with response prevention plan. The ERP plan is the heart of cognitive behavior therapy (CBT) for pediatric OCD. It guides the treatment and provides a path forward for youth, parents, and clinicians. The ERP plan is so central to the success of CBT for pediatric OCD, we devote an entire chapter to the process of building the ERP plan. Furthermore, clinicians who are new to the psychological treatment of pediatric OCD often have the most questions about building the ERP plan. We hope the next chapter takes some of the mystery out of the process.

———

8

Implementing Graded Exposure and Response Prevention

Julie was afraid that if she did not repeat aloud numbers that she saw, then something bad would happen. Julie and the clinician set up an ERP task. The exposure was to walk down the street searching for house address numbers to elicit her fear, and the response prevention strategy was for her to sing her favorite song softly to prevent herself from saying the numbers aloud. After she and the clinician walked around for 20 minutes, the clinician asked what she had learned. "Well," Julie said, "I learned that even though it feels weird and uncomfortable not saying the numbers to myself, I can do it. And you know what? I kind of got more used to it as I kept going. I think I could definitely do this again."

In this chapter, we describe the basics of implementing graded exposure and response prevention (ERP). We first describe guidelines for conducting effective exposure tasks in general, and then we describe the types of exposure strategies and their application to obsessive–compulsive disorder (OCD) symptom subtypes. We next describe guidelines for implementing response prevention (RP) strategies to accompany graded exposure and the role of parents in supporting ERP tasks in session and out of session.

PREPARING YOUTH AND PARENTS FOR ERP

ERP tasks, by design, are anxiety provoking for youth. To enhance the willingness of youth to undertake this difficult and critical phase of the treatment, we recommend that clinicians review the cognitive behavior model before

http://dx.doi.org/10.1037/0000167-009
Cognitive Behavior Therapy for OCD in Youth: A Step-by-Step Guide, by M. A. Tompkins, D. J. Owen, N. H. Shiloff, and L. R. Tanner

beginning ERP and prior to every ERP task, particularly with early ERP tasks. The clinician can use a training metaphor, particularly with youth who are sports enthusiasts, to underscore the importance of repeatedly facing fears. For example, they could say, "Facing your fear strengthens your resistance muscle. The more you practice, the stronger your resistance muscle gets, and the easier it will be to resist OCD." We often quiz older youth regarding the model and rationale for ERP to verify that they understand the rationale and to encourage them to practice an effective attitude toward OCD, For example, we might ask: "Why do you think you are facing your fear today? What are the good things that will come from facing your fear?" Youth who can recall the rationale for ERP are likely to engage in these tasks, particularly when their motivation is low.

ERP tasks can evoke considerable distress in parents too. For that reason, we recommend that clinicians also prepare parents for this critical phase of treatment of pediatric OCD. Explaining psychoeducation regarding the condition, the cognitive behavior model, and the rationale for ERP will do much to calm anxious parents and help them be effective allies against their child's OCD.

Addressing Safety Concerns with Parents

At times, parents will express concerns regarding ERP tasks and their child's safety or personal hygiene. We recommend that clinicians identify and address these concerns early, certainly prior to implementing any ERP task, to maintain the motivation of youth and parents. For example, many people wash their hands every time they use the toilet, whereas others rarely wash their hands after using the toilet. Although washing one's hands after toilet use is a good practice, not washing one's hands is not necessarily dangerous under most circumstances. We recommend that clinicians discuss with parents the value of living one's life relative to reasonable risk rather than living relative to avoiding risk at all cost. Reasonable risk assumes that the risk of a bad outcome is quite low but is not zero. We often share with parents: "The goal is for your child to become more comfortable with risks that are reasonable rather than to continue to try to eliminate all risk, which is impossible and only keeps OCD powerful in your child's life." We recommend that clinicians introduce to youth and parents the idea of reasonable risk in this way:

> Shane, Mom, and Dad, let's talk about what is and isn't reasonable when it comes to Shane's handwashing. You might not know this: Many, but not all, people wash their hands after toilet use. There are research studies that tell us this. However, OCD doesn't want Shane to take any chances, not even very small ones that other people take every day. That's one of the ways OCD stays in charge. But as Shane faces his fear of germs, his brain will slowly recalibrate, and he'll become more comfortable with the things about which most people are

comfortable. For example, lots of kids don't wash their hands before eating a snack or before lunch at school. When the kids are at home, parents often ask them to wash their hands before eating, but many kids don't do it. I think of reasonable risks as "Shane doing what most kids do."

Sometimes this information alone is not enough to convince parents and youth that living with reasonable risks is both safe and helpful. They may accept that refusing to wash one's hands after toilet use is not dangerous, but they argue that it is not typical either. In these instances, we recommend that clinicians explain how doing things that are not typical can help recalibrate one's brain:

> Of course, OCD isn't comfortable with reasonable risks. OCD expects Shane never to take any risk, even very small ones. However, it's necessary for Shane to take the same risks other kids do to recalibrate his brain, such as not washing his hands in certain situations. Also, to really recalibrate his brain, I'll ask Shane to do things that are actually safe but are not typical, such as eating food off the ground or eating something that has been sitting on a toilet seat. I know that most kids don't do these sorts of things. However, the more you do safe but uncommon things, the faster you recalibrate your brain. I've helped other kids like Shane, and I know that I can help him recalibrate his brain too.

IMPLEMENTING GRADED EXPOSURE

Graded exposure is the process of approaching in stepwise fashion the fear-evoking situations (i.e., triggers), starting with the least feared and working up to the most feared. A graded approach allows youth to experience sufficient anxiety during the exposure to benefit from it but not so much anxiety that they cannot resist engaging in neutralizations. Furthermore, graded exposure results in generalization, whereby fear-evoking items higher on the hierarchy become less fear-evoking as youth complete fear-evoking items that are lower on the hierarchy. Typically, we recommend that clinicians structure each ERP session in the same way, regardless of the exposure strategy. The steps to follow are: (a) identify an ERP task, (b) formulate the expectancy, (c) implement the ERP task, and (d) monitor and reflect.

Identify an ERP Task

Once the clinician and youth (and parents) have developed the ERP hierarchy and discussed the model and rationale for ERP, it is time to implement this core strategy. We recommend that the clinician begin with the lowest trigger on the exposure hierarchy, particularly with the first critical ERP tasks. Some youth will want to leap ahead and tackle very anxiety-evoking ERP tasks. Although we appreciate this enthusiastic wish to regain all the territory lost to OCD as soon as possible, we believe strongly that nothing succeeds like success and therefore encourage youth to begin slowly. There are a number of reasons for this caution. First, the clinician does not know whether the youth can effectively resist neutralizations during an exposure task and, for that matter, which neutralizations the youth might use. Second, the clinician does not know how long it will take for the youth's distress to decrease adequately. Last, the overarching goal of ERP tasks is to strengthen the belief that the youth can tolerate anxiety and distress. Beginning an exposure that youth are unable to complete weakens rather than strengthens that belief.

Select an Exposure Strategy

The ERP plan includes at least three types of exposure strategies: (a) in-office situational exposures, (b) out-of-office situational exposures, and (c) imaginal exposures. Most treatment plans include a combination of these three, although we recommend that clinicians emphasize situational exposures whenever possible, as these are the exposures that are often the most effective in reducing obsessive fear. Staging and selecting among these exposure strategies is generally based on the type of exposure that would be easiest for youth at a particular point in treatment or that would be easiest for the clinician to implement. The reality is that not all exposures are feasible for all therapy practices, regardless of how effective the exposure would be. As a result, we encourage clinicians (a) to identify what would be most effective for the youth, and (b) to determine which aspects of that exposure youth can realistically complete during a session in or outside the office. All three exposure strategies can be used as ERP tasks that youth practice between sessions.

Situational Exposures. Situational exposures typically involve two types: in vivo and in vitro. In vivo situational exposures direct youth to do things that precisely mirror what they could do in the real world but which they avoid (e.g., directing youth to enter and use public restrooms or to touch certain objects at home and school). Situational exposures can also include gradually decreasing the type, duration, and frequency of neutralization strategies (e.g., washing, wiping, spitting, holding breath) used in situations that trigger obsessive fears. In vitro situational exposures are not true situations but artificial situations that involve contrived objects, activities, or situations. In vitro exposures are particularly helpful when in vivo exposures are not readily accessible or appropriate (e.g., directing youth to touch a picture of urine or feces or to touch artificial urine or feces).

In-Office Situational Exposures. In-session in vivo situational exposures include exposure tasks conducted in session with the assistance of the clinician. Situations that trigger repeated checking and counting compulsions as well as avoiding certain (contaminated) objects all lend themselves well to in-session in vivo situational exposures. For example, 16-year-old Adele suffered from health-related obsessions, particularly thoughts that she may have contracted oral herpes. Adele inspected inside and outside her mouth several times a day, often for periods lasting up to an hour. The clinician began the exposure by first triggering the obsession: "It looks as if you might have some dry skin or possibly a sore on the left corner of your mouth." As directed earlier by the clinician, Adele resisted the urge to touch her mouth while the clinician examined Adele's mouth with a neutral and difficult-to-read demeanor. While the clinician discussed the signs and symptoms of herpes for 30 minutes, Adele resisted examining her face in a hand mirror that sat on the desk next to her or touching her mouth. Periodically, the clinician asked Adele to rate her feeling of distress and her confidence that she could continue to resist checking. After about 45 minutes, Adele reported that she still had small urges to check her mouth, but she was confident she could resist them.

In-session in vitro exposures such as touching fake urine or feces can help youth complete in vivo situational exposures that involve possible contact with real urine or feces (e.g., touching the bathroom floor). Other examples of in vitro exposures include watching the clinician use fake vomit to simulate throwing up in a toilet or sniffing butyric acid (a chemical that smells like vomit). Clinicians can set up in vitro exposures to urine by adding yellow food coloring to water to make artificial urine and then adjusting the color (lighter or darker) relative to the youth's fear level. If the youth reports little to no distress when looking at the artificial urine in a clear bottle or cup, the clinician could pour it into a toilet or onto toilet paper to make it look more real. Similarly, clinicians can use rubber dog feces, brown modeling clay in the shape of feces, or fake vomit for ERP tasks. There are a number of effective fake vomit recipes that use canned soup, yogurt, or oatmeal with food coloring. For young children, the clinician first encourages the child to touch artificial urine with a magic wand and then touch items in the clinician's office to contaminate them; then the youth and clinician handle these items.

Out-Of-Office Situational Exposures. Although clinicians can conduct many situational exposures in the office setting, sometimes the clinician and youth need to leave the office to get to create the most effective exposures. Although there can be many obstacles to exposure sessions away from the office, the most common are finding an appropriate location for the ERP tasks and handling confidentiality.

If the office location is unsuitable, the clinician accompanied by the youth (or meeting the youth at the remote location) may need to travel to public restrooms, garbage dumpsters, or city parks if these are relevant anxiety-evoking situations for youth. At times, clinicians can ask parents to assist youth in these remote situational exposures or to contaminate an item and bring it to the therapy session to use. For example, a clinician who was treating a 10-year-old boy with contamination fears asked his parents to walk with him in a park frequented by homeless individuals and bring and leave with the clinician the "contaminated" shoes the youth wore. The shoes were effective exposure items for weeks of work in the office. Because of travel time, clinicians may wish to schedule these meetings at the beginning or end of the day or near lunchtime (if the youth can leave school). Clinicians may wish to schedule longer sessions for out-of-office situational exposures to accommodate the travel time. Also longer ERP sessions are preferred when working on higher level ERP tasks. Advances in technology (e.g., smartphones) sometimes permit clinicians to coach ERP tasks while youth are in the natural setting and the clinician is in the office.

Although youth and parents are seldom concerned with issues of confidentiality when conducting ERP tasks, we recommend that clinicians carefully think through the issue of treating youth outside the confines of an office and discuss the matter with youth and parents. For example, the clinician may wish to discuss with youth and parents how they want to introduce the clinician if they run into someone the youth knows during an out-of-office ERP task. Similarly, the clinician and youth may wish to develop a pre-planned response if asked by strangers what they are doing. For example, if engaged in an ERP task such as touching and smelling books in the local library, the clinician and youth may develop a response such as "we love the smell of old books" to curious questions from strangers. If it is necessary to conduct ERP tasks at the youth's school, the clinician may wish to discuss with the classroom teacher and school personnel the option of the clinician and youth visiting the school and classroom in the morning before school begins or later in the afternoon after school ends.

Imaginal Exposure. Imaginal exposures involve writing out the content of the youth's obsessive fears and then rereading the account repeatedly or reading the story aloud and recording it so that it can be listened to repeatedly later. Imaginal exposures trigger the thoughts and images that fuel the youth's obsessive fear; the more youth interact with the obsessions without neutralizing them, the more tolerance they develop to the distress. Clinicians can use imaginal exposures in three different ways: as primary, secondary, and preliminary exposures. Most clinicians will use all of these at some time during the treatment process.

Primary imaginal exposures involve youth confronting the feared stimulus by imagining it. Clinicians typically include primary imaginal exposures in the youth's ERP hierarchy if the clinician cannot trigger the thought or image in a real-life situation. For example, if the youth's obsessive fear is stabbing siblings or parents, we recommend that clinicians develop narratives or stories that describe the situation in the first person and present tense. Always include in the narrative typical RP strategies that youth use but that in the story fail to work. Also include all thoughts, feelings, and urges youth experience when their obsessive fear is triggered; for example:

> I'm getting ready for school, and I'm running late. My hands feel a little dirty, but I don't have time to wash as I usually do before leaving for school. I tell myself that the feeling won't be so bad this time and try to think about something else. My mom yells at me to get in the car, and we drive away. I'm having an urge to wash, but I can't. The feeling is getting more and more intense. I can't think about anything else but the dirty feeling, and I notice that it's starting to move up my arms. It's past my wrists now. I wipe my hands over and over on my pants, but the feeling keeps building. The feeling is on my forearms now and moving up to my shoulders. I want to scream, but my friends are in the back seat and my mom is already mad at me. I keep hoping the feeling will go away, but it's getting worse and worse. It's moving up the sides of my neck, and then it's in

my mouth. I'm gagging and I want to spit, but I can't because my friends are watching. It's getting worse and worse. I feel like I'm coming out of my skin.

The narrative scripts for imaginal exposures will vary in length and detail depending on how anxiety provoking the clinician and youth want the exposure to be. At first, the clinician may wish to encourage shorter scripts with less detail, particularly when the clinician expects the youth to feel intensely anxious or uncomfortable. As the youth progresses through the imaginal exposures, the clinician can add more detail and elaborate more directly on feared outcomes.

Some parents and clinicians balk at the content of certain imaginal exposure scripts. We often remind parents that their child is likely to already be thinking the thoughts that are in the script. The imaginal exposure is only a way for youth to interact fully with the obsessions they are having to become more comfortable with them. Furthermore, we recommend that clinicians respond unemotionally, regardless of the content. Youth with OCD often worry that even the clinician will find the thoughts horrific and disgusting. We recommend that clinicians strive for a neutral matter-of-fact attitude that speaks for itself: *These thoughts are unimportant.*

Secondary imaginal exposures are effective in conjunction with the corresponding situational exposure and an excellent strategy to evoke fear of a terrible outcome following, at some time in the future, a particular act performed in the situational exposure. For example, with a youth with obsessive thoughts and images of his parents dying in an automobile accident who avoided certain "unlucky" numbers he believed would result in his parents dying, the clinician directed the youth first to write the feared number and then to read the following imaginal exposure that describes the feared outcome:

> Today, I wrote the number 777, even though I didn't want to do it. I couldn't help myself. As I'm thinking about this, my phone rings. It's my dad, and he tells me that my mom died in a horrible car accident. I feel sick, and I start to vomit. I'm sobbing because it's all my fault. I knew it was a mistake to write the number. I should have played it safe, like I always do, but I took a chance. It was stupid, and now my mom is dead and my dad and sister are devastated. I could have prevented this if I had been more careful. I'm a horrible son. I'm horrible.

Secondary imaginal exposures are also effective when designing ERP asks in situations in which youth repeat certain behaviors in response to an obsession, such as walking back and forth through a doorway while thinking a good or neutral thought to neutralize the bad thought. In these cases, clinicians might ask youth to intentionally walk through the doorway while thinking a bad thought. However, the exposure itself is short, and therefore we recommend that youth repeat this exposure many times during a short period of time for an effective exposure. Furthermore, the clinician and youth created the following imaginal script the youth recorded and then listened to when doing the situation exposure (i.e., repeatedly walking through doorways):

> I just walked through the door thinking bad thoughts, and I did nothing about it. Because I did this, bad things are going to happen. Because I chose not to do

something about the bad thought, this means that it's my fault that the something bad happens because I could have prevented it but didn't. Now there's nothing that I can do about it. This means that I'm a bad person, a very bad person.

Preliminary imaginal exposures are effective when youth are extremely anxious about situational ERP tasks and are unwilling to try them. However, preliminary imaginal exposures are no substitute for situational exposures (Rabavilas, Boulougouris, & Stefanis, 1976), and we recommend that clinicians clearly inform youth and parents that preliminary imaginal exposures will make upcoming situational exposures a bit easier, but that situational exposures are essential and forthcoming. For example, James, a 10-year-old boy, engaged in checking compulsions before going to bed to prevent something bad happening to him while he sleeps. He refused situational exposures, such as not checking his bedroom closet or under his bed. James and the clinician agreed to begin with an imaginal exposure before doing the situational exposure:

> I didn't check my closet or under my bed tonight. I decided it was silly to check, but as I'm lying in bed, I hear sounds coming from the closet. I freeze and cover my head with the blanket. Someone is in my room. I can feel him coming for me. I'm paralyzed. I can't scream, and I can't run. I'm going to die, and it's all my fault. I thought it was silly to check, but now I know that if I had checked I wouldn't die tonight.

Formulate Expectancy to Test

The next step in implementing a graded-exposure task is to elicit from youth, particularly older youth who understand the concept of prediction, the predicted outcome or expectation. When formulating the expectancy to test, we recommend that clinicians ask youth for (a) the predicted outcome and how strongly they believe the outcome is likely to be on a scale from 0 to 100, where 100% means that the outcome is guaranteed; (b) the initial distress rating before confronting the obsessive fear (graded on a scale from 0 to 10, where 10 is the most distressed they can imagine feeling); (c) how distressed or anxious they predict they will feel during the ERP task (on a scale of 0 to 10, where 10 is the most distressed they can imagine feeling); and (d) how confident they are that they can handle their distress (on a scale of 0 to 100, where 100% is complete confidence).

Typically, youth overestimate the level of anxiety or distress they experience and underestimate their ability to handle what they feel. Testing these predictions with each ERP task corrects these misappraisals over time and thereby increases the willingness of youth to try more difficult exposure tasks.

Implement the ERP Task

Prior to youth engaging in an ERP task, we recommend that clinicians carefully detail for youth and parents the ERP task to complete. First, include the action or behavior that youth will complete. This is typically the exposure task (e.g., "I will touch the full palm of my right hand to the top of the toilet tank, press my palm against the tank top and hold for three seconds, and then wipe my forehead with the full palm of my right hand"). Second, describe the actions or mental actions that the youth will resist (e.g., "I will not wash my hands or forehead or wipe my hands on my pants or a towel or try to remove the contamination in any way"). Third, describe the length of time and the content on which the youth will focus attention while resisting any neutralizations (e.g., "I will wait 40 minutes and think about the dirty and germy feeling").

Model and Shape

We recommend that clinicians model for youth and parents all exposure tasks prior to youth trying them. Just as we can learn to fear something by observing someone interact in a fearful manner with it, we can learn to be less fearful by observing someone interact with it in a nonfearful manner. For example, the clinician might touch a toilet seat and not wash his hands before asking the youth to do it. With young children, the clinician might instruct the child to watch the clinician engage in the exposure task and "take the bounce-off fear" (i.e., the fear youth feel as they observe the clinician engage in the exposure task) before the youth does it. When appropriate, the clinician can test the youth's predictions by trying it first (e.g., "So I'm going to say '13' three times and see if I go blind. On the zero to 100% scale I taught you, what do you think the chance is that I'll go blind?").

In addition to modeling for youth nonanxious responding, we recommend that clinicians shape approach behavior by encouraging, in small steps, approximations to the full exposure when necessary. Clinicians typically use two shaping strategies: shape relative to proximity and shape relative to duration.

Shape Relative to Proximity. To shape relative to proximity, clinicians direct youth to approach in steps the feared object. For example, the clinician directed 11-year-old Marcus, who feared that he would become homeless if he interacted with a homeless person, to walk down a street where a homeless person sat on a bus bench. At first, Marcus and the clinician repeatedly walked on the sidewalk across the street from the homeless person. Then they repeatedly walked on the sidewalk near the homeless person. After more practice, the clinician directed Marcus to make eye contact and smile at the homeless person. Finally, the clinician directed Marcus to place a dollar bill in the homeless person's hand and to say "you're welcome" when the homeless person thanked him.

When treating youth with contamination symptoms, a common strategy to shape relative to proximity is "the thing, that touched the thing, that touched the thing." For example, 7-year-old Christopher reported that it was too hard for him to touch the floor of the clinician's office. The clinician then suggested that Christopher touch the floor with a pen and then hold the pen fully in his hand. If Christopher had balked at this small step, the clinician might drop a tissue on the floor and ask Christopher to rub the pen on the tissue and then hold the pen fully in his hand.

Shaping Relative to Duration. Another method of shaping ERP tasks is to gradually increase the duration that youth remain in the feared situation without engaging in neutralizations. As youth become less anxious, the clinician can add more time to the ERP task, eventually assisting youth to complete the ERP task fully. Remember that the goal of any ERP task is to evoke sufficient anxiety to benefit from the exposure itself. If the duration of an exposure is too short, the youth is not likely to experience enough anxiety to benefit from the exposure task.

Ending the Exposure Task

To benefit fully from this critical core strategy, youth must complete ERP tasks as planned. Youth who discontinue an ERP task prematurely reinforce the belief that they cannot tolerate high levels of anxiety without engaging in neutralization strategies. We recommend careful planning of exposures, particularly early ones when the clinician is unfamiliar with the youth's response to anxiety. First, consider longer exposure periods, perhaps 90 minutes, particularly during the critical early exposures. More exposure time increases the likelihood that youth will learn what the clinician hopes they will learn: that they can tolerate their anxiety and that their anxiety decreases within an ERP task over time. Second, we recommend that clinicians begin with ERP tasks near the bottom of the ERP hierarchy even when youth report they wish to begin with more difficult ERP tasks. It is better for youth to complete an easy ERP task, particularly early in treatment, than to discontinue an ERP task that is too difficult. Third, we recommend that clinicians explain to youth the importance of continuing an ERP task for an agreed-upon duration. Typically, it is appropriate to discontinue an exposure once the youth's subjective units of distress (SUD) is 50% of the maximum anxiety. For example, when an exposure task results in a maximum of 60, the exposure continues until the youth's SUD ratings are 30 or less. When it appears that the youth may not reach this mark within the remaining session time, we recommend that the clinician discontinue the exposure and direct the youth to continue the exposure, if possible, in the clinician's waiting room or in the car on the drive home. The overarching goal of all ERP tasks is for youth to learn that they can handle their anxiety and fear over time while resisting neutralizations. As the strength of this belief increases, their willingness to approach and remain in anxiety-evoking situations increases too.

Monitor and Reflect

Monitoring the youth's learning during and after the youth completes ERP tasks is a critical final step in the treatment process. Generally, we recommend that clinicians monitor both the SUDs and the strength of belief in an expected outcome or prediction. After the youth completes ERP tasks, we recommend that the clinician help the youth reflect on what was learned. In particular, we encourage youth to reflect on their predicted outcome. Did it happen or not? Many times, the predicted outcome is not testable, such as the fear of going to hell if certain thoughts are not neutralized. In these instances, clinicians engineer ERP tasks such that youth can test their predictions regarding features of the distress or anxiety that accompany the uncertainty of future outcomes. For example, through ERP tasks, youth might test their predictions regarding their experience with uncertainty (e.g., "How anxious will I feel not knowing whether I will go to hell? How long will I feel the maximum anxiety? Will I be able to cope or handle my predicted level of distress? Will I be able to tolerate not knowing with certainty?"). Clinicians can download a blank ERP Practice Form (see http://pubs.apa.org/books/supp/tompkins, Web Form 8.1) to use to track the progress of youth during an ERP task.

IMPLEMENTING RESPONSE PREVENTION

Youth will not fully benefit from graded exposure when they engage in mental or physical neutralizations; therefore, it is important that clinicians implement RP during the exposure process in a thoughtful and planned manner. Also, decreasing neutralizations outside of formal exposure tasks results in a decrease in obsessive fear; therefore, that is an important part of the treatment process. In this section, we describe strategies for managing neutralizations during graded-exposure tasks and shaping and decreasing spontaneous neutralizations to triggers apart from planned exposure tasks.

Response Prevention During Exposure Tasks

Before the clinician begins exposure tasks with youth, we recommend that the clinician ask youth to describe all neutralization strategies they anticipate they will be using during exposure tasks. Asking about this beforehand allows the clinician and youth to identify appropriate strategies to resist the urge to neutralize; thus, the likelihood increases that the youth will successfully resist these urges during the exposure task. Typically, as youth progress through their ERP tasks, clinicians permit neutralizations for situations not yet targeted in the graded-exposure hierarchy. For example, for youth with contamination fears, the clinician might permit youth to wash their hands when they touch the bathroom counter at home (6 on the exposure hierarchy) but resist washing when they touch the kitchen counter at home (3 on the exposure hierarchy).

Shifting Importance of Thoughts

Reevaluating the importance of a thought can help youth resist neutralizations during exposure tasks; however, we recommend that clinicians take great care in teaching youth this approach. It can be a slippery slope because reevaluation of a thought can become a neutralization itself. For example, a youth might think, "Oh, this thought does not really matter," in response to an obsession. Thoughts, such as, "this is actually okay," "I don't have to feel scared of this," or "this thought isn't so bad" are likely reassurance neutralizations because the youth's intention is to reassure herself. If the youth thinks instead to an obsession (e.g., "I can handle this thought. I do not have do what OCD is telling me to do. I can wait for the thought to go away"), then the youth's intention is to engage in the obsessive fear while resisting the urge to neutralize.

Furthermore, in order to assist youth to resist urges to neutralize, we recommend that clinicians teach youth to tell themselves: "No matter how scary this thought is, I'm not going to do what OCD tells me to do." Similarly, in order to assist youth to tolerate uncertainty and its associated anxiety, clinicians can teach youth to say to themselves: "I know the thought I might hurt my brother is my OCD but I'm going to take a chance and sit next to my brother anyway."

Distraction in the Service of Acceptance of Discomfort

Youth will often distract themselves from obsessions and the discomfort that arises during ERP tasks. We recommend that clinicians explain to youth that distraction functions in the same way as neutralizations when they distract themselves to feel less anxious. Once youth understand this, clinicians can direct youth to focus on the thought, image, or urge that evokes their distress. However, at times, we encourage youth to get on with their lives in the process of an exposure. Although this strategy appears similar to distraction, its function is quite different. For example, a youth with a symmetry obsession may wish to balance out repeatedly how he sits in a chair. To encourage youth to resist neutralizations and tolerate uncertainty and discomfort, the clinician might suggest a game or activity (e.g., "Rather than trying to be sure you're even, let's play a game of Uno while you sit there with the uneven feeling"). Again, it is essential that clinicians understand the function of an activity. In this case, the function of the game is to enable youth to accept discomfort rather than distract from discomfort.

Limit Access to Neutralizations

Although limiting access to neutralization strategies is not always possible, it is one of the most effective ways to assist youth to resist urges to neutralize. For example, removing the means to wash (e.g., soap, hand sanitizer, wipes) during exposure can help. For checking neutralizations, one could conduct the exposure when youth are away from the object they wish to check (e.g., doors, windows). Similarly, directing youth to close their eyes so they cannot see the object they have the urge to check is effective, particularly when the neutralization is a quick glance. We recommend that clinicians begin by blocking the youth's access to neutralizations and work toward the youth resisting urges to neutralize when access to neutralizations is available. For example, start by directing the youth to touch contaminated objects without access to soap, water, or other means to wash; then work youth toward resisting the urge to wash when soap and water are available to them.

Identify and Disengage From Mental Neutralizations

Mental neutralizations are some of the most challenging neutralizations to manage during exposure tasks. For that reason, during exposure tasks we recommend that clinicians check with youth whether they are using any type of mental neutralization. Simple questions could be used, such as: "Are you telling yourself something right now to get the OCD bully to go away?" "Are you doing anything in your head right now to feel less anxious or frightened?" "Are you repeating any words or phrases to yourself right now to feel less anxious or to get the bad thought to go away?" Once youth understand the function of mental neutralizations and can separate these from the thoughts that generate their anxiety and discomfort, the better able they will be to resist mental neutralizations. For example, a 16-year-old boy who feared that he would become addicted to drugs or alcohol would immediately repeat what he was doing if he had a thought about drugs or alcohol. The youth appeared to do very well during his first exposure task in which he looked at photos of drug paraphernalia. At the end of the exposure task, however, the clinician noticed that the youth hesitated slightly before standing to leave. When the clinician asked the youth about this, he reported that he wanted to make certain he had cleared his head of all the bad thoughts before he stood. The clinician pointed out that this neutralization undid all his hard work during the exposure. They then repeated the exposure, but this time, when the youth stood to leave the office, the clinician directed the youth to intentionally think about the photos of drug paraphernalia and to describe what he saw in the photos to block mental neutralizations.

Decrease Neutralizations in Response to Natural Triggers

Although ERP tasks (i.e., the combination of exposure and response prevention) are critical to effective cognitive behavior therapy (CBT) for pediatric OCD, youth can benefit from decreasing neutralizations in response to natural triggers, rather than to planned exposure tasks. Once the youth and clinician complete the RP hierarchy, the clinician assists the youth to select a specific physical neutralization to resist on a daily basis. If at all possible, we recommend that clinicians work with youth to stop the targeted neutralization altogether. However, many times youth cannot stop all neutralizations completely, and the clinician will take a graded approach to RP. That is, the clinician works with youth to drop out one neutralization after another, typically from easiest to most difficult, relative to the RP hierarchy. As youth move through the RP hierarchy, we recommend that clinicians delay youth from moving to the next step in the RP hierarchy until they demonstrate that they can consistently and effectively resist the targeted neutralization.

Decrease the Frequency of Neutralizations

One of the more common strategies for resisting physical neutralizations is to shape the frequency with which youth engage in neutralizations. For example, for youth who engage in ritualized neutralizations (e.g., counting to 7 fourteen times), the clinician might direct the youth to count to 7 fewer times. Decreasing the number of times by half is often a good place to begin.

Reassurance-seeking is a common neutralization; clinicians need to help youth and parents decrease the frequency with which youth seek reassurance as well as the frequency with which parents provide reassurance. The intuitive response of caring parents is to reassure their anxious child. Clinicians who ask parents to stop reassuring their distressed child often encounter resistance, in part because many parents view withholding reassurance as being mean or punishing. We recommend that clinicians explain to parents that for their child to recover from OCD, it is necessary that they learn to parent counterintuitively (i.e., respond counter to the messages from their caring parent guts). Before they create a plan to fade reassurance, we recommend that clinicians review with families the family accommodation cycle. Clinicians can download the Family Accommodation Cycle handout (http://pubs.apa.org/books/supp/tompkins, Web Form 7.1) and use it when discussing with parents the role that seeking and providing reassurance plays in the maintenance of the condition. Once parents understand the negative long-term consequences of reassuring their child, they are usually willing to discontinue providing reassurance. We recommend that clinicians coach parents and others to respond to requests for reassurance by first alerting youth that the reassurance-seeking is an OCD symptom and then with a caring but firm manner remind youth that reassurance is not forthcoming (e.g., "Sounds like this is OCD looking for reassurance again; I'm not going to answer these kinds of questions from OCD anymore").

For youth who continue to seek reassurance, clinicians can implement a response cost strategy. Each morning parents determine the price of their reassurance and give the child a set number of tokens. When seeking reassurance, the child must purchase it from parents with one of the tokens. After the child uses all tokens, parents will no longer answer any reassurance questions. If the child has tokens at the end of the day, the child may then trade them for small rewards such as extra TV time or a later bedtime. For older children and teens, parents can apply the same strategy but use money (a dollar or two in change) as the token. The price of reassurance varies relative to the age of the youth (younger youth generally are satisfied with a lower price) as well as the richness of the reinforcement baseline. For example, youth will resist reassurance-seeking more if the value of the token is high. That is, the fewer tokens, the fewer opportunities to seek reassurance; therefore, the more valuable each token becomes. We strive for a reinforcement baseline that is just below the typical frequency that the youth seeks reassurance. If youth seek reassurance 10 times a day, give them five or six tokens. In order to maintain an acceptable reinforcement baseline, youth may not save tokens to purchase reassurance the next day. Youth may only use tokens to purchase reassurance on the day parents gave youth the tokens. Response cost procedures are quite effective, and clinicians can use this strategy to decrease the frequency of any neutralization that involves the youth and parents.

Delay Neutralizations

When youth report that they are unable to resist the urge to neutralize, we recommend that clinicians assist youth to delay neutralizations. Typically, we negotiate with youth a delay period based on their confidence that they can adhere to the period. For example: "How confident are you on a 0% to 100% scale that you can delay washing your hands for 5 minutes?" Strive for 90%-or-greater confidence. If the youth reports low confidence, decrease the length of the delay to achieve 90%. After youth consistently meet the delay goal, gradually increase the length of the delay period based on confidence ratings.

Do the Opposite

Often youth who agree to discontinue neutralizations are unsure what to do instead. This is particularly true for neutralizations that involve avoiding particular actions: avoid stepping on sidewalk cracks, or use a foot to flush the toilet. The clinician instructs the youth to do the opposite of what OCD tells the youth to do. If OCD tells the youth not to step on a sidewalk crack, the youth steps on all sidewalk cracks. Similarly, if OCD tells the youth to avoid touching doorknobs, the youth agrees to do the opposite (i.e., grasp doorknobs).

Perform the Neutralization Wrong

For many neutralizations, the most effective RP strategy is to direct youth to do neutralizations incorrectly. This is particularly effective with youth who engage in neutralizations during routine daily activities, such as dressing or grooming. For example, a 13-year-old youth who dressed each morning in a rigid and exact manner agreed to change the routine in small ways each morning. Rather than putting her right arm through her shirt first, she agreed to put her left arm through first. However, after a few days this new routine became a neutralization too. The clinician then numbered the activities (e.g., 1: left arm in shirt first; 2: right arm in shirt first; 3: head in shirt first) and directed the youth to roll a die to decide which dressing activity to complete first, then second, and so on.

For speaking neutralizations, such as praying or repeating a certain phrase, doing it wrong might involve singing the neutralization to a funny tune or saying it in a silly voice. This not only changes the neutralization but also shifts the emotional response (i.e., from fear to fun). Doing it wrong can also include counting to the wrong number, repeating an action the wrong number of times, or completing a sequence out of order.

Set a Time Limit for Neutralizations

Rituals often involve an elaborate sequence of neutralizations that must be completed in an exact manner. For example, a youth with contamination obsessions and showering neutralizations might (a) wash the hair with three pumps of shampoo (rinse, and repeat two times); (b) wash all body parts with soap starting with hands, then arms, then torso, and then legs (rinse and repeat two times); (c) rinse hair and body two more times; and (d) turn off the water and check body and hair to make sure it is completely clean. For elaborate rituals like this one, it is often difficult for the youth to drop a specific behavior in a chain of related behaviors. Therefore, the clinician may want to direct the youth to complete the ritual but in less time. The first step is for the clinician to establish the time it currently takes the youth to complete the ritual. Often parents and youth are agonizingly aware of the amount of time a ritual consumes. However, when in doubt, we recommend that clinicians direct youth and parents to time the ritual for 3 days and then average the times. The clinician then negotiates with the youth a new time amount to begin the shaping process; for example:

CLINICIAN: So it looks like it takes you 20 minutes to complete your shower in the morning. How confident, on a 0 to 100% scale, are you that you'll complete your shower in 15 minutes?

YOUTH: I don't think I can do that. I'm maybe 70% confident.

CLINICIAN: Okay. Let's shoot for 90% confidence. Right now, you're 100% confident or close to it that you can complete your shower in 20 minutes. That's what you averaged over the last 3 days. To hit that 90% confidence mark, how long are you willing to shower?

YOUTH: Probably about 18 minutes. It would be hard, but I'm 90% confident I could finish in 18 minutes.

CLINICIAN: Okay. Let's start with 18 minutes. Now remember, you can do every step in the ritual during the 18 minutes, but when the timer goes off, you will turn off the water and get out of the shower.

Eliminate Neutralizations by Proxy

At times, youth request, demand, or trick parents, siblings, other family members, and even teachers into completing the youth's neutralizations when the youth is unable to do so. For example, a child who is exhausted at bedtime might convince a parent to check the locks and windows according to the child's specific instructions. Youth with contamination fears might ask siblings to open doors or flush toilets for them. Youth who repeatedly go through doors might ask a grandmother to bring something to him rather than to leave the room and trigger the urge to repeat.

As with other physical neutralizations, stopping all neutralizations immediately is the ideal option, if youth will do this. However, neutralizations by proxy can also be decreased in a stepwise fashion. We recommend that clinicians discourage parents from eliminating all neutralizations by proxy if they have not discussed the matter with the youth and clinician, particularly if the youth is not on board with that plan. Instead, we encourage parents, in collaboration with their child and the clinician, to develop a plan or hierarchy to gradually decrease their responses to their child's requests. Also, clinicians can use the response cost strategy described earlier to decrease the youth's requests of others to complete neutralizations for the youth.

Eliminate Mental Neutralizations

In the past, individuals with OCD who had no overt behavioral compulsions were often referred to as having pure obsessions. However, a more accurate way to think about this type of OCD is pure mental neutralizations. Youth still engage in neutralizations, but they are covert mental neutralizations. Most youth engage in both physical and mental neutralizations. The function of mental neutralizations is the same as the function of physical neutralizations: to decrease obsessive anxiety and fear. Mental neutralizations include praying, counting, replacing a bad thought or image with a good thought or image, and mentally replaying events to check. A child with harm obsessions might replace violent thoughts with happy or neutral thoughts. A young girl with scrupulosity obsessions might mentally recite a specific prayer multiple times in response to her obsessions. A teen with sexual obsessions might mentally replay events to make sure he did not experience sexual arousal.

Spoil or Undo Mental Neutralizations

One of the most effective ways to deal with mental neutralizations is to teach youth to spoil or to undo the neutralization. For example, a boy who recites a prayer in response to a blasphemous thought would first recognize the prayer as a neutralization (e.g., "The prayer just now was a mental compulsion"), and then spoil the neutralization by repeating to himself, "It doesn't matter if I prayed. I am still a bad person for having these thoughts." In this way, the boy spoils the neutralization by reconfirming his core fear that these blasphemous thoughts do, in fact, mean that he is a bad person. Clinicians might direct teens who mentally check if they feel aroused by their sexual obsessions to spoil the checking neutralization by saying, "Just because I checked doesn't mean that I wasn't aroused. I may be aroused and not even know it."

Slow Mental Neutralizations

Mental neutralizations occur quickly and automatically. For this reason, we recommend that clinicians teach youth strategies to slow their mental neutralizations prior to assisting youth to discontinue mental neutralizations altogether. For example, we often teach youth to describe in detail all thoughts and images that arise from the moment the obsession begins to the moment the neutralization ends. To assist youth to practice this strategy, we trigger an obsession (near the bottom of the ERP hierarchy) in session and then direct the youth to describe all thoughts that are part of the mental neutralization:

> Okay, let's have you look at this photo of a girl in a swimsuit. That will trigger your gay doubts. Remember, those gay doubts are the obsessions. Now, as you look at the photo, I want you to describe aloud everything that you are thinking and feeling. Remember: it's okay to do your mental neutralizations. I'm not asking you to resist them. That comes later. For now, you're just practicing slowing your thoughts. This will increase your awareness of which thoughts are obsessions and which thoughts are neutralizations. Once you know the difference, I'll teach you to resist the mental neutralizations and accept the obsessions. This will help you later when you begin to practice resisting the mental neutralizations.

Use Competing Mental Actions to Interrupt Mental Neutralizations

At times, clinicians can teach youth to disengage from mental neutralizations by directing them to engage in an alternative and competing action. This strategy is most helpful for mental neutralizations such as checking and counting. We recommend that clinicians first explain to youth that it is more difficult to engage in a mental neutralization when they are engaged in other mental activities. Then, clinicians work with the youth to identify a competing mental action. For example, clinicians might direct youth who count in their heads to sing a song or to describe the objects (e.g., door, window, carpet, light) around them when they notice an urge to count.

A competing mental action can become a new mental neutralization, however, when the competing mental action serves the same function as the mental neutralization, particularly for youth who use thought replacement mental neutralizations (i.e., replace a bad thought with a good thought). For this reason, we recommend that clinicians avoid teaching youth with thought replacement mental neutralizations the competing mental action strategy.

Design and Monitor ERP Action Plans

Just as we recommend that clinicians provide detailed descriptions of what youth will do during in-session exposures, we also recommend that clinicians provide youth and parents with a detailed set of ERP instructions for out-of-session practice tasks or action plans. Typically we include what, when, where, and how. For example, Jena agreed to touch the doorknob on her front door, then the doorknobs that lead into the kitchen and the garage. She agreed to touch each doorknob four times: Monday, Wednesday, Friday, and Sunday. After each practice, she agreed to sit at the kitchen counter and look at her hands and to think about the feeling of contamination while resisting the urge to wash and waiting for the feeling to decrease. She agreed to wait for at least 30 minutes, or until her urge to wash had decreased by 50% of the maximum during the exposure.

Because exposure tasks are difficult for youth, they do not always prioritize their ERP practice. Therefore, we recommend that clinicians direct parents and youth to identify optimal times to practice the ERP tasks. When possible, we recommend that youth avoid practicing ERP tasks just before bed or when hungry or tired. In addition, we recommend that youth practice ERP tasks when they are not already overly anxious about something else. For example, if the youth is anxious about an exam the next day, we recommend scheduling the ERP practice after the exam.

For younger youth, we recommend that clinicians review with parents their roles and responsibilities regarding the ERP practice. Will the parents remind the child when it is time to do the ERP practice? Will the parents facilitate the exposure and how (e.g., contaminate an object for the child to use during the ERP homework)? What will the parent do if the child refuses to complete the ERP practice? If the clinician has trained the parents to be effective ERP coaches, they likely know the answers to these questions. It is worth reminding parents that if the youth refuses to complete the agreed-upon ERP practice, they are not to reason, to cajole, to threaten, or to punish the youth. Instead, we recommend that parents note the days and times the youth refused to do the ERP practice, how the youth refused, and how the parents responded to the refusal. The clinician will then review these notes with parents and brainstorm possible solutions to improve the youth's adherence with future ERP action plans.

Master the Top of the ERP Hierarchy

Youth who master the early (low) steps on the ERP hierarchy begin to feel more confident and less anxious in general. By the middle of the ERP hierarchy, they begin to feel considerably less anxious and may (along with their parents) suggest that it is time to end treatment. However, mastering the most fear-evoking hierarchy items in varied contexts can enhance the durability of the treatment (Bouton, 2002).

We recommend that clinicians explain to youth and parents at the first meeting the importance of mastering the topmost ERP item and to convey this message repeatedly as youth move up their ERP hierarchies. Furthermore, we recommend that clinicians strive to engage youth in the most feared hierarchy items around the last third of treatment. Typically, clinicians will require extra time to assist youth to master these particularly difficult steps using a variety of exposure and RP strategies.

Build Self-Management Strategies

Near the end of treatment, we recommend that clinicians shift to building self-management strategies. The overarching objective of ERP for pediatric

OCD is to help youth develop and maintain a recovery attitude. A recovery attitude includes a willingness to approach rather than avoid anxiety-evoking situations and, just as important, search for opportunities to practice the skills learned in treatment. The self-management phase is focused on strategies to enable youth and parents to benefit fully from the ERP strategies they have learned throughout treatment, and to build and reinforce a viable recovery attitude.

Do-Overs

After months or years of utilizing mental and physical neutralizations to decrease obsessive fear, these mental and physical acts have become second nature to youth. Many times they respond to an obsession with a neutralization before they realize it. Do-overs provide youth and parents with the opportunity to practice ERP when they slip and respond in the old way, such as when the youth washes his hands before he realizes this is a neutralization. We recommend that clinicians explain to youth that do-overs are opportunities to give themselves treatment. Clinicians may wish to demonstrate a do-over in session (e.g., touch a counter and wash hands, then retouch the counter and not wash hands) and direct youth and parents as an out-of-session action plan to record instances in which youth engaged in do-overs.

Regain Ground

Following treatment, youth will likely discover that certain objects, activities, and situations that, because of treatment, no longer make them anxious occasionally make them feel quite anxious again. Youth may then fall back into a pattern of neutralizing or avoiding. We recommend that clinicians teach youth and parents a method to regain ground to prevent full relapse of the condition. To regain ground, the youth and parents step down one step in the ERP hierarchy and begin with that ERP task. Similarly, for a difficult exposure task, the clinician teaches youth and parents to apply the process of breaking down the exposure task into steps as they learned and practiced during treatment.

Self-Directed ERP Tasks

The goal of self-directed ERP tasks is to enhance the willingness of youth to engage in ERP tasks without prompts or encouragement from parents or the clinician. Self-directed ERP tasks set the stage for the lifestyle ERP tasks we describe next. We recommend that clinicians first develop a practice schedule that includes the top third (most difficult) of the youth's ERP hierarchy. We recommend that the clinician ask the youth to practice one or more of the ERP tasks listed in the practice schedule. We recommend that youth practice self-directed ERP tasks on a schedule rather than in response to their anxiety level. When the decision to practice ERP tasks is left exclusively to youth, they may delay the practice until they feel less anxious. In addition, we recommend that clinicians introduce randomness into self-directed ERP tasks. Randomness counters the youth's tendency to favor one ERP task over another, as well as actively introduces uncertainty. We recommend that clinicians include at least six tasks (numbered 1–6) on the self-directed practice schedule, then direct youth to toss a die to determine the self-directed exposure to perform that day. For example, if the youth tosses a 5, the youth performs ERP Task 5 on the self-directed practice plan. Direct the youth to record the results of the self-directed ERP task on a form and bring this form to follow-up meetings with the clinician. The clinician can download a blank copy of this form (http://pubs.apa.org/books/supp/tompkins, Web Form 8.2) to use when developing a self-directed ERP practice plan.

Lifestyle ERP Tasks

Lifestyle ERP tasks are a practical way to assist youth to incorporate a recovery attitude into their day-to-day life, rather than something that is done only as part of treatment. We recommend that clinicians repeatedly emphasize the importance of an effective recovery attitude early and often in treatment to reinforce the idea that treatment enhances this essential attitude over time. The clinician may wish to first brainstorm with the youth the lifestyle ERP opportunities that may arise before the next session: eating food in a restaurant, using the toilet at home, washing hands before dinner, or hanging out with peers. Next, develop an appropriate response to a lifestyle exposure: eat food without examining it or asking parents if it's okay to eat; sit directly on the toilet seat; wash hands for only 20 seconds and not in an exact way; permit peers to touch belongings, or share belongings with peers. Last, direct youth to list new obsessions, compulsions, or triggers on this form. Then, direct the youth to write the successful completion of these spontaneous lifestyle ERP tasks on a form and bring this form to follow-up meetings with the clinician. The clinician can download a blank copy of this form (http://pubs.apa.org/books/supp/tompkins, Web Form 8.3) to use when developing lifestyle ERP tasks. The clinician may wish to assist youth to develop imaginal exposures to these lifestyle practice opportunities and practice in session to establish that the youth is responding appropriately to the obsessions and distress triggered through the imaginal exposure.

CONCLUSION

Graded exposure with response prevention is the critical core strategy in CBT for pediatric OCD. The effectiveness of the treatment rests on the ability of clinicians to implement effectively a variety of exposure and response prevention strategies. Furthermore, in order for youth to benefit fully from ERP and to generalize treatment gains to the world in which youth live, they must practice ERP tasks consistently and correctly in sessions with the clinician and between sessions with parent support.

In the next chapter, we describe step-by-step guidelines for developing and implementing a relapse prevention plan with youth and parents. Pediatric OCD is a chronic condition, and teaching youth and parents to anticipate and manage the breakthrough of symptoms following treatment prevents the reemergence of the condition. A comprehensive and thoughtful relapse prevention plan adds to the durability of the treatment and to the confidence of youth and parents that they have the tools to manage the ups and downs of the condition over time.

Developing and Implementing a Relapse Prevention Plan

Gemma is thrilled that she is in charge of her land again. However, her recovery from obsessive–compulsive disorder (OCD) has not been easy. It took 6 months for 6-year-old Gemma and her parents to push Bossy-Face off her land, and there were many ups and downs, tears, and tantrums. It's understandable that Gemma and her parents do not want to think that Bossy-Face might return. Yet, as Gemma's clinician explains to them, although Bossy-Face is much weaker than he was when they first began to meet, he's still very tricky, and it's essential that Gemma and her parents watch for any sign that Bossy-Face is plotting a comeback. "It's very important," the clinician says, "that Bossy-Face knows that we're watching for him and that you and your mom and dad know what to do the moment he tries to steal back some of your land."

OCD is a chronic condition, and although the risk of relapse for youth who successfully complete cognitive behavior therapy (CBT) for their OCD is low, it is not zero (Mancebo et al., 2014). Therefore, it's essential that clinicians develop a plan to minimize the likelihood of relapse of the condition as they begin the process of ending formal treatment. Relapse prevention includes a series of strategies that help youth and parents anticipate the reemergence of OCD symptoms and implement a plan to manage breakthrough symptoms to avoid the return of the condition. In this chapter, we present step-by-step guidelines for developing and implementing a relapse prevention plan with youth and parents.

http://dx.doi.org/10.1037/0000167-010
Cognitive Behavior Therapy for OCD in Youth: A Step-by-Step Guide, by M. A. Tompkins, D. J. Owen, N. H. Shiloff, and L. R. Tanner

INTRODUCE TERMINATION AND REVIEW TREATMENT PROGRESS

The first step in relapse prevention is to introduce the idea of ending treatment as part of the discussion of treatment gains and progress toward treatment goals. Over the course of treatment, the clinician has periodically reviewed treatment progress using several measures, as described in Chapter 4, this volume. We recommend that clinicians graph these measures over the course of treatment and review these measures with youth and parents. The graph provides a clear and compelling rationale for the discussion of termination (see Figure 9.1).

In Jack's case, the decrease in both Jack's depressive (Beck Depression Inventory; A. T. Beck, Ward, Mendelson, Mock, & Erbaugh, 1961) and OCD symptoms (Children's Florida Obsessive-Compulsive Inventory; Storch et al., 2009) demonstrate that he benefited from treatment and it is time to terminate. In cases in which the data show little progress or stalled progress, the graph can set the stage for discussions with youth and parents about changing the current treatment plan (see Chapter 4).

In addition, we recommend that clinicians review the domains with youth and parents in which OCD symptoms were reported as most disruptive (e.g., home, school, social situations) and solicit specific examples of progress (e.g., "The last time we met with Joey's teacher, she said that he wasn't getting up during class to go wash his hands. She also said that he seems more focused on his work and happier").

Typically, youth and parents are thrilled that they have progressed enough to end treatment. However, some youth and parents are surprisingly reluctant to terminate. There are many reasons for this. Some parents worry that the youth will relapse without ongoing treatment and assistance from the clinician. Parents who have suffered many years with the day-to-day stress of parenting a child with OCD may worry that they do not have the resources or the skills to handle their child's OCD without ongoing assistance from the clinician. Other parents are often pleased with the improvement in their relationship with each other over the course of treatment and worry that their relationship will worsen again if they discontinue treatment of their child's OCD.

At times, the youth and a parents may introduce other problems (e.g., marital difficulties, a parent's substance use, the youth's social anxiety) and want to continue treatment to resolve these problems. Therefore, it is important that the clinician begin the discussion of treatment termination by soliciting the concerns of the youth and parents about the timing and process of termination itself. The clinician may wish to do this first with the youth alone and then with the parents alone so that each feels free to discuss their concerns without fear of undermining the youth's accomplishments. Alternatively, the clinician may wish to give the youth and parents the option of discussing these concerns separately or as a family.

The answers youth and parents give to the clinician's questions determine when and how to proceed with termination. For example, if the family

FIGURE 9.1. Jack's Treatment Progress

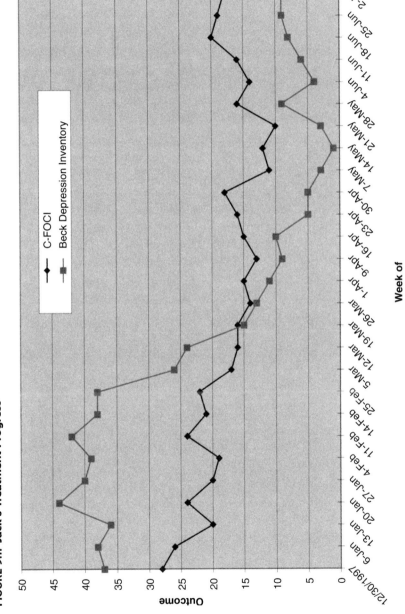

C-FOCI = Children's Florida Obsessive-Compulsive Inventory.

introduces new problems, the clinician may wish to graduate youth to celebrate the resolution of their OCD and mark the close of this treatment and then refocus treatment on the new problem.

INTRODUCE THE RELAPSE PREVENTION PLAN

Introducing the relapse prevention plan as a gradual and collaboratively planned process reassures many youth and parents regarding termination of treatment. Termination and relapse prevention plans include tapering meetings over time by extending the time between sessions, scheduling follow-up sessions, and offering booster sessions if required. In fact, the relapse prevention plan builds the confidence of youth and parents that they now have the skills and knowledge to manage OCD over time. Clinicians may wish to introduce termination and relapse prevention to young children in this way:

> Congratulations, Gemma! You've run Bossy-Face off your land, and now you're free from that big bad bully. You've worked very hard, and you've shown that you're very brave. You bossed back the big bad bully and have taken back all your land. Now I think it's time for you to defend your land on your own. That doesn't mean I and your mom and dad won't be here to help you if you want it, and we won't stop meeting right away. But I think it's time to make a plan that will help build your confidence that you have all the smarts, all the courage, and all the know-how to defend your land yourself. How does that sound?
>
> Of course, keeping the big-bad-bully off your land is important, but there's so much more to life than just being free from that bully. Often, kids have been bugged by the OCD bully for years, and because of that, they've missed out on some things. Either they didn't have the time to do fun things because the OCD bully took so much of their time or they were exhausted fighting the bully and didn't have the energy or desire to do more than just get through the day. So your plan will include two things: steps to keep the big bad bully out of your life and steps to help you get the most out of life now and in the future. What do you think?

For older youth, clinicians may wish to introduce termination and relapse prevention in this way:

> You know, Jacob, we've been working together for several months now. It's been quite a trip, hasn't it? It's like we've been pilot and copilot flying our plane through ups and downs, twists and turns, but always with the same destination in mind: to free you from OCD. I've been the pilot for most of the trip, but now it's time for you to take charge and slide over into the pilot's seat. From here on out, you're flying solo. That doesn't mean you can't call air traffic control for some help. You can certainly call me if you hit a bit of turbulence, but it's important that you show yourself and your parents that you can fly this plane all by yourself. We'll meet a little less often over the next few months. Perhaps we'll meet every other week at first, or whatever you, I, and your parents agree makes sense. These are short trips to build your confidence as the pilot, not too far away from air traffic control, but far enough away to give you a chance to fly the plane on your own. After a while, though, you'll be ready to fly cross-country. How does that sound?

In a minute, we'll work together to develop a Flight Plan for you. Now, every flight has some turbulence, so the Flight Plan will include the strategies that have helped the most in pushing OCD out of your life. Of course, keeping OCD out of your life is important, but there's so much more to life than just being free from OCD. Often, teens have been bugged by OCD for years, and because of that, they've missed out on some things. Either they didn't have the time to do fun things because OCD took so much of their time or they were exhausted fighting OCD and didn't have the energy or desire to do more than just get through the day. So, your Flight Plan will include two things: directions to keep OCD out of your life and directions to help you get the most out of life now and in the future. That's your Flight Plan. What do you think?

EDUCATE YOUTH AND PARENTS ABOUT RELAPSE

The first step in relapse prevention is to educate youth and parents about the difference between relapse and lapse. A lapse or slip is a brief return of OCD symptoms. The youth may begin to wash his hands a bit more or seek a bit more reassurance from parents or teachers. Lapses are common in chronic conditions such as OCD, particularly when youth are stressed or when they are ill or fatigued. A relapse, on the other hand, is a complete return of the disorder. Clinicians might explain to the parents the difference between *lapse* and *relapse* in this way:

> Remember in one of our first meetings when I explained what OCD was and what mental health professionals mean when we use the term *disorder*? The D in OCD just means that the O and the C are so severe that they've created a great deal of distress and disruption in your child's and your lives. The goal of treatment then was to decrease the O and the C until the D disappears. Well, with your help and support, your son's O and C are low now and the D has disappeared. That doesn't mean that the O and the C are completely gone. Every kid at the end of treatment has a little O and a little C and—you know what?—it's fine to have a little O and C. Kids can be successful and happy with a little O and C.
>
> Sometimes, when kids are stressed, or tired, or when they're sick, the O and C may increase a little. We call this a *lapse*. That's fine so long as you and your son continue to do the things you learned in treatment that decrease the OCD symptoms. However, if your son returns to his old ways of thinking and acting, such as more handwashing, and doesn't resist these compulsions the way he learned to do in therapy, then he might *relapse*. Relapse is a complete return of the D. Similarly, if you begin to accommodate or reassure him again, the way you did before treatment, the O and C symptoms will increase and the D might reappear. However, lapses don't have to lead to relapses if you have a plan to prevent this and you follow it.

In the meeting with the youth, the clinician might explain lapse and relapse in this way:

> Joey, in a minute we're going to put together your Flight Plan, but before we do that, I want to explain to you the difference between what we call a *lapse* and what we call a *relapse*. A lapse is like a slip. That's when Voldemort slips past both you and your parents and tries to make a comeback. He's sneaking around, but he hasn't taken back any of your land yet. He's looking for an opportunity to

trick you into doing the things that made him strong before. Relapse happens when Voldemort tricks you into doing the things that made him strong before you bossed him off your land. Do you remember some of the things Voldemort made you do that made him strong enough to take over your land?

DEVELOP A RELAPSE PREVENTION PLAN

The lower relapse rates of CBT versus pharmacotherapy may result from the youth's internalization of not only the ERP strategies that youth and parents learned but, perhaps more important, the attitude they developed toward anxiety, fear, and discomfort (i.e., an attitude of approaching and interacting with fear or discomfort, rather than escaping and avoiding fear or discomfort). The goal of relapse prevention is to reinforce the attitude and tasks of the treatment as well as to build the confidence of youth and parents so they can successfully manage OCD symptoms in the absence of the clinician's direct guidance and instruction. We develop relapse prevention plans for the youth and for the parents. We refer to these relapse prevention plans as Flight Plans. Clinicians can download blank Flight Plan forms (see http://pubs.apa.org/books/supp/tompkins, Web Forms 9.1 and 9.2) to use when developing relapse prevention plans with youth and parents. The process of developing a relapse prevention plan includes several steps.

Identify Early Warning Signs of a Lapse

Educating youth and parents regarding relapse versus lapse reassures the family that slips or lapses are not failures but a natural feature of any chronic mental health condition. The clinician also signals that there is always a risk of relapse no matter how effective the treatment has been. This becomes the rationale for the importance of developing and practicing a relapse prevention plan. In the meeting with youth and parents, clinicians might solicit signs of a lapse in this way:

CLINICIAN: Joey, I'd like us to list all the signs—little ones and big ones—that Voldemort is lurking around your land. The signs that he's lurking are the things he tricked you into doing that made him strong and helped him take so much of your land. Do you remember any of those things?

JOEY: Yeah. He made me wash my hands a lot even when I didn't want to. He made me take long showers too. He was really mean.

CLINICIAN: Yes, he was really mean to you, Joey. What else did he make you do that kept him strong and in charge of your land?

JOEY: Well, he made me stop touching things, like my backpack or my schoolbooks. I couldn't do my homework because I couldn't touch my school stuff. That really made me mad. I like school.

CLINICIAN: Yes, I know you love school, and Voldemort made it really hard for you to keep up with your schoolwork. Anything else?

JOEY: I can't think of anything else.

MOTHER: Is it okay if I add something? I remember how Voldemort made you come to me for reassurance. Do you remember that?

JOEY (to clinician): Oh, yeah. I remember now. He made me go to my mom all the time and ask her if I was going to die or get sick. If she didn't tell me, I'd get really mad at her. I feel bad about that.

MOTHER: Oh, that's okay, honey. That was the mean old Voldemort. I understand you didn't want to do that.

CLINICIAN: Joey, that was Voldemort at his worst. Anything else?

JOEY: I can't think of anything else.

CLINICIAN: Nice work, Joey. So, there are a couple of signs that OCD is trying to make a comeback: more handwashing, more showers, more seeking reassurance from your mom, and more avoiding touching things. In a minute we're going to add those things to your Flight Plan. Those are the things to watch for because those are the signs that Voldemort is trying to make a comeback. You'll want to watch for those things, and your mom and dad will too. We don't want Voldemort to come back. Let's write these in the Signs OCD is Trying to Make a Comeback part of your Flight Plan. Okay?

Develop Guidelines for Normal Living

For some youth, it may help to include response prevention guidelines in the "to stay in shape, I will . . ." section of their Flight Plan. For example, youth with health and disease obsessions can benefit from Guidelines for Normal Health Diligence. These guidelines list normal health practices or routines, such as attending a yearly physical, waiting a reasonable time before calling the advice nurse, or restricting Internet research regarding symptoms. Similarly, youth with contamination obsessions and washing compulsions might benefit from Guidelines for Living in a Contaminated World. These guidelines list restrictions on washing and cleaning behaviors, such as washing hands for only 20 seconds after toilet use. Again, these guidelines are primarily response prevention guidelines with which the youth and parents are already familiar because they have practiced adhering to the guidelines over the course of treatment.

Review Values-Driven Smart Attitude Self-Talk

We recommend that clinicians review with youth and parents the values-driven smart attitude self-talk youth used to motivate themselves to engage in ERP tasks. Remind youth that the values-driven smart attitude they practiced over the course of treatment is the reason, in large measure, they overcame their fears. Include in the youth's Flight Plan the most helpful smart attitude self-talk, and practice these again with youth and parents.

Identify Appropriate Responses to Triggers

We recommend that clinicians review with parents and youth the appropriate responses to triggers. For example, clinicians may wish to review with youth and parents the statements parents used to respond to the youth's symptoms during treatment. Perhaps the clinician taught the youth to alert the parents of urges to engage in compulsions: "Voldemort is telling me I have to wash my hands." Parents learned to respond: "That's Voldemort alright. I'm your mom, and I say let's go put a puzzle together while we wait for Voldemort to get bored and go away." We recommend that clinicians check with parents whether they use other strategies when youth alert them regarding OCD symptoms and then identify whether these strategies are adaptive or maladaptive responses. If maladaptive, clinicians explain why, and they ask parents to use the adaptive strategies that the clinician taught them during treatment.

Last, we recommend that clinicians ask youth to identify the strategies that are the most helpful to them and explain why, as well as solicit from youth the unhelpful strategies they used in the past and why they were unhelpful. Furthermore, clinicians may want to check with youth whether they use any maladaptive strategies from the past or new ones the clinician has not identified. We recommend that clinicians also review two other responses that youth and parents learned during treatment: do-overs and regaining ground (see Chapter 8).

Practice Appropriate Response to Trigger in Imagination

Youth benefit from symbolic rehearsal of desired responses to trigger situations (Bandura, 1977). Symbolic rehearsal enables youth to practice an appropriate response repeatedly to build confidence in their ability to initiate the response, particularly when anxious or distressed.

In symbolic rehearsal, the youth imagines several typical trigger situations and imagines the appropriate response learned in treatment. Often, the appropriate response is to resist the urge to engage in a compulsion or to step toward the feared object or situation. Through symbolic rehearsal, the youth also rehearses other features of the adaptive response, such as subvocalizing the values-driven smart attitude self-talk (e.g., "In order to have more friends and fun, I accept that I cannot be certain that my hands are clean or dirty, and I choose not to wash them"). We recommend that clinicians ask youth to rate their confidence level (0% to 100%) before and after symbolic rehearsal. Because the goal of symbolic rehearsal is to increase the confidence of youth that they can respond appropriately to a trigger situation, even when anxious, it is important that clinicians monitor the increase in their confidence level throughout this process.

Record Unplanned Acts of Bravery

In addition to youth and parents following the practice plan, we recommend that youth and parents record unplanned acts of bravery. This strategy enhances a self-management attitude for youth. Clinicians encourage youth to scan their environments for opportunities to approach a feared object, situation, or activity and thereby face uncertainty. Youth record these unplanned acts of bravery for which they receive rewards (including praise from parents) using the reward system developed during treatment. During relapse prevention or booster sessions, clinicians review with youth the list of unplanned acts of bravery and, of course, praise the youth with unbounded enthusiasm.

Record Public Service Announcement

A public service announcement is a fun and effective strategy that youth internalize the skills and attitude necessary to maintain their recovery (Kendall, Chu, Gifford, Hayes, & Nauta, 1998). The clinician asks the youth to record a public service announcement for kids with OCD. While the clinician records, the youth recalls and describes his or her particular OCD symptoms, examples of ways the OCD disrupted the youth's life, and the strategies and ideas the youth learned and used to recover from OCD. These public service announcements are fun and very compelling. Most youth are eager to send a message of hope to other kids. Once the youth records the public service announcement, the youth and clinician develop a list of people to whom the youth wishes to show it. Some youth and parents have organized congratulation parties around the public service announcement. One family invited special friends and family members to a premier of this special movie of success.

MANAGE BOOSTER SESSIONS AND MEDICATION TAPER

Booster sessions are an important part of the relapse prevention process and follow the structure of treatment sessions. The clinician begins the session by soliciting from the youth (and parents) specific examples of the successful application of the strategies learned in treatment, particularly examples of the youth approaching and remaining in situations when anxious.

Clinicians then question the youth and parents regarding an increase in particular symptoms, new symptoms, and whether the youth and family are experiencing or anticipating new stressors. Clinicians then review each strategy or tool and solicit from the youth specific examples of her or his successful application of specific tools, such as resisting compulsions or spontaneous self-initiated exposures. We recommend during booster sessions that clinicians also repeat with the youth the most important imaginal exposures from their imaginal exposure catalog or practice an important situational exposure in session.

Last, clinicians may wish to schedule telephone check-ins between booster sessions, particularly if the youth and parents are struggling to manage the relapse prevention plan between meetings. Telephone check-ins are typically brief and focused on coaching youth and parents to follow the features in their respective Flight Plans. If the clinician observes that a family is having persistent difficulties following the relapse prevention plan, we recommend that clinicians schedule more frequent booster sessions.

For youth who participated in both CBT and pharmacotherapy, clinicians may want to discuss when and how to taper medications. Refer to Chapter 11 for suggestions to collaborate effectively with prescribers when organizing a medication taper. Regardless of whether or not youth and parents plan to taper or discontinue medications, it is important that clinicians emphasize to youth and parents that the youth is primarily responsible for decreasing OCD symptoms and that medication merely helped. In order to decrease the likelihood of relapse during a medication taper, it is essential that youth attribute a successful treatment outcome to their efforts and to the skills that they learned and practiced rather than to the medication. The clinician might convey that information in this way:

> You know some kids used water wings or floaties when they were learning to swim. The floaties just kept their heads above the water, but if they wanted to swim across the pool, they kicked their feet and flapped their arms and swam across the pool themselves. Medicine is a little like a floatie. It helped keep your head above the water when you were battling the OCD bully, but it didn't win back your land. You did that. How do I know that? Because when we first started working together, you were already taking some medicine, and the OCD bully was still in charge of your land. The doctor who prescribed medicine to weaken the OCD bully didn't change the medicine at all over the last few months, and now you have back all your land. Although the medicine helped, it didn't get you to where you are today. You did!

Last, we recommend that clinicians remind parents to contact the clinician if the prescriber plans to taper medications and to schedule additional booster sessions during the taper. These booster sessions can help youth and parents use the ERP strategies learned in CBT to manage the breakthrough of OCD symptoms as the prescriber gradually withdraws medication.

IDENTIFY ANTICIPATED AND UNANTICIPATED STRESSORS AND DEVELOP SKILLS TO MANAGE

For certain youth, it is not sufficient to treat only OCD. Some youth lack particular skills to manage the problems that may arise following termination of treatment. For these youth, it is important not only to identify anticipated and unanticipated stressors but also to teach youth the skills necessary to manage these problems if and when they arise.

A description of all the skills and how to teach them is beyond the scope of this book. However, we recommend that clinicians teach youth particular stress management strategies that will help them manage the academic or social stress that accompanies other conditions, such as attention-deficit/hyperactivity disorder (ADHD), specific learning disabilities, or autism spectrum disorders. Typical skills include problem solving, or responding to peer provocation, assertiveness, and effective communication. These and other skills may help youth who struggle with anger or depression as well.

In addition, we encourage clinicians to urge parents to schedule booster sessions to help the family manage stress during predictable transitions, such as when the youth transitions from middle school to high school, or to unexpected changes in life of youth, such as a best friend moving out of town, or unexpected family stressors, such as the death of a grandmother, or a parent losing a job.

SCHEDULE FUN AND PROUD ACTIVITIES TO PROTECT TIME

For many youth, OCD has consumed hours each day and restricted many daily activities of youth and their parents. For example, youth with contamination obsessions and washing compulsions might spend many hours each day washing their hands or taking very long showers. The parents of a child who engages in long showers and handwashing compulsions late into the evening likely stay awake too, trying to limit the compulsive cleaning and washing. Youth may avoid attending school, soccer, or even parties because they are afraid that these activities or events may trigger their OCD. In an effort to manage their child's OCD, parents may limit their own activities, doing only what is necessary, such as going to work or grocery shopping. Soon the lives of youth and parents shrink with few fun or productive activities.

Once youth begin to regain time, it is essential that youth and parents work to fill this time with productive and rewarding activities. Free time leaves room for obsessions and compulsions to return. The clinician might introduce the rationale for scheduling fun and productive activities in this way:

> Bossy-Face took a lot away from you, and you've worked very hard to win back your land from him. When Bossy-Face was in charge, there just wasn't any room in your land for activities that were fun or that made you feel proud. Now that you have your land again, it's important to protect that land from Bossy-Face. Bossy-Face loves empty land because that's usually how he sneaks back into your life. I'd like to start planning more fun and proud activities for you and your family. Let's fill your land with some fun. How does that sound?

For youth and parents who in the past lived busy lives filled with fun and meaningful activities, this is a straightforward task. For youth and parents who primarily filled their lives with work or school and engaged in few fun activities, this can be more complicated. There are likely reasons that the youth (and parents) did so little before the onset of OCD. Perhaps the youth has social anxiety also and this anxiety disorder caused the youth to avoid activities with others or performance-related activities, such as sports or chorus. Perhaps the youth has another co-occurring condition, such as autism spectrum disorder, and engaged in a very few interests beyond the youth's specific and limited interests prior to the onset of OCD. Regardless of the reason, it is important that clinicians work to build more fun and proud activities into the youth's life and into the lives of parents as well.

Activity scheduling includes two general steps: identify fun (pleasant) and proud (mastery) activities, and then schedule these activities each week. Clinicians meet with youth and parents and solicit fun and proud activities youth engaged in prior to the onset or worsening of OCD symptoms, such as playing a board game, walking the dog, or listening to music. Clinicians may wish to show youth and parents a list of typical pleasant activities. For a list of typical pleasant activities for youth, see Creed, Reisweber, and Beck (2011, Appendix 4.1, p. 156). Once youth have identified fun and proud activities, clinicians then schedule these activities using the Activity Scheduling Form (see http://pubs.apa.org/books/supp/tompkins, Web Form 9.3). Typically, clinicians ask youth to rate the level of fun or proud feeling next to each activity. In addition, clinicians may wish to encourage youth to add and rate fun and proud activities as they discover them.

GRADUATION

We recommend a formal graduation ceremony for several reasons. First, it marks the end of formal treatment and the start of the maintenance phase of treatment that includes relapse prevention, and a graduation ceremony is a great way to introduce relapse prevention. We have found that clearly marking these distinct phases clarifies the goals of relapse prevention and sets the stage for the role of booster sessions as part of the maintenance phase.

Second, prior to treatment, youth with OCD often felt great shame regarding their thoughts and embarrassed because they were not able to resist or hide their compulsions. Not only is a graduation ceremony for youth a public statement of their success and renewed self-confidence, but it normalizes in a formal manner both the condition and how youth go about managing it.

Third, a graduation ceremony is fun. It's fun for the youth, for the parents, and for the clinician. The graduation ceremony includes three features: brag session, graduation ceremony, and notifications.

Brag Session

The clinician meets with youth and parents and organizes a discussion of the youth's accomplishments over the course of treatment. The clinician begins the brag session, then asks the parents to share, and finishes with the youth:

> Well, Joey, it's time to celebrate your success, and there's a lot of success to celebrate. I'm going to start off the brag session, if that's okay with you. Then

we'll hear from your mom and dad. I know they'll want to brag a bit about you. Then, we'll hear from you. It's okay to brag about yourself. You've worked very hard to push Voldemort off your land, and that's a big deal. You've earned the right to brag about yourself to us.

During the brag session, the clinician begins the process and praises the youth. We recommend that clinicians offer specific examples of the youth's courage and perseverance throughout treatment. Also, if the clinician and youth completed Map of My Land forms over the course of treatment, the clinician may wish to review all the Map of My Land forms with the youth during the termination process to demonstrate the youth's progress; for example:

> I remember when we first started meeting, Joey. Voldemort had beat you down pretty bad. He was in charge of a lot of your land. See how much of your land he owned when we first met. And you were feeling very scared and had big doubts about whether you could win the war against Voldemort. But you didn't give up. I've helped a lot of kids over the years, and you're one of the bravest I've ever met. Remember when you started to cry when we licked lollipops that we had wiped across the floor? But you did it, Joey. This is the Map of My Land form you completed after that exposure. You can see that exposure helped you win back a lot of your land. When you did that exposure, I knew right then that Voldemort didn't have a chance. I'm very, very proud of you Joey. Now, Mom and Dad, I bet you want to brag about this terrific son of yours.

After the parents have bragged about the youth, the clinician encourages the youth to brag about what he or she accomplished through the treatment process. For young youth, they might brag about the land they recaptured from OCD and how they accomplished this.

Not all youth are comfortable bragging about themselves. We recommend that the clinician encourage youth to say at least one great thing about themselves and what they accomplished but not push them to say more if they are not comfortable doing this.

Graduation Ceremony

Now for the fun part: the graduation ceremony. Following the brag session, the youth puts on a black mortarboard and gown furnished by the clinician. The clinician, youth, and parents then stand while the clinician plays a recording of Edward Elgar's "Pomp and Circumstance." When the music ends, the clinician reads the diploma and gives the diploma to the youth. Clinicians can download a Graduation Diploma form (see http://pubs.apa.org/books/supp/tompkins, Web Form 9.4) to complete and include in the graduation ceremony. Last, the clinician gives a brief speech:

> Joey, in recognition of your courage and hard work, I'm honored to give you this graduation diploma. I've signed it, and your mom and dad will sign it too. I hope you will show this diploma to your grandmother or to your cousins, perhaps even to your teacher or your best friend. In fact, I hope you'll show it to anyone you want, because it's important that your friends and family know what you've accomplished. Congratulations, Joey! You are an amazing kid.

The clinician then poses for photos with youth (if they want to do this) and shares cookies or other treats with the entire family. We recommend that clinicians also take this opportunity to normalize the return to treatment and booster sessions. Some youth with OCD may feel embarrassed or ashamed about returning to therapy following a relapse or even for booster sessions. They may think that returning to treatment means that they have failed, so we recommend that clinicians anticipate and normalize this for youth and parents; for example:

> Joey, one of the cool things about being a kid is that you'll have many graduations over the years. You'll graduate from middle school and then high school, and then college, and if you go to graduate school or medical school or law school, you'll have a graduation then too. That's the way I think about therapy too. You've had this graduation, but one day Voldemort might capture a bit of your land again. You might want to come back for a few meetings with me. If that happens, it's okay. We'll just run him off your land again, and you get to have another graduation. I've graduated some kids more than once, and it's always been great.

Notifications

The graduation ceremony is a great time to discuss with youth and parents the value of notifications. It's important that youth correct the views many family members and friends have developed about youth because of their OCD. Teachers may have viewed the youth with OCD as being too fragile or weak to handle what other students handle and given the youth work that is too easy. Friends may have viewed the youth as weird or afraid and avoided the youth at school or declined playdates. Family members may have viewed the youth with OCD as less capable or as having a behavior problem. Notifications of success begin to correct these misperceptions so that others treat youth as the capable and courageous children that they are. Although youth and parents may not wish to share the news of their success, we recommend that clinicians encourage youth to tell at least one peer (e.g., a best friend) or a trusted adult (e.g., a grandmother).

Notifications can take many forms. Examples include showing photos of the youth with the graduation diploma to others, having congratulation parties at which youth shows the public service video they recorded, or writing a few sentences in the Victory Book (see Chapter 5) to other kids who come for help with OCD.

CONCLUSION

Relapse prevention is an important feature of CBT for OCD and adds to the durability of the treatment and the confidence of youth and parents that they have the skills necessary to carry them forward for years to come. An effective relapse prevention plan includes many features, several of them quite important. We encourage clinicians to resist rushing this important pro-cess to ensure that youth and parents have a relapse prevention plan that is workable and effective.

In the next chapter, we present several pediatric cases to demonstrate the process of gathering information, developing a case conceptualization, and implementing the core strategies of CBT for pediatric OCD. We strived to include cases that capture a range of developmental ages, co-occurring condi-tions, and degrees of youth and parent engagement.

PUTTING IT ALL TOGETHER

INTRODUCTION

In Part III, we begin with a description of the application of the core strategies to three cases of youth with obsessive–compulsive disorder (OCD; Chapter 10). We selected cases that covered three developmental age periods as well as different primary OCD symptoms and secondary factors, such as co-occurring conditions or different degrees of family accommodation and parent effectiveness. The cases are composites of youth and their families; they do not describe any particular youth or parent or their particular circumstances.

Next, we take up the topic of pharmacotherapy for pediatric OCD (Chapter 11). We begin with a brief review of typical medications for pediatric OCD and offer guidelines and suggestions for introducing the topic of pharmacotherapy to youth and parents, incorporating pharmacotherapy into cognitive behavior therapy (CBT) with youth, and collaborating with prescribers who are tapering up or down or discontinuing medications for youth with OCD. In the final chapter (Chapter 12), we describe typical obstacles that arise when implementing the core strategies of CBT for pediatric OCD and suggest modifications of the core strategies to overcome these obstacles.

10

Structuring the Treatment

RENEE

Renee is a 4 1/2-year-old girl who lives with her mother, Liz, and her 6-year-old sister, Lisa. Renee's biological father ended the relationship with Renee's mother when he discovered she was pregnant with Renee. Renee has never met or spoken with her father. Renee is slow to warm to adults but is friendly and talkative during playdates with neighborhood children. Liz is a thoughtful, caring mother, but she is overwhelmed by the demands of raising two young children on her own. Liz brought Renee to therapy after her pediatrician insisted that Renee meet with a clinician to help Renee overcome her fear of eating.

Gathering Information

The clinician first met with Renee's mother, Liz, alone following Renee's discharge from the hospital. At the initial meeting, Liz reported that Renee had always been a picky eater, but her refusal to eat had both frightened and puzzled Liz. She also reported that Renee had always been "very clean and tidy," but her preoccupation with germs and cleanliness increased after a preschool teacher read a book to her class about little germ monsters on food. At about this time, Renee started to wash her hands multiple times before eating, examining carefully all of her food prior to eating it, and asking her mother to reassure her that the food was clean. In the weeks leading up to the hospitalization, Liz reported that her reassurances no longer calmed Renee,

http://dx.doi.org/10.1037/0000167-011
Cognitive Behavior Therapy for OCD in Youth: A Step-by-Step Guide, by M. A. Tompkins,
D. J. Owen, N. H. Shiloff, and L. R. Tanner

and soon after, Renee's handwashing became ritualized. She washed exactly the same way every time and started over if she felt she had not washed enough or correctly. Within days of these behaviors, Renee stopped eating altogether for 3 days at which time Renee's pediatrician hospitalized her. After discharge, Renee was eating, but she continued to wash her hands before meals repeatedly, ate only food from home, and continued to seek her mother's reassurance about germs.

Because of Renee's age, the clinician asked Renee's mother to complete the Family Accommodation Scale (Pinto, Van Noppen, & Calvocoressi, 2013), the OCD Disturbance Scale (Geffken et al., 2005), and the Child Obsessive-Compulsive Impact Scale (Piacentini & Jaffer, 1999). These measures indicated that Renee's washing and reassurance-seeking behaviors caused significant interference at home and school. Furthermore, Liz engaged in numerous accommodation behaviors, primarily reassuring her daughter, but also washing food carefully for Renee and permitting Renee to avoid any activity that appeared to make her more anxious. The clinician also administered the Children's Yale–Brown Obsessive Compulsive Scale (CY-BOCS; Scahill et al., 1997) to Renee's mother and identified several other obsessions, such as the need for exactness, and minor collecting and checking behaviors. Obsessions regarding health and germs were the most significant, however, along with washing and cleaning compulsions.

For the second assessment session, the clinician met with Renee and her mother together. The clinician used the session to determine the extent to which Renee could and would participate in therapy sessions and the extent to which she would require Renee's mother's participation in the exposure and response prevention (ERP) tasks. Although Renee was very shy, she did tell the clinician that she was afraid to eat dirty food but could not identify the feared consequence other than feeling sick. To assess Renee's avoidance behaviors, the clinician invited Renee to play with plastic food and dishes. During the play, the clinician commented that some of the food looked dirty. Renee agreed and pointed to the "dirty" food and directed her mother or the clinician to move the food off the plate. When the clinician pretended to eat the "dirty" food, Renee gasped and looked away.

Developing the Case Conceptualization and Treatment Plan

Because of Renee's age, the clinician developed the case conceptualization and treatment plan with Liz only. The clinician reviewed with Liz the completed CY-BOCS and asked for examples of Renee's current neutralizations (washing compulsions and reassurance seeking) and the objects, situations, and activities that Renee repeatedly avoided when at school, at home, and when visiting with friends and family members. The clinician asked Liz to identify Renee's level of distress at high, medium, and low levels for the specific situations, and he underscored the importance of identifying low-level anxiety-evoking situations. With Liz, the clinician developed Renee's general exposure hierarchy (see Figure 10.1). The clinician recommended beginning

FIGURE 10.1. Renee's General Exposure Hierarchy

	Exposure Item From Hierarchy	SUD (0–100)
1.	Use only a wipe (no soap and water) before dinner.	45
2.	Use only water to wash hands.	50
3.	Don't wash hands before dessert.	55
4.	Eat snack without washing hands.	60
5.	Eat food off the table.	65
6.	Use fork after it falls on the floor.	70
7.	Rub hands on table, and then eat something.	75
8.	Wash hands for only 3 seconds.	80
9.	Eat without washing hands.	85
10.	Drink from mother's glass, or take a bite of mother's ice cream cone.	90
11.	Lick the kitchen table.	95
12.	Eat food off the floor.	100
13.		
14.		
15.		
16.		

SUD = subjective units of distress (0 = *low*; 100 = *high*).

the ERP process with low-level anxiety-provoking situations to familiarize Renee and Liz with the approach and to build Renee's confidence that she can tolerate her distress. In addition, Liz and the clinician speculated that Renee's feared consequence was that she believed that if she consumed dirty food she would become sick.

Next, the clinician and Liz focused on developing Renee's response prevention plan. Renee's primary contamination-related neutralizations included washing her hands before eating, checking her food for contaminants, and asking her mother for reassurance. Liz reported that Renee's handwashing interfered the most with her daily activities, so the clinician and Liz agreed to target washing compulsions first. The clinician asked Liz to observe Renee's washing compulsions over the next week, particularly the frequency and duration, as well as all steps and other behaviors, Renee exhibited when she washed her hands. The clinician also asked Liz to record the nature of any covert neutralizations, such as counting, checking, or holding a neutralizing thought or image in her mind. To do this, the clinician recommended that Liz matter-of-factly ask Renee, "What just happened?" when Liz observed Renee stop and restart washing her hands.

Once the clinician had a detailed functional understanding of the washing ritual, they developed a response prevention plan that listed the steps of the washing ritual that Renee would stop and the order in which she would stop them. The clinician did not develop a response prevention plan for Renee's checking neutralizations. The clinician reasoned, and shared with Liz, that these behaviors would likely naturally decrease as Renee progressed through the ERP tasks for the washing neutralizations. The clinician then compiled the neutralization targets into a response prevention hierarchy (see Figure 10.2).

Engaging Youth and Parents in the Treatment Approach

The clinician developed a reinforcement system to engage Renee in the treatment process. The clinician suggested stickers as tokens for adherence with ERP practice and recommended a simple three-column sticker chart. Renee was to place a sticker in the STUC (Show-That-You-Can) column immediately after she completed the ERP task (i.e., shortened or eliminated the hand-washing period). Renee also placed a sticker in the GUTI (Get-Used-To-It) column after she demonstrated that she had tolerated her anxiety for the period specified in the ERP task. Last, Renee placed a sticker in the IDIM (I-Did-It-Myself) column when she did more than what she, her mother, and the clinician planned for the week. These self-initiation ERP tasks encouraged Renee to cultivate an approach-rather-than avoid attitude that is critical for long-term management of OCD. Once Renee earned five or more stickers, Liz would arrange a playdate for Renee with one of her friends.

In addition, the clinician taught Liz to provide social reinforcement (praise and positive attention) to her daughter for initiation and completion of core strategies, such as ERP. When Renee agreed to begin her GUTI practice, Liz rewarded her with big smiles and verbal praise: "I love that you want to boss back that mean old worry bully. Great job!" After Renee completed the ERP task, Liz played any game Renee chose for 10 to 15 minutes. If Renee refused to practice, Liz responded in a calm and matter-of-fact manner: "Okay. Let me know when you're ready to do your GUTI practice. Remember, you can earn another sticker if you decide to do the GUTI." Liz would then go about her business and give Renee as little attention as possible for at least 30 minutes.

Psychoeducation With Youth and Parents

The clinician took great care to explain to Liz the role of ERP in the treatment of OCD and to answer her questions. Liz was open to most of the suggested ERP tasks the clinician proposed. However, Liz balked when the clinician suggested that more difficult ERP tasks would include Renee and the clinician eating food that had fallen on the floor. When Liz asked the clinician whether

FIGURE 10.2. Renee's Response Prevention Hierarchy

Description of neutralization: Washing		
	Response prevention item	DTR (0–100)
1.		5
2.		10
3.		15
4.		20
5.		25
6.		30
7.		35
8.	Do not wash hands before going to bed.	40
9.		45
10.	Do not wash hands when entering house.	50
11.		55
12.	Do not wash hands before touching toys.	60
13.	Will not wash hands immediately when entering house from the outside.	65
14.		70
15.	Will wash hands once in 10 seconds before eating dry food.	75
16.	Do not wash hands and face after hugs and kisses from mother.	80
17.	Will wash hands once in 5 seconds before eating dry food.	85
18.	Will not wash hands before eating dry food.	90
19.	Will wash hands once in 5 seconds before eating wet food.	95
20.	Will not wash hands before eating wet food.	100

DTR = difficulty to resist (0 = *low*; 100 = *high*).

it was okay for children to eat food that had fallen on the floor, the clinician explained the importance of Renee becoming more comfortable with acceptable risks:

> When a typical kid, and I bet you've seen this, drops food on the floor, the kid picks it up and eats it. They only think about how yummy the food is. They aren't thinking about the dirt and possible germs that may be on the food. They just want to be a kid and eat yummy food. OCD has kept Renee from acting like

a typical kid. I know asking her to eat food that dropped on the floor sounds weird, but this is the best way to recalibrate her brain. Facing her germ fears will change her brain from functioning like an OCD brain to functioning like a typical kid brain again.

Liz agreed with the clinician's point. With Liz on board, the clinician met with Liz and Renee together to explain OCD to Renee and to help her give OCD a nickname (Worry Bully). The clinician then explained the rationale for ERP and for the Act Brave Ladder (i.e., exposure hierarchy) and that they would build the ladder together. Because of Renee's age, the clinician did not teach Renee cognitive resistance strategies, such as "bossing back talk." Instead, she taught this strategy to Liz and asked her to model the strategy during ERP practices. Although Renee periodically attended sessions with the clinician, the majority of the sessions were with Liz alone and focused on solving problems that arose during the implementation of ERP tasks at home with Renee. Liz developed into an excellent cotherapist.

Working With the Family

The clinician targeted a variety of Liz's accommodation behaviors. Renee was not required to eat the food that Liz prepared. Liz also routinely packed a special snack for Renee when she visited with friends rather than leaving her to eat what her friends ate during the playdate. Liz also gave Renee significant positive attention about her food fears. For example, to lessen Renee's anxiety about eating during playdates, Liz visited her daughter and ate a snack with her away from the other children.

The clinician explained to Liz the disadvantages of these accommodation behaviors and of her general parenting approach. Liz agreed to work with the clinician to decrease the accommodation behaviors and improve her effectiveness as a parent. For example, as Renee benefited from her ERP exercises, she began to eat different foods. The clinician then recommended that Liz stop bringing a special snack to the playdates for Renee to eat. Prior to Renee's next playdate, the clinician asked Liz to explain to Renee that if she refused to eat the snacks offered at the playdate, Liz would end the playdate and take Renee home. When Renee chose to return home to eat her snack, Liz did not give Renee positive attention and instead told Renee that she was going to clean the house and Renee would have to play by herself. Alternatively, when Renee chose to stay at the playdate and eat the snack provided by the host family, Liz arranged a playdate with Renee's favorite friend for the next day.

The clinician also worked with Liz to improve her communication skills with her daughter. Liz had a habit of asking rather than directing her daughter (e.g., "Would you please pick up your shoes?"). Not surprisingly, Renee often said "no." Similarly, Liz asked rather than directed Renee to start her ERP practice (e.g., "Are you ready to try your GUTI practice?"). Either Renee ignored the question and continued what she was doing or she began to cry and protest if Liz asked again. The clinician taught Liz to give Renee commands rather than requests and with a timeline (e.g., "Please start your GUTI practice now").

Although Liz was an excellent cotherapist, she would sometimes fail to follow through with the clinician's directions. At these times, the clinician scheduled additional sessions to provide Liz with additional support and to work through a particular obstacle in the treatment.

Implementing Graded Exposure and Response Prevention

The clinician implemented ERP tasks primarily through play, whimsy, and fun during sessions with Renee. For example, the clinician contaminated game pieces by rubbing them on the floor, and then they played the game with the "dirty" game pieces while they munched on snacks. Similarly, Renee and the clinician touched gummy bears on the floor and then ate them. Combining ERP with arts and crafts (always a favorite for children), the clinician and Renee made magic wands with cardboard tubes, colored construction paper, colored markers, and glitter. With their magic wands, they first touched the wand to dirt or other "dirty" surfaces and touched food they then ate together. Renee enjoyed being the "dirt fairy" and used the dirty magic wand in her ERP tasks at home.

The clinician found ways to make response prevention fun too. To increase Renee's willingness to resist washing compulsions and other neutralizations, the clinician reminded Renee of the name she had given the OCD: the worry bully. The clinician reminded Renee to resist her washing compulsions by ignoring the mean old worry bully, "The worry bully will try to scare you and make you wash your hands, but you don't have to listen to the worry bully. Tell the worry bull to get off your land!" The clinician coached Liz to encourage Renee and, of course, to praise and reward her using the reinforcement system that they had developed.

The clinician incorporated play into response prevention strategies to increase Renee's engagement in these tasks. For example, to decrease the duration and complexity of Renee's handwashing compulsions, Renee and her mother would have fast-handwashing races. Renee earned a sticker each time she finished washing her hands before her mother. Later, she earned stickers for beating her own best handwashing time. To decrease Renee's tendency to check her food carefully, Renee and the clinician made blindfolds from construction paper and string and decorated them with colored glitter. They then dropped candies on the floor and searched for them on their hands and knees. Each time Renee or the clinician found a candy, they ate it.

As the clinician predicted, Renee's germ-related washing compulsions decreased over the course of treatment. However, her reassurance-seeking behaviors continued. The clinician and Liz met and prepared to target these reassurance neutralizations. At the start of the next session with Liz and Renee, the clinician explained the function of reassurance seeking:

> Renee, you're doing great. Every day, you're getting stronger and the worry bully is getting weaker, but the worry bully is very tricky. He's tricked your mom into feeding him, and every time your mom feeds him, he gets a little stronger.

We don't want him to grow stronger. We want him to get weaker. Are you ready to stop feeding him?

Renee replied that she wanted her mom to stop feeding the worry bully. Liz, according to the plan, then asked the clinician, "But how do I stop feeding that mean old worry bully?" The clinician explained to Renee that every time she asked her mother to check or to wash her food or to tell her whether her food is okay to eat, and her mother did these things, she gave the worry bully a little snack. When Renee said that she did not like this, the clinician suggested that her mother respond in a different way. The clinician asked, "Renee, do you know the game I Spy With My Little Eye?" Renee said she did, and the clinician explained,

> Well, when your mom catches the worry bully bugging you, she'll say, "I spy with my little eye the worry bully" and she will then tell the worry bully, "Stop bugging my little girl, you mean old worry bully. Go away. I am not going to give you a snack. I am going to pretend that I didn't even hear you."

The clinician then suggested Liz and Renee do something fun while they "wait for the worry bully to go away." Renee agreed to this plan, and the clinician asked Renee and her mother to role-play the response. First, Liz played the worry bully, and the clinician modeled the response for Liz. Then Renee pretended to be the worry bully and asked her mother for reassurance, to which Liz responded in the new way. Once Renee seemed comfortable with the role-play, the clinician suggested that Renee and Liz divide the day in half and begin by practicing the new response to reassurance seeking in the morning and over the next week work to eliminate reassurance seeking for the entire day.

Developing and Implementing Relapse Prevention

Renee responded well to treatment, and within a few weeks her mother reported that her symptoms were much reduced. Renee had stopped washing her hands in a ritualized fashion and frequently skipped washing them all together. She no longer asked for reassurance about germs and ate what her mother prepared for her at preschool and at home. Near the end of treatment, Renee willingly engaged in dirty food play with the clinician and happily declared that all the food was dirty and that they were going to "feast on the dirty food."

In response to Renee's significant improvement, the clinician proposed they develop a relapse prevention plan and taper treatment sessions. The clinician proposed a relapse prevention plan that included fun GUTI practices, such as "camp at home days," in which the mother, Renee, and her sister ate only finger foods and would not wash their hands all day the way they would if they were really camping. The clinician and Liz identified signs of an OCD lapse or early warning signs, such as the reappearance of brief handwashes, reassurance seeking, and difficulties with bedtime routines and preschool drop-offs. The clinician also explained that the emergence of new OCD symptoms or subtypes was common as children matured, and he briefly described the subtypes of OCD and the manner each might appear as Renee grew from preschooler to high schooler.

Finally, the clinician explained to Liz the role of change and stress in the reemergence of OCD symptoms. They identified upcoming stressors (Renee beginning kindergarten, Liz taking a new job with a longer commute, a grandmother who is growing frail) and developed coping plans and work-arounds for these stressors. The clinician completed the relapse prevention phase by meeting with Liz and Renee together. With the clinician's help, they listed the tools Renee had used to run the worry bully off her land as well as the ways that the worry bully might try to trick her and take back some land in the future.

At the end of the session, the clinician recommended that Liz and Renee fly solo and return in 2 weeks for a check-in appointment. At this session, the clinician worked with Liz and Renee to develop a relapse prevention plan to help Renee maintain her treatment gains (see Figure 10.3). The clinician then proposed to graduate Renee at the next appointment. The clinician asked Renee to invite her sister and one or two friends, if she liked, to her gradua-tion. A few weeks later, Renee arrived with her sister and best friend. The clinician dressed Renee in a cap and gown, played pomp and circumstance, and ended the ceremony with a diploma and speeches from the clinician, her mother, her sister, and her best friend, all who attested to Renee's courage. At the end of the graduation ceremony, they all munched on "dirty" cookies.

COLE

Cole is a 9-year-old boy who lives with his mother and 5-year-old sister. Cole's parents recently divorced, and he and his sister travel back and forth between his parents' homes. His parents contacted the clinician because Cole had become increasingly anxious and was often up late at night arranging items in his room. He had started to miss school because he would not leave for school until everything in his room was just right. A few nights before the first meeting with the clinician, Cole insisted that his mother remain in his room while he repeatedly moved a family photo up and down. He repeated this behavior for over an hour while his mother watched and asked him to stop. Cole was in tears, sobbing and freaking out.

Gathering Information

The clinician first met with Cole's parents alone. They reported that over the past few months Cole had become more anxious about his room and "blew up" when anyone touched his possessions. His parents observed Cole order and reorder the objects on his desk and in his closet until they were in the correct spot and often refuse to begin his homework until everything was right. They had also noticed Cole repeatedly tied and retied his shoes, and

FIGURE 10.3. Renee's Relapse Prevention Plan

Early warning signs	Increase in reassurance-seeking
	Increase in quick handwashes or length of handwashes
	Wiping hands on clothes
	Refusing to eat certain foods
	Eating only parts of foods
	Asking about blemishes or spots on food
	An increase in anxiety at drop-off or when routines change
Encourage these skills	Do the opposite of what OCD tells you.
	Show that you can say no to OCD washing.
	Boss back OCD.
Remind her of what she has learned	"You don't get sick if I don't wash my hands before I tuck you into bed."
	"OCD is telling you that you'll get sick, but you know OCD is trying to trick you."
	"You can handle feeling a little dirty. In fact, dirt looks good on you."
Routine ERP practice	Playful GUTI practices one to two times each month. Roll a die to select the top six GUTI tasks from the ERP tasks.
	Have at-home "campouts." Do not wash or shower for 2 days.
Praise and reward self-initiation	Praise and reward Renee with one token when OCD tells her to wash her hands and she refuses.
	Praise and reward Renee with three tokens when she tells you to watch her touch something and resist handwashing before and after.
Next wellness checkup	March 3, 2018

ERP = exposure and response prevention; GUTI = get used to it.

repeatedly pulled his socks on and off while he became more and more frustrated and anxious. He was often late to school or to soccer practice because he was caught up in a cycle of dressing and redressing or taking off his socks and shoes only to put them on again, over and over.

Cole's parents reported that he never liked people touching his things, but the arranging and organizing behaviors seemed to arise suddenly. They both agreed that the behaviors appeared shortly after they announced the divorce to their children and worsened as Cole and his sister began to split time between their homes. Cole's mother reported that she suffers from generalized anxiety disorder and Cole's maternal uncle has OCD. Cole's parents did not report a streptococcal infection prior to onset of his symptoms, nor did Cole's pediatrician, and the clinician ruled out pediatric autoimmune neuropsychiatric disorders associated with streptococcal infections.

The clinician asked each of Cole's parents to complete the Family Accommodation Scale, the OCD Disturbance Scale, and the Child Obsessive-Compulsive Impact Scale, as well as the Child Behavior Checklist (Achenbach, 1991a). The clinician asked Cole to complete the Children's Depression Inventory (Kovacs & Beck, 1977), the Multidimensional Anxiety Scale for Children (March & Staff, 1997), and the Children's Florida Obsessive-Compulsive Inventory (Storch et al., 2009). These measures indicated that Cole was experiencing mild-to-moderate depressive symptoms, was anxious and worried, and reported a number of obsessions and compulsions, including aggressive and need-for-completeness obsessions and a number of compulsions, particularly repeating, rearranging, and reassurance seeking. Also, his parents, particularly Cole's mother, were participating in a number of accommodation behaviors. She frequently reassured Cole when he was anxious and excused him from a number of his usual responsibilities at home, such as putting away his clothes and taking out the garbage. Both parents wrote letters to his teacher to excuse him when he was late to school, and they no longer expected him to complete all his homework.

The clinician also administered the CY-BOCS, first to Cole's parents together and then to Cole. Before administering the CY-BOCS to Cole, the clinician devoted an entire session to building rapport. The clinician inquired about Cole's interests and about his recent birthday party and summer vacation. The clinician asked to hear Cole's favorite joke and about his favorite treat (apple pie). In addition, the clinician paid close attention to Cole's interests. The clinician would draw on these interests during the psychoeducation phase of the treatment. After 10 to 15 minutes of chatting, the clinician asked Cole why he thought his parents had brought him to meet the clinician. Cole said that his parents were worried about him. When the clinician asked Cole whether he was worried, Cole said yes and began to cry. The clinician then told Cole that he meets many kids who worry a lot and many of them have scary thoughts:

> I'd like to ask you about the kind of worries that scare you. I've helped kids for many years, and I think I've heard pretty much every worry and every scary thought, so, if you tell me a worry or a scary thought I haven't heard, I'll give you this 5-dollar bill. I always like to learn new things.

Cole paused and then in almost a whisper told the clinician his worries. When Cole did not mention harm obsessions, the clinician inquired about them. Cole cried and then said that he worried that he might kill his parents or his little sister while they slept. The clinician nodded, took notes, and said,

> Cole, thanks for telling me about these worries. I can definitely help you with them. Unfortunately, I've heard all these worries before. A 6-year-old girl just the other day told me that she was afraid that she was going to hurt her new baby brother. So, I appreciate you telling me about your worries, but you don't win the 5 dollars. I've heard worries like this many times. However, you can have the 5 dollars anyway because you were very brave to share these worries with me.

Cole blinked his eyes and smiled. Now that Cole was more comfortable, the clinician asked him if he agreed or disagreed with the symptoms his parents noted on the CY-BOCS and to give specific examples of any symptom that he reported. Last, the clinician wanted to establish the function of Cole's compulsions. Cole might engage in rearranging and repeating compulsions to prevent him from harming his parents, to satisfy his need for exactness, or both. Cole responded that sometimes he moved things around because he did not feel comfortable: "But I'm not scared. I just get mad." However, he reported that he had to pick up and put down certain objects "to get a scary worry out of my head, like hurting my sister. That's when I feel really scared. I hate those worries."

Developing the Case Conceptualization and Treatment Plan

To show solidarity against Cole's OCD, the clinician insisted that both parents, as well as Cole, participate in treatment planning. Although initially hesitant because the divorce was recent, Cole's parents agreed. Before creating a plan, the clinician and family identified all of Cole's OCD behaviors and the feared consequence he sought to avoid by performing these behaviors. In Cole's case, he avoided his parents and certain objects that triggered harm obsessions, seeking reassurance from his parents, and, arranging and ordering objects in his room and in his locker at school. Cole identified his feared consequences clearly: "If I don't put things in place, then I might hurt or even kill my parents and sister," and "If I don't straighten my things, then I'll feel so horrible I won't be able to stand it."

Once they had identified the functions of Cole's OCD behaviors and his feared consequences, Cole's family agreed to a plan that included learning about OCD and the strategies that would help Cole get rid of his pesky OCD. The clinician explained that Cole and the family would build three ladders to help Cole overcome the OCD. The ladders would target three symptom subtypes: aggression–harm symptoms, morality–scrupulosity symptoms, and "just-so" symptoms. Cole wanted to begin working on his aggression–harm symptoms. These symptoms occupied the most time during his day and were the most disruptive at school.

The clinician met with Cole and his parents together to solicit current examples of these symptoms and to build the ERP hierarchy (see Figure 10.4).

FIGURE 10.4. Cole's Exposure With Response Prevention Hierarchy

Exposure Item From General Hierarchy: Harm

	Exposure Type	Item	SUD (0–100)
1.	Situ:	Write words *knife*, *stab*, *kill*, and say them aloud.	40
	Imag:	Think about stabbing your father in his hand.	45
	Intr:		
2.	Situ:	Sit with knife at dinner with mom and sister.	50
	Imag:	Think about the bad things that will happen to your family now.	55
	Intr:		
3.	Situ:	Move photo of family once, and stop while thinking of stabbing them.	60
	Imag:	Think about walking into your mother's bedroom with a knife.	65
	Intr:		
4.	Situ:	Move photo of family once, and stop while thinking the word *kill*.	70
	Imag:	Think about stabbing your mother while she sleeps.	70
	Intr:		
5.	Situ:	Enter sister's bedroom while she's sleeping, and think of strangling her.	80
	Imag:	Think about your sister eating candy that you poisoned.	75
	Intr:		
6.	Situ:	Stand behind your mom while holding a knife, and think of stabbing her.	90
	Imag:	Think about smothering your sister while she sleeps.	80
	Intr:		
7.	Situ:	Before bed, move the "magic" things in your room three times and stop.	100
	Imag:	Think about stabbing your mother and sister while they sleep.	90
	Intr:		

SUD = subjective units of distress (0 = *low*; 100 = *high*); Situ = situational exposure; Imag = imaginal exposure; Intr = interoceptive exposure.

The clinician first asked for examples of behavioral neutralizations (compulsions) because these symptoms are easily observed by youth and parents. The clinician then asked for examples of situations, objects, and activities that Cole avoided because they triggered compulsions. The clinician also inquired about particular words or phrases that triggered harm obsessions, such as *knife, stab,* and "I might kill them when they're sleeping." As the conversation proceeded, the clinician wrote each of these triggers on a slip of paper and then asked Cole to rate his level of distress (on a fear thermometer, rated from 0 to 10) for each one. On the back of each slip of paper, the clinician then wrote the type of neutralization Cole typically used when the particular situation triggered the OCD. The clinician explained that during ERP Cole would not engage in these behaviors.

Engaging Youth and Parents in the Treatment Approach

Cole loved soccer, so the clinician decided to present the treatment approach as a competition: OCD on one side and Cole, his parents, and the clinician on the other. Cole understood the importance of practice, persistence, and working hard when competing in soccer, so he quickly understood the rules of the game when it came to beating OCD.

The clinician also included a bit of fun to lighten Cole's apprehension regarding the treatment and the clinician. At the end of every session, the clinician and Cole agreed to play 5 minutes of office soccer in which they kicked a small Nerf™ ball around the office. The clinician also gave Cole a short quiz during sessions to test Cole's knowledge of what the clinician taught him about OCD and its treatment. Every time Cole answered a quiz question correctly, the clinician game him a piece of candy. Cole also agreed to quiz the clinician about soccer.

Although Cole was very motivated to overcome the obsessive fear of harming his parents and sister, he was less motivated to overcome the just-so feelings that influenced his need for order and exactness. The clinician decided to develop and implement a reinforcement plan to assist their work on his harm-related symptoms and later implement this same plan when they shifted to working on the exactness-related symptoms.

The clinician proposed Connect-the-Dots as a reinforcement plan. For his big prize, Cole chose a trip to a local professional soccer game with his father. They cut out a picture of the soccer team from a soccer magazine and traced its outline on a piece of graph paper. At each point that the picture touched a line, they drew a dot. The clinician then explained how Cole and his parents would use Connect-the-Dots. Once Cole connected all the dots, he and his father would attend a professional soccer game. In addition, for every third dot Cole connected, Cole's parents agreed to give him 20 minutes additional video game time during the week but only after he had completed all his homework. The clinician also explained the idea of dot detours and assured Cole that dot detours would not occur in the first 2 weeks and perhaps not at all.

Psychoeducation With Youth and Parents

The clinician met with Cole and his parents together and began the psycho-education process. The clinician explained that fear is the body's danger alarm. The clinician compared Cole's OCD-related fears to a smoke detector alarm that sounds when there is a fire. He asked, "But, Cole, when the smoke detector alarm sounds but there's no fire, what do we call that?" Cole smiled and replied, "A false alarm." Carrying the alarm analogy further, the clinician explained that OCD loved to sound false alarms in Cole's brain: "OCD pushes the alarm button when you think that you may hurt someone or do some-thing wrong." Cole and the clinician discussed the impact of paying attention to his OCD false alarms. The clinician then explained to Cole that the first step in pushing OCD out of his life was to learn the difference between OCD false alarms and real alarms that mean real danger. Cole and the clinician listed all of Cole's OCD-related thoughts, images, and urges. The clinician suggested that Cole name his OCD and Cole quickly suggested "False-Alarmer." To encourage detachment from his obsessions, the clinician suggested Cole say to himself, "Oh, that's just a False-Alarmer. No need to pay attention to that nonsense!"

The clinician then moved to psychoeducation regarding Cole's just-so obsessions. The clinician explained that Cole's just-so discomfort was similar to how it feels to get into a pool of cold water: "It feels really cold at first, but if you stay in the water, after some time you get used to the cold water and it doesn't feel so cold anymore. But you never get used to it if you jump out of the pool." The clinician then explained that the tightness of Cole's shoelaces or the stiffness of his school uniform pants are uncomfortable feelings, but that he will never get used to those feelings if he keeps jumping out of the pool. Cole and the clinician then listed the ways Cole jumps out of the pool (e.g., repeatedly tugging at his socks, cutting the labels out of his shirts, tying and retying his shoelaces, or refusing to wear long pants).

Working With the Family

Cole's parents engaged in several accommodation behaviors, but by far the most frequent accommodation behavior was reassuring him when he was anxious. The clinician explained to both parents the role of reassurance in maintaining Cole's OCD symptoms. The clinician explored with each parent the ways she or he reassured Cole, and added, "It's difficult for many parents to stop reassuring their child. Why do you think it may be difficult for you?" The parents admitted that following the divorce, they both worried that their children would begin to see them as the bad parent. As Cole's father explained, "I guess I reassured Cole more for me than for him sometimes." The clinician praised both parents for their honesty: "It's clear to me that although you don't always get along, you both deeply care about Cole and are committed to helping your son recover from the OCD." The parents nodded their heads in agreement. The clinician explained to the parents that they had fallen into the overprotection trap:

> Overprotection is a bit like keeping a bandage on a wound too long. After a while the bandage delays the healing process because the wound needs air to form a scab. Although the bandage protects the wound, the wound doesn't heal. If you want your son to heal, it's really important that you both stop reassuring him when he's anxious.

Cole's parents agreed and were open to developing a plan to fade their reassurance behaviors. The clinician then met with Cole and his parents to negotiate a nonreassuring response to Cole's reassurance seeking. The clinician explained that Cole was the first line of defense against the False-Alarmer, and his job was to boss back the False-Alarmer when he had urges to seek reassurance from his parents. If the False-Alarmer snuck past the first line of defense, Cole's parents agreed to be the second line of defense and call out the False-Alarmer, They could say, "That sounds like a False-Alarmer question to me," or "That sounds like the False-Alarmer is trying to trick you." and encourage resistance: "Don't let the False-Alarmer get the best of you. Tell that False-Alarmer to go away." If the False-Alarmer persisted with other questions or pleas for reassurance, the parents agreed to say, "You know the answer to that question," or "What is the answer to that question?" Last, after the parents helped their son recognize the presence of OCD and encouraged him to resist the compulsion (i.e., reassurance seeking), the clinician asked the parents to redirect Cole to an engaging activity or task, such as kicking a soccer ball around the backyard.

The clinician also targeted other accommodation behaviors. For example, prior to treatment, Cole's parents permitted him to stop doing certain tasks, such as completing his homework, cleaning his room, or setting the table before meals. This was perhaps understandable at the time. After all, these tasks tended to trigger Cole's OCD symptoms, particularly his organizing and repeating behaviors. However, as treatment progressed, the clinician noted that Cole no longer avoided certain tasks or situations that had triggered his OCD, but he continued to refuse to do homework, or household jobs, often throwing a tantrum, slamming doors, and screaming at his parents.

The clinician met with Cole's parents, and they agreed that it was time for Cole to begin to do his share at home and, in particular, to comply with their directions. The clinician first taught the parents to communicate their directions directly. Both parents, and particularly Cole's father, tended to ask Cole rather than to direct him to begin homework or household tasks. The clinician modeled the desired communication behavior for the parents and, through multiple role-plays, increased their confidence and comfort with commanding rather than asking or pleading. At the same time, the clinician helped the parents distinguish those behaviors that they would ignore from those behaviors that they would manage directly, primarily through response cost (see Chapter 7).

The Connect-the-Dots reinforcement plan had worked exceedingly well for Cole. To handle Cole's pushback behaviors, the clinician explained again the concept of dot detours (response cost) to Cole and his parents. Dot detours added three dots to Cole's path to the big reward. Although a dot detour added only three dots, the detour delayed Cole's progress toward the big reward nonetheless. The clinician and parents identified three tasks (i.e., completing homework, setting the table for meals, and clearing the table after meals) to target with the response cost strategy. The clinician then explained that they would give Cole a dot when he started the task after they directed him to begin and complete the task in a reasonable amount of time. However, if Cole refused to start and complete the task after his parents directed him to begin, his parents would give him one warning: "A dot detour is around the corner." If he did not comply then, he would take a dot detour. After only two dot detours, Cole was complying with his parents' commands without complaint or argument.

Implementing Graded Exposure and Response Prevention

Once Cole understood the types of tricks OCD plays on his brain, he was ready to learn OCD response prevention strategies. The clinician worked with Cole on six main strategies to fight back against his OCD: waiting to do his neutralization for a certain amount of time, changing neutralizations, dropping steps from multistep rituals or reducing the time he checks or adjusts objects, doing neutralizations in a silly way, ignoring urges to neutralize, and doing the opposite of the neutralization.

ERP Tasks for Harm-Related Symptoms

Cole and the clinician made a ladder of words and phrases that triggered the harm obsessions: *kill, die, knife, smother, strangle,* "I'll kill them while they're asleep," "I could lose it today and kill my little sister." The clinician created a recording of the three lowest anxiety words: *knife, strangle,* and *smother.* Cole then listened to the recording repeatedly. During this process, the clinician asked Cole about mental neutralizations. Cole reported that at times he told himself, "This is just a recording." The clinician suggested that Cole undo that neutralization when it arose by repeating to himself, "Yes, it's a recording, and listening to it might make me hurt my family." The clinician directed Cole to listen to the recording throughout the day at home with his earbuds and smartphone. The clinician suggested that Cole use a phone application that looped the recording repeatedly.

    Next, the clinician and Cole focused on a series of situational exposures taken from the ERP hierarchy: sitting with a knife when the family had dinner, entering his sister's room while she was sleeping and imagining strangling her, reading articles about teenagers who killed their parents, moving objects incorrectly while he imagined stabbing his mother or father, and standing behind his mother while holding a knife. Prior to implementing these ERP tasks, the clinician informed Cole's parents that they planned to move ahead with these situational ERP tasks. The clinician then reviewed again with them the rationale for ERP in general and these ERP tasks in particular: "These are things Cole is already thinking. We're just triggering these thoughts and images so that he can practice hanging out with them. Over time, these thoughts and images will lose their power over Cole." The parents granted the clinician permission and agreed to support Cole as he completed these ERP tasks in session and to support him to repeat the ERP tasks at home as action plans.

ERP Tasks for Just-So Symptoms

Once Cole had worked successfully up the harm-related ERP hierarchy, he agreed to work on his just-so symptoms. Cole and the clinician agreed to begin with the lowest step on the just-so ladder, which was Cole's shoelaces. Cole was very particular about the tightness of his shoes and for this first exposure, Cole agreed to tie his shoes one time and not redo the laces regardless how loose or tight they felt. With the clinician's assistance, Cole began this ERP task in session. He tied his laces and then accompanied the clinician as they walked around the block. Periodically, the clinician requested Cole report his level of distress. Within a few minutes, Cole's distress level was half of the maximum when they began the ERP task. Once they were back in the office, the clinician directed Cole to repeat the ERP task: untie and tie his laces again and walk around the block with the clinician. At the end of the session, Cole was surprised but very pleased with himself. The clinician then met with Cole and his parents and described to the parents what they had done and asked them to repeat this practice: Cole would resist adjusting the laces regardless of his discomfort. When he arrived at school, which was a 40-minute car ride with his mom or dad, he could adjust the laces if he wished but would earn extra dots if he did not. If he absolutely had to adjust the laces at school, he could do so one time. To assist Cole to resist neutralizations during ERP practice at home, the clinician modified Cole's access to the neutralization. The clinician directed Cole to keep his hands in his pants pockets immediately after he put on his shoes and to walk out the door to the car. Cole and the clinician developed other strategies to resist the OCD urges. If Cole absolutely could not resist the urge to retie his shoes, he agreed to tie them in a silly way (i.e., pretending to be a bunny when making bunny ears of the laces) to shift his emotion and weaken the ritual. Last, the clinician recommended Cole to complete ERP at home that directed him to tie his shoes, sit on the sofa, and focus on the feeling of discomfort for a specific time period, based on a time ladder that Cole and the clinician developed (from 2 minutes to 30 minutes). Cole agreed to use a timer and resist urges to adjust his shoes until the timer sounded.

Involving the Classroom Teacher in ERP Tasks

Although not as often as when he was home, Cole did engage in the just-so neutralizations when at school. To generalize the gains to the classroom, the clinician asked Cole's classroom teacher to send Cole home with a just-so report card. The clinician explained to the teacher that Cole could retie his shoes one time after he arrived at school, per the first ERP plan but no more and described how she would mark the report card. On the basis of the report card, Cole would earn dots for his progress at school. The clinician explained to the teacher and parents that the report card would focus only on neutralizations on which Cole and the clinician were currently working and would change over time as Cole worked his way up the ERP hierarchy. The clinician directed the parents to bring the report cards for the week to each session. They would then review them with Cole and praise and reward him for his work.

Developing and Implementing Relapse Prevention

Once Cole had successfully completed his three fear ladders, the clinician informed the family that it was time to discontinue treatment and develop a relapse prevention plan. Cole and his parents were anxious about terminating treatment, but the clinician reassured them that it was time to do so and that they all had worked very hard to get to this day. At the next session, the clinician introduced the idea of relapse prevention to the family in this way:

> Cole, Mom, and Dad, it's time for you to fly solo. Every flight begins with a Flight Plan. Cole will have a Flight Plan, and, Mom and Dad, you will have Flight Plans too. The Flight Plans will include several parts, and we will develop those today. Once we have a Flight Plan, then you will fly solo. At first these solo flights will be short. You'll fly solo for two weeks before we meet again. Two weeks isn't long, so that means you're still close to the traffic control tower, which is me. That way, I can help if you hit any turbulence. After that, you'll take longer solo flights, perhaps for four weeks or a month before you circle back to the tower. After that, you're ready to fly solo as long and as far as you want.

Cole's Flight Plan included five sections. The first section included his early warning signs, the first signs that False-Alarmer is lurking at the edge of his land. Cole added to the list small urges to check or little thoughts that he might have hurt someone. The clinician reminded Cole that these warning signs signaled that it was time to use the tools he learned to push OCD off his land again. In addition, the clinician helped Cole's parents list the ways OCD tricked them into accommodating, such as the overprotection trap when they excuse Cole from completing tasks at school and home. Also, the clinician worked with Cole's parents to differentiate between Cole's questions and OCD's questions. With the clinician's help, they listed qualities of OCD questions so that his parents could spot these questions quickly if they slipped through Cole's first line of defense.

The clinician and family then completed the remaining sections of the Flight Plan. The second section included ERP tasks to practice each week to keep in shape. The third section included the things I learned about False-Alarmer. The clinician helped Cole list the strategies that Cole believed had helped him the most and that he would use to fight back against any new worries that came his way. They practiced these strategies again in session, such as using boss-back talk to resist False-Alarmers. The fourth section included the times and places that False-Alarmer might try to come back. The fifth and final section included upcoming stressors and plans to manage them. The clinician completed Cole's Flight Plan and gave the plan to the family (see Figure 10.5) and scheduled the next meeting 2 weeks out. The clinician then met with the parents without Cole to develop their Flight Plan. Their Flight

FIGURE 10.5. Cole's Flight Plan

My Flight Plan

_____

Congratulations! You've worked very hard and have pushed OCD out of your life. Now, you're about to fly solo, and today we'll develop your flight plan. We'll include in your flight plan all the things you've learned that will keep OCD from coming back.

We'll begin with short flights. Rather than meeting every week, we'll meet every other week for a while. This gives you time to practice what you've learned. You can always call the control tower, that's me, if you have a question or want a little help. Because every flight has a little turbulence, your flight plan will include all the things that you've learned to fly through the bumps that OCD throws at you and stay on course. So, let's build your flight plan!

Signs False-Alarmer is trying to come back:	I start to have more False-Alarmer thoughts about my family or friends or teachers.
	False-Alarmer makes me arrange things more and in certain ways.
	False-Alarmer makes me ask Mom or Dad to reassure me more.
To stay in shape, I will:	Tell Mom and Dad that False-Alarmer is bugging me again.
	I'll ask Mom to schedule some checkup appointments with my doctor.
	Practice my False-Alarmer exercises with Mom or Dad.
	Do the scariest exercise on my ladder once a week.
At the first sign that False-Alarmer is back, I will remind myself of the things I've learned:	Boss back False-Alarmer with my Boss-Back talk. I'm stronger than False-Alarmer. I beat him once, and I will beat him again.
	Just because False-Alarmer tells me that I'll hurt my family doesn't mean I will do it.
	I can handle my fear and thoughts.

FIGURE 10.5. (Continued)

Times and places that False-Alarmer might try to come back:	Starting fourth grade might be hard. I'll remember to watch for False-Alarmer and tell Mom if he's starting to bug me. I can come for a few booster meetings with my doctor.
	Dad is marrying Glenda. She's nice, but that will be a big change for our family. I can come for a few booster meetings with my doctor, just to talk, even if False-Alarmer isn't bugging me.

Plans included skills they learned, primarily focused on supporting and communicating with Cole and with each other and on minimizing their accommodation behaviors (see Figure 10.6).

Following relapse prevention planning, the clinician excused Cole's parents and met with Cole alone. The clinician praised Cole and suggested that they make a movie in which Cole would tell the world how he had bossed the False-Alarmer off his land. The clinician explained to Cole that this would be a public service announcement; that he could show it to friends, family members, or anyone else; and that whether he showed it or not was completely up to him: "I think you've learned a lot about OCD and how you bossed it back. A video like this would help other kids understand OCD and how they can run OCD off their land as you did."

Cole was eager to make his video. The clinician then recorded Cole telling his story about OCD, how it bugged him, and how he overcame it. Cole called the movie *False-Alarmer and Me*. The clinician then invited the parents back into the session, and Cole showed his parents the video. They discussed whether they wished to show it and to whom to show it. Cole and his parents loved the video and decided to throw a second graduation party in which Cole could show his public service announcement video. It would be a graduation and a movie premier. The clinician then organized the bragging session and gave Cole his diploma. The last few minutes they all ate a slice of apple pie, which was Cole's favorite treat.

ALEX

Alex is a 16-year-old boy and an accomplished athlete. He plays soccer and basketball in community leagues and pitches for his high school baseball team. Alex also does well in school, but his teachers have observed that he is never satisfied with his school performance. He lives with his mother and father and 18-year-old sister, who is leaving for college next year. Alex's father works long

FIGURE 10.6. Cole and Parents Flight Plan

Our Flight Plan

Congratulations! You and your child have worked very hard and pushed OCD out of your lives. Now your family is about to fly solo, and today we'll develop your flight plan to do that. This flight plan is for you. Your child has a flight plan too. Some of the things on your child's flight plan are similar to some of the things we'll include in your plan. Your flight plan will include all the things you've learned as parents that if you continue to do them will keep OCD from coming back.

We'll begin with short flights. Rather than meeting every week, we'll meet every other week for a while. This gives you and your child time to practice what you've learned. You can always call the control tower, that's me, if you have a question or want a little help. Because every flight has a little turbulence, your flight plan will include all the things that you've learned to fly through the bumps that OCD throws at you and your child to stay on course. So let's build your flight plan!

Signs that we're slipping back into our old patterns:	We start arguing more about pickups and drop-offs.
	We start using our kids to send messages to each other rather than talking with each other about the problem.
Signs that we've started to accommodate the OCD again:	We reassure Cole that the family is safe rather than remind him that this is the OCD.
	We calm Cole rather than warning him that a consequence is coming if he continues to refuse to comply with our requests.
	We excuse Cole from doing his homework, attending school or after-school activities, or performing his jobs at home.
Communication and coaching skills that help:	We will direct Cole, rather than asking him to do something, in a calm, clear manner.
	We will not argue, beg, or negotiate with Cole. We will tell him what we want him to do, give him a single warning, and then administer an appropriate consequence.

FIGURE 10.6. (Continued)

To stay in shape, we will	We will meet once each week for at least 10 minutes to discuss any problem we are having with the kids or with each other and develop solutions together.
	We will try to be on time with pickups and drop-offs and spend 3 minutes updating each other about Cole before we leave.
	Once per month, we will review the reinforcement plan with Cole to make certain we are implementing correctly. We will also meet once each week for a family meal or activity. We will make family time a priority.
	We will look for opportunities to praise Cole about the many good things he does, not just when he bosses back the OCD.
	We will ignore the small stuff when it comes to our kids and to each other.

hours and spends very little time with his wife and children. Although he is well-meaning, he is often stressed and irritable. Alex's mother is not employed outside the home and is very involved in Alex's life. She worries about Alex, but as she tells people she meets, she worries about everything.

Gathering Information

The clinician first met alone with Alex's parents. Although it was difficult to get his father into the office, the clinician insisted that both parents attend the initial consultation and that he would not treat their son unless both parents attended all meetings the clinician requested them to attend. They arrived on time to the clinician's office. During this meeting, they reported that Alex was excellent at everything: sports, school, friendships. However, they had different opinions about how Alex managed his stress level. His father viewed his son as hardworking and dedicated, just like himself. Alex's mother, on the other hand, was worried about her son. She reported that his teachers were concerned that Alex was often very hard on himself. She reported several recent times when Alex was very upset with himself after he made a poor pass in a soccer game and missed two problems on a math test. Both parents agreed that Alex pushed himself very hard. He did not often hang out with friends. He complained about his homework load but refused to cut corners even when his parents and teachers encouraged him to do so.

The clinician administered a number of measures to the parents and Alex. The parents completed the Family Accommodation Scale (FAS), OCD

Disturbance Scale, and Child Obsessive-Compulsive Impact Scale, as well as the Child Behavior Checklist. Items related to providing reassurance and excusing Alex from household tasks were elevated on the FAS, particularly as reported by Alex's mother. The clinician also administered the CY-BOCS to the parents together.

The clinician reviewed the measures Alex completed: Children's Depression Inventory, Multidimensional Anxiety Scale for Children, and Children's Florida Obsessive-Compulsive Inventory. These measures indicated that Alex was experiencing moderate depressive symptoms, and he was anxious and worried. He reported a number of obsessions: a need for exactness and a need for neatness, and perfectionism. He reported a number of compulsions, particularly repeating, checking, and reassurance seeking.

The clinician then met with Alex alone and reviewed the CY-BOCS the clinician completed in the meeting with the parents. Alex agreed with his parents on a number of symptoms. He admitted that he repeatedly checked and rechecked the school website to make certain that he knew the correct homework assignment for the day. When working on the homework, he repeatedly checked that he had answered the questions correctly. If he did not fully understand a homework assignment, he repeatedly asked his parents to explain it to him, or he texted friends for reassurance. He often worked 2 hours or more on a single homework assignment that friends typically completed in 20 minutes. Alex reported that homework was very stressful and took too much time to complete, but he insisted that, as exhausting as the process was for him, it was better than making a mistake.

The clinician explained that the goal of treatment was to help Alex feel less stressed in general and less stressed about school work in particular. The first step was to gather data regarding Alex's work process. At first, Alex objected: "I can't keep up with the work I have, and you want me to do more?" However, the clinician assured him that the data collection process would be simple and require little effort and time. The clinician and Alex then developed a form to use each week. The form noted several categories of checking behavior: repeatedly checking homework assignments on the school website; repeatedly checking the correctness of homework assignments; repeatedly asking parents, friends, and teachers about homework assignments; repeatedly checking his soccer bag; repeatedly checking his gym locker; repeatedly checking his school locker; and, repeatedly checking his backpack. The clinician asked Alex to place a tally mark next to each category when he engaged in that behavior. The clinician then folded several of the blank forms to make a small notebook.

Developing the Case Conceptualization and Treatment Plan

Alex and the clinician met a second time to create collaboratively a case conceptualization and treatment plan. First they discussed the function of Alex's checking behaviors. Alex clearly stated that certainty was extremely important to him: "I can't stand the feeling of not knowing for sure. It feels like torture to me." The clinician explored with Alex the costs and benefits of striving for certainty. On the benefit side of the equation, Alex believed that striving for certainty prevented mistakes, ensured that he did his best, and helped him live to his full potential. On the cost side, Alex admitted that his need for certainty created a great deal of stress and worry.

The clinician decided to begin with response prevention to the triggers Alex experienced every day: completing school homework, getting items out of his locker, packing his backpack, and checking with others. The clinician and Alex created a response prevention hierarchy. Alex identified that cutting back on the frequency he checked with others was a good place to begin. Alex reported that even when he checked with his parents and friends and they reassured him, he usually still checked, often multiple times, because "the other person could be wrong or careless." In collaboration with Alex and after reviewing Alex's self-monitoring forms, he and the clinician created a response prevention plan (see Figure 10.7).

Engaging Youth and Parents in the Treatment Approach

Typically, perfectionistic youth can be very challenging to engage in treatment because often they strongly believe in the value of perfectionistic behavior. Parents can also stoke the fires of perfectionism because their high-achieving child provides a sense of pride or mirrors their own values, as is the case with Alex's father. While Alex did agree that his checking was cumbersome, he hesitated to agree to decrease the checking even a little.

To engage him in treatment, the clinician suggested Alex reflect on his life before OCD. Alex remembered his days in middle school and early high school. He was still an excellent athlete and student, but he felt less stressed. He even remembered having time to do fun things, such as sorting his baseball cards and playing video games with friends. Although he admitted that he still enjoyed these activities, he now viewed them as a waste of time or felt guilty when he considered setting aside time to do them. He also remembered easier times when he laughed and messed around with friends between classes rather than rechecking his locker and rushing to class or to the library.

Next, the clinician asked Alex to complete a values card sort. The clinician directed Alex to examine a stack of 100 cards and select 10 cards that reflected values that were the most important to him. Alex identified family, friends, and adventure as very important. He shared that family, friends, and adventure came in second to his need to achieve. The clinician explored with Alex which values he wanted to occupy a bigger part of his daily life and what he would have to compromise (e.g., check and seek reassurance less) to do so. As the clinician gently explored with Alex his core values, Alex admitted that his friends were becoming annoyed with his repeated questions about tests, grades, and assignments. He acknowledged that he did not want to lose his friends to OCD.

FIGURE 10.7. Alex's Response Prevention Plan

My Response Prevention Plan

Follow these response prevention instructions:

1. Do not ask friends about assignments, or limit it to only one time.

2. Do not check the school website more than twice each day.

3. Do not repeatedly read emails to teachers or texts to friends before sending.

4. Do not ask my coach for reassurance before, during, or after a game or practice.

5. Do not repeatedly check first drafts of papers or other assignments.

6. Do not ask parents for reassurance on assignments.

Remember:

Every compulsion, no matter how small or how brief, feeds my OCD. Even small neutralizations interfere with my progress. Time is on my side. The longer I wait, the less intense the urge to engage in the compulsion becomes.

A mistaken belief or assumption is triggering the urge to engage in a compulsion. Remember what I learned: I don't really need to check my work repeatedly to feel better or to do well in school.

Alternatives to Compulsions:

Find someone to talk with, and ask that person to stay with me until the urge passes.

Leave the situation for a time (if possible) to get away from reminders that trigger urges to engage in a compulsion.

Negotiate a delay with the urge. Set a small goal to delay the compulsion (for example, 5 minutes, 10 minutes, whatever length of time I am 90% confident that I can delay giving into the urge). After I have successfully reached my goal of delaying for 10 minutes, for example, negotiate another 10 minutes, if I am 90% confident that I can resist the urge for that time. If not, set a smaller goal, such as 5 minutes or 2 minutes.

If I slip and engage in a compulsion, undo it in some way (for example, make a change to an assignment and do not recheck it). Immediately record slips on my self-monitoring form, and discuss it with my therapist.

Once Alex started to get on board with treatment, the clinician worked to engage his parents in treatment, particularly the importance of Alex's mother decreasing her accommodation behaviors:

CLINICIAN: While I completely understand how hard it can be to see your child in distress and tolerate his angry tantrums, I bet you've tolerated this kind of thing in the past with Alex. Did Alex ever want something at a store and you refused to buy it for him?

MOTHER: Oh, yes! Alex has always been persistent. Looking at him now you would never guess it, but he was a chubby kiddo. He always wanted me to buy cookies at the grocery store. We would have standoffs that were hard for me. I always felt really embarrassed when he screamed in the store.

CLINICIAN: How did you hold your ground?

MOTHER: I remembered that Alex's dentist told me that if he got one more cavity, he'd have more cavities than any kid he'd ever treated. I felt like a terrible mother. So I kept my cool. I just smiled at the other parents and shrugged my shoulders, but I did not buy the treats.

CLINICIAN: Bravo! So you were able to do something that was hard for you, and you did it because you knew that's what a good mom does.

MOTHER: Yes. I want to be the best mom I can be to Alex.

Psychoeducation With Youth and Parents

Psychoeducation with Alex and his family emphasized recognizing that OCD had taken many things from all of them. In Alex's case, OCD had robbed him of sleep, relaxation, and easy and fun time with friends. Through careful inquiry, the clinician helped Alex recognize that OCD had likely decreased his performance in school and sports, not improved it. The clinician explained the negative reinforcement cycle of OCD and how the relief he feels after checking or seeking reassurance is temporary and maintains the OCD cycle.

The clinician then addressed with Alex and his family the difference between seeking information and seeking reassurance. The clinician explained to the parents that it was important to understand the function of any questions Alex asks: "Is he missing an important piece of information, or does he have the information but is not certain that it is correct or complete?" The clinician informed the parents that this was not always clear but that they would learn strategies to help them and Alex in these situations.

Working With the Family

Because Alex's ERP plan included primarily response prevention strategies, the clinician worked with his parents to decrease their accommodation behaviors, beginning with a plan decrease the frequency with which they reassure Alex when he was anxious about his school work. They agreed to begin by limiting reassurance to twice per day. The clinician wrote the word *reassurance* on two colored index cards and gave these to Alex. When Alex asked for reassurance, his parents requested one of the cards and then reassured him. After Alex used both cards, his parents were directed to tell Alex in a calm and neutral voice, "I'm sorry but you used your two reassurance cards for today. I'll give you two new cards tomorrow." Alex's mother started to deliver the message with a funny accent, which decreased the tension and often resulted in a giggle or two. She reported that the strategy often defused the situation, and the clinician encouraged her to continue this strategy as long as it did not escalate Alex's distress.

The clinician worked with Alex and his parents to set up a reinforcement plan. Alex was desperate to use the family car and agreed to earn access to driving time. The clinician created a Connect-the-Dots chart and explained the process to the family. Alex would earn dots when he completed ERP tasks in session and out of session. At first, Alex complained that the Connect-the-Dot system was "babyish," but he later agreed that it was the simplest way to track his progress and to earn driving time. The clinician explained to Alex that he earned an extra dot for each reassurance card he did not use for the day.

The clinician also sought permission from Alex's parents to contact the school and Alex's soccer coaches. Initially, Alex's parents did not want the clinician to contact the school and share information regarding Alex's diagnosis and treatment plan. They did not want this information to negatively affect his academic record. The clinician validated their concerns and then explained that involving the school likely would improve Alex's success in treatment. The clinician underscored the importance of including classroom teachers in the treatment plan to prevent them from unintentionally responding to Alex's OCD in an unhelpful manner. The clinician made a similar request with a similar rationale for informing Alex's soccer coaches too. The parents agreed, and the clinician negotiated with them what the clinician would and would not include when communicating with Alex's teachers and coaches.

Implementing Graded Exposure and Response Prevention

With the clinician's assistance, Alex worked through his ERP plan diligently with only a few bumps during periods of increased stress (e.g., final exams, an important soccer game). The reinforcement plan helped maintain Alex's motivation, and periodic meetings with Alex's parents helped them manage their accommodation behaviors. As is often the case, the clinician identified new neutralizations and in some cases neutralizations that the clinician failed to identify during the assessment phase. For example, as Alex's parents refused to reassure him, Alex asked his sister for reassurance or, rather than asking friends directly for reassurance, he instead told his friends what he believed to be the correct answer to a question and hoped that they would agree or disagree with him. Either way, Alex would feel a little better because he escaped the anxiety of uncertainty. In addition, Alex often sought reassurance through repeatedly reviewing text chains among friends regarding school assignments. The clinician created a response prevention hierarchy for text messages, and Alex increased the delay between urges to check.

Within the last few weeks of ERP tasks, the clinician recommend that Alex go "over the top." The clinician explained the process of overlearning in which individuals with OCD go above and beyond what typical people do and thereby deepen their learning and protect themselves from future relapse. The clinician convinced Alex to include a mistake in a homework assignment. The clinician told Alex that he would earn five dots for each intentional mistake, which increased Alex's motivation considerably. Alex agreed to begin with English, which was his easiest course, and work up to including a mistake in his math homework. Alex learned two important lessons from his intentional mistake practice. First, he learned that he could tolerate making mistakes and the uncertainty of what his teachers and friends might think about him. Second, he learned that homework mistakes were not the end of the world. The over-the-top practice increased Alex's confidence greatly and added to the durability of his treatment.

Developing and Implementing Relapse Prevention

Alex and his family made consistent progress over several months. Alex had become more comfortable with uncertainty and had decreased his perfectionistic behaviors. Although the intentional-mistake ERP tasks were difficult for him initially, he had learned that avoiding any mistake at all costs was unnecessary and only added anxiety and stress to his life. The clinician introduced the topic of ending treatment with Alex and his parents:

> Alex, you've worked very hard over the last few months. I think we've made a great team. At the beginning, I was mostly the therapist, but then you stepped up and became a great cotherapist. You had some great ideas for ERP tasks, and you practiced them consistently. Nice job! Now I think it's time for you to take over and be your own therapist. We'll do this in steps, and in a minute we'll develop a plan to do this. I think you're ready. What do you think?

The clinician, Alex, and his parents created Alex's relapse prevention plan. In the section of the plan that noted early warning signs, Alex added: "checking my school website and homework more than usual" and "asking for more reassurance from my parents and friends." The clinician reminded him that these early warning signs signaled that it was time to use the tools he had learned, and they linked these to the warning signs. In the second section of the plan, Alex noted, "If I start to check my homework more, I'll try to make a mistake on an assignment." Also Alex was to practice tolerating the consequences of a mistake (usually minor, if at all) and remind himself that perfection is not necessary. In addition, the clinician asked Alex's parents to list in their own plans the first signs that they had slipped into the overprotection trap, such as excusing Alex from household responsibilities and reassuring him when he was anxious about schoolwork. To assist Alex to respond appropriately to early warning signs, the clinician and Alex developed Guidelines for Normal Academic Diligence (see Figure 10.8).

The clinician and family then completed the remaining sections of the relapse prevention plan. The third section included ERP tasks to practice each week to keep in shape. Alex agreed to make intentional mistakes on his school assignments and when at soccer practice (e.g., make a bad pass to a team member). The fourth section included a plan to fill the time that was now available to Alex after he was engaged in less checking, reassurance seeking, and over studying. The clinician helped Alex schedule time during

FIGURE 10.8. Alex's Response Prevention Hierarchy

	Response Prevention Hierarchy	SUD (0–100)
1.	Only ask one friend for reassurance about one assignment per night.	35
2.	Only ask parents for reassurance twice per day; ask coach for reassurance about how well I am playing two times per practice or game.	40
3.	Only check homework assignments on school website three times per day.	45
4.	Only ask two teachers for reassurance on assignments (e.g., understanding directions or the quality of my work) one time per class. Do not ask for reassurance in any of my other classes.	50
5.	Only recheck assignments two times each.	55
6.	Only edit papers after I have written the full first draft without any editing.	60
7.	Send an email to my mother without rereading before sending.	65
8.	Send an email to my teacher without rereading before sending.	70
9.	Go through an entire soccer practice/game without asking for any reassurance from the coach about my playing.	75
10.	Go through an entire day of school without getting any reassurance from teachers or peers.	80
11.	Hand in an assignment that is ungraded (students just get credit for completion) without checking it over.	85
12.	Hand in a graded assignment without checking it over.	90
13.	Print and hand in a paper without checking it over after writing the final draft.	95
14.	Hand in an assignment with a small error on it.	100

SUD = subjective units of distress (0 = *low*; 100 = *high*).

the week and on weekends to hang out with friends. Alex also agreed to begin activities that had always been fun for him, such as skateboarding and mountain biking, and build those activities into his week. The clinician asked Alex's parents to do their share to encourage him in a balanced life as well as transport Alex and his friends to these activities. In the final section, the clinician, Alex and his family identified upcoming stressors and developed plans to manage them. For example, he would soon begin the process of applying to colleges. The clinician assumed, and Alex and his parents agreed, that this would be a stressful period for the entire family. The clinician then worked with the family to develop a plan for this process that was reasonable. For example, they would limit the number of colleges to which Alex applied, and restrict extra work, such as studying excessively for the SAT. The clinician then gave the completed relapse prevention plan to the family and scheduled a follow-up meeting in 2 weeks (see Figure 10.9).

Alex agreed that he was ready to graduate. The clinician organized a discussion with Alex and his parents. The clinician asked each to share the most important lessons from treatment. Alex shared: "Trying to be perfect is impossible and way too stressful. Not trying to be perfect makes my life easier, and I still do great." Alex's mother shared that she had learned that the protection trap was just that: "It's a trap for me and Alex. I learned that Alex can handle a lot, and so can I. I still slip into overprotecting Alex, but I've learned that

FIGURE 10.9. Alex's Relapse Prevention Plan

My Relapse Prevention Plan

Early warning signs:	Checking my school website and homework more than usual
	Asking for more reassurance from my parents and friends
Encourage these skills:	If I start to check my homework more, I'll try to make a mistake on an assignment.
	Remind myself that perfection isn't necessary.
Routine ERP practice:	Complete intentional mistakes on two school assignments and when at soccer practice (e.g., make a bad pass to a team member every two weeks).
	When I have urges to check my backpack, lockers, or school websites, I'll delay checking for 30 minutes.
Fun and proud activities:	Hang out with friends at least once per week and on the weekend.
	Spend 1 day a week skateboarding or mountain biking with friends.
Upcoming stressors:	Apply to six colleges only.
	Take an SAT study course, and study only 3 hours each week for the test.

ERP = exposure and response prevention.

helping like that isn't really helping Alex. It's holding him back." Last, Alex's father shared: "I learned a lot from Alex through this entire thing. I was caught up in my own perfectionism, and seeing Alex fight it and win has helped me cut back on work and spend more time with my family."

The clinician invited Alex to enter something in the Victory Book (see Chapter 5) in the clinician's office. Alex liked the idea of passing on what he had learned to other youth with OCD. As Alex entered a short paragraph, he smiled at the clinician and said, "I just misspelled two words."

CONCLUSION

These three cases provide clinicians with an overview of the implementation of the core strategies described in this book. We selected clinical situations that reflect the complexities of youth with OCD to illustrate the importance of case formulation in designing effective treatment plans for the condition. Furthermore, we hope these cases illustrate the ways clinicians can flexibly and creatively apply the core strategies in routine clinical practice.

In the next chapter, we describe pharmacotherapy for pediatric OCD. Although not every child with OCD requires combined (CBT and medication) treatment, many do. Therefore, we recommend that clinicians who treat pediatric OCD understand the evidence base for pharmacotherapy, CBT, and the combination of these treatment approaches so that they are prepared to explain to parents and youth the benefits and risks of these treatment options.

11

Combining Cognitive Behavior Therapy and Pharmacotherapy

A consistent and growing body of empirical evidence supports the efficacy of psychosocial and pharmacological treatments for youth with obsessive–compulsive disorder (OCD; Freeman, Garcia, et al., 2014; Pediatric OCD Treatment Study [POTS] Team, 2004).

In this chapter, we briefly review the evidence base for pharmacotherapy, cognitive behavior therapy (CBT), and the combination of these evidence-based treatment approaches. As in other chapters, we limit our review to information we believe to be of primary interest to clinicians when consulting with parents and youth regarding the condition and the evidence-based options to treat it.

EFFICACY OF COGNITIVE BEHAVIOR THERAPY

CBT is the most studied psychosocial treatment for OCD and is considered the first-line psychosocial treatment for children and adolescents (ages 7–18) with mild-to-moderate cases of OCD (Geller, March, & AACAP Committee on Quality Issues [CQI], 2012). The evidence base for CBT as the psychological treatment of choice comes from numerous studies of CBT for pediatric OCD focused on exposure with response prevention. The research consistently demonstrates remission rates between 40% and 85% across studies in children and adolescents with OCD (Barrett, Healy-Farrell, & March, 2004; Pediatric OCD

http://dx.doi.org/10.1037/0000167-012
Cognitive Behavior Therapy for OCD in Youth: A Step-by-Step Guide, by M. A. Tompkins, D. J. Owen, N. H. Shiloff, and L. R. Tanner

Treatment Study [POTS] Team, 2004). Meta-analyses of randomized controlled trials of CBT for pediatric OCD exhibit large effect sizes (Abramowitz, Franklin, Schwartz, & Furr, 2003; Watson & Rees, 2008), and other studies support CBT alone as being more efficacious than medication alone (de Haan, Hoogduin, Buitelaar, & Keijsers, 1998; Pediatric OCD Treatment Study [POTS] Team, 2004). Additionally, studies support the durability of CBT for pediatric OCD for at least 18 months posttreatment (Barrett, Farrell, Dadds, & Boulter, 2005; March, Mulle, & Herbel, 1994).

The treatment studies to date have a number of limitations, including their generalizability to populations with comorbid disorders (Barrett, Farrell, Pina, Peris, & Piacentini, 2008). The available data indicate that psychosocial treatment response may be mediated by pretreatment functioning. Greater symptom severity at baseline, as well as worse anxiety, and the level of impairment in academic and social functioning may predict poorer treatment outcomes (Barrett et al., 2005; Piacentini, Bergman, Jacobs, McCracken, & Kretchman, 2002). The literature also shows strong support for the use of CBT to treat pediatric OCD, regardless of the youth's medication status at baseline (Piacentini et al., 2002). In addition, CBT may be the psychological treatment of choice for pediatric autoimmune neuropsychiatric disorders associated with streptococcal infections subtypes (Valderhaug, Larsson, Götestam, & Piacentini, 2007).

EFFICACY OF PHARMACOTHERAPY

Selective serotonin reuptake inhibitors (SSRIs, a class of antidepressant medications commonly prescribed for anxiety, mood disorders, and OCD) are the pharmacologic first-line treatment for pediatric OCD. The most commonly prescribed SSRI medications for pediatric OCD are paroxetine, fluoxetine, fluvoxamine, and sertraline. A meta-analysis of randomized controlled medication trials for children and adolescents including SSRIs and clomipramine (Geller, Biederman, Stewart, Mullin, Martin, et al., 2003) found significant pooled effects of medication versus placebo, and an overall effect size of 0.46 or a 4- to 6-point decrease in Children's Yale–Brown Obsessive Compulsive Scale (CY-BOCS; Scahill et al., 1997) between active and placebo conditions. The results of four standardized measures indicated that youth who took medication with active ingredients had a significant reduction in symptoms compared with participants in the placebo group. Furthermore, the study confirmed that the SSRIs appear to have similar effects; therefore, the decision to use one medication over another may depend more on managing side effects than on efficacy. At least two randomized controlled multisite psychopharmacological trials of pediatric OCD have demonstrated improvements in psychosocial functioning of youth who accepted a trial of SSRIs (Geller et al., 2001; Liebowitz et al., 2002). Medications that selectively effect norepinephrine have not been found to be effective for pediatric OCD (Leonard et al., 1989) as well.

At this time, only fluoxetine (for ages 7 and above), fluvoxamine (for ages 8 and above), and sertraline (for ages 6 and above) are FDA-approved for use in the treatment of pediatric OCD. Although the FDA has not approved some SSRIs (e.g., paroxetine, citalopram), and some non-SSRI medications (e.g., venlafaxine) for the treatment of pediatric OCD, physicians occasionally do prescribe these medications for youth with the condition. It is important to note that although SSRIs do carry the potential for side effects, such as increased anxiety, jitteriness, nausea, diarrhea, and insomnia, most side effects subside over time. Most youth tolerate these medications well, but some youth continue to experience side effects throughout the medication treatment period.

When youth fail to respond adequately to first-line treatments such as SSRIs, clinicians may suggest a trial of clomipramine, a tricyclic antidepressant medication. Some studies show clomipramine to have superior efficacy over SSRIs (Geller, Biederman, Stewart, Mullin, Martin, et al., 2003), but others do not (Abramowitz, Whiteside, & Deacon, 2005). Regardless, clomipramine is not a first-line treatment for pediatric OCD, in part because of recurrent adverse events (DeVeaugh-Geiss et al., 1992; Puig-Antich et al., 1987) and the need for ongoing medical monitoring (e.g., electrocardiograms and blood panels) for arrhythmogenic effects (Geller, Biederman, Stewart, Mullin, Martin, et al., 2003).

The most common question parents and youth ask clinicians and prescribers about antiobsessional medications concerns their short- and long-term safety. A review of the literature on the safety and side effects of medications for pediatric OCD found that although these medications result in side effects, variously labeled as activation, akathisia, disinhibition, impulsivity, and hyperactivity, there is no strong evidence that these medications significantly increase the relative risk of suicidal thoughts or behaviors (Nischal, Tripathi, Nischal, & Trivedi, 2012). Although risk for suicidal ideation does exist for youth taking SSRIs, there are no reported cases of actual suicides because of SSRIs (Blier, Habib, & Flament, 2006). Nevertheless, we recommend that clinicians, in collaboration with the prescriber, closely monitor suicidal thoughts and behaviors for every youth taking SSRIs.

EFFICACY OF COMBINING COGNITIVE BEHAVIOR THERAPY AND PHARMACOTHERAPY

Several studies have compared the effectiveness of medication combined with CBT to treat pediatric OCD, but the Pediatric Obsessive-Compulsive Disorder Treatment Study (POTS) is the most notable (Pediatric OCD Treatment Study [POTS] Team, 2004). The multisite POTS study deemed that the combination of individual CBT and sertraline met the criteria of probably efficacious (Chambless et al., 1998; Chambless & Hollon, 1998). The combination of medication and CBT was superior to medication alone: however, the combination did not differ significantly from CBT alone (Pediatric OCD Treatment

Study [POTS] Team, 2004). The rate of remission in the POTS study does not demonstrate CBT or CBT plus medication to be unilaterally effective treatments for youth; however, the evidence is persuasive regarding the potential efficacy of CBT alone or in combination with medication for the treatment of pediatric OCD (Pediatric OCD Treatment Study [POTS] Team, 2004). Guidelines by the American Academy of Child and Adolescent Psychiatry for the treatment of pediatric OCD recommend a combination of CBT and medications for severe cases of OCD (American Academy of Child and Adolescent Psychiatry, 2012).

COLLABORATING WITH MEDICATION PRESCRIBERS

It is common for adults who seek therapy to arrive for treatment already taking a psychotropic medication, but it is far less common for youth. This means two things for nonprescribing clinicians treating pediatric OCD. First, the nonprescribing clinician may be the first mental health professional to present the option of medication, alone or in combination with CBT, to youth and parents. Second, because the combination of medication and CBT is a first-line treatment for certain youth with pediatric OCD, clinicians are likely to find themselves working closely with a prescriber currently or in the future. For an excellent book on this topic, see *Combining CBT and Medication: An Evidence-Based Approach* (Sudak, 2011).

Advantages of Collaborative Care

Collaborative care (Gabbard, 2006) is a team approach whereby the prescriber and nonprescriber work together to provide a consistent, coordinated, and effective treatment. Collaborative care in the treatment of pediatric OCD has several advantages. First, it can reinforce adherence to the goals and tasks of each therapeutic approach (pharmacotherapy and CBT). Second, collaborative care provides greater support to youth and parents, particularly during crises. Third, it is likely that the nonprescribing clinician will have more clinical contact with youth and parents than the prescriber when starting, changing, or stopping medication. The nonprescribing clinician can then provide more frequent updates to the psychiatrist regarding the youth's response to the medication (including side effects) and work with youth and parents to follow the medication treatment plan. Last, collaborative care is particularly important in community clinic settings when clinicians and trainees rotate in an out of the clinical setting. Youth and parents who meet with at least one member of the collaborative care team will feel less anxious during these transitions in care.

The Cooperative Relationship of Collaborative Care

Collaborative care rests on establishing and maintaining the cooperative relationship on which collaborative care rests.

Communication

Clear communication is the foundation of a collaborative relationship between the prescribing and nonprescribing clinician, particularly when one or both treatments are not going well. Anxious parents may have great trouble assisting their child to adhere to the medication or exposure plans. At such times, parents might complain that the prescriber or the nonprescribing clinician is incompetent or that the respective treatments are too difficult, or seek reassurance about some aspect of one or both treatment approaches. For example, parents may ask nonprescribing clinicians repeatedly about whether the medication is safe, if a particular side effect is typical, or how long the youth must remain on the medication. Similarly, parents may ask the prescriber whether exposure is safe, whether it is necessary for them to follow the clinician's recommendations regarding withdrawing accommodations, or whether their child with OCD can be successful in life. Of course, these questions are best addressed by the respective professionals early in the treatment process.

Education

Although most psychiatrists understand CBT for pediatric OCD, not all understand the essential role of exposure in the process of change. Furthermore, primary care physicians and pediatricians who most often prescribe medications, even psychotropic medications, to youth may not understand exposure-based therapies at all (Mark, Levit, & Buck, 2009). These physicians may emphasize skills over exposure when they discuss with parents CBT for OCD. Often, this means that the clinician must work harder to convince the parents in the consultation meeting of the benefits of exposure-based therapy. In addition, some psychiatrists (as well as other mental health professionals) view exposure as dangerous and traumatizing for all youth and do not explicitly support this approach (Deacon et al., 2013). For these reasons, we recommend that both prescribing and nonprescribing clinicians teach each other. For nonprescribing clinicians, it is essential that they know the typical medications prescribed for pediatric OCD, including augmentation agents, the side effects of these medications, and what to look for in terms of treatment response and adverse effects. To that end, we recommend that clinicians discuss these topics and read the fine books written for nonprescribing clinicians on the topic of pharmacotherapy with youth (Elliott, 2006; Preston, O'Neal, & Talaga, 2015; Wilens & Hammerness, 2016).

Respect

Both CBT and pharmacotherapy are evidence-based treatments for pediatric OCD; therefore, both are valid treatment approaches. It is essential that both the prescribing and nonprescribing clinician respect the advantages and disadvantages of each approach and work to help youth and parents adhere to the respective treatment plans. Collaboration is quite powerful in establishing and maintaining treatment adherence, and we encourage prescribing clinicians to ask youth and parents the following: "Are you [youth and parents] meeting regularly and at the frequency that the nonprescribing clinician recommended?" "Are you [youth] doing the assigned exposures in and out of session?" "Are you [parents] implementing the changes the nonprescribing clinician recommended regarding your parenting?" "What are you [youth and parents] learning that is helping?" "What skills are you [youth and parents] learning, and how are they helpful?"

WHEN TO CONSIDER MEDICATION AS AN OPTION

We recommend that nonprescribing clinicians discuss the option of medication with parents during the initial consultation session. There are several advantages to this. First, medication is an evidence-based option for pediatric OCD, and introducing rather than avoiding discussing this option communicates to parents that the nonprescribing clinician is open to that option if the parents wish to pursue it. For parents who are not open to that option, introducing the topic of medication at the first meeting provides an opportunity for them to discuss their concerns and preferences. Also, it permits nonprescribing clinicians to present their recommendations regarding medication given the particular youth's and family's clinical situation. Last, introducing the option of medication early makes the discussion a bit easier if over the course of therapy medication becomes a more pressing option to consider. Generally, we say something like this:

> As you may know, there are three evidence-based options for the treatment of pediatric OCD. The first option is CBT alone. I'll say more about this treatment in a moment. The second option is medication alone, which is also an evidence-based option for pediatric OCD. The third option is a combination of CBT and medication. I'll describe best practice guidelines for those three options, and, based on my evaluation of your child's unique strengths and weaknesses and your particular situation, I'll offer my recommendations.

Many parents will consider medication when CBT alone does not result in a significant change in their child's OCD symptoms. Other parents, however, will still oppose including a medication trial for their child along with CBT in spite of their child's failure to respond to CBT alone. In these circumstances, we recommend that clinicians refer youth to a higher level of care, such as intensive outpatient or residential OCD treatment programs. Intensive OCD programs provide youth with many hours of daily supervised or independent exposure and response prevention (ERP) practice. The intensive and consistent massed ERP practice that these programs provide can greatly benefit youth with severe OCD that have not responded to routine outpatient CBT. For a list of intensive outpatient and residential OCD treatment programs in the United States, check http://www.iocdf.org.

INTRODUCING THE OPTION OF MEDICATION

The decision to add medications to CBT is not an easy one for most parents, particularly parents who may be anxious or even have OCD themselves. However, there are several good reasons to add medication to CBT. First, the combination of CBT and medication may be the most effective option for complicated youth with multiple co-occurring conditions, such as youth with trauma histories, co-occurring tic disorders, or pervasive developmental delays. Similarly, youth (or one or more parents) with co-occurring attention-deficit/hyperactivity disorder (ADHD) can struggle to remember and to follow through with essential ERP tasks. When evaluating complicated youth and parents, we recommend that clinicians consider a combined treatment approach and introduce that recommendation early with an appropriate rationale for the recommendation. For example,

> Your son has OCD and ADHD as well as some social anxiety. This is a complicated clinical picture. I recommend that you consider adding medication to CBT for your son's OCD. The most important thing is for your son's treatment to be successful, and I believe a combined treatment is the best way to ensure that.

In such cases, prescribers might consider prescribing other medications in addition to an SSRI, such as stimulant medication for ADHD or mood stabilizer for mood disorders.

A second reason to consider adding medication to the treatment plan is when youth are significantly disabled by their OCD symptoms. For example, if the youth is not able to attend school or is taking showers that last 2 or 3 hours. Furthermore, medication makes sense when youth are reluctant to begin CBT and, in particular, when they balk at the prospect of exposure-based therapy. Last, when the youth's response to CBT is low, both youth and parents may be more open to adding medication to the treatment plan. Furthermore, when youth fail to respond to conventional CBT for their OCD, we recommend that clinicians discuss treatment alternatives sooner rather than later to avoid further demoralizing youth and parents.

Once the clinician introduces the topic of medication, parents will have many questions. We recommend that clinicians assist youth and parents through a thoughtful analysis of the costs and benefits of starting and not starting medication. At times, parents or youth may identify a minus for medication that is based on misinformation or a misperception. At those times, clinicians can provide accurate information to correct these misunderstandings. When youth and parents identify a real problem with taking medication, such as the cost, clinicians can move into problem-solving.

One last word about medications. We do not recommend, in general, the use of benzodiazepines for the treatment of pediatric OCD. Although medical professionals rarely prescribe benzodiazepines to youth, particularly children, they sometimes do. This is most common in cases of a co-occurring condition such as panic disorder or chronic pain disorders. Youth are not likely to benefit fully from exposure-based treatments such as ERP if they take a benzodiazepine before an exposure trial (Marks et al., 1993). If benzodiazepine is prescribed, it is important to educate youth, parents, and the prescriber regarding the effects of the drug's use during CBT and to work out a plan to taper benzodiazepine use prior to or during CBT.

MANAGING FEARS REGARDING MEDICATION

When youth with OCD are too afraid to take medications, we recommend that clinicians target this fear using the exposure strategies presented earlier in the book. The first step is to revisit the case conceptualization developed for the youth's OCD. Fears of vomiting, choking, or the ill effects of medication itself may drive the youth's reluctance or refusal to take medication. It is essential that clinicians understand the focal fear and target it with the exposure strategies (situational, imaginal, and interoceptive) described earlier. Figure 11.1 shows a typical situational ERP plan related to health obsessions and medication.

ROLE OF CBT WHEN STARTING MEDICATION OR INCREASING THE DOSE

CBT can assist the process of increasing or tapering medications. As mentioned, exposure-based strategies are useful for overcoming the anxiety and fears youth may have when starting medication or with each incremental increase in medication. Furthermore, once youth are on a maintenance dose of medication, exposure-based strategies can decrease the

FIGURE 11.1. Situational Hierarchy for Medication-Related Obsessive Fears

Fear rating[a]	Situation
100	Swallow full pill of medication.
90	Swallow half-pill of medication.
80	Hold half-pill of medication in mouth but do not swallow.
70	Touch pill to tongue and swallow saliva.
60	Touch moist pill to closed lips and swallow saliva.
50	Touch dry pill to closed lips and swallow saliva.
40	Touch moist pill in closed hand.
30	Hold dry pill in closed hand.
20	Touch inside of pill bottle.
10	Hold outside of pill bottle.

[a]0 = *low*, 100 = *high*.

residual breakthrough symptoms common for youth on medication alone (Simpson et al., 2008), particularly when youth experience medication-related obsessive fears.

ROLE OF CBT WHEN DISCONTINUING MEDICATION

We recommend that clinicians include ERP booster sessions during medication withdrawal. Although research has not categorically established the optimal duration of treatment on SSRI medications, most prescribers recommend 9 to 18 months before tapering off the medication (March et al., 1997). Typically, prescribers taper down or lower medication dosage by 25%, waiting for 2 to 3 months before lowering again. The goal of this slow taper is to identify the minimum dose of medication and CBT that manages the symptoms. With youth who received CBT alone, the dose might be no medication and a yearly wellness checkup. For other youth, a low-dose of SSRI and a wellness checkup every 3 months might be sufficient. In addition, a slow taper allows both the prescriber and nonprescribing clinician to watch for signs of relapse. Relapse is common with discontinuation of medication (Flament et al., 1990; Leonard et al., 1993), and prescribers can lessen the likelihood of relapse by increasing the medication dosage for a time. Long-term maintenance on medication is recommended after three to four mild relapses or two to three severe relapses (March et al., 1997).

MANAGING MEDICATION NONADHERENCE IN COGNITIVE BEHAVIOR THERAPY

Poor medication adherence can be a problem for some youth with OCD who receive CBT and medication. J. S. Beck (2001) classified nonadherence problems as either practical, psychological, or a combination of the two.

Practical Problems or Nonpsychological Factors

Examples of practical problems include overwhelmed parents who do not have the time or the capacity to supervise the youth's medication adherence; youth who move between the homes of divorced parents, making the logistics of remembering, finding, and taking medications more complicated; or the single mother with five children and a full-time job who rightfully complains that she is too overwhelmed to track whether or not her son takes his medication. It is important that clinicians help youth and parents identify and solve the real practical problems that contribute to the difficulties they have in adhering with the medication plan. We recommend that clinicians teach youth and parents problem-solving skills that they can use to solve the current and future medication-adherence problems, as well as other problems that arise in their lives. For example, Carl is 14 years old and often fails to take his medication when he visits his father's house, although he typically remembers to take the medication when he is in his mother's house. We might assist Carl to solve this practical problem in this way:

CLINICIAN: So, Carl, it looks like you tend to remember to take your medications when you're at your mom's house but often forget when you're at your dad's place. Have you always forgotten to take your medications when you were at your dad's house?

CARL: No, I was pretty good at first. I'd take them at my dad's and my mom's places.

CLINICIAN: I see. Do you remember when you started to forget to take your medications at your dad's place?

CARL: Yes. I think it was when I started soccer practice. Sometimes my dad picked me up from soccer, and sometimes my mom did. My dad is great, but he forgets things more than my mom. My mom never forgets anything. Sometimes my dad works at home at night and then he forgets to remind me to take my medications.

CLINICIAN: So if you're at your dad's place, he's busy at night and sometimes forgets to remind you to take your medication. I'll speak to your dad about trying to remind you when you're at his place. At the same time, I think it's important for you to depend on yourself a little more when it comes to taking your medications. How about if we use the problem-solving tool I taught you? We'll list all the possible solutions to this problem and the pluses and minuses of each solution. You remember how we've done this before. You start, okay?

CARL: Well, I guess I could set an alarm in my phone to remind me. The plus is that I'm pretty sure it will work if I get up right away and take my medications. The minus is that sometimes I'm in the middle of something, and then I forget.

CLINICIAN: Okay. So, a reminder on your phone could work, but if you don't take your medications immediately, then you might forget. How about other solutions for this problem?

CARL: I guess I could set up repeating reminders, but the minus is that constant beeping is really annoying. The plus is that it would help me remember.

CLINICIAN: That's a solution. Other possible solutions?

CARL: Maybe I could keep the medication in my bathroom. I could leave it by my toothbrush. That would remind me to take it.

CLINICIAN: That's a solution. What are the pluses and minuses?

CARL: I guess the plus is that I would see my medication and take it. The last thing I do at night is brush my teeth, so I'm not going to be doing anything else, and I'll definitely see the medication bottle. The minus is that my stepsister is pretty young, and my dad doesn't like me to keep my medication out so that she can reach it.

CLINICIAN: Good point. Other solutions?

CARL: Well, maybe I could move my toothbrush. Right now, my toothbrush is on the counter, but I could move it to the top shelf of the medicine cabinet. I could put my medication right next to it. My stepsister can't reach that, and I think my dad would be good with that.

CLINICIAN: That's a solution. Other solutions?

CARL: No. That's it.

CLINICIAN: Okay. Which solution do you want to try first?

CARL: I like the idea of moving my toothbrush to the medicine cabinet and putting my medication next to it. I think that would work best.

CLINICIAN: Okay. We'll bring your dad in now and check to see whether he's cool with this plan. Then you can try it. You did a great job of solving this one on your own. Well done!

Psychological Factors

Many youth and parents refuse medication trials or fail to adhere to the medication treatment plan because they have incorrect information. For example, some youth and parents believe SSRI medications are addictive, that SSRI medications affect the youth's ability to think clearly and to learn in the classroom, or that SSRI medications increase the youth's risk of using alcohol and drugs in the future (research suggests that the opposite is true). We recommend that clinicians explore with parents and youth what they know about medication and from where they gathered their information. Similarly, we recommend that clinicians ask them what they know about OCD and how often medications are prescribed for the condition. Ask them if they know anyone who takes medication and what they have observed. Last, ask them to tell you their concerns about medication—small and large—and refer them to appropriate information on the topic.

At times, poor medication adherence can be influenced by the OCD itself, as we described earlier. For example, Kami is a 16-year-old with OCD who was terrified of becoming addicted to drugs and therefore refused to take OCD medications because these medications had been stored in a pharmacy along with addictive medications (which of course is true). In addition to providing

Kami with correct information about the addiction potential of OCD medications, the clinician also targeted Kami's medication-related obsessive fears with ERP.

Still other youth refuse medication because of what they believe taking a medication means about themselves or others. They might believe that taking medication means that they are weak and that taking medications is a crutch. Youth with ADHD might refuse to use reminder systems because they believe that they will remember and that using a reminder system takes too much effort. Perfectionistic youth may refuse rewards offered for medication adherence because they believe that they do not deserve rewards for something they believe that they should do. Nonadherence thoughts like these are common, and we recommend that clinicians target these thoughts and behaviors and utilize typical cognitive behavior strategies to alter them (J. S. Beck, 2001).

Combination of Practical and Psychological Factors

In our experience, medication nonadherence in youth is often caused by psychological factors creating practical problems. Youth with OCD and co-occurring ADHD may be the best example of this. It is common for youth with ADHD to forget to take their medication or forget that they have taken it. Clinicians can use a host of prompting strategies, such as pairing the taking of medication with a routine daily activity such as brushing teeth or feeding pets. Youth can set an alarm (or include an alert in their phone) to remind them to take medication. They can use medication organizers to help them remember that they took their medication. In addition, clinicians can encourage cognitive rehearsal (imagine in detail taking the medication) to help youth remember to take medication or to identify potential obstacles and develop plans to work through them. Finally, clinicians can encourage youth and parents to monitor medication adherence. On a form, youth and parents enter each dose taken, the points youth earned for taking it, as well as noting any side effects.

CONCLUSION

Both CBT and pharmacotherapy are evidence-based treatments for pediatric OCD; the combination of CBT and medications is generally recommended for severe cases of the disorder or complex cases with multiple co-occurring conditions. Therefore, it is likely that the topic of medication will arise during therapy and, once broached, will require thoughtful discussion with youth and parents and then careful planning with the prescriber, if applicable.

In the next chapter, we describe typical obstacles that arise when conducting CBT for pediatric OCD, such as working with overanxious parents or when the motivation of youth decreases, and strategies to overcome them.

12

Overcoming Obstacles

Ample clinical evidence supports the effectiveness of the core strategies, particularly exposure and response prevention (ERP), in the psychological treatment of pediatric obsessive–compulsive disorder (OCD). However, the effectiveness of a core strategy depends on clinicians' implementing it correctly. In our experience, particularly with clinicians who are new to cognitive behavior therapy (CBT), most obstacles arise in routine practice because of poor implementation of a core strategy. For example, clinicians may develop exposure tasks that fail to target the youth's core fear, which thereby results in inadequate response to exposure. Or they may fail to adjust the value of reinforcers or the reinforcement baseline in response to a drop in the motivation of youth. In this chapter, we describe typical obstacles that arise when implementing the core strategies and offer suggestions to overcome them.

GATHERING INFORMATION

An effective treatment plan depends in part on the quality of data that clinicians gather during the assessment process. Two common obstacles arise as clinicians gather information from youth, and both involve self-monitoring. Self-monitoring is a critical core strategy that builds self-awareness, particularly regarding covert experiences such as the frequency and nature of obsessions

http://dx.doi.org/10.1037/0000167-013
Cognitive Behavior Therapy for OCD in Youth: A Step-by-Step Guide, by M. A. Tompkins,
D. J. Owen, N. H. Shiloff, and L. R. Tanner

and mental neutralizations, and assists in treatment planning. The first obstacle to effective self-monitoring is a feature of OCD itself, and the second is related to ability of youth to identify their covert experiences.

When Youth Record Compulsively

The strategy of self-monitoring is a task, and like many tasks in which youth with OCD participate, they can engage in self-monitoring compulsively. Youth who record every detail of an OCD episode are soon overwhelmed by the task. They may give up in exasperation, or they may provide information that is overly detailed and difficult for the clinician to interpret or use effectively for treatment planning.

When this occurs, we recommend that clinicians place limits on the self-monitoring process. For example, the clinician can create a sheet that lists relevant triggers, obsessions, and neutralizations. The clinician then directs youth to check a box when triggered. The clinician can also ask youth to monitor one piece of information (e.g., triggers) each day. This breaks self-monitoring into smaller steps that limits overrecording. In addition, they can ask youth to describe the situation in just a few words (e.g., bullet points) per incident to capture rather than describe each situation in well-constructed and detailed sentences. If these strategies fail, clinicians can ask parents to record for youth who reports the features of the situation (e.g., trigger, obsession, neutralization). Last, clinicians can target compulsive recording and design an ERP hierarchy to treat these symptoms.

When Youth Have Poor Self-Awareness

At times, youth may have very poor self-awareness, and this influences their ability to self-record. This is particularly true for youth with specific or pervasive learning disorders in which awareness of thoughts and emotions is often a core deficit. Clinicians can overcome this through focused training with youth. For example, clinicians can trigger the youth's OCD in session and then ask the youth to "talk aloud" to describe obsessions and neutralizations. Similarly, clinicians can ask youth to imagine a recent trigger situation and "talk aloud" to describe covert mental events. Also clinicians can direct older youth with greater self-awareness to set reminders on their smartphones to prompt them to self-record.

Clinicians can ask parents, when they observe that their child is anxious or distressed or when the child is in typical trigger situations, to prompt the child to self-record. Some parents, however, have great trouble prompting their child, perhaps because they have similar neurocognitive weaknesses. Clinicians can direct the parent who is better able to prompt to assume this task, or they may recommend visual prompts in typical trigger situations (e.g., Post-it notes on the dinner table to capture food-related triggers). Clinicians can also encourage parents to set alarms on their mobile devices to remind them to prompt their child to record an event.

ENGAGEMENT

Engagement is an ongoing process that begins at the first meeting and continues through to the last. CBT for pediatric OCD is a difficult treatment, particularly the ERP tasks that are critical to recovery from the condition, and the motivation of youth and their parents to engage in ERP will fluctuate.

Review Rationale of Core Strategies

Youth and parents can lose sight of the reason for engaging in a core strategy, particularly ERP tasks. We recommend that clinicians provide the rationale for each core strategy before asking youth and parents to implement the strategy, particularly early in treatment. This can be quick, such as "self-recording helps you know when OCD is lurking in the weeds" or "facing your fears is difficult, but over time, as you face your fears, you'll learn that there is nothing to fear in the first place." As treatment progresses, we recommend that clinicians ask youth and parents to tell the clinician the rationale for the core strategy; for example: "So please tell me why it's important to not reassure your child when he is anxious."

Metaphors are an excellent strategy to enhance engagement, and we recommend that clinicians work with youth to find the metaphor that works for them. For some youth, the idea of a false alarm resonates with their OCD experience, whereas other youth connect with the idea of a bully that frightens them. Feel free to ask youth for ideas of the best way to present rationales for core strategies (e.g., "How would you tell a friend why facing fears helps?").

When Youth Overvalue OCD

Youth who overvalue the perceived benefits of OCD are particularly difficult to engage in the treatment process. When clinicians encounter this obstacle, we recommend that they assist youth to remember life before OCD (e.g., "Did you have more fun before OCD started to boss you around?" "Are there things that OCD won't let you do anymore that you miss?"). Youth who can connect to a time when they were happier or less anxious are more likely to work in therapy to reconnect with those times again. For many youth, the greatest benefit of recovering from OCD is to regain time to do things that they enjoy and value. We recommend that clinicians revisit the youth's values (e.g., "Once you've pushed OCD out of your life, what do you want to fill it with again?").

When the Reinforcement Baseline Is Too Rich

In some families, youth receive many privileges and rewards without having to do anything to earn them. Sleepovers with friends, sweet treats, screen time, shopping trips, and staying up late are all part of their daily lives. This makes for an overrich reinforcement baseline that decreases the motivation of youth to work for additional incremental reinforcers. To overcome this obstacle, clinicians can try one of two strategies. First, clinicians can work with parents to identify those reinforcers that are "free" versus those for which the youth is expected to earn. For example, parents can give their child 30 minutes of screen time per day after the child has completed all school homework. But the child must earn additional screen time, perhaps in 5-minute increments up to a maximum per day. Second, clinicians can brainstorm with parents a larger reward that the youth does not receive and link this to the reinforcement plan (e.g., a trip to an amusement park with three friends).

When Reinforcers Become Stale

In some cases, reinforcers become stale when youth receive them too often. In such cases, the clinician and the youth can brainstorm new rewards that the youth is eager to earn. For example, clinicians might suggest as rewards one-on-one time with a parent, a special job at home, preferred seating in the car or dinner table, or the privilege of deciding where the family sits in a restaurant. Also we recommend that parents take particular rewards out of circulation from time to time to maintain their value. For example, if a youth enjoys a particular video game, parents can withhold that video game for several months and reintroduce the game later as a reinforcer.

When Youth Decline Rewards

At times, certain youth will decline rewards. Typically, this occurs with youth who are perfectionistic or who suffer with scrupulosity (i.e., an excessive concern with right or wrong or morality). These youth may believe that it is wrong to be rewarded for working to overcome OCD or that they should do ERP tasks because that is what the clinician and parents expect them to do. In these instances, we recommend that clinicians and youth examine the pluses and minuses of two attitudes: "do it because I think I should" versus "accept rewards because I'm doing something that is more difficult than other things I do." In addition, clinicians can facilitate a discussion with youth and parents who then give the youth permission to accept rewards for the hard work of ERP tasks.

At other times, youth who are depressed will decline rewards because they do not see the point or they no longer enjoy activities that were once rewarding and pleasurable in the past (i.e., anhedonia). In these cases, we recommend that clinicians identify rewards and activities that the youth once found pleasurable and include these items in the reward list. As the youth earns these rewards and enjoys them, they will likely begin to feel less depressed. Reinforcers will then feel more rewarding, and this will further enhance the youth's motivation. The clinician can then work with the youth to add new rewards to the reinforcement list.

When Youth Do Not Respond to Time-Outs

Time-outs are effective, but only when done correctly. Three typical obstacles arise when parents implement time-out procedures with their child. First, some parents delay the time-out and instead fall into the trap of teaching, negotiating, or even arguing with the child. This only increases the likelihood of a tantrum. Furthermore, parents can become angry and throw their own tantrum. We recommend that clinicians remind parents to direct their child to time-out quickly and without hesitation and role-play this repeatedly with parents until they are confident that they can do this.

Second, some parents increase the frequency of tantrums or other push-back behaviors by inadvertently reinforcing them. The best example of this is the parent who directs the child to his room for time-out where he has easy access to toys and video games. It does not take the child long to discover the formula for more video game time. We recommend that clinicians remind parents that time-out means time-out from rewards and attention. The clinician then helps parents to locate a time-out spot that is free from reinforcers, such as the kitchen, bathroom, or hallway. At times, the child's room is the only viable time-out spot; in this case, we recommend that parents remove all reinforcers from the child's room and establish a "play" area in another part of the residence.

Third, some parents view a time-out as a teaching moment and then explain to the child why she received a time-out. This often results in another time-out and an escalation of pushback behavior. If parents must say something at the end of time-out, we recommend only "please tell me why you got this time out." If the child does not know, then provide a very brief explanation and move on.

Last, parents might remove a demand or command given prior to the time-out. For example, if the parent instructed the child to pick up her backpack and carry it to her room, the parent might do this while the child is in time-out. We recommend that the clinician instruct parents to direct youth to complete any task that preceded the time-out.

When Youth Are Unmotivated for Treatment

Some youth, no matter how hard the clinician works on engagement, are unmotivated for treatment. With older youth, we recommend that clinicians use motivational interviewing strategies (see Chapter 5, this volume). For youth who continue to reluctantly and inadequately engage in treatment, we recommend that clinicians discuss with youth and parents whether it is the right time for the family to engage in treatment. For some youth with mild OCD, their symptoms may not be sufficiently distressing or disruptive to motivate them to engage in CBT. For these families, we recommend that the family wait until the youth's symptoms worsen and motivation increases before returning to treatment. When low motivation is because of high family accommodation, we recommend that the clinician discontinue ongoing meetings with the youth and work intensely with parents to decrease their accommodation behaviors. For some youth, focusing on decreasing family accommodation behaviors is sufficient to significantly reduce OCD symptoms (Lebowitz et al., 2012). For youth with severe OCD, we recommend that the clinician speak with parents regarding the addition of medication to the treatment plan or a referral to an intensive OCD treatment program. At times, the discussion of these less desirable treatment alternatives is sufficient to engage youth in outpatient CBT.

Working with unmotivated youth can at times discourage clinicians. We encourage clinicians not to take the youth's low engagement personally. Instead, we recommend that the clinician remain curious about the reasons the youth is not interested in help with the OCD. An open and curious attitude can lead to frank conversations with youth that can strengthen the therapeutic alliance and perhaps enhance the willingness of youth to recommit to treatment or consider treatment alternatives. Furthermore, at these times parents can pressure the clinician to "convince" their child to engage in treatment or to "force" their child to do ERP practices. These situations can be difficult for clinicians, but we encourage clinicians to remember that our job is not to convince youth to engage in treatment when they are not open to it. Our job is to assess whether youth are ready for appropriate evidence-based treatment and offer that treatment when they are open to trying it.

PSYCHOEDUCATION

Psychoeducation typically covers a number of topics that clinicians introduce and reintroduce throughout treatment. Psychoeducation involves primarily imparting information to youth and parents to instill hope, to destigmatize the condition, and to engage the family in the treatment process.

When Youth Are Easily Bored or Distracted

Psychoeducation includes considerable information and often in great detail. At times, easily distracted or overwhelmed youth may disengage from the psychoeducation process. If this is the case, we recommend that clinicians avoid lecturing in favor of imparting information through storytelling, metaphors, and with younger youth play. Also, we recommend that clinicians use strategies to increase the likelihood youth will remember key points. For example, write important points in different colors on a whiteboard and draw designs or cartoons to illustrate the points. Give youth periodic quizzes on the material covered for which they earn rewards for correct answers. Break a topic into smaller chunks, and introduce these minitopics throughout a session rather than presenting a topic for 30 minutes without interruption.

When Youth Have Trouble Labeling the Degree of Anxiety

Some youth have difficulty labeling on the fear thermometer the degree of anxiety they are experiencing. For example, youth with need for exactness obsessions may struggle to decide whether they feel 3 or 4 on the fear ther-mometer. In these cases, we recommend that the clinician encourage youth to "estimate" the number or to convert this task into an ERP task, and reward youth for taking a chance that the number they select may be wrong and tolerating the discomfort that they are not certain it is correct. Other youth may benefit from using colors rather than numbers to identify their anxiety level (e.g., red is high, yellow is moderate, blue is low). The clinician may want to spend extra time with youth to anchor the fear thermometer ratings to trigger situations (e.g., trigger situations at home are high, trigger situa-tions in school or medium, trigger situations in the car are low). Similarly, clinicians can help youth link anxiety levels to physical sensations (e.g., "When your hands tremble, that's an 8 on the fear thermometer"). Last, the clinician can use the observations of parents and teachers to build the youth's fear thermometer.

WORKING WITH THE FAMILY

Parents are important allies in the battle against OCD, but they can at times inadvertently undermine their child's progress in treatment. Often, parenting strategies that were only moderately effective prior to the onset of OCD become less effective and often contribute to an amplification of their child's OCD symptoms.

When Parents Push Too Hard

Once parents observe the power of ERP to decrease their child's OCD symp-toms, they may begin to push their child to move through ERP tasks faster. In this instance, we recommend that clinicians explain the difference between forced and planned exposure tasks. We remind parents that successful ERP tasks depend on the willingness of youth to engage in them. Providing youth with the choice of which ERP task to try and when to try it enhances their willingness to participate in the most difficult part of the treatment process. We remind parents that the objective of the reinforcement system is to pull rather than push youth through the treatment process. Youth who feel pushed by parents will likely push back. We recommend that clinicians assist parents to encourage rather than push their child to remain in the anxiety-evoking situation and resist neutralizations through the use of praise and tangible rewards. Furthermore, for out-of-session ERP practice, we instruct parents to prompt and support their child to practice only the ERP tasks that the child and clinician have agreed that the child will do.

When Parents Blame Their Child for OCD

A key objective of psychoeducation is to educate youth and parents about the condition, particularly the youth's neutralizations and the great difficulty they have in resisting these neutralizations even when the youth views these actions as unreasonable. At times, parents believe that youth could stop the compulsions if they tried harder and blame them for a condition that is not their fault. Youth can begin to feel ashamed and guilty and push back against the clinician and parents, or youth may conceal symptoms rather than sharing them as they arise. In these instances, we recommend that clinicians sympathize with the distress the parents feel while offering an analogy that they may understand (e.g., "If your child had the flu and couldn't stop coughing, would you punish or criticize him?").

At times, parents may blame their child because they do not know how to respond to their child's symptoms in a constructive manner. We recommend that clinicians meet with parents and review basic parenting strategies, such as how to respond to their distressed child in a way that assists the child to recognize OCD, encourages the child to resist neutralizations, and praises the child for standing up to OCD (e.g., "It looks like OCD is bugging you right now. How about if we ignore him and wait for him to go away? I know you can do it").

When Parents Are Overanxious

Because anxious youth often have anxious parents, many parents feel quite anxious when implementing response prevention plans. They may worry that their child will have a tantrum if they refuse to participate in the youth's neutralizations, as the youth likely has done in the past. If this is the case, we recommend that clinicians review key parenting strategies, particularly ways to manage pushback behaviors and schedule additional parent-only meetings in which clinicians assist parents to practice adaptive responding through repeated role play exercises.

Some anxious parents are overly concerned that dropping certain neutralizations may be unsafe or unhealthy for their child. For example, parents may balk when the clinician suggests that their child no longer wash his hands after returning from school or the playground or to not wash before eating. Although not washing in these situations may increase the risk of exposure to germs and thus illness, the inherent risk is small, and therefore handwashing can only decrease the risk of illness below a level of risk that is already quite low. We recommend that clinicians remind parents, however, that if their child continues to engage in these handwashing behaviors, the risk is high that the child will continue to struggle with OCD and suffer significant short- and long-term consequences.

When Parents Have Negative Views Regarding Rewards

At times, parents view rewards as bribery. They tell clinicians that they do not believe in rewarding their child for doing what they expect the child to do. To support this view, parents will tell the clinician that when they were children, their parents did not reward or praise them for doing what their parents told them to do. In these instances, we recommend that the clinician describe to parents the difference between rewards and bribes. For example, rewards are given after the youth exhibits the desired behavior, whereas bribes are given before the youth exhibits the desired behavior. The clinician might state, "It's never a good idea to reward your child before he does what you've asked him to do."

In addition, we recommend that clinicians normalize the use of rewards in motivating people to complete tasks, particularly difficult tasks. They might say, "Rewards motivate all of us. You receive a paycheck and paid holidays. Would you go to work every day if your company didn't pay you?" Even little rewards motivate us. Remind parents, "That cup of coffee in the morning gets me out of bed. Does that cup of coffee in the morning motivate you too?"

IMPLEMENTING GRADED EXPOSURE WITH RESPONSE PREVENTION

Graded exposure with response prevention is the critical core strategy in the treatment of pediatric OCD. Therefore, it is critical that clinicians implement this core strategy correctly.

When Exposures Overwhelm Youth

Certain youth may be easily overwhelmed by a particular exposure and therefore reluctant to engage in the ERP task. In these cases, we recommend that clinicians break down the exposure into smaller more manageable steps. However, it is necessary that youth experience some anxiety during exposures to benefit from them. If youth refuse to engage in even very small ERP tasks, we recommend that clinicians revisit psychoeducation. The clinician can then reexplain the role of exposure in overcoming OCD and mention that exposure, by definition, includes some anxiety and that some anxiety is necessary to benefit from the process. Also clinicians may wish to review and adjust the reinforcement plan to increase the youth's motivation.

When Youth Are Poor Imagers

Imaginal exposure is an effective exposure strategy, particularly when combined with situational exposures. However, the effectiveness of imaginal exposure depends on the youth's ability to bring forth and hold rich and detailed images, and not all youth can do this easily. When this obstacle arises, we recommend that the clinician provide some imagery training. Typically, imagery training involves instructing youth to imagine a fun scene, such as swimming in a warm pool, and to instruct youth to describe aloud all features of the scene (what they hear, see, feel, and smell). As youth bring forth the image, the clinician asks youth to rate the intensity of the image from 0 to 10, where 10 is "technicolor intense," and repeat this process until youth report intense images. The clinician then assigns additional imagery practice as an action plan at home.

When the Clinician Is Distressed by Content of Imaginal Exposures

At times, clinicians who are new to exposure therapy may wonder whether the content of imaginal exposures is appropriate. It is not necessary to embellish the content of the imaginal exposure beyond the content of the youth's actual obsessions. Typically, youth are already experiencing many of the distressing thoughts and images that the clinician would include in an imaginal exposure script. We find it helps to remember that distressing thoughts will enter the youth's mind no matter what the clinician does because this is the nature of an obsession.

When Youth Have Obsessions About OCD Itself

Youth will sometimes report obsessions or doubts about whether they have OCD, whether a new symptom is OCD, whether they are doing the ERP tasks correctly, or whether OCD will return. In these cases, we recommend that the clinician explain to youth and parents that this is a variation of OCD and target these obsessions for treatment. Typically, clinicians use a combination of imaginal and situational exposures to target obsessions about OCD, and they implement the strategies in the same manner. Clinicians also use typical response prevention strategies for obsessions about OCD, particularly for youth seeking subtle reassurance from the clinician: "Do you think I'll get better? Do you think this is OCD?"

When Progress Is Slow

At times, youth are progressing in treatment but the progress is very slow. Typically, two obstacles arise that hamper progress in treatment: inconsistent resistance to neutralizations and minineutralizations or stealth neutralizations during ERP tasks.

When Youth Do Not Consistently Resist Neutralizations

To fully benefit from treatment of pediatric OCD, youth must resist neutralizations consistently. This certainly includes resisting neutralizations during graded-exposure tasks but also resisting neutralizations outside of formal exposure tasks when an event or activity triggers the youth's OCD during the course of the day. Youth who resist neutralizations some of the time intermittently reinforce neutralizations and thereby maintain and strengthen the urges to neutralize. When we observe this, we explain the function of the intermittent reinforcement machine using the analogy of a slot machine:

> Well, it is a little like playing a slot machine. Most of the time when OCD pulls the lever on the slot machine, he doesn't get anything because you resist the urge to do the compulsion. However, every once in a while when OCD pulls the lever, you do the compulsion and OCD hits the jackpot. OCD likes jackpots, and when he hits one, he thinks the next jackpot is just around the corner. That's

why OCD keeps pulling the lever over and over, trying harder and harder to get you to give in. If you give in, OCD hits the jackpot again. If you want OCD to go away and stay away, he can't win any jackpots. That means you can't give in to any of the OCD urges. Eventually, OCD will get bored and stop pulling the lever.

When Youth Engage in Minirituals or Stealth Rituals

At times, youth engage in minirituals or stealth rituals that undermine the effectiveness of exposure tasks. Some youth know that they are engaging in minirituals or stealth rituals. Other youth engage in these minirituals automatically without realizing they are doing them. Mental reassurance is a typical type of stealth ritual. For example, a youth with contamination fears may resist urges to wash by telling himself, "I haven't touched anything dirty today, so it's okay not to wash my hands." The same youth may also engage in minirituals, such as wiping his hands on his jeans before he touches other things rather than washing his hands. We recommend that clinicians repeatedly check with youth about the presence of these minirituals or stealth rituals and explain the role of these neutralizations in the maintenance of their OCD. The clinician might say,

> The OCD is snacking. It can't get a big meal from you as it does when you wash your hands, but if it snacks all day on little meals, such as when you wipe your hands, that can still make OCD bigger and stronger. Do you think you could stop wiping off your hands to stop feeding the OCD these snacks?

RELAPSE PREVENTION

Relapse prevention is the final core strategy in CBT for pediatric OCD. The great news about CBT for pediatric OCD is that it is a durable treatment. That is, most youth get better and stay better. At the same time, some youth and parents are reluctant to end treatment or seek frequent contact with the clinician after termination of treatment.

When Youth or Parents Are Reluctant to End Treatment

Often, families have lived through many months and sometimes years of distress. They have grown desperate and hopeless and wondered whether there was anything that could be done to eliminate OCD from their lives. Now that they are feeling better, they are reluctant to end treatment, even after the youth has fully recovered from OCD. At the same time, it is essential that youth and parents gain confidence that they can manage the condition on their own. When parents or youth report that they are anxious about ending treatment, we recommend that clinicians negotiate a longer taper phase with youth and parents. Rather than meeting every other week for 1 month and then every third week for the next month, the clinician might meet with the family every other week for 3 months and then every third week for the next 3 months. Often, the family gains confidence that they have the skills to manage the condition and terminate treatment before finishing the extended treatment taper plan.

Managing Frequent Contact Following Termination

Some youth and parents will contact the clinician repeatedly during the treatment taper phase and at times long after treatment has ended. We recommend that clinicians manage frequent contact in several ways. First, when parents or youth call, strive for a neutral nonreinforcing attitude on the telephone. Keep the conversations brief, and refer the family to the skills learned in treatment. Second, the goal of treatment has been to enhance the family's confidence that they have the skills and knowledge to manage the OCD on their own. To that end, we encourage youth and parents to keep notes from sessions and other information in a therapy notebook. When the family calls, refer them to the therapy notebook first (e.g., "Before I help you, please look through your therapy notebook and find something that might be useful right now"). Last, we recommend that the clinician consider inviting youth and parents in for one or two sessions focused on imaginal exposures to their fears of terminating treatment. At times, these are obsessive fears of OCD returning, and we recommend that clinicians target these for ERP practice.

CONCLUSION

In this the final chapter, we identified common obstacles that arise as clinicians implement the core strategies and then provided suggestions to work through these obstacles. If poor treatment continues after reviewing and adjusting the implementation of core strategies, we recommend that clinicians revisit the case conceptualization of the youth. At times, clinicians may have missed a vital factor, such as targeting the wrong or less important core fear, or ongoing substance use that undermines treatment response. Reconceptualizing the case can yield a more effective treatment plan that results in greater treatment progress. Last, if the response to treatment remains poor, we recommend that clinicians seek consultation with cognitive behavior clinicians experienced in treating pediatric OCD. Often, a second pair of ears and a few suggestions are all that is required to reinvigorate a flagging treatment.

In conclusion, CBT is an effective and durable treatment for pediatric OCD. The effectiveness of the approach rests on a compassionate and respectful therapeutic relationship that enables the thoughtful, flexible, and creative application of the core treatment strategies.

REFERENCES

Abramowitz, J. S. (1996). Variants of exposure and response prevention in the treatment of obsessive–compulsive disorder: A meta-analysis. *Behavior Therapy, 27,* 583–600. http://dx.doi.org/10.1016/S0005-7894(96)80045-1

Abramowitz, J. S. (2006). *Understanding and treating obsessive-compulsive disorder: A cognitive behavioral approach.* Mahwah, NJ: Lawrence Erlbaum Associates.

Abramowitz, J. S., Deacon, B. J., & Whiteside, S. P. H. (2011). *Exposure therapy for anxiety: Principles and practice.* New York, NY: Guilford Press.

Abramowitz, J. S., Franklin, M. E., Schwartz, S. A., & Furr, J. M. (2003). Symptom presentation and outcome of cognitive-behavioral therapy for obsessive–compulsive disorder. *Journal of Consulting and Clinical Psychology, 71,* 1049–1057. http://dx.doi.org/10.1037/0022-006X.71.6.1049

Abramowitz, J. S., Whiteside, S. P., & Deacon, B. J. (2005). The effectiveness of treatment for pediatric obsessive–compulsive disorder: A meta-analysis. *Behavior Therapy, 36,* 55–63. http://dx.doi.org/10.1016/S0005-7894(05)80054-1

Achenbach, T. M. (1991a). *Manual for the Child Behavior Checklist/4-18 and 1991 Profile.* Burlington: University of Vermont Department of Psychiatry.

Achenbach, T. M. (1991b). *Manual for the Youth Self-Report and 1991 Profile.* Burlington: University of Vermont Department of Psychiatry.

Adams, G. B., Waas, G. A., March, J. S., & Smith, M. C. (1994). Obsessive–compulsive disorder in children and adolescents: The role of the school psychologist in identification, assessment, and treatment. *School Psychology Quarterly, 9,* 274–294. http://dx.doi.org/10.1037/h0088290

Addis, M. E., & Jacobson, N. S. (2000). A closer look at the treatment rationale and homework compliance in cognitive-behavioral therapy for depression. *Cognitive Therapy and Research, 24,* 313–326. http://dx.doi.org/10.1023/A:1005563304265

Addis, M. E., & Krasnow, A. D. (2000). A national survey of practicing psychologists' attitudes toward psychotherapy treatment manuals. *Journal of*

Consulting and Clinical Psychology, 68, 331–339. http://dx.doi.org/10.1037/0022-006X.68.2.331

Alexander, J. M., Fabricius, W. V., Fleming, V. M., Zwahr, M., & Brown, S. A. (2003). The development of metacognitive causal explanations. *Learning and Individual Differences, 13,* 227–238. http://dx.doi.org/10.1016/S1041-6080(02)00091-2

Allsopp, M., & Verduyn, C. (1990). Adolescents with obsessive–compulsive disorder: A case note review of consecutive patients referred to a provincial regional adolescent psychiatry unit. *Journal of Adolescence, 13,* 157–169. http://dx.doi.org/10.1016/0140-1971(90)90005-R

American Academy of Child and Adolescent Psychiatry. (2012). Practice parameter for assessment and treatment of children and adolescents with obsessive-compulsive disorder. *Journal of the American Academy of Child and Adolescent Psychiatry, 51,* 98–113. http://dx.doi.org/10.1016/j.jaac.2011.09.019

American Psychiatric Association. (2013). *Diagnostic and statistical manual of mental disorders* (5th ed.). Arlington, VA: Author.

Amir, N., Freshman, M., & Foa, E. B. (2000). Family distress and involvement in relatives of obsessive–compulsive disorder patients. *Journal of Anxiety Disorders, 14,* 209–217. http://dx.doi.org/10.1016/S0887-6185(99)00032-8

Andreoli, E., Finore, E. D., Provini, A., & Paradisi, M. (2008). Dermatiti da auto-aggressione: Un caso in età pediatrica [Self-inflicted dermatitis: A case in pediatric age]. *Minerva Pediatrica, 60,* 355–359.

Annon, J. S. (1975). *The behavioral treatment of sexual problems: I: Brief therapy.* Oxford, England: Enabling Systems.

Arch, J. J., & Abramowitz, J. S. (2015). Exposure therapy for obsessive–compulsive disorder: An optimizing inhibitory learning approach. *Journal of Obsessive–Compulsive and Related Disorders, 6,* 174–182.

Arch, J. J., Twohig, M. P., Deacon, B. J., Landy, L. N., & Bluett, E. J. (2015). The credibility of exposure therapy: Does the theoretical rationale matter? *Behaviour Research and Therapy, 72,* 81–92. http://dx.doi.org/10.1016/j.brat.2015.05.008

Arkowitz, H., Westra, H. A., Miller, W. R., & Rollnick, S. (Eds.). (2008). *Motivational interviewing in the treatment of psychological problems.* New York, NY: Guilford Press.

Armbruster, P., & Fallon, T. (1994). Clinical, sociodemographic, and systems risk factors for attrition in a children's mental health clinic. *American Journal of Orthopsychiatry, 64,* 577–585. http://dx.doi.org/10.1037/h0079571

Assion, H.-J., Brune, N., Schmidt, N., Aubel, T., Edel, M.-A., Basilowski, M., . . . Frommberger, U. (2009). Trauma exposure and post-traumatic stress disorder in bipolar disorder. *Social Psychiatry and Psychiatric Epidemiology, 44,* 1041–1049. http://dx.doi.org/10.1007/s00127-009-0029-1

Bandelow, B., Michaelis, S., & Wedekind, D. (2017). Treatment of anxiety disorders. *Dialogues in Clinical Neuroscience, 19,* 93–107.

Bandura, A. (1977). Self-efficacy: Toward a unifying theory of behavioral change. *Psychological Review, 84,* 191–215. http://dx.doi.org/10.1037/0033-295X.84.2.191

Bandura, A. (1988). Self-efficacy conception of anxiety. *Anxiety Research, 1,* 77–98. http://dx.doi.org/10.1080/10615808808248222

Barlow, D. H., & Hersen, M. (1984). *Single-case experimental designs: Strategies for studying behavior change* (2nd ed.). New York, NY: Pergamon Press.

Barmish, A. J., & Kendall, P. C. (2005). Should parents be co-clients in cognitive-behavioral therapy for anxious youth? *Journal of Clinical Child & Adolescent Psychology, 34,* 569–581. http://dx.doi.org/10.1207/s15374424jccp3403_12

Barrett, P., Farrell, L., Dadds, M., & Boulter, N. (2005). Cognitive-behavioral family treatment of childhood obsessive–compulsive disorder: Long-term follow-up and predictors of outcome. *Journal of the American Academy of Child & Adolescent Psychiatry, 44,* 1005–1014. http://dx.doi.org/10.1097/01.chi.0000172555.26349.94

Barrett, P., Healy-Farrell, L., & March, J. S. (2004). Cognitive-behavioral family treatment of childhood obsessive–compulsive disorder: A controlled trial. *Journal of the American Academy of Child & Adolescent Psychiatry, 43,* 46–62. http://dx.doi.org/10.1097/00004583-200401000-00014

Barrett, P., Shortt, A., & Healy, L. (2002). Do parent and child behaviours differentiate families whose children have obsessive–compulsive disorder from other clinic and non-clinic families? *Journal of Child Psychology and Psychiatry, 43,* 597–607. http://dx.doi.org/10.1111/1469-7610.00049

Barrett, P. M., Farrell, L., Pina, A. A., Peris, T. S., & Piacentini, J. (2008). Evidence-based psychosocial treatments for child and adolescent obsessive–compulsive disorder. *Journal of Clinical Child & Adolescent Psychology, 37,* 131–155. http://dx.doi.org/10.1080/15374410701817956

Beck, A. T., Ward, C. H., Mendelson, M., Mock, J., & Erbaugh, J. (1961). An inventory for measuring depression. *Archives of General Psychiatry, 4,* 561–571. http://dx.doi.org/10.1001/archpsyc.1961.01710120031004

Beck, J. S. (1995). *Cognitive therapy: Basics and beyond.* New York, NY: Guilford Press.

Beck, J. S. (2001). A cognitive therapy approach to medication compliance. In J. Kay (Ed.), *Integrated psychiatric treatment for psychiatric disorders* (pp. 113–141). Washington, DC: American Psychiatric Publishing.

Becker, K., Jennen-Steinmetz, Ch., Holtmann, M., El-Faddagh, M., & Schmidt, M. H. (2003). Komordibität bei Zwangsstörungen im Kindes- und Jugendalter [Comorbidity of compulsive disorders in childhood and adolescence]. *Zeitschrift für Kinder- und Jugendpsychiatrie und Psychotherapie, 31,* 175–185. http://dx.doi.org/10.1024/1422-4917.31.3.175

Beidel, D. C., & Turner, S. M. (1998). *Shy children, phobic adults: Nature and treatment of social phobia.* Washington, DC: American Psychological Association. http://dx.doi.org/10.1037/10285-000

Bell-Dolan, D., & Suarez, L. (2001). Obsessive compulsive disorder. In H. Orvaschel, J. Faust, & M. Hersen (Eds.), *Handbook of conceptualization and treatment of child psychopathology* (pp. 267–287). Oxford, England: Elsevier Science. http://dx.doi.org/10.1016/B978-008043362-2/50014-7

Benazon, N. R., Ager, J., & Rosenberg, D. R. (2002). Cognitive behavior therapy in treatment-naive children and adolescents with obsessive–compulsive disorder: An open trial. *Behaviour Research and Therapy, 40,* 529–539. http://dx.doi.org/10.1016/S0005-7967(01)00064-X

Beutler, L. E., & Harwood, T. M. (2000). *Prescriptive psychotherapy: A practical guide to systematic treatment selection.* New York, NY: Oxford University Press. http://dx.doi.org/10.1093/med:psych/9780195136692.001.0001

Bjork, R. A. (1994). Memory and metamemory considerations in the training of human beings. In J. Metcalfe and A. Shimamura (Eds.), *Metacognition: Knowing about knowing* (pp. 185–205). Cambridge, MA: MIT Press.

Black, D. W., Gaffney, G. R., Schlosser, S., & Gabel, J. (2003). Children of parents with obsessive–compulsive disorder—A 2-year follow-up study. *Acta Psychiatrica Scandinavica, 107,* 305–313. http://dx.doi.org/10.1034/j.1600-0447.2003.02182.x

Blake, J. J., Kim, E. S., Lund, E. M., Zhou, Q., Kwok, O., & Benz, M. R. (2016). Predictors of bully victimization in students with disabilities: A longitudinal examination using a national data set. *Journal of Disability Policy Studies, 25,* 1–10.

Blanchard, E. B. (1970). Relative contributions of modeling, informational influences, and physical contact in extinction of phobic behavior. *Journal of Abnormal Psychology, 76,* 55–61. http://dx.doi.org/10.1037/h0029635

Blanco, C., Alegría, A. A., Petry, N. M., Grant, J. E., Simpson, H. B., Liu, S.-M., . . . Hasin, D. S. (2010). Prevalence and correlates of fire-setting in the United States: Results from the National Epidemiologic Survey on Alcohol and Related Conditions (NESARC). *The Journal of Clinical Psychiatry, 71,* 1218–1225. http://dx.doi.org/10.4088/JCP.08m04812gry

Blier, P., Habib, R., & Flament, M. F. (2006). Pharmacotherapies in the management of obsessive–compulsive disorder. *The Canadian Journal of Psychiatry/ La revue Canadienne de psychiatrie, 51,* 417–430. http://dx.doi.org/10.1177/070674370605100703

Bluett, E. J., Homan, K. J., Morrison, K. L., Levin, M. E., & Twohig, M. P. (2014). Acceptance and commitment therapy for anxiety and OCD spectrum disorders: An empirical review. *Journal of Anxiety Disorders, 28,* 612–624. http://dx.doi.org/10.1016/j.janxdis.2014.06.008

Boileau, B. (2011). A review of obsessive–compulsive disorder in children and adolescents. *Dialogues in Clinical Neuroscience, 13,* 401–411.

Bolton, D., Luckie, M., & Steinberg, D. (1995). Long-term course of obsessive–compulsive disorder treated in adolescence. *Journal of the American Academy of Child & Adolescent Psychiatry, 34,* 1441–1450. http://dx.doi.org/10.1097/00004583-199511000-00010

Borntrager, C. F., Chorpita, B. F., Higa-McMillan, C., & Weisz, J. R. (2009). Provider attitudes toward evidence-based practices: Are the concerns with the evidence or with the manuals? *Psychiatric Services, 60,* 677–681. http://dx.doi.org/10.1176/ps.2009.60.5.677

Bouton, M. E. (2002). Context, ambiguity, and unlearning: Sources of relapse after behavioral extinction. *Biological Psychiatry, 52,* 976–986. http://dx.doi.org/10.1016/S0006-3223(02)01546-9

Brakoulias, V., Starcevic, V., Sammut, P., Berle, D., Milicevic, D., Moses, K., & Hannan, A. (2011). Obsessive–compulsive spectrum disorders: A comorbidity and family history perspective. *Australasian Psychiatry, 19,* 151–155. http://dx.doi.org/10.3109/10398562.2010.526718

Calvocoressi, L., Lewis, B., Harris, M., Trufan, S. J., Goodman, W. K., McDougle, C. J., & Price, L. H. (1995). Family accommodation in obsessive–compulsive disorder. *The American Journal of Psychiatry, 152,* 441–443. http://dx.doi.org/10.1176/ajp.152.3.441

Caporino, N. E., Morgan, J., Beckstead, J., Phares, V., Murphy, T. K., & Storch, E. A. (2012). A structural equation analysis of family accommodation in pediatric obsessive–compulsive disorder. *Journal of Abnormal Child Psychology, 40,* 133–143. http://dx.doi.org/10.1007/s10802-011-9549-8

Carter, A. S., & Pollock, R. A. (2000). Obsessions and compulsions: The developmental and familial context. In A. J. Sameroff & M. Lewis (Eds.), *Handbook of developmental psychopathology* (2nd ed., pp. 549–566). Dordrecht, Netherlands: Kluwer. http://dx.doi.org/10.1007/978-1-4615-4163-9_29

Castle, D. J., & Groves, A. (2000). The internal and external boundaries of obsessive–compulsive disorder. *Australian and New Zealand Journal of Psychiatry, 34*, 249–255.

Cautela, J. R., & Kearney, A. J. (1990). Behavior analysis, cognitive therapy, and covert conditioning. *Journal of Behavior Therapy and Experimental Psychiatry, 21*, 83–90. http://dx.doi.org/10.1016/0005-7916(90)90013-B

Chabane, N., Delorme, R., Millet, B., Mouren, M. C., Leboyer, M., & Pauls, D. (2005). Early-onset obsessive–compulsive disorder: A subgroup with a specific clinical and familial pattern? *Journal of Child Psychology and Psychiatry, 46*, 881–887. http://dx.doi.org/10.1111/j.1469-7610.2004.00382.x

Chambless, D. L., Baker, M. J., Baucom, D. H., Beutler, L. E., Calhoun, K. S., Crits-Cristoph, P., . . . Woody, S. R. (1998). Update on empirically validated therapies. II. *Clinical Psychologist, 51*, 3–16.

Chambless, D. L., & Hollon, S. D. (1998). Defining empirically supported therapies. *Journal of Consulting and Clinical Psychology, 66*, 7–18. http://dx.doi.org/10.1037/0022-006X.66.1.7

Chang, K., Frankovich, J., Cooperstock, M., Cunningham, M. W., Latimer, M. E., Murphy, T. K., . . . Swedo, S. E., & the PANS Collaborative Consortium. (2015). Clinical evaluation of youth with pediatric acute-onset neuropsychiatric syndrome (PANS): Recommendations from the 2013 PANS Consensus Conference. *Journal of Child and Adolescent Psychopharmacology, 25*, 3–13. http://dx.doi.org/10.1089/cap.2014.0084

Chansky, T. E. (2000). *Freeing your child from obsessive–compulsive disorder: A powerful, practical program for parents of children and adolescents.* New York, NY: Crown.

Chaturvedi, S. K. (1993). Neurosis across cultures. *International Review of Psychiatry, 5*, 179–191. http://dx.doi.org/10.3109/09540269309028309

Chorpita, B. F., Daleiden, E. L., & Weisz, J. R. (2005a). Identifying and selecting the common elements of evidence based interventions: A distillation and matching model. *Mental Health Services Research, 7*, 5–20. http://dx.doi.org/10.1007/s11020-005-1962-6

Chorpita, B. F., Daleiden, E. L., & Weisz, J. R. (2005b). Modularity in the design and application of therapeutic interventions. *Applied & Preventive Psychology, 11*, 141–156. http://dx.doi.org/10.1016/j.appsy.2005.05.002

Chorpita, B. F., Taylor, A. A., Francis, S. E., Moffitt, C. E., & Austin, A. A. (2004). Efficacy of modular cognitive behavior therapy for childhood anxiety disorders. *Behavior Therapy, 35*, 263–287. http://dx.doi.org/10.1016/S0005-7894(04)80039-X

Chorpita, B. F., Weisz, J. R., Daleiden, E. L., Schoenwald, S. K., Palinkas, L. A., Miranda, J., . . . Gibbons, R. D., & the Research Network on Youth Mental Health. (2013). Long-term outcomes for the Child STEPs randomized effectiveness trial: A comparison of modular and standard treatment designs with usual care. *Journal of Consulting and Clinical Psychology, 81*, 999–1009. http://dx.doi.org/10.1037/a0034200

Christenson, G. A., Mackenzie, T. B., Mitchell, J. E., & Callies, A. L. (1991). A placebo-controlled, double-blind crossover study of fluoxetine in trichotillomania. *The American Journal of Psychiatry, 148*, 1566–1571. http://dx.doi.org/10.1176/ajp.148.11.1566

Coffey, B. J., & Park, K. S. (1997). Behavioral and emotional aspects of Tourette syndrome. *Neurologic Clinics, 15*, 277–289. http://dx.doi.org/10.1016/S0733-8619(05)70312-1

Cohen, J. A., Deblinger, E., Mannarino, A. P., & Steer, R. A. (2004). A multisite, randomized controlled trial for children with sexual abuse–related PTSD symptoms. *Journal of the American Academy of Child & Adolescent Psychiatry, 43,* 393–402. http://dx.doi.org/10.1097/00004583-200404000-00005

Comer, J. S., Furr, J. M., Cooper-Vince, C. E., Kerns, C. E., Chan, P. T., Edson, A. L., . . . Freeman, J. B. (2014). Internet-delivered, family-based treatment for early-onset OCD: A preliminary case series. *Journal of Clinical Child & Adolescent Psychology, 43,* 74–87. http://dx.doi.org/10.1080/15374416.2013.855127

Cone, J. D. (1999). Introduction to the special section on self-monitoring: A major assessment method in clinical psychology. *Psychological Assessment, 11,* 411–497. http://dx.doi.org/10.1037/1040-3590.11.4.411

Constantino, M. J., Castonguay, L. G., & Schutt, A. J. (2002). The working alliance: A flagship for the scientist-practioner model in psychotherapy. In G. S. Tryon (Ed.), *Counseling based on process research: Applying what we know* (pp. 81–131). Boston, MA: Allyn & Bacon.

Craske, M. G., Kircanski, K., Zelikowsky, M., Mystkowski, J., Chowdhury, N., & Baker, A. (2008). Optimizing inhibitory learning during exposure therapy. *Behaviour Research and Therapy, 46,* 5–27. http://dx.doi.org/10.1016/j.brat.2007.10.003

Craske, M. G., & Mystkowski, J. L. (2006). Exposure therapy and extinction: Clinical studies. In M. G. Craske, D. Hermans, & D. Vansteenwegen (Eds.), *Fear and learning: From basic processes to clinical implications* (pp. 217–233). Washington, DC: American Psychological Association. http://dx.doi.org/10.1037/11474-011

Craske, M. G., Treanor, M., Conway, C. C., Zbozinek, T., & Vervliet, B. (2014). Maximizing exposure therapy: An inhibitory learning approach. *Behaviour Research and Therapy, 58,* 10–23. http://dx.doi.org/10.1016/j.brat.2014.04.006

Creed, T. A., Reisweber, J., & Beck, A. T. (2011). *Cognitive therapy for adolescents in school settings.* New York, NY: Guilford Press.

Cuijpers, P. (1998). A psychoeducational approach to the treatment of depression: A meta-analysis of Lewinsohn's "Coping with Depression" course. *Behavior Therapy, 29,* 521–533. http://dx.doi.org/10.1016/S0005-7894(98)80047-6

Cusack, K. J., Grubaugh, A. L., Knapp, R. G., & Frueh, B. C. (2006). Unrecognized trauma and PTSD among public mental health consumers with chronic and severe mental illness. *Community Mental Health Journal, 42,* 487–500. http://dx.doi.org/10.1007/s10597-006-9049-4

Dattilio, F. M., & Hanna, M. A. (2012). Collaboration in cognitive-behavioral therapy. *Journal of Clinical Psychology, 68,* 146–158. http://dx.doi.org/10.1002/jclp.21831

Davidson, R. J. (1998). Affective style and affective disorders: Perspectives from affective neuroscience. *Cognition and Emotion, 12,* 307–330. http://dx.doi.org/10.1080/026999398379628

Deacon, B. J., Farrell, N. R., Kemp, J. J., Dixon, L. J., Sy, J. T., Zhang, A. R., & McGrath, P. B. (2013). Assessing therapist reservations about exposure therapy for anxiety disorders: The Therapist Beliefs about Exposure Scale. *Journal of Anxiety Disorders, 27,* 772–780. http://dx.doi.org/10.1016/j.janxdis.2013.04.006

de Haan, E., Hoogduin, K. A., Buitelaar, J. K., & Keijsers, G. P. (1998). Behavior therapy versus clomipramine for the treatment of obsessive–compulsive disorder in children and adolescents. *Journal of the American Academy of Child & Adolescent Psychiatry, 37*, 1022–1029. http://dx.doi.org/10.1097/00004583-199810000-00011

Delorme, R., Golmard, J.-L., Chabane, N., Millet, B., Krebs, M.-O., Mouren-Simeoni, M. C., & Leboyer, M. (2005). Admixture analysis of age at onset in obsessive–compulsive disorder. *Psychological Medicine, 35*, 237–243. http://dx.doi.org/10.1017/S0033291704003253

de Oliveira, S. K., & Pelajo, C. F. (2010). Pediatric autoimmune neuropsychiatric disorders associated with streptococcal infection (PANDAS): A controversial diagnosis. *Current Infectious Disease Reports, 12*, 103–109. http://dx.doi.org/10.1007/s11908-010-0082-7

de Silva, P. (2006). Culture and obsessive–compulsive disorder. *Psychiatry, 5*, 402–404. http://dx.doi.org/10.1053/j.mppsy.2006.08.006

DeVeaugh-Geiss, J., Moroz, G., Biederman, J., Cantwell, D., Fontaine, R., Greist, J. H., . . . Landau, P. (1992). Clomipramine hydrochloride in childhood and adolescent obsessive–compulsive disorder—A multicenter trial. *Journal of the American Academy of Child & Adolescent Psychiatry, 31*, 45–49. http://dx.doi.org/10.1097/00004583-199201000-00008

Diniz, J. B., Rosario-Campos, M. C., Shavitt, R. G., Curi, M., Hounie, A. G., Brotto, S. A., & Miguel, E. C. (2004). Impact of age at onset and duration of illness on the expression of comorbidities in obsessive–compulsive disorder. *The Journal of Clinical Psychiatry, 65*, 22–27. http://dx.doi.org/10.4088/JCP.v65n0104

Donker, T., Griffiths, K. M., Cuijpers, P., & Christensen, H. (2009). Psychoeducation for depression, anxiety and psychological distress: A meta-analysis. *BMC Medicine, 7*, 79. http://dx.doi.org/10.1186/1741-7015-7-79

Douglass, H. M., Moffitt, T. E., Dar, R., McGee, R., & Silva, P. (1995). Obsessive–compulsive disorder in a birth cohort of 18-year-olds: Prevalence and predictors. *Journal of the American Academy of Child & Adolescent Psychiatry, 34*, 1424–1431. http://dx.doi.org/10.1097/00004583-199511000-00008

Eichstedt, J. A., & Arnold, S. L. (2001). Childhood-onset obsessive–compulsive disorder: A tic-related subtype of OCD? *Clinical Psychology Review, 21*, 137–157. http://dx.doi.org/10.1016/S0272-7358(99)00044-6

Eisen, A. R., & Silverman, W. K. (1998). Prescriptive treatment for generalized anxiety disorder in children. *Behavior Therapy, 29*, 105–121. http://dx.doi.org/10.1016/S0005-7894(98)80034-8

Eisen, J. L., Rasmussen, S. A., Phillips, K. A., Price, L. H., Davidson, J., Lydiard, R. B., . . . Piggott, T. (2001). Insight and treatment outcome in obsessive–compulsive disorder. *Comprehensive Psychiatry, 42*, 494–497. http://dx.doi.org/10.1053/comp.2001.27898

Elliott, G. R. (2006). *Medicating young minds: How to know if psychiatric drugs will help or hurt your child*. New York, NY: Stewart, Tabori & Chang.

Emmelkamp, P. M. G., de Haan, E., & Hoogduin, C. A. L. (1990). Marital adjustment and obsessive–compulsive disorder. *The British Journal of Psychiatry, 156*, 55–60. http://dx.doi.org/10.1192/bjp.156.1.55

Emmelkamp, P. M. G., & Kraanen, J. (1977). Therapist-controlled exposure in vivo versus self-controlled exposure in vivo: A comparison with obsessive–compulsive patients. *Behaviour Research and Therapy, 15*, 491–495. http://dx.doi.org/10.1016/0005-7967(77)90005-5

England, E. L., Herbert, J. D., Forman, E. M., Rabin, S. J., Juarascio, A., & Goldstein, S. P. (2012). Acceptance-based exposure therapy for public speaking anxiety. *Journal of Contextual Behavioral Science, 1*, 66–72. http://dx.doi.org/10.1016/j.jcbs.2012.07.001

Essau, C. A., Conradt, J., & Petermann, F. (2002). Course and outcome of anxiety disorders in adolescents. *Journal of Anxiety Disorders, 16*, 67–81. http://dx.doi.org/10.1016/S0887-6185(01)00091-3

Falloon, I. R. H. (Ed.). (1988). *Handbook of behavioral family therapy.* New York, NY: Guilford Press.

Felling, R. J., & Singer, H. S. (2011). Neurobiology of Tourette syndrome: Current status and need for further investigation. *The Journal of Neuroscience, 31*, 12387–12395. http://dx.doi.org/10.1523/JNEUROSCI.0150-11.2011

Ferrão, Y. A., Shavitt, R. G., Bedin, N. R., de Mathis, M. E., Carlos Lopes, A., Fontenelle, L. F., . . . Miguel, E. C. (2006). Clinical features associated to refractory obsessive–compulsive disorder. *Journal of Affective Disorders, 94*, 199–209. http://dx.doi.org/10.1016/j.jad.2006.04.019

Fireman, B., Koran, L. M., Leventhal, J. L., & Jacobson, A. (2001). The prevalence of clinically recognized obsessive–compulsive disorder in a large health maintenance organization. *The American Journal of Psychiatry, 158*, 1904–1910. http://dx.doi.org/10.1176/appi.ajp.158.11.1904

Flament, M. F., Koby, E., Rapoport, J. L., Berg, C. J., Zahn, T., Cox, C., . . . Lenane, M. (1990). Childhood obsessive–compulsive disorder: A prospective follow-up study. *The Journal of Child Psychology and Psychiatry, 31*, 363–380. http://dx.doi.org/10.1111/j.1469-7610.1990.tb01575.x

Flament, M. F., Whitaker, A., Rapoport, J. L., Davies, M., Berg, C. Z., Kalikow, K., . . . Shaffer, D. (1988). Obsessive compulsive disorder in adolescence: An epidemiological study. *Journal of the American Academy of Child & Adolescent Psychiatry, 27*, 764–771. http://dx.doi.org/10.1097/00004583-198811000-00018

Flessner, C. A., Sapyta, J., Garcia, A., Freeman, J. B., Franklin, M. E., Foa, E., & March, J. (2011). Examining the psychometric properties of the Family Accommodation Scale-Parent-Report (FAS-PR). *Journal of Psychopathology and Behavioral Assessment, 33*, 38–46. http://dx.doi.org/10.1007/s10862-010-9196-3

Foa, E. B., Abramowitz, J. S., Franklin, M. E., & Kozak, M. J. (1999). Feared consequences, fixity of belief, and treatment outcome in patients with obsessive–compulsive disorder. *Behavior Therapy, 30*(4), 717–724. http://dx.doi.org/10.1016/S0005-7894(99)80035-5

Foa, E. B., Huppert, J. D., & Cahill, S. P. (2006). Emotional processing theory: An update. In B. O. Rothbaum (Ed.), *Pathological anxiety: Emotional processing in etiology and treatment* (pp. 3–24). New York, NY: Guilford Press.

Foa, E. B., & Kozak, M. J. (1986). Emotional processing of fear: Exposure to corrective information. *Psychological Bulletin, 99*, 20–35. http://dx.doi.org/10.1037/0033-2909.99.1.20

Foa, E. B., Kozak, M. J., Steketee, G. S., & McCarthy, P. R. (1992). Imipramine and behavior therapy in the treatment of depressive and obsessive–compulsive symptoms: Immediate and long-term effects. *British Journal of Clinical Psychology, 31*, 279–292. http://dx.doi.org/10.1111/j.2044-8260.1992.tb00995.x

Foa, E. B., & McNally, R. J. (1995). Mechanisms of change in exposure therapy. In R. B. Rapee (Ed.), *Current controversies in the anxiety disorders* (pp. 329–343). New York, NY: Guilford Press.

Foa, E. B., Steketee, G. S., Grayson, J. B., Turner, R. M., & Latimer, P. R. (1984). Deliberate exposure and blocking of obsessive–compulsive rituals: Immediate and long-term effects. *Behavior Therapy, 15,* 450–472. http://dx.doi.org/10.1016/S0005-7894(84)80049-0

Foa, E. B., Steketee, G., & Milby, J. B. (1980). Differential effects of exposure and response prevention in obsessive–compulsive washers. *Journal of Consulting and Clinical Psychology, 48,* 71–79. http://dx.doi.org/10.1037/0022-006X.48.1.71

Foa, E. B., Steketee, G., Turner, R. M., & Fischer, S. C. (1980). Effects of imaginal exposure to feared disasters in obsessive–compulsive checkers. *Behaviour Research and Therapy, 18,* 449–455. http://dx.doi.org/10.1016/0005-7967(80)90010-8

Fontenelle, L. F., Mendlowicz, M. V., Marques, C., & Versiani, M. (2004). Transcultural aspects of obsessive–compulsive disorder: A description of a Brazilian sample and a systematic review of international clinical studies. *Journal of Psychiatric Research, 38,* 403–411. http://dx.doi.org/10.1016/j.jpsychires.2003.12.004

Fontenelle, L. F., Mendlowicz, M. V., & Versiani, M. (2005). Impulse control disorders in patients with obsessive–compulsive disorder. *Psychiatry and Clinical Neurosciences, 59,* 30–37. http://dx.doi.org/10.1111/j.1440-1819.2005.01328.x

Franklin, M. E., Flessner, C. A., Woods, D. W., Keuthen, N. J., Piacentini, J. C., Moore, P., . . . the Trichotillomania Learning Center-Scientific Advisory Board. (2008). The child and adolescent trichotillomania impact project: Descriptive psychopathology, comorbidity, functional impairment, and treatment utilization. *Journal of Developmental & Behavioral Pediatrics, 29,* 493–500. http://dx.doi.org/10.1097/DBP.0b013e31818d4328

Frare, F., Perugi, G., Ruffolo, G., & Toni, C. (2004). Obsessive–compulsive disorder and body dysmorphic disorder: A comparison of clinical features. *European Psychiatry, 19,* 292–298. http://dx.doi.org/10.1016/j.eurpsy.2004.04.014

Freeman, J., Garcia, A., Frank, H., Benito, K., Conelea, C., Walther, M., & Edmunds, J. (2014). Evidence base update for psychosocial treatments for pediatric obsessive–compulsive disorder. *Journal of Clinical Child and Adolescent Psychology, 43,* 7–26. http://dx.doi.org/10.1080/15374416.2013.804386

Freeman, J., Sapyta, J., Garcia, A., Compton, S., Khanna, M., Flessner, C., . . . Franklin, M. (2014). Family-based treatment of early childhood obsessive–compulsive disorder: The Pediatric Obsessive–Compulsive Disorder Treatment Study for Young Children (POTS Jr)—A randomized clinical trial. *JAMA Psychiatry, 71,* 689–698. http://dx.doi.org/10.1001/jamapsychiatry.2014.170

Freeston, M. H., Ladouceur, R., Thibodeau, N., & Gagnon, F. (1991). Cognitive intrusions in a non-clinical population. I. Response style, subjective experience, and appraisal. *Behaviour Research and Therapy, 29,* 585–597. http://dx.doi.org/10.1016/0005-7967(91)90008-Q

Gabbard, G. (2006). The rationale for combining medication and psychotherapy. *Psychiatric Annals, 36,* 315–319.

Garcia, A. M., Freeman, J. B., Himle, M. B., Berman, N. C., Ogata, A. K., Ng, J., . . . Leonard, H. (2009). Phenomenology of early childhood onset obsessive compulsive disorder. *Journal of Psychopathology and Behavioral Assessment, 31,* 104–111. http://dx.doi.org/10.1007/s10862-008-9094-0

Geffken, G. R., Storch, E. A., Lewin, A., Adkins, J., Merlo, L. J., & Murphy, T. K. (2005, March). *Development of the Pediatric OCD Disturbance Scale: Assessing egosyntonic OCD.* Paper presented at the Anxiety Disorders Association of America Annual Conference, Seattle, WA.

Geller, D., Biederman, J., Jones, J., Park, K., Schwartz, S., Shapiro, S., & Coffey, B. (1998). Is juvenile obsessive–compulsive disorder a developmental subtype of the disorder? A review of the pediatric literature. *Journal of the American Academy of Child & Adolescent Psychiatry, 37*, 420–427. http://dx.doi.org/10.1097/00004583-199804000-00020

Geller, D. A. (2006). Obsessive–compulsive and spectrum disorders in children and adolescents. *Psychiatric Clinics of North America, 29*, 353–370. http://dx.doi.org/10.1016/j.psc.2006.02.012

Geller, D. A., Biederman, J., Faraone, S., Agranat, A., Cradock, K., Hagermoser, L., . . . Coffey, B. J. (2001). Developmental aspects of obsessive compulsive disorder: Findings in children, adolescents, and adults. *Journal of Nervous and Mental Disease, 189*, 471–477. http://dx.doi.org/10.1097/00005053-200107000-00009

Geller, D. A., Biederman, J., Faraone, S. V., Cradock, K., Hagermoser, L., Zaman, N., . . . Spencer, T. J. (2002). Attention-deficit/hyperactivity disorder in children and adolescents with obsessive–compulsive disorder: Fact or artifact? *Journal of the American Academy of Child & Adolescent Psychiatry, 41*, 52–58. http://dx.doi.org/10.1097/00004583-200201000-00011

Geller, D. A., Biederman, J., Griffin, S., Jones, J., & Lefkowitz, T. R. (1996). Comorbidity of juvenile obsessive–compulsive disorder with disruptive behavior disorders. *Journal of the American Academy of Child & Adolescent Psychiatry, 35*, 1637–1646. http://dx.doi.org/10.1097/00004583-199612000-00016

Geller, D. A., Biederman, J., Stewart, S. E., Mullin, B., Farrell, C., Wagner, K. D., . . . Carpenter, D. (2003). Impact of comorbidity on treatment response to paroxetine in pediatric obsessive–compulsive disorder: Is the use of exclusion criteria empirically supported in randomized clinical trials? *Journal of Child and Adolescent Psychopharmacology, 13*(Suppl. 1), S19–S29. http://dx.doi.org/10.1089/104454603322126313

Geller, D. A., Biederman, J., Stewart, S. E., Mullin, B., Martin, A., Spencer, T., & Faraone, S. V. (2003). Which SSRI? A meta-analysis of pharmacotherapy trials in pediatric obsessive–compulsive disorder. *The American Journal of Psychiatry, 160*, 1919–1928. http://dx.doi.org/10.1176/appi.ajp.160.11.1919

Geller, D. A., March, J. S., & AACAP Committee on Quality Issues (CQI). (2012). Practice parameter for the assessment and treatment of children and adolescents with obsessive–compulsive disorder. *Journal of the American Academy of Child & Adolescent Psychiatry, 51*, 98–113. https://dx.doi.org/10.1016/j.jaac.2011.09.019

Gillespie, M., Smith, J., Meaden, A., Jones, C., & Wane, J. (2004). Clients' engagement with assertive outreach services: A comparison of client and staff perceptions of engagement and its impact on later engagement. *Journal of Mental Health, 13*, 439–452. http://dx.doi.org/10.1080/09638230400006767

Ginsburg, G. S., & Schlossberg, M. C. (2002). Family-based treatment of childhood anxiety disorders. *International Review of Psychiatry, 14*, 143–154. http://dx.doi.org/10.1080/09540260220132662

Goodman, W., Rasmussen, S., Foa, E., & Price, L. (1994). Obsessive–compulsive disorder. In R. Prien & D. Robinson (Eds.), *Clinical evaluation of psychotropic drugs: Principles and guidelines* (pp. 431–466). New York, NY: Raven Press.

Goodman, W. K., & Price, L. H. (1992). Assessment of severity and change in obsessive compulsive disorder. *The Psychiatric Clinics of North America, 15*, 861–869. http://dx.doi.org/10.1016/S0193-953X(18)30214-4

Goodman, W. K., Price, L. H., Rasmussen, S. A., Mazure, C., Fleischmann, R. L., Hill, C. L., . . . Charney, D. S. (1989). The Yale–Brown Obsessive Compulsive Scale. I. Development, use, and reliability. *Archives of General Psychiatry, 46,* 1006–1011. http://dx.doi.org/10.1001/archpsyc.1989.01810110048007

Grant, J. E., & Kim, S. W. (2007). Clinical characteristics and psychiatric comorbidity of pyromania. *The Journal of Clinical Psychiatry, 68,* 1717–1722. http://dx.doi.org/10.4088/JCP.v68n1111

Grant, J. E., Kim, S. W., & Crow, S. J. (2001). Prevalence and clinical features of body dysmorphic disorder in adolescent and adult psychiatric inpatients. *The Journal of Clinical Psychiatry, 62,* 517–522. http://dx.doi.org/10.4088/JCP.v62n07a03

Grant, J. E., & Odlaug, B. L. (2008). Cleptomania: Características clínicas e tratamento [Kleptomania: Clinical characteristics and treatment]. *Revista Brasileira de Psiquiatria, 30*(Suppl. 1), S11–S15.

Greco, L. A., & Hayes, S. C. (2008). *Acceptance and mindfulness treatments for children and adolescents: A practitioner's guide.* Oakland, CA: New Harbinger.

Groves, P. M., & Thompson, R. F. (1970). Habituation: A dual-process theory. *Psychological Review, 77,* 419–450. http://dx.doi.org/10.1037/h0029810

Guy, W. (1976). *ECDEU assessment manual for psychopharmacology.* (DHEW Pub. No. ABM 76-388). Washington, DC: U.S. Government Printing Office.

Hanna, G. L. (1995). Demographic and clinical features of obsessive–compulsive disorder in children and adolescents. *Journal of the American Academy of Child & Adolescent Psychiatry, 34,* 19–27. http://dx.doi.org/10.1097/00004583-199501000-00009

Hayes, S. C., Strosahl, K. D., & Wilson, K. G. (1999). *Acceptance and commitment therapy: An experiential approach to psychotherapy.* New York, NY: Guilford Press.

Herzog, D. B., Nussbaum, K. M., & Marmor, A. K. (1996). Comorbidity and outcome in eating disorders. *Psychiatric Clinics of North America, 19,* 843–859. http://dx.doi.org/10.1016/S0193-953X(05)70385-3

Hibbs, E. D., Hamburger, S. D., Lenane, M., Rapoport, J. L., Kruesi, M. J., Keysor, C. S., & Goldstein, M. J. (1991). Determinants of expressed emotion in families of disturbed and normal children. *The Journal of Child Psychology and Psychiatry, 32,* 757–770. http://dx.doi.org/10.1111/j.1469-7610.1991.tb01900.x

Hodgson, R., Rachman, S., & Marks, I. M. (1972). The treatment of chronic obsessive–compulsive neurosis: Follow-up and further findings. *Behaviour Research and Therapy, 10,* 181–189. http://dx.doi.org/10.1016/S0005-7967(72)80012-3

Hollander, E., Kwon, J. H., Stein, D. J., Broatch, J., Rowland, C. T., & Himelein, C. A. (1996). Obsessive–compulsive and spectrum disorders: Overview and quality of life issues. *The Journal of Clinical Psychiatry, 57*(Suppl. 8), 3–6.

Houghton, S., & Saxon, D. (2007). An evaluation of large group CBT psychoeducation for anxiety disorders delivered in routine practice. *Patient Education and Counseling, 68,* 107–110. http://dx.doi.org/10.1016/j.pec.2007.05.010

Huebner, D. (2007). *What to do when your brain gets stuck: A kid's guide to overcoming OCD.* Washington, DC: American Psychological Association.

Huynh, M., Gavino, A. C., & Magid, M. (2013). Trichotillomania. *Seminars in Cutaneous Medicine and Surgery, 32,* 88–94. http://dx.doi.org/10.12788/j.sder.0007

Iervolino, A. C., Perroud, N., Fullana, M. A., Guipponi, M., Cherkas, L., Collier, D. A., & Mataix-Cols, D. (2009). Prevalence and heritability of compulsive hoarding: A twin study. *The American Journal of Psychiatry, 166,* 1156–1161. http://dx.doi.org/10.1176/appi.ajp.2009.08121789

Israel, A. C., Guile, C. A., Baker, J. E., & Silverman, W. K. (1994). An evaluation of enhanced self-regulation training in the treatment of childhood obesity. *Journal of Pediatric Psychology, 19,* 737–749. http://dx.doi.org/10.1093/jpepsy/19.6.737

Israel, A. C., Stolmaker, L., Sharp, J. P., Silverman, W. K., & Simon, L. G. (1984). An evaluation of two methods of parental involvement in treating obese children. *Behavior Therapy, 15,* 266–272. http://dx.doi.org/10.1016/S0005-7894(84)80028-3

Ivanov, V. Z., Mataix-Cols, D., Serlachius, E., Lichtenstein, P., Anckarsäter, H., Chang, Z., . . . Rück, C. (2013). Prevalence, comorbidity and heritability of hoarding symptoms in adolescence: A population based twin study in 15-year olds. *PLoS One, 8*(7), e69140. http://dx.doi.org/10.1371/journal.pone.0069140

Ivarsson, T., & Winge-Westholm, C. (2004). Temperamental factors in children and adolescents with obsessive–compulsive disorder (OCD) and in normal controls. *European Child & Adolescent Psychiatry, 13,* 365–372. http://dx.doi.org/10.1007/s00787-004-0411-1

Ivey, A. E., & Ivey, M. B. (2003). *Intentional interviewing and counseling: Facilitating client development in a multicultural society.* Pacific Grove, CA: Thomson/Brooks/Cole.

Jacoby, R. J., & Abramowitz, J. S. (2016). Inhibitory learning approaches to exposure therapy: A critical review and translation to obsessive–compulsive disorder. *Clinical Psychology Review, 49,* 28–40. http://dx.doi.org/10.1016/j.cpr.2016.07.001

Jefferys, D. E., & Castle, D. J. (2003). Body dysmorphic disorder—A fear of imagined ugliness. *Australian Family Physician, 32,* 722–725.

Johnson, J. G., Cohen, P., Kotler, L., Kasen, S., & Brook, J. S. (2002). Psychiatric disorders associated with risk for the development of eating disorders during adolescence and early adulthood. *Journal of Consulting and Clinical Psychology, 70,* 1119–1128. http://dx.doi.org/10.1037/0022-006X.70.5.1119

Kadesjö, B., & Gillberg, C. (2000). Tourette's disorder: Epidemiology and comorbidity in primary school children. *Journal of the American Academy of Child & Adolescent Psychiatry, 39,* 548–555. http://dx.doi.org/10.1097/00004583-200005000-00007

Kalra, S. K., & Swedo, S. E. (2009). Children with obsessive–compulsive disorder: Are they just "little adults"? *The Journal of Clinical Investigation, 119,* 737–746. http://dx.doi.org/10.1172/JCI37563

Kanfer, F. H. (1977). The many faces of self-control, or behavior modification changes its focus. In R. B. Stuart (Ed.), *Behavioral self-management: Strategies, techniques, and outcomes* (pp. 1–48). New York, NY: Brunner/Mazel.

Kazantzis, N., Fairburn, C. G., Padesky, C. A., Reinecke, M., & Teesson, M. (2014). Unresolved issues regarding the research and practice of cognitive behavior therapy: The case of guided discovery using Socratic questioning. *Behaviour Change, 31,* 1–17. http://dx.doi.org/10.1017/bec.2013.29

Kazdin, A. E. (1979). Therapy outcome questions requiring control of credibility and treatment-generated expectancies. *Behavior Therapy, 10,* 81–93. http://dx.doi.org/10.1016/S0005-7894(79)80011-8

Kazdin, A. E. (2001). *Behavior modification in applied settings* (6th ed.). Belmont, CA: Wadsworth/Thomson Learning.

Kazdin, A. E., Bass, D., Ayers, W. A., & Rodgers, A. (1990). Empirical and clinical focus of child and adolescent psychotherapy research. *Journal of Consulting and Clinical Psychology, 58*, 729–740. http://dx.doi.org/10.1037/0022-006X.58.6.729

Kazdin, A. E., Holland, L., & Crowley, M. (1997). Family experience of barriers to treatment and premature termination from child therapy. *Journal of Consulting and Clinical Psychology, 65*, 453–463. http://dx.doi.org/10.1037/0022-006X.65.3.453

Kendall, P. C., Chu, B., Gifford, A., Hayes, C., & Nauta, M. (1998). Breathing life into a manual: Flexibility and creativity with manual-based treatments. *Cognitive and Behavioral Practice, 5*, 177–198. http://dx.doi.org/10.1016/S1077-7229(98)80004-7

Kendall, P. C., Flannery-Schroeder, E., Panichelli-Mindel, S. M., Southam-Gerow, M., Henin, A., & Warman, M. (1997). Therapy for youths with anxiety disorders: A second randomized clinical trial. *Journal of Consulting and Clinical Psychology, 65*, 366–380. http://dx.doi.org/10.1037/0022-006X.65.3.366

Kendall, P. C., & Sugarman, A. (1997). Attrition in the treatment of childhood anxiety disorders. *Journal of Consulting and Clinical Psychology, 65*, 883–888. http://dx.doi.org/10.1037/0022-006X.65.5.883

Kessler, R. C., Berglund, P., Demler, O., Jin, R., Merikangas, K. R., & Walters, E. E. (2005). Lifetime prevalence and age-of-onset distributions of DSM-IV disorders in the National Comorbidity Survey Replication. *Archives of General Psychiatry, 62*, 593–602. http://dx.doi.org/10.1001/archpsyc.62.6.593

Kessler, R. C., Chiu, W. T., Demler, O., & Walters, E. E. (2005). Prevalence, severity, and comorbidity of 12-month DSM-IV disorders in the National Comorbidity Survey Replication. *Archives of General Psychiatry, 62*, 617–627. http://dx.doi.org/10.1001/archpsyc.62.6.617

Kinney, A. (1991). Cognitive-behavior therapy with children: Developmental considerations. *Journal of Rational-Emotive & Cognitive-Behavior Therapy, 9*, 51–61. http://dx.doi.org/10.1007/BF01060637

Klein, D. N., Schwartz, J. E., Santiago, N. J., Vivian, D., Vocisano, C., Castonguay, L. G., . . . Keller, M. B. (2003). Therapeutic alliance in depression treatment: Controlling for prior change and patient characteristics. *Journal of Consulting and Clinical Psychology, 71*, 997–1006. http://dx.doi.org/10.1037/0022-006X.71.6.997

Korotitsch, W. J., & Nelson-Gray, R. O. (1999). An overview of self-monitoring research in assessment and treatment. *Psychological Assessment, 11*, 415–425. http://dx.doi.org/10.1037/1040-3590.11.4.415

Kovacs, M. (1992). *Children's depression inventory manual.* Toronto, Ontario, Canada: Multi-Health Systems.

Kovacs, M., & Beck, A. T. (1977). An empirical-clinical approach toward a definition of childhood depression. In J. G. Schulterbrandt & A. Raskin (Eds.), *Depression in childhood: Diagnosis, treatment, and conceptual models* (pp. 1–25). New York, NY: Raven Press.

Lambert, M. J., Harmon, C., Slade, K., Whipple, J. L., & Hawkins, E. J. (2005). Providing feedback to psychotherapists on their patients' progress: Clinical results and practice suggestions. *Journal of Clinical Psychology, 61*, 165–174. http://dx.doi.org/10.1002/jclp.20113

Lambert, M. J., & Shimokawa, K. (2011). Collecting client feedback. *Psychotherapy, 48*, 72–79. http://dx.doi.org/10.1037/a0022238

Lang, A. J., Craske, M. G., & Bjork, R. A. (1999). Implications of a new theory of disuse for the treatment of emotional disorders. *Clinical Psychology: Science and Practice, 6,* 80–94. http://dx.doi.org/10.1093/clipsy.6.1.80

Lang, R., Didden, R., Machalicek, W., Rispoli, M., Sigafoos, J., Lancioni, G., . . . Kang, S. (2010). Behavioral treatment of chronic skin-picking in individuals with developmental disabilities: A systematic review. *Research in Developmental Disabilities, 31,* 304–315. http://dx.doi.org/10.1016/j.ridd.2009.10.017

Langley, A. K., Bergman, R. L., McCracken, J., & Piacentini, J. C. (2004). Impairment in childhood anxiety disorders: Preliminary examination of the child anxiety impact scale-parent version. *Journal of Child and Adolescent Psychopharmacology, 14,* 105–114. http://dx.doi.org/10.1089/104454604773840544

Lazarus, A. A. (1974). Multimodal behavioral treatment of depression. *Behavior Therapy, 5,* 549–554. http://dx.doi.org/10.1016/S0005-7894(74)80045-6

Leadbeater, B., & Hoglund, W. (2006). Changing the social contexts of peer victimization. *Journal of the Canadian Academy of Child and Adolescent Psychiatry/ Journal de l'Académie canadienne de psychiatrie de l'enfant et de l'adolescent, 15,* 21–26.

Lebowitz, E. R., & Omer, H. (2013). *Treating childhood and adolescent anxiety: A guide for caregivers.* Hoboken, NJ: Wiley. http://dx.doi.org/10.1002/9781118589366

Lebowitz, E. R., Panza, K. E., Su, J., & Bloch, M. H. (2012). Family accommodation in obsessive–compulsive disorder. *Expert Review of Neurotherapeutics, 12,* 229–238. http://dx.doi.org/10.1586/ern.11.200

Lebowitz, E. R., Scharfstein, L. A., & Jones, J. (2014). Comparing family accommodation in pediatric obsessive–compulsive disorder, anxiety disorders, and nonanxious children. *Depression & Anxiety, 31,* 1018–1025. http://dx.doi.org/10.1002/da.22251

Lebowitz, E. R., Vitulano, L. A., & Omer, H. (2011). Coercive and disruptive behaviors in pediatric obsessive compulsive disorder: A qualitative analysis. *Psychiatry: Interpersonal and Biological Processes, 74,* 362–371. http://dx.doi.org/10.1521/psyc.2011.74.4.362

Leckman, J. F., & Cohen, D. J. (1999). *Tourette's syndrome—tics, obsessions, compulsions: Developmental psychopathology and clinical care.* Hoboken, NJ: Wiley.

Leonard, H. L., Freeman, J., Garcia, A., Garvey, M., Snider, L., & Swedo, S. E. (2001). Obsessive–compulsive disorder and related conditions. *Pediatric Annals, 30,* 154–160. http://dx.doi.org/10.3928/0090-4481-20010301-09

Leonard, H. L., Goldberger, E. L., Rapoport, J. L., Cheslow, D. L. S., & Swedo, S. E. (1990). Childhood rituals: Normal development or obsessive–compulsive symptoms? *Journal of the American Academy of Child & Adolescent Psychiatry, 29,* 17–23. http://dx.doi.org/10.1097/00004583-199001000-00004

Leonard, H. L., Lenane, M. C., Swedo, S. E., Rettew, D. C., Gershon, E. S., & Rapoport, J. L. (1992). Tics and Tourette's disorder: A 2- to 7-year follow-up of 54 obsessive–compulsive children. *The American Journal of Psychiatry, 149,* 1244–1251. http://dx.doi.org/10.1176/ajp.149.9.1244

Leonard, H. L., Swedo, S. E., Lenane, M. C., Rettew, D. C., Hamburger, S. D., Bartko, J. J., & Rapoport, J. L. (1993). A 2- to 7-year follow-up study of 54 obsessive–compulsive children and adolescents. *Archives of General Psychiatry, 50,* 429–439. http://dx.doi.org/10.1001/archpsyc.1993.01820180023003

Leonard, H. L., Swedo, S. E., Rapoport, J. L., Koby, E. V., Lenane, M. C., Cheslow, D. L., & Hamburger, S. D. (1989). Treatment of obsessive–compulsive disorder with clomipramine and desipramine in children and adolescents. A double-blind crossover comparison. *Archives of General Psychiatry, 46,* 1088–1092. http://dx.doi.org/10.1001/archpsyc.1989.01810120030006

Lewin, A. B., Wood, J. J., Gunderson, S., Murphy, T. K., & Storch, E. A. (2011). Phenomenology of comorbid autism spectrum and obsessive–compulsive disorder among children. *Journal of Developmental and Physical Disabilities, 23,* 543–553. http://dx.doi.org/10.1007/s10882-011-9247-z

Lewis, S. (1974). A comparison of behavior therapy techniques in the reduction of fearful avoidance behavior. *Behavior Therapy, 5,* 648–655.

Liberman, R. P., Mueser, K. T., & Glynn, S. (1988). Modular behavioral strategies. In I. R. H. Falloon (Ed.), *Handbook of behavioral family therapy* (pp. 27–50). New York, NY: Guilford Press.

Liebowitz, M. R., Turner, S. M., Piacentini, J., Beidel, D. C., Clarvit, S. R., Davies, S. O., . . . Simpson, H. B. (2002). Fluoxetine in children and adolescents with OCD: A placebo-controlled trial. *Journal of the American Academy of Child & Adolescent Psychiatry, 41,* 1431–1438. http://dx.doi.org/10.1097/00004583-200212000-00014

Maia, T. V., Cooney, R. E., & Peterson, B. S. (2008). The neural bases of obsessive–compulsive disorder in children and adults. *Development and Psychopathology, 20,* 1251–1283. http://dx.doi.org/10.1017/S0954579408000606

Mancebo, M. C., Boisseau, C. L., Garnaat, S. L., Eisen, J. L., Greenberg, B. D., Sibrava, N. J., . . . Rasmussen, S. A. (2014). Long-term course of pediatric obsessive–compulsive disorder: 3 years of prospective follow-up. *Comprehensive Psychiatry, 55,* 1498–1504. http://dx.doi.org/10.1016/j.comppsych.2014.04.010

Mancebo, M. C., Garcia, A. M., Pinto, A., Freeman, J. B., Przeworski, A., Stout, R., . . . Rasmussen, S. A. (2008). Juvenile-onset OCD: Clinical features in children, adolescents and adults. *Acta Psychiatrica Scandinavica, 118,* 149–159. http://dx.doi.org/10.1111/j.1600-0447.2008.01224.x

March, J. (2012). *Multidimensional Anxiety Scale for Children* (2nd ed.). North Tonawanda, NY: Multi-Health Systems. http://dx.doi.org/10.1037/t05050-000

March, J., & Albano, A. (1996). Assessment of anxiety in children and adolescents. *American Psychiatric Press Review of Psychiatry, 15,* 405–427.

March, J. S. (1995). Cognitive-behavioral psychotherapy for children and adolescents with OCD: A review and recommendations for treatment. *Journal of the American Academy of Child & Adolescent Psychiatry, 34,* 7–18. http://dx.doi.org/10.1097/00004583-199501000-00008

March, J. S., & Benton, C. M. (2006). *Talking back to OCD: The program that helps kids and teens say "No way" and parents say "Way to go."* New York, NY: Guilford Press.

March, J. S., Frances, A., Carpenter, D., & Kahn, D. A. (1997). The expert consensus guideline series: Treatment of obsessive–compulsive disorder. *The Journal of Clinical Psychiatry, 58*(Suppl. 4), 1–72.

March, J. S., Franklin, M. E., Leonard, H. L., & Foa, E. B. (2004). Obsessive–compulsive disorder. In T. L. Morris & J. S. March (Eds.), *Anxiety disorders in children and adolescents* (pp. 212–240). New York, NY: Guilford Press.

March, J. S., Leonard, H. L., & Swedo, S. E. (1995). Obsessive–compulsive disorder. In J. S. March (Ed.), *Anxiety disorders in children and adolescents* (pp. 251–275). New York, NY: Guilford Press.

March, J. S., & Mulle, K. (1998). *OCD in children and adolescents: A cognitive-behavioral treatment manual.* New York, NY: Guilford Press.

March, J. S., Mulle, K., & Herbel, B. (1994). Behavioral psychotherapy for children and adolescents with obsessive–compulsive disorder: An open trial of a new protocol-driven treatment package. *Journal of the American Academy of Child & Adolescent Psychiatry, 33,* 333–341. http://dx.doi.org/10.1097/00004583-199403000-00006

March, J. S., & Staff, M. (1997). *Multidimensional Anxiety Scale for Children Technical Manual.* Toronto, Ontario, Canada: Multi-Health System.

Mark, T. L., Levit, K. R., & Buck, J. A. (2009). Datapoints: Psychotropic drug prescriptions by medical specialty. *Psychiatric Services, 60,* 1167. http://dx.doi.org/10.1176/ps.2009.60.9.1167

Marks, I. M., Swinson, R. P., Başoğlu, M., Kuch, K., Noshirvani, H., O'Sullivan, G., . . . Wickwire, K. (1993). Alprazolam and exposure alone and combined in panic disorder with agoraphobia: A controlled study in London and Toronto. *The British Journal of Psychiatry, 162,* 776–787. http://dx.doi.org/10.1192/bjp.162.6.776

Masi, G., Perugi, G., Toni, C., Millepiedi, S., Mucci, M., Bertini, N., & Akiskal, H. S. (2004). Obsessive–compulsive bipolar comorbidity: Focus on children and adolescents. *Journal of Affective Disorders, 78,* 175–183. http://dx.doi.org/10.1016/S0165-0327(03)00107-1

Mataix-Cols, D., Rosario-Campos, M. C., & Leckman, J. F. (2005). A multidimensional model of obsessive–compulsive disorder. *The American Journal of Psychiatry, 162,* 228–238. http://dx.doi.org/10.1176/appi.ajp.162.2.228

May, A. C., Rudy, B. M., Davis, T. E., III, & Matson, J. L. (2013). Evidence-based behavioral treatment of dog phobia with young children: Two case examples. *Behavior Modification, 37,* 143–160. http://dx.doi.org/10.1177/0145445512458524

McLeod, B. D. (2011). Relation of the alliance with outcomes in youth psychotherapy: A meta-analysis. *Clinical Psychology Review, 31,* 603–616. http://dx.doi.org/10.1016/j.cpr.2011.02.001

McLeod, B. D., Islam, N. Y., Chiu, A. W., Smith, M. M., Chu, B. C., & Wood, J. J. (2014). The relationship between alliance and client involvement in CBT for child anxiety disorders. *Journal of Clinical Child & Adolescent Psychology, 43,* 735–741. http://dx.doi.org/10.1080/15374416.2013.850699

Merlo, L. J., Lehmkuhl, H. D., Geffken, G. R., & Storch, E. A. (2009). Decreased family accommodation associated with improved therapy outcome in pediatric obsessive–compulsive disorder. *Journal of Consulting and Clinical Psychology, 77,* 355–360. http://dx.doi.org/10.1037/a0012652

Merlo, L. J., Storch, E. A., Adkins, J. W., Murphy, T. K., & Geffken, G. R. (2007). Assessment of pediatric obsessive–compulsive disorder. In E. A. Storch, G. R. Geffken, & T. K. Murphy (Eds.), *Handbook of child and adolescent obsessive–compulsive disorder* (pp. 67–107). Mahwah, NJ: Lawrence Erlbaum.

Meyer, V., & Levy, R. (1973). Modification of behavior in obsessive–compulsive disorders. In H. E. Adams & P. Unikel (Eds.; pp. 77–137), *Issues and trends in behavior therapy.* Springfield, IL: Charles C Thomas.

Meyer, V., Levy, R., & Schnurer, A. (1974). A behavioral treatment of obsessive–compulsive disorders. In H. R. Beech (Ed.), *Obsessional states.* London, England: Methuen.

Miller, W., & Rollnick, S. (2002). *Motivational interviewing: Preparing people for change* (2nd ed.). New York, NY: Guilford Press.

Miller, W. R., Benefield, R. G., & Tonigan, J. S. (1993). Enhancing motivation for change in problem drinking: A controlled comparison of two therapist styles. *Journal of Consulting and Clinical Psychology, 61,* 455–461. http://dx.doi.org/10.1037/0022-006X.61.3.455

Mills, H. L., Agras, W. S., Barlow, D. H., & Mills, J. R. (1973). Compulsive rituals treated by response prevention: An experimental analysis. *Archives of General Psychiatry, 28,* 524–529. http://dx.doi.org/10.1001/archpsyc.1973.01750340058010

Mineka, S., Davidson, M., Cook, M., & Keir, R. (1984). Observational conditioning of snake fear in rhesus monkeys. *Journal of Abnormal Psychology, 93,* 355–372. http://dx.doi.org/10.1037/0021-843X.93.4.355

Moretti, G., Pasquini, M., Mandarelli, G., Tarsitani, L., & Biondi, M. (2008). What every psychiatrist should know about PANDAS: A review. *Clinical Practice and Epidemiology in Mental Health, 4,* 13. http://dx.doi.org/10.1186/1745-0179-4-13

Moyers, T. B., Miller, W. R., & Rollnick, S. (1998). *Motivational interviewing: Professional training series.* Albuquerque: University of New Mexico.

Murphy, C. M., & Bootzin, R. R. (1973). Active and passive participation in the contact desensitization of snake fear in children. *Behavior Therapy, 4,* 203–211. http://dx.doi.org/10.1016/S0005-7894(73)80029-2

Murphy, T. K., Kurlan, R., & Leckman, J. (2010). The immunobiology of Tourette's disorder, pediatric autoimmune neuropsychiatric disorders associated with *Streptococcus,* and related disorders: A way forward. *Journal of Child and Adolescent Psychopharmacology, 20,* 317–331. http://dx.doi.org/10.1089/cap.2010.0043

Murphy, T. K., Sajid, M., Soto, O., Shapira, N., Edge, P., Yang, M., . . . Goodman, W. K. (2004). Detecting pediatric autoimmune neuropsychiatric disorders associated with streptococcus in children with obsessive–compulsive disorder and tics. *Biological Psychiatry, 55,* 61–68. http://dx.doi.org/10.1016/S0006-3223(03)00704-2

Myers, K. M., & Davis, M. (2007). Mechanisms of fear extinction. *Molecular Psychiatry, 12,* 120–150. http://dx.doi.org/10.1038/sj.mp.4001939

Naar-King, S., & Suarez, M. (2010). *Motivational interviewing with adolescents and young adults.* New York, NY: Guilford Press.

Nelson, R. O. (1977). Assessment and therapeutic functions of self-monitoring. In M. Hersen, R. M. Eisler, & P. M. Miller (Eds.), *Progress in behavior modification* (Vol. 5; pp. 263–308). New York, NY: Academic Press.

Nicolini, H., Salin-Pascual, R., Cabrera, B., & Lanzagorta, N. (2017). Influence of culture in obsessive–compulsive disorder and its treatment. *Current Psychiatry Reviews, 13,* 285–292. http://dx.doi.org/10.2174/2211556007666180115105935

Niler, E. R., & Beck, S. J. (1989). The relationship among guilt, dysphoria, anxiety and obsessions in a normal population. *Behaviour Research and Therapy, 27,* 213–220. http://dx.doi.org/10.1016/0005-7967(89)90039-9

Nischal, A., Tripathi, A., Nischal, A., & Trivedi, J. K. (2012). Suicide and antidepressants: What current evidence indicates. *Mens Sana Monographs, 10,* 33–44. http://dx.doi.org/10.4103/0973-1229.87287

Nock, M. K., Ferriter, C., & Holmberg, E. (2007). Parent beliefs about treatment credibility and effectiveness: Assessment and relation to subsequent treatment participation. *Journal of Child and Family Studies, 16,* 27–38. http://dx.doi.org/10.1007/s10826-006-9064-7

Norcross, J. C. (Ed.). (2011). *Psychotherapy relationships that work: Evidence-based responsiveness* (2nd ed.). New York, NY: Oxford University Press. http://dx.doi.org/10.1093/acprof:oso/9780199737208.001.0001

Odlaug, B. L., & Grant, J. E. (2010). Pathologic skin picking. *The American Journal of Drug and Alcohol Abuse*, *36*, 296–303. http://dx.doi.org/10.3109/00952991003747543

Okasha, A., Saad, A., Khalil, A. H., El Dawla, A. S., & Yehia, N. (1994). Phenomenology of obsessive–compulsive disorder: A transcultural study. *Comprehensive Psychiatry*, *35*, 191–197. http://dx.doi.org/10.1016/0010-440X(94)90191-0

O'Kearney, R. (2007). Benefits of cognitive-behavioural therapy for children and youth with obsessive–compulsive disorder: Re-examination of the evidence. *Australian & New Zealand Journal of Psychiatry*, *41*, 199–212. http://dx.doi.org/10.1080/00048670601172707

Ollendick, T. H. (2000, November). *Discussant in T. L. Morris (Chair), Innovative approaches to the treatment of child anxiety: Conceptual issues and practical constraints.* Paper presented at the Association for Advancement of Behavior Therapy, New Orleans, LA.

Ollendick, T. H., & Francis, G. (1988). Behavioral assessment and treatment of childhood phobias [Special issue]. *Behavior Modification*, *12*, 165–204. http://dx.doi.org/10.1177/01454455880122002

Ollendick, T. H., Grills, A. E., & King, N. J. (2001). Applying developmental theory to the assessment and treatment of childhood disorders: Does it make a difference? *Clinical Psychology & Psychotherapy*, *8*, 304–314. http://dx.doi.org/10.1002/cpp.311

Ollendick, T. H., & King, N. J. (1994). Diagnosis, assessment, and treatment of internalizing problems in children: The role of longitudinal data. *Journal of Consulting and Clinical Psychology*, *62*, 918–927. http://dx.doi.org/10.1037/0022-006X.62.5.918

Oranje, A. P., Peereboom-Wynia, J. D., & De Raeymaecker, D. M. (1986). Trichotillomania in childhood. *Journal of the American Academy of Dermatology*, *15*, 614–619. http://dx.doi.org/10.1016/S0190-9622(86)70213-2

Ougrin, D., Tranah, T., Leigh, E., Taylor, L., & Asarnow, J. R. (2012). Practitioner review: Self-harm in adolescents. *Journal of Child Psychology and Psychiatry*, *53*, 337–350. http://dx.doi.org/10.1111/j.1469-7610.2012.02525.x

Palinkas, L. A., Weisz, J. R., Chorpita, B. F., Levine, B., Garland, A. F., Hoagwood, K. E., & Landsverk, J. (2013). Continued use of evidence-based treatments after a randomized controlled effectiveness trial: A qualitative study. *Psychiatric Services*, *64*, 1110–1118. http://dx.doi.org/10.1176/appi.ps.004682012

Panza, K. E., Pittenger, C., & Bloch, M. H. (2013). Age and gender correlates of pulling in pediatric trichotillomania. *Journal of the American Academy of Child & Adolescent Psychiatry*, *52*, 241–249. http://dx.doi.org/10.1016/j.jaac.2012.12.019

Parikh, S. V., Zaretsky, A., Beaulieu, S., Yatham, L. N., Young, L. T., Patelis-Siotis, I., . . . Streiner, D. L. (2012). A randomized controlled trial of psychoeducation or cognitive-behavioral therapy in bipolar disorder: A Canadian Network for Mood and Anxiety Treatments (CANMAT) study [CME]. *The Journal of Clinical Psychiatry*, *73*, 803–810. http://dx.doi.org/10.4088/JCP.11m07343

Pauls, D. L., Alsobrook, J. P., II, Goodman, W., Rasmussen, S., & Leckman, J. F. (1995). A family study of obsessive–compulsive disorder. *The American Journal of Psychiatry*, *152*, 76–84. http://dx.doi.org/10.1176/ajp.152.1.76

Pediatric OCD Treatment Study (POTS) Team. (2004). Cognitive-behavior therapy, sertraline, and their combination for children and adolescents with obsessive–compulsive disorder: The Pediatric OCD Treatment Study (POTS) randomized controlled trial. *JAMA, 292*, 1969–1976. http://dx.doi.org/10.1001/jama.292.16.1969

Persons, J. B. (1989). Case formulation: Why cognitive-behavior therapists need one. *International Cognitive Therapy Newsletter, 5*, 3.

Persons, J. B. (2008). *The case formulation approach to cognitive-behavior therapy*. New York, NY: Guilford Press.

Persons, J. B., & Tompkins, M. A. (1997). Cognitive-behavioral case formulation. In T. D. Eells (Ed.), *Handbook of psychotherapy case formulation* (pp. 314–339). New York, NY: Guilford Press.

Persons, J. B., & Tompkins, M. A. (2007). Cognitive-behavioral case formulation. In T. D. Eells (Ed.), *Handbook of psychotherapy case formulation* (2nd ed., pp. 290–316). New York, NY: Guilford Press.

Peterson, B. S., Pine, D. S., Cohen, P., & Brook, J. S. (2001). Prospective, longitudinal study of tic, obsessive–compulsive, and attention-deficit/hyperactivity disorders in an epidemiological sample. *Journal of the American Academy of Child & Adolescent Psychiatry, 40*, 685–695. http://dx.doi.org/10.1097/00004583-200106000-00014

Phillips, K. A., Menard, W., Pagano, M. E., Fay, C., & Stout, R. L. (2006). Delusional versus nondelusional body dysmorphic disorder: Clinical features and course of illness. *Journal of Psychiatric Research, 40*, 95–104. http://dx.doi.org/10.1016/j.jpsychires.2005.08.005

Piacentini, J., Bergman, R. L., Chang, S., Langley, A., Peris, T., Wood, J. J., & McCracken, J. (2011). Controlled comparison of family cognitive behavioral therapy and psychoeducation/relaxation training for child obsessive–compulsive disorder. *Journal of the American Academy of Child & Adolescent Psychiatry, 50*, 1149–1161. http://dx.doi.org/10.1016/j.jaac.2011.08.003

Piacentini, J., Bergman, R. L., Jacobs, C., McCracken, J. T., & Kretchman, J. (2002). Open trial of cognitive behavior therapy for childhood obsessive–compulsive disorder. *Journal of Anxiety Disorders, 16*, 207–219. http://dx.doi.org/10.1016/S0887-6185(02)00096-8

Piacentini, J., Bergman, R. L., Keller, M., & McCracken, J. (2003). Functional impairment in children and adolescents with obsessive–compulsive disorder. *Journal of Child and Adolescent Psychopharmacology, 13*(Suppl. 1), S61–S69. http://dx.doi.org/10.1089/104454603322126359

Piacentini, J. C., & Jaffer, M. (1999). *Measuring functional impairment in youngsters with OCD: Manual for the Child OCD Impact Scale (COIS)*. Los Angeles, CA: UCLA Department of Psychiatry.

Pichichero, M. E. (2009). The PANDAS syndrome. *Advances in Experimental Medicine and Biology, 634*, 205–216. http://dx.doi.org/10.1007/978-0-387-79838-7_17

Pinto, A., Van Noppen, B., & Calvocoressi, L. (2013). Development and preliminary psychometric evaluation of a self-rated version of the Family Accommodation Scale for Obsessive-Compulsive Disorder. *Journal of Obsessive-Compulsive and Related Disorders, 2*, 457–465. http://dx.doi.org/10.1016/j.jocrd.2012.06.001

Podell, J. L., Kendall, P. C., Gosch, E. A., Compton, S. N., March, J. S., Albano, A.-M., . . . Piacentini, J. C. (2013). Therapist factors and outcomes in CBT for anxiety in youth. *Professional Psychology: Research and Practice, 44*, 89–98. http://dx.doi.org/10.1037/a0031700

Preston, J. D., O'Neal, J. H., & Talaga, M. C. (2015). *Child and adolescent clinical psychopharmacology made simple* (3rd ed.). Oakland, CA: New Harbinger.

Puig-Antich, J., Perel, J. M., Lupatkin, W., Chambers, W. J., Tabrizi, M. A., King, J., . . . Stiller, R. L. (1987). Imipramine in prepubertal major depressive disorders. *Archives of General Psychiatry, 44*, 81–89. http://dx.doi.org/10.1001/archpsyc.1987.01800130093012

Purdon, C., & Clark, D. A. (1993). Obsessive intrusive thoughts in nonclinical subjects. Part I. Content and relation with depressive, anxious and obsessional symptoms. *Behaviour Research and Therapy, 31*, 713–720. http://dx.doi.org/10.1016/0005-7967(93)90001-B

Rabavilas, A. D., Boulougouris, J. C., & Stefanis, C. (1976). Duration of flooding sessions in the treatment of obsessive–compulsive patients. *Behaviour Research and Therapy, 14*, 349–355. http://dx.doi.org/10.1016/0005-7967(76)90022-X

Rachman, S. (1997). A cognitive theory of obsessions. *Behaviour Research and Therapy, 35*, 793–802. http://dx.doi.org/10.1016/S0005-7967(97)00040-5

Rachman, S. (2003). *The treatment of obsessions.* New York, NY: Oxford University Press. http://dx.doi.org/10.1093/med:psych/9780198515371.001.0001

Rachman, S., & de Silva, P. (1978). Abnormal and normal obsessions. *Behaviour Research and Therapy, 16*, 233–248. http://dx.doi.org/10.1016/0005-7967(78)90022-0

Rapoport, J. L., Inoff-Germain, G., Weissman, M. M., Greenwald, S., Narrow, W. E., Jensen, P. S., . . . Canino, G. (2000). Childhood obsessive–compulsive disorder in the NIMH MECA study: Parent versus child identification of cases. *Journal of Anxiety Disorders, 14*, 535–548. http://dx.doi.org/10.1016/S0887-6185(00)00048-7

Rasmussen, S. A., & Eisen, J. L. (1990). Epidemiology of obsessive compulsive disorder. *The Journal of Clinical Psychiatry, 51*(Suppl.), 10–13.

Renshaw, K. D., Steketee, G., & Chambless, D. L. (2005). Involving family members in the treatment of OCD. *Cognitive Behaviour Therapy, 34*, 164–175. http://dx.doi.org/10.1080/16506070510043732

Rescorla, R. A. (1988). Pavlovian conditioning: It's not what you think it is. *American Psychologist, 43*, 151–160. http://dx.doi.org/10.1037/0003-066X.43.3.151

Rescorla, R. A., & Wagner, A. R. (1972). A theory of Pavlovian conditioning: Variations in effectiveness of reinforcement and nonreinforcement. In A. H. Black & W. F. Prokasy (Eds.), *Classical conditioning II: Current research and theory* (pp. 64–99). New York, NY: Appleton-Century-Crofts.

Rettew, D. C., Swedo, S. E., Leonard, H. L., Lenane, M. C., & Rapoport, J. L. (1992). Obsessions and compulsions across time in 79 children and adolescents with obsessive–compulsive disorder. *Journal of the American Academy of Child & Adolescent Psychiatry, 31*, 1050–1056. http://dx.doi.org/10.1097/00004583-199211000-00009

Riggs, D. S., & Foa, E. B. (1993). Obsessive compulsive disorder. In D. H. Barlow (Ed.), *Clinical handbook of psychological disorders: A step-by-step treatment manual* (2nd ed., pp. 189–239). New York, NY: Guilford Press.

Ritter, B. (1968). The group desensitization of children's snake phobias using vicarious and contact desensitization procedures. *Behaviour Research and Therapy, 6*, 1–6. http://dx.doi.org/10.1016/0005-7967(68)90033-8

Robertson, M. M. (2011). Gilles de la Tourette syndrome: The complexities of phenotype and treatment. *British Journal of Hospital Medicine, 72*, 100–107. http://dx.doi.org/10.12968/hmed.2011.72.2.100

Russell, A. J., Mataix-Cols, D., Anson, M., & Murphy, D. G. (2005). Obsessions and compulsions in Asperger syndrome and high-functioning autism. *The British Journal of Psychiatry, 186*, 525–528. http://dx.doi.org/10.1192/bjp.186.6.525

Rutter, M., & Sroufe, L. A. (2000). Developmental psychopathology: Concepts and challenges. *Development and Psychopathology, 12*, 265–296. http://dx.doi.org/10.1017/S0954579400003023

Sameroff, A., & Haith, M. (1996). *The five to seven year shift: The age of reason and responsibility*. Chicago, IL: University of Chicago Press.

Sauter, F. M., Heyne, D., & Michiel Westenberg, P. (2009). Cognitive behavior therapy for anxious adolescents: Developmental influences on treatment design and delivery. *Clinical Child and Family Psychology Review, 12*, 310–335. http://dx.doi.org/10.1007/s10567-009-0058-z

Scahill, L., Riddle, M. A., McSwiggin-Hardin, M., Ort, S. I., King, R. A., Goodman, W. K., . . . Leckman, J. F. (1997). Children's Yale–Brown Obsessive Compulsive Scale: Reliability and validity. *Journal of the American Academy of Child & Adolescent Psychiatry, 36*, 844–852. http://dx.doi.org/10.1097/00004583-199706000-00023

Schlosser, S., Black, D. W., Blum, N., & Goldstein, R. B. (1994). The demography, phenomenology, and family history of 22 persons with compulsive hair pulling. *Annals of Clinical Psychiatry, 6*, 147–152.

Schotte, C. K. W., Van Den Bossche, B., De Doncker, D., Claes, S., & Cosyns, P. (2006). A biopsychosocial model as a guide for psychoeducation and treatment of depression. *Depression & Anxiety, 23*, 312–324. http://dx.doi.org/10.1002/da.20177

Seiden, D. (1999). The effect of research on practice in cross-cultural behavior therapy: A single case study (you're the case). *The Behavior Therapist, 22*, 200–201.

Shaffer, D., Fisher, P., Dulcan, M. K., Davies, M., Piacentini, J., Schwab-Stone, M., . . . Regier, D. A. (1996). The NIMH Diagnostic Interview Schedule for Children Version 2.3 (DISC-2.3): Description, acceptability, prevalence rates, and performances in the MECA study. *Journal of the American Academy of Child & Adolescent Psychiatry, 35*, 865–877. http://dx.doi.org/10.1097/00004583-199607000-00012

Shirk, S. R., Karver, M. S., & Brown, R. (2011). The alliance in child and adolescent psychotherapy. *Psychotherapy, 48*, 17–24. http://dx.doi.org/10.1037/a0022181

Shulman, S. T. (2009). Pediatric autoimmune neuropsychiatric disorders associated with streptococci (PANDAS): Update. *Current Opinion in Pediatrics, 21*, 127–130. http://dx.doi.org/10.1097/MOP.0b013e32831db2c4

Sica, C., Novara, C., Sanavio, E., Dorz, S., & Coradeschi, D. (2002). Obsessive compulsive disorder cognitions across cultures. In R. O. Frost & G. Steketee (Eds.), *Cognitive approaches to obsessions and compulsions: Theory, assessment, and treatment* (pp. 371–384). Oxford, England: Elsevier Science. http://dx.doi.org/10.1016/B978-008043410-0/50024-6

Silverman, W. K., & Albano, A. M. (2004). *Anxiety Disorders Interview Schedule (ADIS-IV): Child and Parent Versions*. New York, NY: Oxford University Press.

Silverman, W. K., & Kurtines, W. M. (1996). Transfer of control: A psychosocial intervention model for disorders in youth. In E. D. Hibbs & P. Jensen (Eds.),

Psychosocial treatment of child and adolescent disorders: Empirically based strategies for clinical practice (pp. 63–81). Washington, DC: American Psychological Association. http://dx.doi.org/10.1037/10196-003

Silverman, W. K., Pina, A. A., & Viswesvaran, C. (2008). Evidence-based psychosocial treatments for phobic and anxiety disorders in children and adolescents. *Journal of Clinical Child & Adolescent Psychology, 37,* 105–130. http://dx.doi.org/10.1080/15374410701817907

Simpson, H. B., Foa, E. B., Liebowitz, M. R., Ledley, D. R., Huppert, J. D., Cahill, S., . . . Petkova, E. (2008). A randomized, controlled trial of cognitive-behavioral therapy for augmenting pharmacotherapy in obsessive–compulsive disorder. *The American Journal of Psychiatry, 165,* 621–630. http://dx.doi.org/10.1176/appi.ajp.2007.07091440

Singer, H. S. (2011). Tourette syndrome and other tic disorders. In W. J. Weiner & E. Tolosa (Eds.), *Handbook of clinical neurology* (pp. 641–657). New York, NY: Elsevier.

Singh, N. N., & Singh, S. D. (2001). Developmental considerations in treatment. In H. Orvaschel, J. Faust, & M. Hersen (Eds.), *Handbook of conceptualization and treatment of child psychopathology* (pp. 9–38). Oxford, England: Elsevier Science. http://dx.doi.org/10.1016/B978-008043362-2/50003-2

Sisemore, T. A. (2010). *Free from OCD: A workbook for teens with obsessive–compulsive disorder.* Oakland, CA: New Harbinger.

Snider, L. A., & Swedo, S. E. (2000). Pediatric obsessive–compulsive disorder. *JAMA, 284,* 3104–3106. http://dx.doi.org/10.1001/jama.284.24.3104

Snider, L. A., & Swedo, S. E. (2004). PANDAS: Current status and directions for research. *Molecular Psychiatry, 9,* 900–907. http://dx.doi.org/10.1038/sj.mp.4001542

Southam-Gerow, M. A., Weisz, J. R., & Kendall, P. C. (2003). Youth with anxiety disorders in research and service clinics: Examining client differences and similarities. *Journal of Clinical Child & Adolescent Psychology, 32,* 375–385. http://dx.doi.org/10.1207/S15374424JCCP3203_06

Steiner, H. (2004). *Handbook of mental health interventions in children and adolescents.* San Francisco, CA: Jossey-Bass.

Steketee, G., & Van Noppen, B. (2003). Abordagem familiar no tratamento do transtorno obsessivo-compulsivo [Family approaches to treatment for obsessive compulsive disorder]. *Revista Brasileira de Psiquiatria, 25,* 43–50. http://dx.doi.org/10.1590/S1516-44462003000100009

Steketee, G. S. (1993). *Treatment of obsessive compulsive disorder.* New York, NY: Guilford Press.

Stewart, S. E., Geller, D. A., Jenike, M., Pauls, D., Shaw, D., Mullin, B., & Faraone, S. V. (2004). Long-term outcome of pediatric obsessive–compulsive disorder: A meta-analysis and qualitative review of the literature. *Acta Psychiatrica Scandinavica, 110,* 4–13. http://dx.doi.org/10.1111/j.1600-0447.2004.00302.x

Stewart, S. E., Jenike, M. A., & Keuthen, N. J. (2005). Severe obsessive–compulsive disorder with and without comorbid hair pulling: Comparisons and clinical implications. *The Journal of Clinical Psychiatry, 66,* 864–869. http://dx.doi.org/10.4088/JCP.v66n0709

Stoddard, J. A., & Williams, K. N. (2012). *CBT for mood disorders in children and adolescents.* Paper presented at the Rady Children's Outpatient Psychiatry Seminar Series, Oceanside, CA.

Storch, E. A., Geffken, G. R., Merlo, L. J., Mann, G., Duke, D., Munson, M., . . . Goodman, W. K. (2007). Family-based cognitive-behavioral therapy for pediatric obsessive–compulsive disorder: Comparison of intensive and weekly approaches. *Journal of the American Academy of Child & Adolescent Psychiatry, 46*, 469–478. http://dx.doi.org/10.1097/chi.0b013e31803062e7

Storch, E. A., Geffken, G. R., & Murphy, T. K. (Eds.). (2007). *Handbook of child and adolescent obsessive–compulsive disorder*. Mahwah, NJ: Lawrence Erlbaum.

Storch, E. A., Khanna, M., Merlo, L. J., Loew, B. A., Franklin, M., Reid, J. M., . . . Murphy, T. K. (2009). Children's Florida Obsessive Compulsive Inventory: Psychometric properties and feasibility of a self-report measure of obsessive–compulsive symptoms in youth. *Child Psychiatry and Human Development, 40*, 467–483. http://dx.doi.org/10.1007/s10578-009-0138-9

Storch, E. A., Lack, C. W., Merlo, L. J., Geffken, G. R., Jacob, M. L., Murphy, T. K., & Goodman, W. K. (2007). Clinical features of children and adolescents with obsessive–compulsive disorder and hoarding symptoms. *Comprehensive Psychiatry, 48*, 313–318. http://dx.doi.org/10.1016/j.comppsych.2007.03.001

Storch, E. A., Larson, M. J., Muroff, J., Caporino, N., Geller, D., Reid, J. M., . . . Murphy, T. K. (2010). Predictors of functional impairment in pediatric obsessive–compulsive disorder. *Journal of Anxiety Disorders, 24*, 275–283. http://dx.doi.org/10.1016/j.janxdis.2009.12.004

Storch, E. A., Ledley, D. R., Lewin, A. B., Murphy, T. K., Johns, N. B., Goodman, W. K., & Geffken, G. R. (2006). Peer victimization in children with obsessive–compulsive disorder: Relations with symptoms of psychopathology. *Journal of Clinical Child & Adolescent Psychology, 35*, 446–455. http://dx.doi.org/10.1207/s15374424jccp3503_10

Storch, E. A., Milsom, V. A., Merlo, L. J., Larson, M., Geffken, G. R., Jacob, M. L., . . . Goodman, W. K. (2008). Insight in pediatric obsessive–compulsive disorder: Associations with clinical presentation. *Psychiatry Research, 160*, 212–220. http://dx.doi.org/10.1016/j.psychres.2007.07.005

Storch, E. A., Murphy, T. K., Geffken, G. R., Soto, O., Sajid, M., Allen, P., . . . Goodman, W. K. (2004). Psychometric evaluation of the Children's Yale–Brown Obsessive–Compulsive Scale. *Psychiatry Research, 129*, 91–98. http://dx.doi.org/10.1016/j.psychres.2004.06.009

Sudak, D. M. (2011). *Combining CBT and medication: An evidence-based approach*. Hoboken, NJ: Wiley. http://dx.doi.org/10.1002/9781118093368

Sukhodolsky, D. G., do Rosario-Campos, M. C., Scahill, L., Katsovich, L., Pauls, D. L., Peterson, B. S., . . . Leckman, J. F. (2005). Adaptive, emotional, and family functioning of children with obsessive–compulsive disorder and comorbid attention deficit hyperactivity disorder. *The American Journal of Psychiatry, 162*, 1125–1132. http://dx.doi.org/10.1176/appi.ajp.162.6.1125

Swedo, S. E., Leckman, J. F., & Rose, N. R. (2012). From research subgroup to clinical syndrome: Modifying the PANDAS criteria to describe PANS (pediatric acute-onset neuropsychiatric syndrome). *Pediatrics & Therapeutics: Current Research, 2*(2), 1–8. http://dx.doi.org/10.4172/2161-0665.1000113

Swedo, S. E., Rapoport, J. L., Leonard, H., Lenane, M., & Cheslow, D. (1989). Obsessive–compulsive disorder in children and adolescents: Clinical phenomenology of 70 consecutive cases. *Archives of General Psychiatry, 46*, 335–341. http://dx.doi.org/10.1001/archpsyc.1989.01810040041007

Thienemann, M., Murphy, T., Leckman, J., Shaw, R., Williams, K., Kapphahn, C., . . . Swedo, S. (2017). Clinical Management of Pediatric Acute-Onset Neuropsychiatric Syndrome: Part I-Psychiatric and Behavioral Interventions. *Journal of Child and Adolescent Psychopharmacology, 27,* 566–573. http://dx.doi.org/10.1089/cap.2016.0145

Timpano, K. R., Exner, C., Glaesmer, H., Rief, W., Keshaviah, A., Brähler, E., & Wilhelm, S. (2011). The epidemiology of the proposed DSM-5 hoarding disorder: Exploration of the acquisition specifier, associated features, and distress. *The Journal of Clinical Psychiatry, 72,* 780–786. http://dx.doi.org/10.4088/JCP.10m06380

Tolin, D. F., Franklin, M. E., Diefenbach, G. J., Anderson, E., & Meunier, S. A. (2007). Pediatric trichotillomania: Descriptive psychopathology and an open trial of cognitive behavioral therapy. *Cognitive Behaviour Therapy, 36,* 129–144. http://dx.doi.org/10.1080/16506070701223230

Tolin, D. F., Meunier, S. A., Frost, R. O., & Steketee, G. (2010). Course of compulsive hoarding and its relationship to life events. *Depression and Anxiety, 27,* 829–838. http://dx.doi.org/10.1002/da.20684

Tracey, T. J., Wampold, B. E., Lichtenberg, J. W., & Goodyear, R. K. (2014). Expertise in psychotherapy: An elusive goal? *American Psychologist, 69,* 218–229. http://dx.doi.org/10.1037/a0035099

Trepka, C., Rees, A., Shapiro, D. A., Hardy, G. E., & Barkham, M. (2004). Therapist competence and outcome of cognitive therapy for depression. *Cognitive Therapy and Research, 28,* 143–157. http://dx.doi.org/10.1023/B:COTR.0000021536.39173.66

Tseng, W. (1997). Overview: Culture and psychopathology. In W. Tseng & J. Streltzer (Eds.), *Culture and psychopathology* (pp. 1–27). New York, NY: Brunner/Mazel.

Tükel, R., Ertekin, E., Batmaz, S., Alyanak, F., Sözen, A., Aslantaş, B., . . . Özyıldırım, I. (2005). Influence of age of onset on clinical features in obsessive–compulsive disorder. *Depression and Anxiety, 21,* 112–117. http://dx.doi.org/10.1002/da.20065

Turner, S. M., Hersen, M., Bellack, A. S., Andrasik, F., & Capparell, H. V. (1980). Behavioral and pharmacological treatment of obsessive–compulsive disorders. *Journal of Nervous and Mental Disease, 168,* 651–657. http://dx.doi.org/10.1097/00005053-198011000-00003

Turrell, S. L., & Bell, M. (2016). *ACT for adolescents: Treating teens and adolescents in individual and group therapy.* Oakland, CA: Context Press.

Valderhaug, R., Larsson, B., Götestam, K. G., & Piacentini, J. (2007). An open clinical trial of cognitive-behaviour therapy in children and adolescents with obsessive–compulsive disorder administered in regular outpatient clinics. *Behaviour Research and Therapy, 45,* 577–589. http://dx.doi.org/10.1016/j.brat.2006.04.011

Valleni-Basile, L. A., Garrison, C. Z., Jackson, K. L., Waller, J. L., McKeown, R. E., Addy, C. L., & Cuffe, S. P. (1995). Family and psychosocial predictors of obsessive compulsive disorder in a community sample of young adolescents. *Journal of Child and Family Studies, 4,* 193–206. http://dx.doi.org/10.1007/BF02234095

VanElzakker, M. B., Dahlgren, M. K., Davis, F. C., Dubois, S., & Shin, L. M. (2014). From Pavlov to PTSD: The extinction of conditioned fear in rodents, humans, and anxiety disorders. *Neurobiology of Learning and Memory, 113,* 3–18. http://dx.doi.org/10.1016/j.nlm.2013.11.014

Vinker, M., Jaworowski, S., & Mergui, J. (2014). [Obsessive compulsive disorder (OCD) in the ultra-orthodox community—Cultural aspects of diagnosis and treatment]. *Harefuah, 153*, 463–466, 498, 497.

Vygotsky, L. (1978). Interaction between learning and development. In M. Cole, V. John-Steiner, S. Scribner, & E. Souberman (Eds.), *Mind and Society* (pp. 79–91). Cambridge, MA: Harvard University Press.

Waters, T. L., Barrett, P. M., & March, J. S. (2001). Cognitive-behavioral family treatment of childhood obsessive–compulsive disorder: Preliminary findings. *American Journal of Psychotherapy, 55*, 372–387. http://dx.doi.org/10.1176/appi.psychotherapy.2001.55.3.372

Watson, H. J., & Rees, C. S. (2008). Meta-analysis of randomized, controlled treatment trials for pediatric obsessive–compulsive disorder. *Journal of Child Psychology and Psychiatry, and Allied Disciplines, 49*, 489–498. http://dx.doi.org/10.1111/j.1469-7610.2007.01875.x

Watson, J. P., Gaind, R., & Marks, I. M. (1971). Prolonged exposure: A rapid treatment for phobias. *BMJ: British Medical Journal, 1*(5739), 13–15. http://dx.doi.org/10.1136/bmj.1.5739.13

Watts, F. N. (1979). Habituation model of systematic desensitization. *Psychological Bulletin, 86*, 627–637. http://dx.doi.org/10.1037/0033-2909.86.3.627

Weg, A. H. (2011). *OCD treatment through storytelling: A strategy for successful therapy.* New York, NY: Oxford University Press. http://dx.doi.org/10.1093/med:psych/9780195383560.001.0001

Weissman, M. M., Bland, R. C., Canino, G. J., Greenwald, S., Hwu, H. G., Lee, C. K., . . ., & the The Cross National Collaborative Group. (1994). The cross national epidemiology of obsessive compulsive disorder. *The Journal of Clinical Psychiatry, 55*(Suppl.), 5–10.

Weisz, J. R., & Chorpita, B. F. (2012). Mod squad for youth psychotherapy: Restructuring evidence-based treatment for clinical practice. In P. C. Kendall (Ed.), *Child and adolescent therapy: Cognitive-behavioral procedures* (4th ed., pp. 379–397). New York, NY: Guilford Press.

Weisz, J. R., Chorpita, B. F., Palinkas, L. A., Schoenwald, S. K., Miranda, J., Bearman, S. K., . . . Gibbons, R. D., & the Research Network on Youth Mental Health. (2012). Testing standard and modular designs for psychotherapy treating depression, anxiety, and conduct problems in youth: A randomized effectiveness trial. *Archives of General Psychiatry, 69*, 274–282. http://dx.doi.org/10.1001/archgenpsychiatry.2011.147

Weisz, J. R., Donenberg, G. R., Han, S. S., & Weiss, B. (1995). Bridging the gap between laboratory and clinic in child and adolescent psychotherapy. *Journal of Consulting and Clinical Psychology, 63*, 688–701. http://dx.doi.org/10.1037/0022-006X.63.5.688

Weisz, J. R., & Kazdin, A. E. (Eds.). (2010). *Evidence-based psychotherapies for children and adolescents.* New York, NY: Guilford Press.

Wergeland, G. J., Fjermestad, K. W., Marin, C. E., Haugland, B. S., Silverman, W. K., Öst, L. G., . . . Heiervang, E. R. (2015). Predictors of dropout from community clinic child CBT for anxiety disorders. *Journal of Anxiety Disorders, 31*, 1–10. http://dx.doi.org/10.1016/j.janxdis.2015.01.004

White, M. (1986). Negative explanation, restraint, and double description: A template for family therapy. *Family Process, 25*, 169–184. http://dx.doi.org/10.1111/j.1545-5300.1986.00169.x

White, M., & Epston, D. (1990). *Narrative means to therapeutic ends*. New York, NY: Norton.

Wilens, T. E., & Hammerness, P. G. (2016). *Straight talk about psychiatric medications for kids* (4th ed.). New York, NY: Guilford Press.

Wilhelm, S., Keuthen, N. J., Deckersbach, T., Engelhard, I. M., Forker, A. E., Baer, L., . . . Jenike, M. A. (1999). Self-injurious skin picking: Clinical characteristics and comorbidity. *The Journal of Clinical Psychiatry, 60*, 454–459. http://dx.doi.org/10.4088/JCP.v60n0707

Zohar, A. H. (1999). The epidemiology of obsessive–compulsive disorder in children and adolescents. *Child and Adolescent Psychiatric Clinics of North America, 8*, 445–460. http://dx.doi.org/10.1016/S1056-4993(18)30163-9

Zohar, A. H., & Felz, L. (2001). Ritualistic behavior in young children. *Journal of Abnormal Child Psychology, 29*, 121–128. http://dx.doi.org/10.1023/A:1005231912747

INDEX

ABOUT THE AUTHORS

Michael A. Tompkins, PhD, ABPP, is codirector of the San Francisco Bay Area Center for Cognitive Therapy, assistant clinical professor at the University of California–Berkeley, and board certified in behavioral and cognitive psychology. He is the author or coauthor of numerous articles and chapters on cognitive behavior therapy and related topics, as well as ten books. Dr. Tompkins serves on the advisory board of Magination Press, the children's press of the American Psychological Association, and provides evidence-based treatments for adults, adolescents, and children.

Daniela J. Owen, PhD, is the assistant director of the San Francisco Bay Area Center for Cognitive Therapy, and assistant clinical professor at the University of California–Berkeley. She is the coauthor of several peer-reviewed articles and chapters. Dr. Owen has presented locally and nationally on evidence-based treatments for pediatric disorders.

Nicole H. Shiloff, PhD, is an adjunct clinical faculty member at Stanford University School of Medicine and diplomate of the Academy of Cognitive Therapy. She has a private practice in Menlo Park where she specializes in the treatment of anxiety disorders in children, adolescents, and adults.

Litsa R. Tanner, MS, MFT, is a cofounder of the Santa Rosa Center for Cognitive Behavioral Therapy. Ms. Tanner specializes in the treatment of pediatric obsessive–compulsive disorder and obsessive–compulsive spectrum disorders.